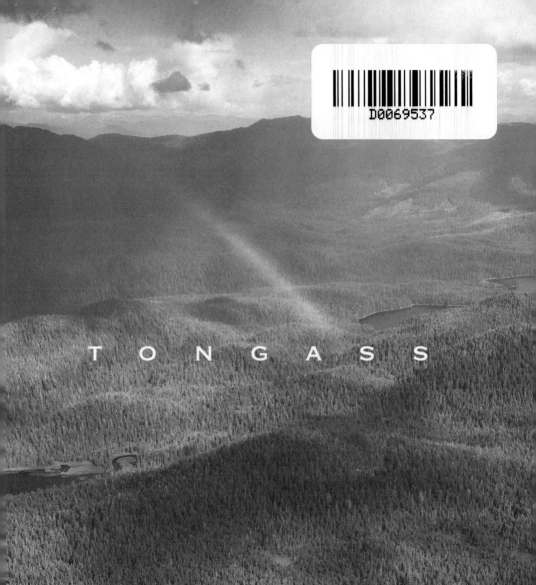

TONGASS

Yakutat Fiord
Russell Fiord
Yakutat Bay
Yakutat
Alsek River
Skagway
Haines
GLACIER BAY NATIONAL PARK AND PRESERVE
Lynn Canal
CANADA
UNITED STATES
Cross Sound
Icy Strait
JUNEAU
TONGASS
Chichagof Island
Admiralty Island
ADMIRALTY ISLAND NATIONAL MONUMENT WILDERNESS
Chatham Strait
Stephens Passage
Baranof
Sitka
Island
NATIONAL
Frederick Sound
River
Kuiu
Kupreanof Island
Petersburg
Mitkof
Stikine
PACIFIC
Strait
Sumner Strait
Zarembo
Wrangell
Wrangell Island
Etolin
OCEAN
Island
FOREST
MISTY FIORDS NATIONAL MONUMENT WILDERNESS
Prince of Wales Island
Clarence Strait
Behm Canal
Revillagigedo Island
Craig
Ketchikan
Annette Island
ALASKA
Map Area
Proposed International Boundary
DIXON ENTRANCE
Prince Rupert

TONGASS

Pulp Politics
and the
Fight for the Alaska Rain Forest

by

Kathie Durbin

SECOND EDITION

Oregon State University Press
Corvallis

Publication of this book was made possible
in part by contributions from
THE COMPTON FOUNDATION
THE LAZAR FOUNDATION
The Oregon State University Press is grateful for their support

Cover photo by Trygve Steen.

The paper in this book meets the guidelines for permanence and durability of the Committee on Production Guidelines for Book Longevity of the Council on Library Resources and the minimum requirements of the American National Standard for Permanence of Paper for Printed Library Materials Z39.48-1984.

Library of Congress Cataloging-in-Publication Data
Durbin, Kathie.
Tongass : pulp politics and the fight for the Alaska rain forest / second edition by Kathie Durbin.
   p.   cm.
Includes bibliographical references and index.
ISBN 0-87071-056-7 (alk. paper)
1. Tongass National Forest (Alaska)—Management. 2. Logging—Environmental aspects—Alaska—Tongass National Forest.
3. Wood-pulp industry—Environmental aspects—Alaska—Tongass National Forest. 4. Rain forest conservation—Alaska—Tongass National Forest. I. Title.
SD428.T6D87   1999
333.75'13'097982—dc21   99-40408
                                                             CIP

Oregon State University Press
102 Adams Hall
Corvallis OR 97331-2005
541-737-3166 •fax 541-737-3170
http://oregonstate.edu/dept/press

TABLE OF CONTENTS

"I hold few convictions so deeply as my belief that a profound transgression has taken place here, by devastating an entire forest rather than taking from it selectively and in moderation. Yet whatever judgment I might make against those who cut it down, I must also make against myself. I belong to the same nation, speak the same language, vote in the same elections, share many of the same values, avail myself of the same technology, and owe much of my existence to the same vast system of global exchange. There is no refuge in blaming only the loggers or their industry or the government that deeded this forest to them. The entire society—one in which I take active membership—holds responsibility for laying this valley bare."

—Richard Nelson, "The Forest of Eyes"
in *The Island Within*

An ancient Sitka spruce growing from karst, Prince of Wales Island.
Photo by Trygve Steen.

PRINCE OF WALES ISLAND

I t is March in Southeast Alaska. The Taquan Air flight from Ketchikan to Craig crosses Clarence Strait and passes over the east coast of Prince of Wales Island, then heads up Kasaan Bay toward the island's midsection. A heavy cloud cover dissipates; below, morning light gleams off frozen lakes. There is snow on the muskeg, snow in the high country. As the clouds part, a stark vista is revealed.

Clearcuts extend from ridgetops to streambanks to the edges of muskeg bogs. Rough logging roads wind up river valleys. Except for a few remnant old conifers, shaggy-limbed and wind-battered, and budding willows along some of the larger streams, these valleys are shorn of trees. With their vegetative cover removed, the underlying landforms are revealed, naked and exposed to the Alaska Panhandle's torrential rains. Environmentalists call this place Prisoner of War Island. In a brief half-century, much of it has been defiled by the short-sighted acts of governments and men.

Some of its logged valleys lie within the Tongass National Forest. For forty-three years, most of the federal timber from these lands fed a pulp mill in Ketchikan. The rest, including the denuded mountain that looms into view as the plane descends, is the property of Alaska Native corporations, which logged their land rapidly and virtually without restriction beginning in 1980.

The clearcutting of Prince of Wales Island has ravaged salmon spawning streams and erased habitat for Sitka black-tailed deer, a staple of life for the wolves and humans who call this place home. The construction of poorly built logging roads has triggered thousands of landslides and opened the wilderness to poaching. The removal of trees growing on karst bedrock has destroyed cave features and buried archeological remains. Prince of Wales Island is Southeast Alaska's sacrifice zone. War has been waged here. The foe appears to be nature itself.

IN 1879, THE NATURALIST JOHN MUIR traveled from Puget Sound by mail steamer through the Alexander Archipelago, with stops in Fort Sitka and Fort Wrangell, eventually making his way north to Glacier Bay. Muir rhapsodized over the endless beauty that unfolded before him: "So numerous are the islands that they seem to have been sown broadcast; long tapering vistas between the largest of them open in every direction," he wrote. " . . . in these coast landscapes there is such indefinite, on-leading expansiveness, such a multitude of features without apparent redundance, their lines graduating delicately into one another in endless succession, while the whole is so fine, so tender, so ethereal, that all penwork seems hopelessly unavailing. Tracing shining ways through fiord and sound, past forests and waterfalls, islands and mountains and far azure headlands, it seems as if surely we must at length reach the very paradise of the poets, the abode of the blessed."

The Tlingit and Haida who claim this region as their ancestral homeland know its forests and waterfalls, its islands and mountains, its fiords and sound, intimately. But for most outsiders, the Alexander Archipelago Muir described in 1879 remained a largely unexplored paradise well into the twentieth century. And even after nearly a half-century of industrial logging, it still holds many places of surpassing beauty.

Prince of Wales is a large island, covering 2,231 square miles. Along its 990 miles of coastline are secluded bays and deep winding inlets carved by glacial ice. Its mountains rise 3,000 feet from tidewater. It holds deep U-shaped glacial valleys, chains of lakes where trumpeter swans stop over on their long migrations, rare karst formations and limestone caves. Eleven other large satellite islands and hundreds of small ones cluster around it, some of them exposed to the open Pacific. Here, in the South Tongass, were the largest trees and the most productive forests in the 500-mile-long archipelago. At the heads of some coves and estuaries, modern-day explorers have found giants 200 feet tall that escaped the chainsaw because there was no way to bring out the logs.

THE ALASKA PANHANDLE IS ICE-CARVED, lapped by Pacific waves and washed by coastal rains. When glaciers retreated from the North Pacific coast ten thousand years ago, the level of the sea rose and filled the channels the ice fields had left, creating the wide straits and narrow fiords of today's archipelago. On the mainland, the Stikine and Taku rivers sliced through the steep, glaciated coastal mountains that form today's Alaska-British Columbia boundary. The forest that grew up on these islands and on the

Muskeg bogs, which cover large areas of the Alexander Archipelago, grow only stunted bull pine (Pinus contorta) and other dwarf plants, which are aesthetically pleasing but have no commercial value. Photo by Trygve Steen.

narrow mainland shelf is a mosaic of muskeg, alpine scrub and lichen-draped conifer rainforest. It is dominated by western hemlock, interspersed with Sitka spruce and small amounts of western red cedar and prized Alaska yellow cedar. The largest trees grow only below 2,000 feet. The forest floor is a nearly impenetrable jumble of toppled trees, spiky Devil's club and densely matted berries and forbs.

It is coastal temperate rain forest, a forest type that flourishes only where summers are cool and annual rainfall exceeds 55 inches. It draws nourishment from the cycling of water between land and sea. Pacific weather fronts bumping up against the coast mountains spend themselves as rain at lower elevations and as snow in the high country. Some parts of the Panhandle receive more than 200 inches of rain each year.

At one time, temperate rain forests were found along the western fringe of every continent except Africa and Antarctica. Today, the rain forests of

Scotland and Ireland have vanished, and only fragments survive in Norway. Larger expanses remain in Chile, New Zealand and Tasmania. But by far the largest contiguous temperate rain forest stretches along the western shelf of North America, from Kodiak Island in the Gulf of Alaska south through the Panhandle and coastal British Columbia to Vancouver Island. Only in Southeast Alaska are significant blocks protected by law.

Until the 1970s, scientists spent little time studying the temperate rain forest. The world's attention was focused on the wholesale destruction of tropical rain forests in Malaysia and Brazil. The temperate forest does not boast the riotous profusion of plant and animal species found in the tropics, but it accumulates and stores more organic material than any other forest type on Earth. Trees may grow to be two thousand years old. The abundant material that passes from forest to ocean enriches the sea as well, supporting incredibly productive marine ecosystems that teem with shellfish, salmon and halibut.

The Alaska rain forest also compensates for its relative lack of biological diversity in geological complexity. It is naturally fragmented by saltwater into islands and peninsulas, punctuated with freshwater muskeg bogs, and limited at its upper reaches by glaciers and subalpine meadows. Fingers of forest enclose short, steep-gradient streams. Wildfire is an infrequent visitor here, but windstorms flatten stands and individual trees, creating a natural mosaic of openings. Fog shrouds the treetops, nourishing a canopy hung with lichens. Muted light pours through holes in the canopy where trees have fallen, illuminating communities of mosses and liverworts. The further north you go in this narrow rain forest zone, the smaller the trees and the harsher the winter climate.

The swift rivers of the Panhandle meet the sea in broad estuaries. Spawning pink and chum salmon crowd into the estuaries in late summer. Their spent bodies feed bald eagles and brown bears and return nutrients to streams and to the land itself. Some streams spill into saltwater rivers known as salt chucks, which penetrate deep inland. Strong tides and powerful currents in these inlets allow a mixing of salt and fresh water that nourishes crabs and other shellfish. At Mitchell Bay on Admiralty Island, the incoming tide creates standing waves far upstream that resemble rapids on a whitewater river.

Throughout the Panhandle, the largest forest stands and individual trees grow on river floodplains, sloping alluvial fans, and uplifted deltas. These stands, where the volume of wood exceeds 30,000 board feet per acre, are the most coveted by timber companies and the most valuable for wildlife as well. Bears amble through these low-lying areas as they move down to feed on spawning salmon. Deer seek cover here from winter snows. At the end of the twentieth century, industrial logging had erased nearly one million acres of this productive forest ecosystem.

To the visitor traveling through by way of the protected waters of the Inside Passage, this loss is not immediately apparent. The beauty that enthralled John Muir still soothes the spirit. A perpetual mist hovers over the Panhandle. It softens the boundaries between forest and sea and blurs the harsh edges of clearcuts. The name the government gave to the national forest that covers most of it—Tongass, for the Tlingit of Tongass Island, at the archipelago's southernmost tip—whispers like wind through spruce boughs.

BEFORE THE FIRST EUROPEAN CONTACT in the late eighteenth century, the Alexander Archipelago was densely populated At the beginning of the nineteenth century, as many as ten thousand indigenous people lived in scattered villages on its islands and on the mainland bordering the coastal mountains. Permanent settlements and seasonal fishing and hunting camps dotted every cove and inlet. Most villages faced saltwater, turning their backs to the wilderness. The Tlingit and Haida ranged far in their dugout canoes, trading with other people up and down the Inside Passage and living well on the bounty of land and sea.

Today, seventy-two thousand people live in fifteen isolated communities in Southeast Alaska. Water and distance separate them; saltwater passages connect them by skiff or floatplane or ferry. Some came to fish, some to log, some to work in the canneries or the pulp mills or the sawmills or the mines. Some came to work for the Forest Service or the Coast Guard. A few hundred, artists and writers and environmentalists mainly, were drawn by the mystique of wilderness. They came to paint this country or photograph it or write poems about it or somehow protect it. They came to explore it, or just to live at the edge of it. All residents of Southeast Alaska have this one thing in common: the Tongass National Forest is woven into the fabric of their lives.

PRINCE OF WALES ISLAND OCCUPIES a significant place in Alaska history. Here, in July of 1741, Aleksei Chirikov, a member of the second Bering expedition, became the first European explorer to have set sail from Siberia and reached

Totem poles near Sea Otter Sound, off the west coast of Prince of Wales Island. Photo by Trygve Steen.

the coast of North America. Chirikov dispatched two landing parties to the island to learn what they could about its natural resources. His men never were heard from again.

In 1799, on the large island to the north that now bears his name, Alexander Baranof established Fort Sitka, which became the capital of Russian Alaska and the prosperous center of the Russian sea otter trade. In 1867 the United States bought Alaska from the Russians for $6.5 million. Twenty years after the Alaska Purchase, hand loggers had moved in to cut trees on this new frontier. They cut timber from slopes close to saltwater and rafted or towed the logs to mills, where they were made into shipping barrels or used to build docks and houses. By 1889, eleven sawmills were operating in Southeast Alaska.

Over the two centuries following Chirikov's ill-fated expedition, beach logging nibbled away at the edges of the great forest. In 1907, President Theodore Roosevelt established the Tongass National Forest, and the following year he consolidated the new national forest with the Alexander

Archipelago Forest Reserve, creating a single national forest of 6,756,362 acres.

In 1920, just fifteen years after the first Tongass timber sale was offered, a forester reported that virtually all the shorelines in Southeast Alaska had been "culled over at least once." The stumps of these giants, notched where loggers inserted springboards to stand on while they cut them down, still rest hidden beneath the undergrowth.

In 1954, soon after a new pulp mill near Ketchikan began turning hemlock and spruce into pulp, a writer for a pulp industry magazine flew to a logging camp on Prince of Wales Island, where the first logs for the new mill were being cut from the Tongass National Forest. He wrote, "The endless green blankets of spruce and hemlock rose and fell on hills and minor mountains of all sizes and descriptions." Over the next forty years, logging transformed Prince of Wales Island, Kosciusko Island, Zarembo Island, northeast Chichagof Island, and many other places. On Prince of Wales, only a few places were spared: the south end of the island, with its deeply incised shoreline; the Karta River drainage; the necklace of lakes in the Thorne River watershed known as Honker Divide.

In 1996 a small party of conservationists launched their sea kayaks in remote waters to search for the largest trees and the highest-volume stands remaining in Southeast Alaska. When they came upon these giants, they photographed them and carefully measured them so they could record them in a national registry. Most of their discoveries were in remote, untouched areas of Prince of Wales Island—tree museums.

At Nasa Creek up Trocadero Bay, they found trees 210 feet tall. At Shaheen Creek near Tuxekan Passage, they found a 180-foot Sitka spruce in a stand containing a phenomenal 113,000 board feet of timber per acre. At Nutwka Sound near Hydaburg, they paddled to the head of an estuary on an eight-foot tide and up a slow-moving stream until they reached a stand of 175-foot hemlocks, measuring six and a half feet in diameter.

IF PRINCE OF WALES ISLAND is a sacrifice zone, there are lessons to be learned from its sacrifice. Over many decades, its streams may recover. Over centuries, its clearcuts and thickets may once again shelter deer through hard winters. Over millennia, the island may become whole. If that is allowed to occur, Prince of Wales Island will have taught us much about the cost of greed, the long life of the forest, the limits of the land.

Photo on opposite page: Hatchery Lake, at the north end of Honker Divide on Prince of Wales Island. Photo by Trygve Steen.

PART I

To 1980

"One well-entrenched social myth, at once pervasive and powerful, yet rarely spoken aloud or critically examined, is the notion of settling frontiers. Empty land is an affront and a challenge."

—Robert B. Weeden, *Messages from Earth: Nature and the Human Prospect in Alaska*

1

THE CONTRACTS

The date was July 14, 1954, the place a sheltered cove north of Ketchikan, Alaska, the occasion the dedication of a new pulp mill. On that day, with great pomp and celebration, the Alaska Territory took a giant stride toward statehood. Forest Service Chief R.E. McArdle, who traveled from Washington, D.C., for the ceremony, proclaimed the event "the realization of a hope which the U.S. Forest Service has cherished for almost 50 years." And for Alaska Territorial Governor B. Frank Heintzleman, the mill's dedication fulfilled a personal lifelong dream.

The sprawling new mill on the shore of Ward Cove, built by two forest products companies at a cost of $52.5 million, was to manufacture dissolving pulp, used in the manufacture of rayon, cellophane and disposable diapers. Its raw material would be supplied from the vast untapped stands of old-growth western hemlock and Sitka spruce that grew on the Tongass National Forest. As inducement to build the mill, the Forest Service guaranteed the newly established Ketchikan Pulp Co. a supply of federal timber adequate to operate the mill for fifty years.

The Ketchikan mill was the largest factory ever built in the Alaska Territory. "It took courage and faith to build this mill–if that is not so, then why did the government offers of low priced wood, with no carrying charges, go begging over thirty years?" the editors of *Pulp and Paper* magazine asked in a special October 1954 issue heralding the new plant.

Overnight, the mill's opening created hundreds of high-paid jobs in Ketchikan and transformed the isolated fishing community at the southern end of the Alaska Panhandle into a bustling timber town. New schools were built, new businesses opened to provide goods and services for the workers, new roads pushed into the forest to open up land for housing.

But more than a pulp mill was launched at Ward Cove that day. By anchoring Alaska's boom-and-bust economy with stable, year-round jobs, the mill would help the nation's sparsely settled northern territory prove its worthiness for statehood. When a Japanese conglomerate agreed to build a second pulp mill near Sitka that same year, a bright future for Southeast Alaska seemed assured.

Statehood, a fervent goal of Alaska territorial leaders since 1912, came five years later. In its constitution, the new state spelled out its principal goal in unambiguous language: to "encourage the settlement of its land and the development of its resources by making them available for maximum use consistent with the public interest."

Charlie Stout came to Alaska in 1954 to log on Prince of Wales Island and soon took a job at the mill. He never left. It was Alaska that attracted him, and Alaska that kept him there. "It was kind of my cup of tea," he said many years later. "I fell in love with the lifestyle. I met a ship millwright who taught me how to flyfish. I went moose-hunting in the Brooks Range. I don't fit anywhere else in the world."

SEEKING STATEHOOD

The campaign to entice a pulp industry to Southeast Alaska began soon after President Theodore Roosevelt signed the proclamation establishing the Tongass National Forest in 1907. Five years later, James Wickersham, the Alaska Territory's congressional delegate, appealed to Congress to confer statehood on Alaska. Like the young Frank Heintzleman, he saw the untapped forests of the Tongass as a path to that end.

In the 1920s, as an assistant district forester, Heintzleman helped survey the old-growth hemlock, spruce and cedar of the nation's largest national forest, which by then encompassed fifteen million acres of the Alaska Panhandle. He concluded that the Tongass was a national resource going to waste. When he let his imagination roam over its forested islands, Heintzleman saw neat clearcuts, vigorous second-growth stands, smokestacks, workers with lunch buckets, growing communities carved from the forest. His agency also saw a chance to break Canada's near-monopoly on the production of newsprint for U.S. markets by chipping Tongass timber for the manufacture of pulp.

The history of the Alaska Territory up to that time had been a history of exploitation. The exploiters had come in waves, seeking sea otter pelts, gold, salmon, crabs from the Aleutians, ivory from the Arctic coast. These raids had depleted Alaska's bounty, produced brief booms and generated great wealth for a few. But Congress wanted evidence that Alaska could build a stable economy with viable communities and a population able to support the obligations that statehood entailed.

Development was hampered by the fact that nearly all of the Alaska Territory's 591,000 square miles were controlled by the federal government. Only small amounts of land had been opened to homesteading. The Tongass National Forest covered nearly all of Southeast Alaska, from Dixon Strait in the south to the Yakutat Forelands in the north. The only private land available surrounded its small towns and villages.

Heintzleman laid out his vision for Southeast Alaska in a 1927 article for *Alaska Magazine*. He wrote that because the soils of the Alaska Panhandle were unsuitable for farming, and neither mining nor commercial fishing provided year-round jobs, timber was destined to become the lifeblood of Southeast Alaska's economy. But because the hemlock and spruce forests of the Tongass were old and riddled with decay, much of their timber would be unsuitable for sawlogs. The highest and best use for the Tongass, he said, would be to chip and pulp its decadent trees and turn them into newsprint.

However, the Forest Service's early attempts to establish a pulp industry in Southeast fell flat. In 1921, Alaska Pulp and Paper Co. bought 100 million board feet of timber and built a pulp mill up Snettisham Inlet southeast of Juneau. The primitive venture used water power to literally grind the wood into pulp. But high shipping costs quickly doomed the venture, and the mill closed soon after it opened.

Undeterred, in 1927 the agency awarded fifty-year contracts to two companies that promised to manufacture pulp for newsprint: Crown-Zellerbach Corp. of San Francisco, which announced that it would build a mill near Ketchikan, and a joint venture of the *San Francisco Chronicle* and the *Los Angeles Times*, which planned to build a mill near the mining town of Juneau. Between them, the contracts, if fulfilled, would consume a whopping ten billion board feet of Alaska rain forest over the fifty years.

The Federal Power Commission had done its part by granting permits for the development of hydroelectric projects to power the two mills. Heintzleman said there would be water power aplenty for other manufacturing enterprises as well—additional paper plants, sawmills, mines, salmon canneries and other local industries. "The long-awaited advent into the Territory of the paper manufacturing industry, which will make use of the hemlock-spruce forests of the southern coastal region, is apparently about to materialize," he wrote in a newspaper column after the contracts were signed. Yet the remoteness of the Alaska Panhandle, its distance from markets, the dominance of the Canadian pulp industry, and the weakness of the world pulp market doomed these projects as well.

In all, the Forest Service signed and awarded ten long-term timber contracts for Tongass timber between 1912 and 1927. In each case the bidder defaulted, usually after long delay and forfeiture of the bid deposit. Not one sale went forward.

THE BEARS OF ADMIRALTY

John Holzworth's *Wild Grizzlies of Alaska*, published in 1930, introduced the world to the brown bears of Admiralty Island. Holzworth, a popular outdoors writer, was guided on his expedition by Alexander Hasselborg, a loner who had lived on the million-acre island for twenty years, sharing it with the bears and the Tlingit Indians of Angoon. Holzworth related several encounters with the great bears and also offered vivid descriptions of the birds and fish, forests and rivers and mountains of Admiralty.

"As we penetrated to the interior of the island I was struck by the almost tropical profusion of flora through which we had to fight our way," he wrote. "It would be a rich field of study for the botanist . . . . We went through thick forests of spruce and hemlock, and even where the trees were thickest there was a solid mass of undergrowth. Ferns with enormous stems grew luxuriantly on the soft spongy ground. The earth itself, save in the game trails, was covered by thick beds of mosses, in which one sank softly as on an Astrakhan rug. Parasitical moss hung from the trees in graceful drooping clusters, thick and long as it does on the live-oaks around Charleston and in the Savannahs of Georgia . . . ."

Holzworth's book captured the imagination of the American public. Here was a place so large and pristine that bears in great numbers could roam at will from mountain slopes to tidewater.

In 1932 the Sierra Club Board of Directors passed a resolution urging the National Park Service to investigate setting aside Admiralty Island to preserve habitat for the Alaska brown bear. The club also urged "the preservation of a typical specimen of Southeast Alaska wilderness in primitive condition . . . to prevent this important region of the Inside Passage from being defaced by unnecessary timber cutting." That same year Holzworth asked a congressional committee to establish Admiralty Island as a national park or bear sanctuary.

Brown bear cubs. Pack Creek, Admiralty Island. Photo by John Schoen.

But within the Forest Service, early arguments for the preservation of Admiralty fell on deaf ears. The agency's master plan designated Admiralty as the source of timber for a pulp mill in Juneau. The Great Depression, however, put these pulp dreams on hold.

During the New Deal, the Forest Service became a conservation agency. The Civilian Conservation Corps put unemployed men to work building roads, trails, bridges and remote recreation cabins in the Tongass. The Forest Service undertook a Works Progress Administration project to preserve outstanding totem poles from the ravages of weather and protect them from looters by moving them to museums in Sitka and Juneau, and hiring Alaska Natives to restore them.

World War II created a temporary demand for lightweight Sitka spruce lumber, which was needed for airplane construction. The First World War had largely depleted spruce stands in the Pacific Northwest. So in 1942 Congress created the Alaska Spruce Log Program. Its goal was to produce 100 million board feet of high-grade spruce annually for the war effort. Independent logging contractors streamed into Southeast Alaska to begin leveling the mammoth trees. A spruce mill was built on the Ketchikan waterfront to cut the logs. Nine logging camps, instant communities, sprang up in remote locations, and the first widescale logging in the Tongass commenced. But the program ended prematurely in early 1944, when the War Production Board announced that metal would take the place of spruce in airplane production. Virtually overnight, the logging camps became ghost towns.

Throughout World War II and the early post-war era, Heintzleman nurtured his dream. He made a standing offer to provide a stable supply of

Tongass timber to any company that would build a pulp mill in Southeast, and he promised that the Forest Service would assist in such an enterprise by building roads, log transfer stations and logging camps in the wilderness. In 1944 Heintzleman dispatched a lieutenant, C.M. Archbold, to head up several cruising parties and complete the maps and reports that would eventually be used to lay out the first of these long-term timber sales. Zellerbach Paper Co. was interested in Heintzleman's offer, but after sending engineers and timber cruisers to review the standing timber, the company, like others before it, backed out of negotiations.

Taking inventory

By the early 1950s, Heintzleman had a good grasp of the extent and types of forest in his domain. He knew that only three million acres of the Tongass grew timber of commercial quality. But his projections of timber yield on those lands were far off the mark. He calculated that Alaska's two national forests, the Tongass and the Chugach, held eighty-five billion board feet of commercial timber between them.

In fact, as late as the 1950s the Forest Service had no way accurately to measure timber volume on the Tongass. Its islands, accessible only by plane or boat, were hard to get to, especially during the long, dark, rainy winter months. Bushwhacking through the tangled undergrowth, over fallen logs and across muskeg bogs, was a treacherous undertaking. Dangerous encounters with brown bears were a constant threat on Admiralty, Baranof and Chichagof islands.

So the Forest Service guessed. It used 1948 aerial photos taken by the Navy to estimate the extent of forest, then calculated timber yields based on formulas used in Oregon and Washington. However, trees in Southeast Alaska did not grow to the behemoth proportions of those in the Pacific Northwest. Few exceeded four feet in diameter and 140 feet in height. The agency's estimates would prove wildly optimistic.

Heintzleman laid out his vision for the liquidation of commercial timber on the Tongass in precise, Soviet-style increments. There would be five pulp mills. Each would produce five hundred tons of newsprint daily. Each would be supplied by a specific area of the national forest. To lure companies to Southeast Alaska, each pulp company would be offered a guaranteed fifty-year supply of timber. There was no room in his equation for such unquantifiable values as salmon, brown bear or black-tailed deer.

NATIVE CLAIMS

One large obstacle stood in the way of development of a pulp industry in the immediate postwar period. That was the matter of unresolved Alaska Native land claims. The Tlingit and Haida claimed title to most of Southeast Alaska by virtue of many thousands of years of occupation. The 1867 Alaska Purchase had not extinguished these claims, and the indigenous people of the Panhandle had not ceded their lands through treaties, nor had they lost them in war. The Alaska Organic Act, which had set forth the principles by which the Alaska Territory would be managed, required Congress eventually to settle Alaska Native claims.

In 1935, as part of the so-called New Deal for Indians, Congress passed the Alaska Reorganization Act, recognizing the right of Alaska's aboriginal tribes to establish village self-government, borrow money from federal credit unions, and defend their traditional hunting and fishing rights. The act specified that no Indian, Eskimo or Aleut could be molested in exercising those rights. But the Office of Indian Affairs did a poor job of administering the act, Congress failed to provide adequate funding, and confusion and inconsistency reigned in its implementation.

The act also authorized Southeast Alaska Natives to seek compensation for land appropriated by the government in the U.S. Court of Claims. But the Alaska Native Brotherhood, the principal voice for the indigenous people of Southeast Alaska, had no standing to press the claim. Founded in 1912 by a group of Alaska Natives educated at Sheldon Jackson College in Sitka, the ANB wielded considerable influence. It reflected the philosophies of the college's founder and namesake, Presbyterian missionary Sheldon Jackson, who favored the eradication of Native languages and the assimilation of Alaska's indigenous people into the territory's political and economic mainstream. The ANB published its own newspaper, and its annual Grand Camp became a must-attend event for Alaska politicians. But because it was not a tribal government in the legal sense, the federal courts ruled that it could not bring a land claim under the 1935 law. So in 1940, Native leaders formed the Central Council of Tlingit and Haida Indians to sue for damages over the loss of land the federal government had appropriated when it established the Tongass National Forest and Glacier Bay National Monument.

The unresolved land claims cast a cloud over the federal government's legal authority to sell timber, oil, minerals or any other commodity in the

Alaska Territory. Investors were unwilling to risk their money as long as the question remained unresolved. In January of 1946, while the Tlingit and Haida lawsuit was pending, U.S. Interior Secretary Harold Ickes brought the issue of Alaska Native land claims to a head when he announced that he had concluded Indians in the Southeast Alaska communities of Hydaburg, Kake and Klawock held "an exclusive possessory right" to a quarter-million acres within the Tongass National Forest.

The following year, Congress offered at least a temporary fix, and allayed investors' concerns, when it passed the Tongass Timber Act. The act authorized the Forest Service to offer fifty-year contracts for Tongass timber in order to jump-start a timber economy in Southeast. To deal with the problem of unresolved Native claims, it directed that proceeds from the long-term contracts be placed in trust for Southeast Alaska Natives.

The Alaska Native Brotherhood had expected a just resolution of land claims. Instead, Congress had given the Forest Service the green light to proceed with selling off the traditional lands of the Tlingit and Haida. The ANB felt betrayed by the law, which it dubbed "Alaska's Teapot Dome." Not until 1959, the year of statehood, did the U.S. Court of Claims rule in favor of the Tlingit and Haida Council. It took nine more years for the court to award them $7.5 million for the 20 million acres the federal government had seized.

A NEW PLAYER

With passage of the Tongass Timber Act, the Forest Service began serious negotiations with prospective pulp mill developers. In 1951, the agency signed a contract with two companies, Puget Sound Pulp & Timber Co. of Bellingham, Washington, and American Viscose Co., the nation's largest manufacturer of rayon, to supply a Ketchikan pulp mill with 8.25 billion board feet of Tongass timber over fifty years. The dissolving pulp produced by the new mill would be used in the manufacture of rayon, not newsprint. But that did not dampen Heintzleman's enthusiasm. He was rewarded for his persistence two years later when President Dwight D. Eisenhower appointed him Alaska's fourteenth territorial governor.

Puget Sound Pulp & Timber, one of the most innovative players in the pulp industry, put the deal together. Its managers assembled the land parcels at Ward Cove, found financing, and negotiated the contract with the Forest Service. In 1953 the newly formed Ketchikan Pulp Company hired Roland

Stanton, a young chemical engineer newly graduated from the University of Washington, to take a manufacturing technology patented by Weyerhaeuser Co. and adapt it to the predominantly hemlock forest of Southeast Alaska. Stanton spent nine months in the basement of Puget Sound Pulp & Timber's Bellingham mill, experimenting with various formulas for bleaching cooked pulp samples, until he found the right recipe for dissolving pulp. The following year Stanton and his wife moved to Ketchikan, where he helped oversee mill startup. The Ketchikan mill was the first designed and built from the ground up specifically to use the magnesium-based process, which allowed the recovery and burning of lignin, a wood waste product also known as "red liquor."

PORTENTS OF TROUBLE

There were several glitches to be worked out in those early months. Stanton recalled the day a river of foam poured out the door of the wash plant. He spent months testing defoamers to control it. And there was the discovery early on that the walls of the mill were dissolving because the stainless steel they were built from contained too little molybdenum, a metal in scarce supply during the Korean War. "The metal became pitted," Stanton said. "We had to replace large sections of the mill."

Before the pulp mill came, Ward Cove and Ward Creek teemed with life. Four kinds of salmon spawned in the creek, along with char, Dolly Varden, and cutthroat and steelhead trout. Shellfish thrived in the cove's cold waters. But portents of trouble surfaced even before the mill began operating.

In 1952, the Alaska Water Pollution Control Board studied the cove and concluded there was virtually no current beneath the top three feet. Whatever the pulp mill dumped into the cove would not easily disperse. The board recommended that the mill pump its wastes out to the mouth of the cove, where they would be diluted by volume, flow and tide. But the outfall extension never was built. Instead, from the beginning, KPC discharged untreated solid and liquid wastes directly into the cove.

A COMPANY TOWN

Ketchikan in the 1950s was Southeast Alaska in microcosm. Perched on the rocky southwestern shore of Revillagigedo Island, named by Captain George Vancouver for an obscure Mexican count, the town is the rainiest in Southeast, getting an average of 160 inches of precipitation a year. It is the first port of call northbound in Alaska, and is surrounded by steep mountains that rise from the deep channel of Tongass Narrows.

Before white settlers arrived, a Tlingit clan camped each summer at the mouth of Ketchikan Creek, the only flat land in the vicinity, to harvest the creek's teeming salmon runs. Soon after the Alaska Purchase, the U.S. government established a military fort at nearby Tongass Island. The first white settlers followed in the 1880s, and built a fish saltery at the creek's mouth.

In 1900, as miners streamed into the area to prospect for copper and platinum on Prince of Wales Island, the residents of Ketchikan petitioned the federal government to declare their settlement a city. In the early part of the twentieth century the settlement became a supply center for more than twenty mines on Prince of Wales Island. Between the two world wars, Ketchikan was a fishing town, home to two big cold storage companies and as many as eleven fish canneries.

A city of wood built on piers grew up around the creek. Rock fill and dredging eventually allowed Ketchikan to expand. "No longer could boats tie up at the foot of St. John's Church on Mission Street," says an account in a local history. "But today, as then, the surge of full moon high tides slips in under downtown buildings to puddle basement floors."

Miners and fishermen stopping off at Ketchikan provided a ready clientele for prostitutes, who were eventually ordered by town fathers to move their businesses from various locations to Creek Street along Ketchikan Creek. For fifty years Ketchikan's notorious red light district prospered, drawing halibut boat and salmon seiner crews, and prospectors who had struck it rich.

Federal and local reformers closed the red light district in 1954, the same year the new pulp mill began operating—perhaps as a signal that Ketchikan had shed its frontier culture and become a suitable place for a working man to raise his family. Creek Street became a historic district, and the most colorful reminder of Ketchikan's frontier past.

"A HE-MAN'S JOB"

Commercial logging began near Hollis, once a mining town of four hundred, across Clarence Strait from Ketchikan on Prince of Wales Island. Trees there grew to impressive size, and the terrain was gentle. A grizzled prospector, owner of the once-famed Lucky Nell gold mine, greeted the first loggers to come ashore.

Early accounts of Prince of Wales describe a primeval world. In 1954, an editor for *Pulp and Paper* Magazine, accompanied by Ketchikan Pulp Co. logging manager Art Brooks, flew over the area that would provide the mill's first supply of pulp logs. "As far as the eye could see, in more than an hour of flying both ways at 85 mph, mostly at 600 feet altitude, there were—trees, trees, trees, nearly all virgin timber," he wrote.

The writer recounted with awe the challenges facing loggers as they began tearing into the green fabric of the rainforest: "Even when the loggers and their construction crews have 'stormed' a beach successfully, a big job in itself, they face many other problems before they even start logging. A considerable amount of muskeg and rock is prevalent in these areas, creating additional problems in building the short road-systems necessary. But it is amazing how so many trees are found growing on only a thin layer of soil over these rocks, and much of it overmature . . . . Over three hunded feet or more above the spar tree and yarder, a logger was clambering around the distant bank like a monkey hooking up the long line to felled trees. Logging in Alaska is a he-man's job. . . ."

With astonishment he described the spectacle of huge tractors hauling bunches of logs off a hillside and snaking them from the landing down to the water: "The route resembled that of a roller coaster. But besides tipping up and down over steep banks, they dragged the logs through deep, oozing muskeg too." It was logging at its most primitive, and environmental safeguards were nonexistent, as this account confirms: ". . . a Lorain two-yard shovel was seen following right up the course of a climbing mountain stream while digging gravel out of the stream bed for road-building. Nature helped with the job, by washing the gravel right there in the stream, as the Lorain dipped its loads in the water and then into Euclid ten-yard dump trucks."

The editor saw seven bears in the woods and several big seals frolicking in the surf during his daylong excursion. He observed enviously that "a logger who had a mind to could go a few feet out in a boat from his bunkhouse and pull in salmon up to 60 pounds, or halibut up to 150 pounds or more." He marveled at spruce six feet in diameter. But he was most impressed with the economics of cutting down this primeval forest: "The Forest Service has figured a complete turnover and fully restored stand of timber in the Tongass forest on the basis of a crop rotation of eighty-five years."

A SPORTSMEN'S CAMPAIGN

The first Alaskans to grasp that the best forests of the Tongass were slated for logging were sportsmen. In 1955, Georgia-Pacific Corporation purchased an option to buy a large timber sale on Admiralty Island and build a mill near Juneau. The following year Corey Frank and Frank DuFresne, the latter a long-time director of the Alaska Game Commission, wrote an article called "Lost Paradise" for *Field and Stream,* in which they recommended that all of Admiralty's one million acres be closed to logging and declared a national game management area. They described an idyllic guided fishing and wildlife viewing trip across Admiralty that offered glimpses of spotted trumpeter swans, harlequin ducks, bald eagles, seals and three-pound Dolly Varden trout, as well as fresh "hat-sized" brown bear tracks. "We halted for a moment, awed into silence by the beauty of this unspoiled paradise," they wrote.

Like the rare trumpeter swan, they said, Admiralty was fighting for its existence. "For this world-famous island, one of the most magnificent wilderness areas in North America, so beautiful that Theodore Roosevelt thought it should be set aside as a national monument, is facing almost sure extinction. The menace is the pulp mill, destroyer of essential timbered watersheds, polluter of clean waters so necessary to the life cycle of the salmon, enemy of all wildlife including the brown bear, ruthless despoiler of a nation's recreational heritage. The progress of the pulp industry in Alaska—a progress that appears to be the pet pride of the Territory's present Governor—does not represent a vague threat lurking somewhere in the future. Its shadow hangs over Admiralty Island at this very moment."

Field and Stream magazine became the unlikely soapbox of hunters and sport fishermen who wanted to protect the Southeast Alaska wilderness from the chainsaw. And Admiralty Island became their rallying point. Georgia-Pacific ultimately would abandon its plan for a Juneau mill.

TIMBER TO REBUILD JAPAN

In 1957, the Forest Service landed its second pulp mill when a newly formed Japanese consortium, headed by the Industrial Bank of Japan, agreed to built a mill in Sitka. In exchange, the Forest Service promised nearly five billion board feet of timber from Baranof and Chichagof islands over fifty years. This second contract was especially popular with President Eisenhower's State Department. They saw Alaska's natural resources—fish from the Bering Sea, timber from the Tongass—as raw material for rebuilding Japan's economy, which was still struggling to rebound from the effects of World War II. They also hoped that access to Alaska fish and timber would keep the nation's vanquished foe from turning to the Soviet Union for economic assistance.

Postwar Japan had a dire need for timber. During the war it had lost access to forests on Sakhalin Island and logs from The Philippines. Its own forest stands had been cut indiscriminately to supply the wartime effort. By war's end Japan's timber acreage had been reduced by nearly half. Young trees were being cut prematurely to meet the nation's need, triggering devastating landslides. If the trend continued, Japan's privately owned softwood forests would be exhausted in fifteen years.

U.S. advisers urged Japanese leaders to take legal steps to conserve their forests, and in 1951 the Japanese Diet did strengthen its forest-practice law. But enforcement of stricter standards threatened to disrupt postwar reconstruction and industrial development. The nation was forced to look abroad for timber.

Softwood timber was abundant in the Soviet Union, but as Alaska Lumber and Pulp Co. explained in a historical account of this era, "It was difficult to realize the import of timber from that country under the international situation prevailing at that time." The largely untapped forests of Southeast Alaska looked more promising. In January of 1952, the Japanese government submitted a petition to General Douglas MacArthur, who had served as Eisenhower's Supreme Commander of the Allied Powers in Japan, asking for permission to procure Alaskan timber.

The response was swift. In June, the American Embassy in Tokyo approved the request, and urged Japanese investors to proceed with incorporating a United States company to produce lumber or pulp. "To promote such an action, the United States Forest Service has several timber units for sale to an organization planning to establish a newsprint or pulpwood mill in Alaska," the embassy wrote. From that point on, it was a matter of negotiating a deal.

Japan sent three representatives to Washington to meet with the Forest Service, and dispatched a technical survey team to Alaska. On August 15, 1953, the Alaska Pulp Co., Ltd. was established in Tokyo. Its shareholders included fourteen chemical fiber and cotton spinning companies, twelve pulp and paper manufacturing companies, four trading companies and several lumber companies. Soon after, APC established a wholly owned Juneau-based subsidiary, Alaska Lumber and Pulp Co. Inc.

The entry of Japanese investors into the American pulp industry drew opposition from the American Paper and Pulp Association, which predicted economic ruin for the domestic wood pulp industry and called on the government to repudiate the plan. But the State Department responded that the Sitka mill would contribute to Alaska's development, and thus be a net gain for the nation.

Sitka, a scenic gem situated on a beautiful sound dotted with small forested islands, was hungry for development in the postwar era. The Sitka Chamber of Commerce moved quickly to bid for the new pulp mill, and launched a signature-collecting drive to thwart opposition from the domestic pulp industry. In 1955 a three-member congressional team visited Alaska and Japan and issued a statement favoring the proposed timber sale.

With opposition silenced, Alaska Lumber and Pulp proceeded to apply for permission to buy timber from the Tongass National Forest. It took the Forest Service twelve days to accept the application. On January 25, 1956, the Forest Service held an auction, and Alaska Lumber and Pulp submitted the only bid on the sale of 5.25 billion board feet of hemlock, spruce and cedar, to be logged over the next half-century from the north end of the Tongass and turned into dissolving pulp.

ALP sent surveyors and engineers to a site on Sawmill Creek, near Sitka on the pristine shore of Silver Bay, to begin laying out the mill. About half the $55 million required to build the mill was raised from U.S. investors through the sale of bonds and bank loans, half from investors in Japan. Construction began in 1958. On Nov. 25, 1959, the mill produced its first batch of finished pulp.

Not all of the Tongass was to be delivered to the two giant pulp companies. The Forest Service planned to set aside one-third of its annual timber offerings for small timber companies and independent loggers to bid on at open auction, so these entrepreneurs who had pioneered the timber industry in Alaska would continue to get a fair chance at federal timber.

But the pulp company managers had other ideas. Collusion between the companies began almost immediately. In January of 1959 Ketchikan Pulp timber manager Art Brooks send a confidential memo to Archie Byers, his counterpart at the Sitka mill. The memo described his company's timber sale agreement with the Forest Service and shared information on how much KPC paid independent loggers for timber. Brooks asked Byers to keep the information "strictly confidential." Two months later, accountants from Alaska Pulp met with KPC officials to obtain more information on logging costs and logging and construction techniques. This was not the behavior of companies that planned to compete for raw material in an open market.

STATEHOOD AT LAST

Statehood came that same year, the culmination of a protracted power struggle between the United States government and its vast, undeveloped northern territory. During the long territorial period, Alaskans had paid federal taxes and been subject to the military draft, but could not vote in federal elections, and had no voting representative in Congress. As Ernest Gruening, former Alaska territorial governor and future U.S. senator, remarked in his keynote address at the Alaska Constitutional Convention of 1955, if a colony is "a geographic area held for political, strategic and economic advantage," the Alaska Territory fitted the description exactly. The bitterness that marked the statehood campaign bred a politics of resentment against the federal government in Alaskans that survives to this day.

President Eisenhower opposed statehood for Alaska. In 1955, he wrote to U.S. Senator Henry Jackson, a Washington Democrat who served on the Senate Interior Committee, that Alaska's strategic importance in the North Pacific demanded full freedom for military action—freedom that would be compromised if statehood were granted. Others argued that the territory's sparsely distributed population, about 200,000 in the early 1950s, could not support a state government. Developing its resources would be too expensive an undertaking to attract private industry, they said, and Alaska's remoteness would isolate it from the main currents of American life. But Alaskans were eager for statehood. And a 1955 poll showed that 82 percent of all Americans agreed.

With statehood came a federal land grant of 104 million acres, an area the size of California, to be selected by the state within twenty-five years. Political leaders were eager to get their hands on the new state's vast undeveloped resources. But most of Alaska remained under the control of the U.S. Department of the Interior and, in Southeast, the Forest Service. The federal government's hegemony continued to remind Alaskans of their longtime second-class status. And the government's continuing strong hand in Alaska's affairs bred a class of chauvinistic Alaska politicians who openly opposed federal control.

Ted Stevens epitomized Alaska's new political class. Born in 1923 in Indianapolis, Indiana, Stevens served in the Army Air Corps in World War II, graduated from Harvard Law School in 1950, and went north to Alaska in 1953 to serve as U.S. attorney. He left Alaska for Washington, D.C. in 1956 to work as legislative counsel to the U.S. Department of the Interior in the final push for Alaska statehood. Afterward he returned to Alaska and served three years in the Alaska House before being appointed to the Senate to fill a vacancy in 1968. Canny, vengeful and zealously pro-development, Stevens was to become the dean of Alaska politics, helping to determine the future of his adopted state.

2

THE CONSERVATIONISTS

The country around Ketchikan was pristine wilderness when Bob and Dixie Baade arrived in the 1940s. Bob Baade had landed a job as an Alaska Department of Fish and Game sport fish biologist. Dixie was an expert on the science of water quality. The Baades' first years in their rainy new home were idyllic. They fished, hunted, and explored the wilderness at their back door on foot, by boat and on cross-country skis. Dixie Baade helped found the Alaska Sports and Wildlife Club, one of the first outdoor recreation groups in Southeast.

After the Ketchikan Pulp Co. mill began operating in 1954, the focus of Dixie Baade's conservation work changed. Her involvement put her face-to-face with the logging that was beginning to scar the mountainsides of Prince of Wales Island. By 1963 entire river drainages on the island—the Rodman, the Harris, the Maybeso—had been stripped of their commercial timber. Some cuts exceeded a thousand acres in size. In one decade, between the early 1950s and the early 1960s, the annual timber harvest on the Tongass National Forest increased six-fold, to 343 million board feet. Ketchikan had become a timber town, and a hostile environment for conservation-minded citizens. The Baades felt this hostility. But Dixie Baade carried on, working to expose harmful logging practices and the pulp mill discharges that were beginning to pollute Ward Cove.

In 1960 Congress passed the Multiple Use-Sustained Yield Act, directing the Forest Service to give equal weight to recreation, timber, forage, wildlife and watershed protection in the management of national forests. In response, the Forest Service in Alaska wrote its first management plan, a "Multiple Use Management Guide for the Alaska Region." Baade threw herself into the planning process, asking hard questions about logging practices on the Tongass. Timber industry leaders put pressure on state fish and game officials to fire Bob Baade if he couldn't "shut his wife up." The Baades were ostracized socially; acquaintances would cross the street to avoid them.

The Baades were not the only ones raising questions about logging practices. Commercial fishermen and kayakers exploring the south end of the Tongass began encountering shocking vistas of scarred mountainsides and sullied salmon streams. State fisheries biologists were among the first to sound the alarm.

Industrial logging spread north after the Alaska Pulp Corporation mill at Sitka began operating in 1959. In 1961, the Alaska Department of Fish and Game asked the Forest Service to protect the abundant salmon runs of the Kadashan River watershed, on Tenakee Inlet in the North Tongass. But the Forest Service was unwilling to forego the sale of timber in the watershed, which lay within the supply area for the Sitka mill.

THE MULTIPLE USE PLAN

In 1964, the Alaska Region of the Forest Service released its Multiple Use Plan. It called for an annual timber sale level of 824 million board feet on the Tongass National Forest—enough, by its calculations, to supply four large pulp mills or other manufacturing plants under long-term contracts, with timber left over for independent purchasers. The ninety-page document plainly stated the agency's bias: "About 95 percent of the commercial forest land of Southeastern Alaska is occupied by overmature stands of hemlock, spruce, and cedar. Silviculturally, these decadent stands should be removed by clear-cutting methods as soon as possible to make way for new stands of fast-growing second-growth timber."

The plan proposed no salmon stream buffers, no wildlife habitat reserves, and no wilderness areas. These omissions prompted an objection from Richard Costley, director of recreation for the Alaska region, who complained in a memo to his superiors that "too few of us recognize Wilderness as a separate resource . . . . It must be protected and other resource uses curtailed, if necessary to do so." This was heresy in the Tongass National Forest of the 1960s.

EARLY WARNINGS

In 1964 Walter Kirkness, commissioner of Alaska Fish and Game, alerted Alaska Governor William Egan in a letter that "all is not as it should be in our logging activities on Forest Service and other land," particularly with regard to impacts on salmon streams. "All must recognize that some damage to salmon production will result from even the best run of logging shows," Kirkness wrote. "What we must attempt to do (ourselves and the Forest Service) is hold it to minimum."

Kirkness said the greatest damage to watersheds was being inflicted by loggers who violated stipulations in their contracts: "They attempt to effect savings in their operation either in time or money to the great detriment of the salmon. It is here that we are having our most trouble. Generally the Forest Service has not taken a firm stand on this type of operation—neither prosecuting nor canceling contracts. They have more field personnel in Southeastern Alaska than does our Department. Their only job is to work with the logging shows, yet we have had instances of the logging getting out of hand . . . ."

He enclosed photographs of an estuary on Chichagof Island, in the North Tongass, where the water ran brown with silt from upstream roads and bridges improperly built. The section of the stream buried in silt had produced three thousand spawning salmon the previous year, Kirkness wrote. But though the Forest Service was aware of the damage, local managers had done nothing until his own biologists brought it to their attention. They responded by closing the operation down for a week while the logger tried to correct the problem, to little effect.

Kirkness said he had avoided going public with criticism of logging on the Tongass because his agency was bound by formal agreement to work entirely through the Forest Service in correcting problems related to logging. "A public appeal," he wrote, "would break down relationships between the two agencies."

Alaska Regional Forester W. Howard Johnson responded arrogantly to complaints from the powerless state agency. Johnson had ascended to the top regional post in 1963, after ten years as regional timber manager, and was thoroughly indoctrinated in the timber culture of the Tongass. When Kirkness asked him to defer logging for 100 years in thirty key salmon watersheds identified by his agency, Johnson retorted that the Tongass was committed to "provide the combination of materials and services from the land that will best meet the needs of the people." He added, without apparent irony: "Resolution of conflicts by favoring one resource over all others will not meet this requirement."

As tourists from the Lower 48 began trickling north on steamers, Forest Service officials faced increasing complaints about their clearcutting practices from outside Alaska. Much of the logging was clearly visible from the shipping lanes used by cruise ships and ferries as they threaded the Inside Passage. The Forest Service responded by establishing regulations that prohibited clearcuts along the narrowest shipping lanes. But as tourism accelerated and clearcutting spread into new watersheds, the friction between the tourism and timber industries intensified. Electing to deal with its problem through better public relations, the agency introduced an interpretive program on the Alaska state ferries to explain why the land looked the way it did.

ENTER THE SIERRA CLUB

In 1967, Peggy Wayburn decided it was high time she and her husband paid a visit to Alaska. Edgar Wayburn, a San Francisco physician, was president of the Sierra Club, the nation's largest and most politically influential conservation organization. In the course of their conservation work the Wayburns had visited the grandest places the American West had to offer. Ed Wayburn had planned something different, a river trip in northern Ontario, for 1967. But Peggy Wayburn pressed her case, and they decided to take their annual "conservation vacation" in Alaska. It was an opportune time; the future of the Great Land was up for grabs.

The Alaska Conservation Society was the only statewide environmental organization in Alaska, and it was stretched thin trying to counter the development pressures that had come with statehood. From the Arctic to the Panhandle, the rush to develop the state's untapped natural resources trove was on.

Celia Hunter, the society's founder, drove the Wayburns from the train station at Mount McKinley National Park to Camp Denali, which she and her partner, Ginny Wood, had established on the Wonder Lake Road. She showed them a hill above Wonder Lake where the National Park Service wanted to build a tourist hotel. Ed Wayburn didn't waste time staking out the Sierra Club's position; in typically blunt fashion, he fired off a letter to the director of the Park Service warning: "You'll put a hotel there over my dead body."

In the late 1960s most of Alaska—290 million acres of "unreserved" federal land in a state of 375 million acres—was administered by the federal Bureau of Land Management. Outside Mt. McKinley National Park, a congressionally designated preserve, and two national monuments established by executive order, at Glacier Bay and on the Katmai Peninsula, virtually all of it was open to development.

The Wayburns met with Alaska BLM Director Burt Silcock, who was attempting to get large expanses of Alaska wilderness protected by executive order. Silcock flew them to see the Arctic Coastal Plain and the jagged peaks of the Wrangell Range.

Eventually the Wayburns arrived in Juneau, where they met local conservationists and paid Regional Forester Johnson a visit. It was Johnson's first encounter with a national conservation group. "He didn't smile," Ed Wayburn recalled. "He brought no people with him. He listened to us, we listened to him. He told us of the great things they were doing, supplying the pulp mills and creating jobs."

The 1964 Wilderness Act had given conservationists a process for winning permanent congressional protection of wilderness. Wayburn asked Johnson how much wilderness he had designated in Alaska. Johnson "sat back and looked hard at me," Wayburn recalled. "Finally he said, 'Wilderness? Wilderness? Man, the whole damn thing is wilderness!' I said, 'That may be true today, but what about tomorrow?'"

Johnson's antipathy toward the idea of congressionally protected wilderness was well-known in the regional office. K .J. Metcalf, a forest planner during Johnson's tenure, recalls Johnson "slamming his fist on the table and saying, 'There will never be one acre of wilderness in the Tongass National Forest!'"

The Wayburns took a ferry south along the Inside Passage in good weather and saw evidence of logging on the Tongass for themselves. The following winter, Ed Wayburn got a letter from Jack Calvin, a biologist and photographer well-known among students of marine biology for co-authoring *Between Pacific Tides*, a classic text on marine life of the Pacific Coast. "I have a wonderful wilderness area and nobody knows anything about it," Calvin wrote. "I'd like to show this to the Sierra Club. I can take up to four people on my boat, the *Ootka*."

That summer the Wayburns flew to Sitka. They traveled by motorboat with Calvin, Brock Evans of the Sierra Club and Evans' wife up the west coast of Chichagof Island, where mountains rise three thousand feet from rocky shores and huge ocean swells roll in from the Pacific. Then they followed the protected east coast, stopping at coves and inlets all along the way. They hiked through areas populated with brown bears at a density of one per square mile. It was on Chichagof that the Wayburns encountered their first brown bear, looming thirty feet ahead of them in the mist as they walked single-file through a clearcut. Calvin let out a string of obscenities and the rest of the party took off running, but Calvin stood his ground, and the bear, no doubt appalled by this encounter with humans, lumbered off into the woods. As a result of that trip, Ed Wayburn put the West Chichagof-Yakobi Island wilderness on the Sierra Club's list of must-save places.

At trip's end, the Wayburns met with Howard Johnson again. This time the regional forester had brought four lieutenants, and he greeted his visitors with a smile. "He said, 'Doctor, I want you to know we have designated four wilderness study areas,'" Wayburn recalled. Wayburn later learned that the four areas were almost exclusively rocks, ice and scrub timber of no commercial value.

Wayburn informed Johnson that he had it in his power to protect a million acres of nearly pristine wilderness at one stroke by designating Admiralty Island as a wilderness reserve. Because Admiralty did not lie within the supply area for either pulp mill, it was not yet committed to wholesale timber production. The island boasted the highest concentrations of brown bears and bald eagles in North America. It was clearly deserving of protection, Wayburn reasoned. But after he made his case, he said, "Mr. Johnson just stared at me, not saying a word."

In fact, the Forest Service had not given up on attracting a third pulp mill to Southeast Alaska, and was offering up the pristine forests of Admiralty as an inducement. In 1965, after Georgia-Pacific Corporation backed out of a deal to build a pulp mill near Juneau, the Forest Service awarded the Admiralty Island sale to St. Regis Paper Co. at public auction. The agency was so eager to commit Admiralty to the chainsaw that it accepted a bid far lower than the going rate for Tongass timber at the time. Yet St. Regis later canceled its option as well. What Wayburn didn't know was that Johnson had quietly arranged to award the Admiralty Island sale to a third company, U.S. Plywood Champion—without benefit of public auction. The sale was awarded in September of 1968. "We didn't hear about this for six or eight months," Wayburn said. "When we heard, we were outraged."

The U.S. Plywood Champion sale area was vast, encompassing the entire west side of Admiralty, portions of the mainland, and an area to the north near Yakutat. At 8.75 billion board feet, the sale would be the largest in the history of the Forest Service.

UNANSWERED QUESTIONS

As Admiralty Island hung in the balance, a high-level Forest Service official sent a remarkable unsigned memo to Richard Cooley, a University of Washington geography professor with a strong interest in Alaska. Cooley forwarded the memo to the Sierra Club. It ended up on Wayburn's desk.

The official expressed deep concern about the direction management of the Tongass was taking, and posed a series of provocative questions. Noting that "the avowed management goal . . . is the liquidation by 2015 of all operable old-growth timber in southeast Alaska," he asked how the agency could then meet its mandate under the Multiple Use-Sustained Yield Act of 1960.

"Why have such large commitments of public land been made within the Alexander Archipelago with no apparent consideration being given to the establishment of wilderness areas?" the dissident official asked. Had anyone considered whether it was in the national interest for the agency to liquidate the old growth at such a rapid rate, and at such high cost to the environment? What was the Forest Service doing to help develop markets for independent logging contractors in Southeast Alaska, given the dominance of the pulp mills? And what was it doing to assure a sustainable timber supply over the long term?

"The Forest Service continues to push for immediate timber development at the price of committing large blocks of timber to one operator, and of selling public timber for a pittance to encourage marginal industry," he wrote. "This has the effect of encouraging marginal silvicultural practices, minimum utilization standards, and of creating monopolies. My question is: Have sufficient economic studies been made to warrant the apparent belief that this policy of rapid exploitation of old-growth timber stock for small immediate financial gain at this time is in the long-term public interest? Have any alternate management policies been considered? At what administrative level is this policy decided, and what are the qualifications of those administrators making these management decisions?"

These were pivotal questions for Congress and the Forest Service. They would remain unanswered for twenty years.

ACTING LOCALLY

By the end of the 1960s, environmental skirmishes were heating up in several Alaska Panhandle communities, and not only over logging. In Juneau, Alaska's capital, increased development pressures threatened the beautiful Mendenhall Wetlands bordering Gastineau Channel. An informal group that called itself the Steller Society, after Georg Wilhelm Steller, a naturalist on the first expedition of Russian explorer Vitus Bering, organized to win protection for the wetlands. Fisheries biologists, birdwatchers and high school students enlisted in the campaign.

Kay Greenough arrived in Juneau in 1965 from Idaho by way of Seattle. Accustomed to the wide open spaces of southeastern Idaho, she felt constrained by Juneau's isolation. "I would walk in the Mendenhall Wetlands with my kids and my dog for solace," she recalls. "I loved the birds and the geese." When proposals to develop the wetlands surfaced, she worked with other activists to fight them. The Steller Society won rerouting of a proposed freeway near the wetland fringe, and in 1976 much of the Mendenhall Wetlands became a state game refuge.

Juneau residents opposed logging of Admiralty Island, at least in principle. "Most people in Juneau didn't know what clearcutting looked like," Greenough said. But she had seen the clearcuts of western Washington and Vancouver Island, and knew well what was at stake.

A new Sierra Club chapter was forming in Anchorage. Juneau activists decided to affiliate with the club too, because of its national membership base and its influence in Washington, D.C. "We judged that they could best help us in our efforts to turn the Forest Service around," said Rich Gordon, a veteran Juneau activist.

In Sitka, local conservationists came together in 1967 as the Sitka Conservation Society to develop Southeast Alaska's first formal wilderness proposal, for permanent protection of Jack Calvin's West Chichagof-Yakobi Island wilderness. The Sierra Club Bulletin and National Parks magazine published feature articles about the area. But the Forest Service actively opposed the plan, arguing that West Chichagof was not true wilderness because it had seen mining and hand logging. The agency ultimately rejected the proposal on grounds that the entire proposed wilderness lay within the Alaska Lumber and Pulp Co. timber supply area.

In Ketchikan, the Southeast Alaska Mountaineering Association was campaigning to save the wild country adjoining East Behm Canal, a steep-sided passageway between Revillagigedo Island and the fiord-carved mainland. To the north, on Mitkof Island, the fishermen of Petersburg were trying to protect the Petersburg Creek watershed in their back yard.

Improved ferry service made it possible for the geographically isolated activists of the Alaska Panhandle to get together. On February 15 and 16, 1969, about seventy of them converged in Juneau to attend a wilderness workshop. Robert Weeden, the president of the Alaska Conservation Society, saw a need for the independent-minded activists of Southeast to coordinate their efforts, learn how the Forest Service was implementing the Wilderness Act, and set an agenda for wilderness protection on the Tongass.

The workshop was a surprisingly amicable affair. Rich Gordon and the new Sierra Club Juneau Group organized it, with help from Regional Forester Howard Johnson. Representatives from the National Park Service, Bureau of Sport Fisheries and Wildlife, Bureau of Land Management, and Alaska Division of Lands made presentations. The Sitka Conservation Society touted its West Chichagof-Yakobi Island Wilderness proposal. Representatives of national conservation groups exhorted the Alaskans to fight for wilderness preservation. "You have great power," John Hall of the Wilderness Society told them. "Your letters can work wonders." Brock Evans of the Sierra Club advised them to "work harder and longer" than their adversaries.

Out of the meeting came the Alaska Wilderness Council, which announced shortly that it had designated five areas of Southeast Alaska—Admiralty Island, West Chichagof-Yakobi Island, part of South Prince of Wales Island, the East Behm Canal area, and Tracy Arm-Holkham Bay, on the mainland east of Admiralty—as high-priority areas for protection. Of the five, only Admiralty had significant stands of high-volume timber.

In December, representatives of Alaska and national conservation groups met in Anchorage to plan a coordinated wilderness campaign. Three grassroots organizations emerged: the Northern Alaska Environmental Center, based in Fairbanks; the Alaska Center for the Environment, in Anchorage; and the Southeast Alaska Conservation Council, in Juneau.

SEACC began as a loose-knit network of middle-class conservationists from the scattered and isolated communities of the Panhandle. Most were appalled at the effect of logging on fish, game, scenery, recreation and the overall quality of life in their communities, but were at a loss about how to slow the damage. And they had a powerful foe in Ted Stevens, Alaska's new U.S. senator, who opposed withdrawing federal land from development for any reason.

In 1969, soon after oil was discovered at Prudhoe Bay, the American Association for the Advancement of Science met in Fairbanks. Ed Wayburn was invited to speak about conservation in the Far North. Stevens also was scheduled to speak. Wayburn had been pleased by Stevens' appointment to fill an unexpired Senate term and looked forward to meeting him. The new U.S. senator had come with a prepared speech, but as Wayburn recalls he set it aside and instead ranted for a full half-hour against scientists and environmentalists. Speaking directly to Wayburn, Stevens demanded to know, "Where were you termites before, and why have you come out of the woodwork now?'

SUING TO SAVE ADMIRALTY

By 1970, Wayburn had determined that the only way to save the forests of Admiralty Island was to sue the Forest Service. But it was not clear that the Sierra Club had legal standing to sue. Karl Lane, a veteran Admiralty Island wilderness guide, was enlisted to be the lead plaintiff. The club also needed an Alaska lawyer. Wayburn eventually found Warren Matthews, a recent Harvard Law graduate practicing in Anchorage, and persuaded him to take the case.

Finding grounds for a lawsuit was problematic. President Nixon had just signed the National Environmental Policy Act. NEPA required an extensive process of public involvement and disclosure for major federal projects. But no implementing regulations had yet been put in place. Little research had been done on the biological effects of logging in the Alaska rain forest.

Matthews settled on a lawsuit asserting that the Admiralty Island sale violated the Forest Service Organic Act and the Multiple Use-Sustained Yield Act. He argued that the agency had entered into the contract "based on inadequate knowledge; giving inadequate consideration to the multiple purposes of the national forests; and failing to assure a sustained yield." "We thought we had a winning case," Wayburn said. "The Forest Service hadn't looked into uses of the forest other than timber at all. They didn't have any knowledge of its biological values. The logging was unsustainable." But proving those contentions was another matter.

The Forest Service made no effort to disguise its disgust with the lawsuit. "Noisy, unscrupulous, and adept in using the big lie and the glittering generality as publicity gimmicks, the Sierra Cub epitomized the idea that the ends justify the means," Forest Service historian Lawrence Rakestraw huffed in an account of the litigation.

Because the Forest Service had kept the Admiralty Island sale under wraps for months, the suit was filed nearly a year after the award of the contract. In a classic Catch-22 argument, the government contended that the case should be thrown out because it had not been challenged in a timely fashion.

But Wayburn had an ace up his sleeve. On his 1969 trip to Juneau, he'd learned quite by accident that U.S. Plywood Champion had hired a team of respected forest scientists to determine whether the Admiralty sale could actually produce as much timber as the Forest Service promised. Starker Leopold, a professor of forestry at the University of California at Berkeley, headed the team. Leopold had formed a consulting firm to help timber companies design environmentally sensitive timber sales. He assured Wayburn that U.S Plywood Champion President Karl Bendetsen was committed to logging the sale responsibly and intended to make the study public.

Leopold hired one of his students, Reginald Barrett, to determine whether U.S. Plywood Champion could achieve a sustained yield of 8.75 billion board feet by logging Admiralty's timber on a 100-year rotation schedule, as the Forest Service claimed. Barrett spent three years on Admiralty and wrote up his findings. Leopold submitted Barrett's first report to U.S. Plywood Champion in 1971. But when the Sierra Club suit went to trial in federal court in November of that year, the club's lawyers still had not seen it.

At the end of a ten-day trial U.S. District Judge Raymond Plummer ruled against the Sierra Club, finding that its claims were not substantiated. Matthews immediately appealed the decision to the 9th U.S. Circuit Court of Appeals, and promised that forthcoming new information would prove his case. Still Leopold did not produce the report. Months passed, then years. Finally Leopold went to Wayburn and told him Bendetsen did not intend ever to release it. He gave the report to Wayburn. Its findings explained why U.S. Plywood Champion had decided to sit on the study.

Barrett and Leopold had concluded that in order to produce the promised volume, the company would have to log Admiralty every fifty years, not every hundred years, as the Forest Service had predicted. That meant the forests of Admiralty, once cut, never would be allowed to mature again. Habitat for Sitka black-tailed deer, and for Admiralty's legendary brown bears, would be irreparably lost.

"As soon as Leopold gave us his findings, we rushed them into court and the 9th Circuit remanded the case back to the trial judge," Wayburn recalled, smiling at the memory. Judge Plummer, who had no love for conservationists, sat on the case for a year. "But U.S. Plywood Champion realized the jig was up, and turned back its $100,000 deposit to the Forest Service," Wayburn said. "The Forest Service then dropped the case." Loggers had nibbled away at Admiralty Island throughout the 1960s. Now it appeared that Admiralty was saved—temporarily.

Yet only action by Congress could protect the island permanently, and Regional Forester Johnson refused even to conduct a wilderness study of Admiralty. Instead, his office developed a modest plan to protect the island's brown bears at two small sanctuaries while proceeding with logging.

In the mid-1970s the Wayburns finally saw Admiralty Island for themselves. They flew to Alexander Lake, and took a cross-island trip by canoe and portage. The mud was deep, the no-see-ums thick, the island's famed brown bears nowhere to be seen. None of that mattered. They were captivated by the forests and waters of Admiralty.

FRESH BLOOD

Bob and Dixie Baade stuck it out in Ketchikan until 1974. She testified at Senate oversight hearings on management of the Tongass, and before the Environmental Protection Agency on pulp mill pollution. In 1974, when Bob Baade retired, the couple moved to Kupreanof Island near Petersburg, where they could continue to fight for protection of the Tongass without the hostility that had surrounded them in the shadow of Ketchikan Pulp.

The demographics of Southeast Alaska were changing. Remote though it was, Alaska was not untouched by the social upheaval taking place in the Lower 48 in the 1970s. Hundreds of adventurers and seekers drifted north. Some had soured on the excesses of the '60s; some were looking for a physically challenging life lived close to nature. Many of them put down roots in Southeast. They began to change the culture of its small weathered fishing villages and its mill towns. Living at the edge of this soggy paradise, kayaking into quiet coves, hiking in the rainforest, they were drawn into the campaign to save the Alaska wild.

The pulp mills attracted environmental scientists and technicians. Don Muller moved to Sitka in 1974 to work as a chemist at the pulp mill's secondary wastewater treatment plant. Muller soon grew disenchanted with the company's cavalier attitude toward water-pollution discharges. He left after two years to start a book store and fight for an end to Alaska Pulp's long-term contract. Muller's slight build and scholarly demeanor disguised an iron will. In later years, he was one of a handful of activists willing to engage in civil disobedience to draw attention to Alaska Pulp's logging and pollution practices.

Larry Edwards landed in Sitka in 1977 with degrees in aeronautical and mechanical engineering. He had been active in a number of California environmental campaigns—fighting pesticide use, working for the protection of wild and scenic rivers, and trying to stop the construction and operation of the Diablo Canyon nuclear power plant. In Wyoming, he had served as director of the Wyoming Outdoor Council and chairman of the Wyoming chapter of the Sierra Club.

Edwards' tenure at Alaska Pulp, like Muller's, was short-lived. His arrival coincided with the beginning of the national campaign to win permanent protection for Alaska wilderness. Alaska Pulp officials opposed designation of wilderness on the Tongass, and expected their workers to do the same. Edwards recalls that two days before a congressional committee held a field hearing in Sitka, Clarence Kramer, a high-level APC executive, called a meeting and warned employees: 'You all know there will be a hearing. You all will testify at the hearing. And you will testify against the bill." As he left the room, he added, "If you value your job."

Edwards submitted his testimony in writing, but he was caught anyway, and received a personal scolding from Kramer. By then he was having other doubts about Alaska Pulp. He had been assured when he took the job that the mill was in full compliance with air and water pollution standards. But he soon found out that was not the case. Edwards quit APC and began his own sea kayaking business, Baidarka Boats. He and Muller founded the Sitka Conservation Society and became leaders in Sitka's small but vocal environmental community.

Like Ketchikan, Sitka was a mill town, with a mill town culture. But it was also a tourist magnet, and a growing regional center for education, health care and government. Although Alaska Pulp Corporation dominated local politics in Sitka, the town still had room for dissident views.

SEEKING WILDERNESS

A few newcomers gravitated to the tiny, remote fishing settlements of Point Baker and Port Protection, on the northwest coast of Prince of Wales Island. One of these pioneers was Alan Stein, a veteran of the University of Wisconsin anti-war movement and former president of the leftist Students for a Democratic Society chapter in Madison. In his junior year, while living in a communist kibbutz in Israel, Stein had developed a fascination with beautiful landscapes. After graduate school, he traveled with his wife across the country, looking for the spiritual peace he had felt while looking out over the Jordan Valley. But no place felt safe from the rapid development overtaking the nation—until he got to Southeast Alaska.

"I went to Seattle, then to Ketchikan, and took a sailboat to Clarence Strait," Stein said. "All I could see was wilderness. I got to Port Protection, climbed a hill surrounded by water and said, 'This is where I want my kids to grow up.'" He and his wife leased an acre of Forest Service land at Wooden Wheel Cove, near Port Protection. Stein built a cabin with a hammer and chainsaw, finishing it just in time for the birth of his son in June of 1973.

Stein had worked briefly as a logger at Shakan Bay, to the south. The destruction he witnessed there had shocked him. "I saw an entire hill denuded of trees," he recalled. "Some of them were twelve feet in diameter. You could smell them bleeding. The equipment dragged them through the moss until there was a slide rut ten feet deep, and it ran mud into the crystal clear water of Shakan Strait. When I saw a guy hit with a log in the head, I told my wife we were going back to Port Protection." He bought a 22-foot boat and took up trolling and halibut fishing. Stein was a long way from the Gallilie.

Port Protection and Point Baker, old Tlingit fishing camps connected by a narrow water passage, had been rediscovered in the 1930s by Petersburg fishermen, who ventured out on day trips to fish the rich waters of Sumner Strait. In the early 1970s a few hippies and Vietnam veterans, attracted by the availability of land and the remoteness of the area, swelled the population of the two outposts to about sixty newcomers and grizzled old-timers. There was no telephone service on North Prince of Wales, no newspaper delivery, no reliable radio reception. The closest real town, Petersburg, was more than forty miles distant, across Sumner Strait and up Wrangell Narrows. Houses nailed together from salvaged lumber and beach logs perched along the shore or sat on pilings. Homesteaders heated their houses with wood,

Roads and clearcuts have transformed North Prince of Wales Island in the past quarter century. Photo by Trygve Steen.

collected rainwater from their rooftops, and coaxed balky generators to keep running so their lamps would stay lit during long winter nights.

Fishing families spent the summer months at sea, selling salmon and halibut right off their boats. In fall, they went deer-hunting in the rain forest that blanketed the nearby hills. In winter they gathered at a floating community center in Point Baker and visited each other in open skiffs. They were self-sufficient, and they had no love for government. "They didn't want taxes, didn't want regulation," Stein said. "They were extreme individualists."

In the early 1970s, Point Baker and Port Protection were still surrounded by wilderness. Most of Kuiu Island to the northwest remained intact, and the north end of Prince of Wales Island still held six hundred thousand acres of forest virtually untouched by logging. No cutting for the Ketchikan Pulp contract had occurred north of El Capitan, about fifteen miles to the southeast. But to the east, at Red Bay, loggers had left behind thousands of acres of clearcuts. And the chainsaws were drawing nearer.

One day in 1972 some government wildlife biologists tied up their skiff at Port Protection and informed Stein and his neighbors that the area was about to be logged. Stein and Darlene Larson wrote a letter to the Ketchikan Daily News calling on the Sierra Club to help stop the logging. At the time, "Sierra Club Kiss My Ax" bumper stickers were commonplace in Ketchikan. Nonetheless, in October of 1973, a delegation of conservationists—Dixie Baade, Jack Hession and Bob Nelson—flew out to Port Protection. "I took them over to Labouchere Bay in my boat," Stein said. "As a result, I was immediately ostracized by half the community."

In February of 1973 the Forest Service began a series of meetings at Port Protection to gather public testimony on a new logging plan covering the entire million-acre Ketchikan Pulp Company timber supply area. The plan called for logging about half the timber on North Prince of Wales Island, an area of six hundred thousand acres, over a period of fifteen years. The proposal divided the fishermen of Point Baker and Port Protection. At a Forest Service hearing, Stein stood up and declared, "You'll carry out those plans over my dead body!" Soon after, he began receiving death threats. "I was shot at in Port Protection after one community meeting," he said.

A LAST-DITCH LAWSUIT

Stein, an old-timer named Herb Zieske and a few others organized the Point Baker Association to appeal the logging plan. Then, in December of 1974, they learned that the Forest Service was about to unload barges of road-building equipment in nearby Labouchere Bay. They took up a collection to send Stein to Juneau, where he met with Alaska Governor Jay Hammond, a Republican with environmental sympathies, and began hunting for a lawyer. "I called every attorney in Southeast Alaska, and half of those in Anchorage," Stein said. "Then I called Dick Folta in Haines." Folta's father, a judge and a great bear hunter in territorial days, had often taken his son on his famous hunts. If Dick Folta could face a charging bear on Admiralty Island, Stein figured, he could surely take on the Forest Service. Folta agreed to take the case for whatever the fishermen could pay him.

An assistant Alaska attorney general provided a list of laws that might work to stop the logging. Folta filed the suit in January 1975 on behalf of Stein, Herb Zieske, and his son Charles. He sued under Alaska water-quality laws and three federal laws: the Multiple Use-Sustained Yield Act of 1960, the Refuse Act, which prohibited dumping debris into the navigable waters of the U.S., and the Forest Service Organic Act of 1897, which prohibited cutting any but dead or dying trees on national forests, and then only if they were individually marked. Though the provision had never been enforced, a federal appeals court in the East had recently upheld its literal interpretation in West Virginia's Monongahela National Forest, and had issued an order blocking clearcutting on national forests in four southern states.

Stein set to work raising money to support the litigation. He got $100 from the Sierra Club and $100 from the Alaska Conservation Foundation. In his spare time, he wrote articles for *National Fisherman* magazine and other publications in an effort to rally Alaska fishermen behind an effort to protect salmon streams from the effects of logging.

In a March 1976 article for the *Ketchikan Daily News*, Stein described the astonishing and largely unreported denuding of Prince of Wales Island: "The U.S. satellite which passed over Prince of Wales Island in July 1973 took a picture of KPC's twenty-year impact . . . . The picture reveals the huge clearcut running along the road to Hydaburg, the great denuded area from Thorne Bay to Coffman Cove, the clearcut many times the size of a large midwestern farm running from Staney Creek half way to the east side of the island, and half of Kosciusko Island stripped of timber. Almost all the beach timber from Pt. Colpoyes to Buster Bay on the north end of the island was also stripped."

Officials from the Forest Service and Ketchikan Pulp Company paid the Point Baker fishermen a visit to discuss the lawsuit. They didn't get far. "We asked for a lot," Charles Zieske recalled. "We wanted no logging from the southeast side of Calder Bay to the northeast side of Red Bay," an area of four hundred thousand acres. "We'd had enough with loggers up here. We didn't care for them anyway." Loggers at one camp had been observed poaching deer and destroying bald eagle nest trees.

During the trial, Herb Zieske, a Point Baker resident since 1944, flew to Juneau to testify about his dependence on deer, and his fear that clearcutting would destroy deer winter cover near his home. Ketchikan Pulp Company sent top officials to keep an eye on the trial. On the afternoon of December 23, 1975, Stein was in the newsroom of the State Capitol in Juneau when John Greeley, an Associated Press reporter, pulled the tape off the machine. "Looks like you won!" he told him. U.S. District Judge James Von der Heyt had granted the Point Baker Association's request for a preliminary injunction. The judge ordered the Forest Service to refrain from commencing logging on four hundred thousand acres—essentially the entire northwest corner of Prince of Wales Island. "The judge said he had no alternative but to rule under the Organic Act because of the Monongahela decision," Stein recalled.

The ruling was a bombshell. Banner headlines up and down the West Coast forecast dire consequences for lumber and newsprint supplies if it was allowed to stand. But Forest Service officials were reluctant to appeal the ruling to the 9th U.S. Circuit Court of Appeals for fear that if they lost, the ban could be widened to apply to all nine states in the appellate court's jurisdiction. Governor Hammond and other political leaders quickly called on Congress to override the injunction.

The Point Baker fishermen were jubilant. But their celebration was short-lived. "The national conservationists were up in arms," recalled Kay Greenough, co-director of SEACC at the time. "They saw what the result would be in Washington. There would be a panic." Sure enough, Congress quickly stepped in to provide a legislative fix for the two precedent-setting court rulings by introducing a National Forest Management Act.

United Fishermen of Alaska paid Stein's way to Washington, D.C., in March of 1976 so he could testify at House and Senate hearings in favor of 300-foot buffer strips along salmon streams in national forests. U.S. Senator Mark Hatfield, an Oregon Republican, chaired the Senate committee hearing at which Stein testified. "I spoke after Ralph Nader," he recalls. "Senator Hatfield said, 'Make it brief. I just want the facts.' I said, 'I've just come over four thousand miles. I've flown over clearcuts all the way.' I said, 'We need buffer strips for fish.'"

But Congress ignored the recommendation, and later that year passed the National Forest Management Act, which restored clearcutting to the national forests and dissolved the Monongahela and Point Baker injunctions. It also required every national forest to prepare a land management plan, to involve the public in the planning process, and to assure the sustainable production not only of timber but of all forest resources. The Forest Service promptly opened North Prince of Wales Island to logging. "The logging camp was built one mile from our community," Stein said. "I wasn't going to see that landscape destroyed. I decided to move to Petersburg." Over the next 21 years, half the timber the Point Baker fishermen had sued to protect was cut.

Charlie Zieske stayed on in Point Baker. To him, the effort was well worth it. Though the lawsuit hadn't stopped the logging permanently, the battle against the Forest Service-pulp mill juggernaut had been joined. "From then on, people realized they weren't God; you could sue them," he said. "But it was a long battle. When you go up against money without money, it's a long haul."

3

ANGOON

The creation myth of the Angoon Tlingit tells the story of wily Raven, who stole the sun to give life to the people, stole the waters to make the rivers, stole the fish from where they were kept in a basket far out in the Pacific Ocean and brought them to spawn in the shining rivers so that even the poorest of the people could partake of their abundance.

Angoon's cultural leader, Matthew Fred Sr., describes his people as natural-born conservationists: "Our ancestors educated us and disciplined us to provide for our grandchildren and their grandchildren. But there are no guarantees. You have to fight for what you want." It is a lesson that residents of this village on Admiralty Island's west coast have had to learn generation after generation since Europeans arrived on their shores.

Angoon today is a village of 750 Tlingit Indians. Its modest wood houses climb the low hills of a peninsula nearly surrounded by the surging waters of Kootznahoo Inlet and Mitchell Bay. There is an elementary school, a high school, a city hall, a grocery store, a community meeting house. The forest begins at the edge of town.

In Angoon, the past is quietly alive. On the shore road that leads to the ferry landing and floatplane dock stand several weathered houses, some missing windows, some uninhabitable. Where the original houses have burned, newer structures with plywood siding stand in their place. But through the eyes of Angoon Mayor Pauline Jim, the faded buildings are living museums. They are tribal houses, owned by the clans and managed by tribal caretakers. Lined up along the street that hugs the bayfront, they perpetuate clan identity. Angoon has the largest surviving community of tribal houses in Southeast Alaska, and though only Raven House bears traditional Tlingit decorations, the mayor knows the clan of each house.

When Gilbert Fred was growing up in Angoon, the village was his extended family. "Respect for my dignity, respect for all of God's creations was strongly instilled in me from the beginning," he says. Sustainability was a bedrock principle. The elders cautioned the young against hunting, fishing, or trapping in overused areas. They taught them the medicinal value of common plants like Devil's club, used by the Tlingit as a compress and taken internally as a drink. "When our elderly first started being admitted to the Pioneer Home, and were not allowed to bring their native foods in, the people perished," he said. When an ailing village elder asks for Devil's club tea, Gilbert Fred goes out into the woods in search of the distinctive "family of five" plant, the one with five stalks growing from a single root. He says a prayer, then peels back the cambium layer, gathers the green stems and steeps them to make the potent tea. "Bringing medicine for the elders is a spiritual thing for me."

BROWN BEAR'S FORT

The story of Angoon began after the last Ice Age, when a seagoing people settled at isolated coves and inlets on both sides of the wide saltwater passage now known as Chatham Strait. Tlingit history recounts that three hunters followed a beaver from one inlet to another, and saw that the isthmus between these inlets, a place nearly surrounded by water, would be a good village site. It was strategically situated at the mouth of an inlet with many arms and tributary streams reaching deep into the heart of their island. The village came to be called Angoon, Tlingit for "isthmus town." The Tlingit called the island xuts nuwu, "brown bear's fort," for its large population of brown bears. On Admiralty Island, the bears always have outnumbered the Tlingit, who regard them with fear and respect.

A Russian census in 1839 found more than 1,800 native people—members of the Auk, Taku, Kake and Hutsnuwu tribes—living in villages scattered along Admiralty's shores. In the late 19th century the populations of these villages consolidated at sites that became Juneau, Kake and Angoon. Today Angoon is the only permanent settlement on Admiralty Island.

The Tlingit clans of Angoon lived in splendid isolation on their isthmus, fighting off invaders and crossing Chatham Strait in long dugout canoes to fish and trade with other villages. Their diet was rich with salmon and halibut, crab and chiton, brown bear and black-tailed deer. Salmon were so abundant that they could catch and preserve thousands of fish each year with minimal effort, allowing them leisure to produce artworks, hold ceremonial events and pursue trade.

Tlingit cultural leader Matthew Fred Sr. in front of the Angoon community building, 1996. Photo by Kathie Durbin.

The Angoon Tlingit followed a practical conservation ethic, periodically resting the areas where they hunted, trapped, fished, gathered shellfish and collected plants, to allow for natural renewal. Their motto, says Matthew Fred, has always been, "Let our island be to you as a dish. Eat off it but do not break it."

Life at Angoon changed little until the arrival of the sea otter trade. The first documented contact between Europeans and the Tlingit of Admiralty occurred in 1794, when Captain George Vancouver surveyed the island after his crew was chased south by the Auk Indians of Juneau. A Russian sea otter trade soon commenced in Chatham Strait. In 1804 hunters killed 1,600 otters there. Over the next half-century the otter population was severely depleted, and the Russians moved on to other waters. Whalers, salmon cannery owners and gold prospectors followed the same boom-and-bust pattern as they moved in to plunder Alaska's riches.

MASSACRE AT KILLISNOO

In 1878 the Northwest Trading Co. established a whaling station on Killisnoo Island near Angoon, and a new Native settlement grew up around it. The cultural divide between whites and Alaska natives here led to a tragedy that would forever color relationships between Angoon and the U.S. government.

Traditional Tlingit society was rigidly class-conscious, and class was based on elaborate property arrangements. Ownership, whether of a fishing site, a clan symbol, a song or a story, was a principle rooted in Tlingit law. Like most Northwest coastal people, the Angoon Tlingit were divided into two moieties, Raven or Eagle. (In Angoon and many other Tlingit communities, the knowledge of one's moiety survives to this day.) If a Raven trespassed on Eagle property or caused insult, injury or death to an Eagle, payment or tribute was required. If an Eagle was responsible, payment was due the Raven. It was this insistence on proper payment for wrongs inflicted that led to the bombardment of Angoon by the U.S. Navy.

K.J. Metcalf, a longtime Forest Service official who moved to Angoon in the early 1980s, and later became an honorary member of the village's Tlingit community, described the tragic incident in *Alaska Geographic:* "In 1882 an Indian was killed by a falling tree that he was cutting for the Northwest Trading Co. whaling plant at Killisnoo. His relatives immediately demanded payment of blankets from the company. The company refused and complained to the government. Cmdr. Merriman, of the Revenue Cutter *Adams*, admonished the Indians, telling them that, as far as white men were concerned, such payments would never be considered now or in the future. He threatened severe punishment if the Indians persisted in their demands. Cmdr. Merriman's words came to pass that October when a Northwest Trading Co. whale gun exploded, killing an Angoon medicine man. The man's relatives stopped working, tied up the whaling boats and painted their faces black, all a part of the mourning process. The medicine man's family demanded 200 blankets for the death of such an important person."

"The white people at Killisnoo became alarmed. Fearing an Indian uprising, they sent to Sitka for help. The Revenue Cutter *Favorite* and a tug, fitted with a cannon, came to the rescue. The misunderstandings between whites and Indians escalated, and the order was given to destroy Angoon along with forty canoes. The village was bombarded, demolishing eighteen of the twenty-nine houses. Six children were said to have died from smoke inhalation. With most of their homes, food and canoes destroyed, winter took a heavy toll on the Angoon people. At the memorial a hundred years later, the village's descendants recounted, through song and story, their suffering that long winter."

In 1973 the U.S. government paid the Tlingit of Angoon $90,000 in compensation. But the government never apologized, and the mistrust and suspicion the Angoon Tlingit harbor toward outsiders have never entirely disappeared.

Because of their remoteness, the Angoon Tlingit were able to shield their traditional cultural practices from the incursions of missionaries and settlers longer than most Southeast Alaska Natives. In Angoon, the elders say, the people never felt the stock market crash of 1929, because their subsistence life protected them from the vagaries of a capitalist economy. Before the Alaska State Ferry added a stop at Angoon, it was the most isolated of the Tlingit communities. Even today, Angoon refuses to allow an airfield built near its village. All passengers and freight arrive by ferry or floatplane.

But even isolated Angoon could not withstand the onslaught of commercial exploitation. By the 1930s the island's shores were dotted with salmon canneries, herring salteries and fish traps, and about twenty commercial fox farms overran small offshore isles. The canneries depleted the wild salmon runs, forcing the Angoon Tlingit to build hatcheries. Then came the Forest Service.

UNDER NEW MANAGEMENT

From the beginning, the Forest Service was indifferent, even hostile, to the land claims of indigenous people in Southeast Alaska. Alaska Regional Forester and later Territorial Governor B. Frank Heintzleman strenuously opposed compensating Alaska Natives for their land. Agency workers routinely burned Indian smokehouses because the owners had not obtained permits to operate them. "The attitude," Metcalf said, "was, 'It's our land. It's under professional management now.'"

The Forest Service began offering timber sales on Admiralty Island to independent loggers in the 1950s. Publicity followed quickly. *Outdoor Life* published an article, "Death Comes to Admiralty Island," that described clearcutting at Whitewater Bay south of Angoon, the site of a permanent Tlingit village, where loggers using A-frame rigs cut trees as far up the valley as their lines could reach. The article gave a national readership its first close-up look at logging practices in Southeast Alaska. "The piece really shook people up," said Matthew Kirchhoff, an Alaska state wildlife biologist. "For the first time, Southeast Alaska and the Forest Service were portrayed in an unfavorable light in the national media." The pro-logging magazine *American Forests* immediately dispatched a writer to undertake damage control.

Metcalf recalls an incident from the late 1960s, when the Forest Service was preparing its Admiralty Island timber sale. "The Forest Service ranger and an interpreter went down to Angoon to talk to the people about where they wanted the bridge across Mitchell Bay. They gave them three options. It was the first time the people of Angoon had heard of the plan to log on Admiralty." Angoon leaders fiercely opposed the logging but were powerless to stop the destruction of their hunting and fishing grounds.

After the Sierra Club lawsuit forced the Forest Service to abandon its plan for logging Admiralty, it appeared that the island was saved. But a discovery in faraway Prudhoe Bay set the stage for a new threat against Admiralty and the Tlingits' subsistence way of life.

THE RUSH TO RESOLVE NATIVE CLAIMS

In 1968, geologists for Atlantic Richfield discovered oil—ten billion gallons of crude—beneath the permafrost at Prudhoe Bay, on Alaska's arctic North Slope. The discovery rocked the petroleum industry and presented the new state of Alaska with the promise of untold wealth. The state, which had selected land bordering Prudhoe Bay, asked the U.S. Interior Department to convey title so it could undertake a competitive bidding program for oil exploration leases. But the Inupiat of Arctic Alaska held unresolved claims to the pipeline corridor right-of-way connecting Prudhoe Bay to the Port of Valdez on Prince William Sound. Before the deep reservoir of black gold could be tapped, the U.S. government would have to settle Alaska Native land claims once and for all.

Legal precedent had been set in a case involving the 27,000-acre Moquawkie Reservation on the west side of Cook Inlet. Indian reservations in Alaska were rare; the Moquawkie was one of eight President Woodrow Wilson had established between 1915 and 1917 to protect Alaska Natives from the incursions of white settlers. In 1962 the U.S. Bureau of Indian Affairs had leased a section of the reservation to an oil company and had placed the receipts in a government fund. The BIA had leased the land without so much as notifying the poverty-stricken residents of the reservation village of Tyonek. Exploratory drilling had already begun when Stanley McCutcheon, an Anchorage attorney, filed suit against the U.S. Department of the Interior on behalf of Tyonek villagers. He won an injunction that halted the drilling, then went on to win a settlement that prevented the government from executing future oil and gas leases on the reservation without the consent of the Tyonek Village Council.

Willie Hensley, an Alaska Native graduate student at the University of Alaska, decided to write his master's thesis on the Native claims issue. His thesis questioned the right of the state of Alaska to select 104 million acres when no treaty or act of Congress had ever extinguished Native title to the land.

In 1966, U.S. Sen. Ernest Gruening of Alaska signaled that the time was ripe to settle Native claims so Alaska could get on with developing its natural resources. Hensley met with Gruening, ran for the Alaska Legislature, and organized the Northwest Alaska Native Association. At about the same time Charles Edwardsen of Barrow and others organized the Arctic Slope Native Association, which vowed to press claims to ninety-six million acres, most of Alaska north of the Brooks Range.

The insurgent Native leaders knew they needed a statewide political organization if they hoped to stop the seizure of their land by the state. But they had no money to bring the leaders of remote Native villages to Anchorage for a meeting. Tyonek, flush with money from its settlement, came to the rescue, loaning the organizers $100,000, and offering to cover travel expenses for tribal leaders.

On Oct. 6, 1966, three hundred delegates from all parts of Alaska met in a deserted fur storeroom on Anchorage's Fourth Avenue and formed the Alaska Federation of Natives. The new federation issued a press release stating that all Alaska Natives were entitled to reparations for the appropriation of their land. Rumors spread that the AFN wanted sixty million acres and $1 billion. An indignant Alaska Gov. Wally Hickel declared, "Just because somebody's grandfather chased a moose across the land doesn't mean he owns it." In fact, the federation hoped to get forty million acres and $500 million. Privately, its leaders doubted they could win even that.

In 1966, U.S. Interior Secretary Stewart Udall acted to bring order from chaos by temporarily freezing all transfers of public land in Alaska pending settlement of Native claims by Congress. U.S. Senator Henry "Scoop" Jackson, a Washington Democrat, took the lead in resolving the issue. A powerful force in Northwest politics, Jackson was a friend to conservationists, but on the Indian question he believed the only hope for Alaska Natives was to bring them into the nation's economic mainstream.

The Federation of Natives pressured the Alaska congressional delegation to introduce a bill settling all Native land claims. Eight separate bills eventually were introduced. With oil fever at a high pitch, the momentum for passage was intense. In 1969, as Hickel was undergoing Senate confirmation to become President Richard Nixon's Interior Secretary, the federation won the governor's reluctant promise that he would not lift Udall's freeze on land transfers, but would instead move forward with a settlement. In exchange, Hickel won AFN's endorsement.

Retired U.S. Supreme Court Justice Arthur Goldberg and former U.S. Attorney General Ramsey Clark agreed to represent the AFN in congressional hearings for free. Native leaders made more than one hundred trips to Washington during negotiations over the settlement. Behind the scenes, internal disputes raged, many of them fanned by lawyers with dollar signs in their eyes who had hired on as advisors to Native groups. Debate flared over how to protect aboriginal hunting and fishing rights, and how to allocate the land.

During the political maneuvering in Washington, D.C., some Native leaders back home remained in the dark about the direction negotiations were taking. "There was zero notification to the tribal governments," recalled Edward Gambel Sr., a member of the Angoon tribal council. "The intent was never clear." Because Arctic oil was driving the campaign, Gambel said, Southeast Natives were not key players in the final, critical negotiations. "We were under the assumption," said Gilbert Fred, a schoolboy in Angoon at the time, "that we were going to win our land and going to be able to live as we had for thousands of years."

DIVIDING THE PIE

Conservationists were apprehensive about the negotiations. The momentum building in Congress for settlement of Native claims took them by surprise. In 1971, Sierra Club President Ed Wayburn flew to Washington, D.C. to attend a wilderness conference. When he arrived, Stewart Brandborg, president of the Wilderness Society, greeted him the with the words: "We have lost everything in ANCSA."

The bill on the table, the Alaska Native Claims Settlement Act, proposed to convey forty-four million acres of federal land to Alaska Natives. Brandborg, Wayburn and other national conservation leaders feared it would doom their campaign to get vast expanses of Alaska set aside as parks, wilderness areas and wildlife refuges. They held an emergency meeting, at which Wayburn urged them to hold off on deciding a course of action until he had talked to Jackson, whom he regarded as an ally.

As Wayburn recalls the meeting, he asked Jackson, "Senator, how could you do this?" Jackson replied, "If we hadn't introduced it, Senator Ted Kennedy was ready to introduce a bill providing sixty million acres and much greater compensation" to settle Alaska Native claims.

Wayburn appealed to Jackson to include language in the act reserving large tracts of Alaska as wilderness. "You've done great things for the state of Alaska and you've done great things for the Alaska Natives," he said. "How about doing something for all the American people?"

"How much do you want?" Jackson asked.

"One hundred fifty million acres," Wayburn said.

"You want too much," Jackson said. "Would eighty million acres satisfy you?"

"No," Wayburn said. "But I'll take it."

Soon after, Jackson inserted language in ANCSA requiring the Interior Secretary to reserve eighty million acres of "land in the national interest." This language, Section (d)2, became part of the final bill—and set the stage for the Alaska wildlands campaign to come.

A CRASH COURSE IN CAPITALISM

On December 14, 1971, with strong support from Alaska's governor, legislature and congressional delegation, Congress passed the Alaska Native Claims Settlement Act. The vote was 307-60 in the House; the Senate approved the bill on a voice vote. President Nixon signed it, and a new era in Alaska was launched.

The act presented Alaska's indigenous people with a trade-off unprecedented in the long and troubled history of U.S.-Indian land settlements. The federal government would convey title to forty-four million acres of federal land and pay $962.5 million. In exchange, Natives would agree to the extinguishment of all land claims forever.

However, neither money nor land would go to tribal governments. Instead, the land and cash would be transferred to twelve regional economic development corporations, and to eligible Alaska Native villages that wished to establish their own corporations. From rainy Klawock in the Southeast to ice-bound Barrow on the Arctic Ocean, each regional and village corporation would be entitled to select land and develop its natural resources, whether oil, hard-rock minerals, fish, or timber.

Every Alaska Native, regardless of residence, would hold stock in one of the state-chartered regional corporations. Those who held stock in village or urban corporations would participate in their regional corporations and receive dividends through these local enterprises. The new corporations would be expected to generate profits for their shareholders. After twenty years, shareholders would be allowed to sell their stock to non-Natives, raising the specter that Alaska Natives could end up with neither land nor dividends.

Southeast Alaska Natives had learned to live in two worlds. As early as the nineteenth century, they had been partners in the sea otter trade. They had worked in the salmon canneries, as loggers, as commercial fishermen. Many were actively engaged in Alaska's political and economic life, yet two centuries of coexistence with Europeans had not severed their material and spiritual ties to the land. They still sustained themselves by hunting, fishing, crabbing, and gathering berries and wild plants. They had expected the settlement to guarantee their right to hunt, fish and gather food in their traditional and customary places. But ANCSA was silent on subsistence. And it was to alter their lives forever.

"DON'T NEVER CONSIDER LOGGING HERE"

ANCSA's passage confronted Angoon's leaders with a difficult dilemma. Village elders opposed all logging on Admiralty Island. Yet now they faced the task of establishing a corporation and selecting lands to be managed for maximum profit. They also faced the threat of land selections by other Native corporations that coveted Admiralty's timber.

ANCSA permitted Southeast Alaska corporations to choose land from the Tongass National Forest in townships adjacent to their villages. It also permitted two "urban corporations" in Juneau and Sitka to select land within a 50-mile radius of their cities. Parts of Admiralty Island lay within range of both cities.

By 1975, the corporations had been chartered and had made their initial land selections. In Southeast, they filed claim to the most productive and accessible timber, much of it in the South Tongass. Shee-Atika, Sitka's Native corporation, and Goldbelt, in Juneau, each selected more than 120,000 acres on Admiralty. Sealaska, the regional corporation for Southeast, selected 370,000 acres on Admiralty, though the legality of that selection was uncertain. In March, James Moorman, an attorney for the Sierra Club Legal Defense Fund, prepared a detailed memo analyzing the few legal options available to conservationists who hoped to thwart the Native land selections.

During the Sierra Club litigation over the Admiralty Island timber sale, Ed and Peggy Wayburn had become acquainted with several Angoon leaders, including Edward Gambel and Matthew Fred. Though the Club and the Angoon Tlingit had different agendas, they shared a commitment to keep the chainsaws off Admiralty. "We were accused of going to bed with the Sierra Club," Gambel recalled. "The Sierra Club had been trying to protect Admiralty Island for fifty years. It just happened that we were now advocating the same thing."

The directors of Angoon's corporation, Kootznoowoo Inc., agreed to oppose logging on Admiralty, though Gambel says outsiders tried to change their minds. "Sealaska took it upon itself to hold a workshop, to help us organize as a corporation," he said. "We were herded from one consultant to another. Top-notch corporate attorneys from D.C. were brought in to talk to us. We were in an ideal situation to be manipulated. We were idealistic; we wouldn't go with the herd. But there was no mistake about what the intent was."

Still, Kootznoowoo Inc.'s 628 shareholders were entitled to dividends. "We knew we couldn't sit around idle," Gambel said. "Uppermost in our minds was that we had to make a profit." Then the directors received an unexpected message that reinforced their first instincts. As Gambel put it, "Someone came along to remind us, 'You guys have no right to take part in the destruction of Admiralty Island.'"

The message arrived via cassette tape from George Davis, an Angoon elder who had married and moved to the village of Hoonah. Davis sent a copy to each of the nine Kootznoowoo Inc. board members. On it, he detailed the family history of each director—in the Tlingit language. "He made the tape so we could know where we came from and who we were," Gambel said. "He told us, 'Don't never consider logging here.' He told us we should not do the wrong thing. We were Tlingit-speaking, Tlingit-understanding people in those days. That's why it carried so much weight."

STERLING BOLIMA

To oversee land use planning and help plot strategy, the board hired Edward Gambel's nephew, Sterling Bolima. Part Tlingit, part Filipino, Bolima was a man of many talents: playwright, photogrammetrist, raconteur. A Vietnam veteran, short and slightly built, Bolima chain-smoked cigarettes, walked hunched over, talked in a slurred manner, and had a bad heart. He had been living on the edge in a rough Seattle neighborhood. It was easy to miss his brilliance.

Gambel and Bolima set to work. "We had a lot of catching up to do," Gambel said. They prepared Kootznoowoo Inc.'s land selection on Admiralty, as the law required, and Bolima went to deliver it to government officials in Anchorage. But when he got there, he changed his mind. Instead, pointing out that all the townships adjacent to Angoon were bodies of water, he asked for a delay,.

Klukwan Inc. had a similar problem; its village, near Haines at the north end of Lynn Canal, was surrounded by state land that was unavailable for selection. Klukwan, Inc., sought permission to choose land on Long Island, in the extreme south end of the Tongass, where the largest trees in Southeast Alaska grew. If Klukwan succeeded in selecting land distant from its village, Bolima calculated, that would set a precedent Angoon could emulate, though it would take an act of Congress to achieve. "Sterling's idea was that if Klukwan could go to Long Island, we could go to Prince of Wales Island," Gambel said. Eventually even the Sierra Club held its nose and agreed to support the exchange.

SHEE-ATIKA'S BETRAYAL

Angoon put pressure on Goldbelt and Shee-Atika to select land elsewhere and leave Admiralty intact. "We couldn't object to their cutting timber," Gambel said. "It would be like objecting to ourselves. So we passed a resolution saying we supported land selections—but only off Admiralty Island. We said, 'Please don't do it in our back yard.'" Goldbelt acquiesced and selected land on the mainland. But Shee-Atika refused to back off, even after Angoon's leaders persuaded the government to offer Shee-Atika land with timber of greater value in the south end of the Tongass. "We said we would work with them to extend the fifty-mile radius to Long Island, where tree regeneration was faster," Gambel recalled. Instead, Shee-Atika laid claim to the land Goldbelt had relinquished, on the west coast of Admiralty.

Various explanations are offered for the corporation's intransigence. Shee-Atika's executive director, a logger from Oregon named Roger Snippen, reportedly bore a deep grudge against the Sierra Club for its efforts to protect wilderness in the Pacific Northwest. He knew the Club had placed Admiralty Island on its list of must-save places. Gambel recalls that during negotiations with a federal mediator, Snippen "told me he had a personal vendetta against the Sierra Club. As long as the Sierra Club tried to keep Shee-Atika off Admiralty Island, he was going to make sure the Sierra Club could never call Admiralty Island 'pristine' again."

A second theory holds that U.S. Sen. Ted Stevens was so infuriated by negotiations between Angoon and Sitka that he was willing to push through legislation to see Admiralty logged. A third is that when Alaska Pulp Corporation loaned Shee-Atika one million dollars to build a posh hotel in Sitka, it set an unwritten condition that Shee-Atika would select land on Admiralty, possibly as a future source of timber for the APC pulp mill in Sitka. At one point, Shee-Atika representatives even approached Kootznoowo

Inc. to propose a joint venture on Admiralty, an offer Angoon's leaders promptly rebuffed. As Gambel recalls, "The tribal council basically said, 'Kiss my ass.'"

During the land selection process, village leaders searched for a way to hold Admiralty permanently. Bolima thought up the idea of asking Congress to establish a national monument on Admiralty. It was an inspired tactic. A national monument under the jurisdiction of the Forest Service would be off-limits to logging, but Angoon's residents could still fish, hunt and gather food there. Angoon was aware of the plight of the Hoonah Tlingit, who faced restrictions on fishing and seal hunting in Glacier Bay after it became a National Park Service monument. "We knew Glacier Bay had been taken away from the Hoonah people," Gambel said. "We didn't want a national park but we didn't want logging either. We wanted the rights of our people to be protected."

In Angoon, Bolima lived and worked in a rundown trailer and immersed himself in the study of federal regulatory management. When the trailer burned to the ground, he moved in with Gambel. "Sterling was not content with accepting the law as it was handed to him," Gambel said. "He was going to take it apart and see what made it work." The two found few allies in Southeast Alaska. "No one wanted to talk to us," Gambel said. "We tried to talk to Hoonah about restoring subsistence rights in Glacier Bay, but they weren't interested. The only people who would talk to us were the Petersburg fishermen. They were fearful of what logging would do to their fishing."

"LIKE THE INDIAN PEOPLE"

By the mid-1970s, a move was afoot to deal with unresolved issues involving Native corporation land selections and subsistence hunting and fishing rights as part of the massive Alaska Lands Act. It was time for Angoon to take its case to Congress. But the first lobbying trip Gambel and Bolima made to Washington was disastrous. "We tried to get doors to open, but no one would even talk to us," Gambel recalled. "We came back with our tails between our legs." Then an attorney for Kootznoowoo Inc., gave them the name of a lobbyist with ties to Alaska. Suddenly they had access.

"Sterling ended up being our day-to-day lobbyist in Washington, D.C.," Gambel said. "He learned how to negotiate like the Indian people." The two befriended powerful Democrats in Congress, including Rep. John

Seiberling of Ohio and Rep. Morris Udall of Arizona. Both Udall and
Seiberling visited Alaska to meet with Angoon's leaders. But Alaska's own
delegation fought Angoon's efforts to protect its homeland.

With Admiralty Island now threatened by Native corporation land
selections, in 1976 Ted Whitesell and Ron Hawk of the Southeast Alaska
Conservation Council hooked up with Bolima to push for protection of
Admiralty in Congress. Bolima quickly became a minor legend in
conservation circles for his work inside the Beltway. "In my opinion there's
no way we could have saved as much as we did on Admiralty without Sterling
Bolima," Whitesell said. "He was more effective than any conservationist I
knew. He went back to D.C. with a bolo tie and a nice turquoise belt
buckle. He was connected to Angoon by family, but he got a lot of street
smarts in the big city. He was basically a streetwise guy from a Filipino
neighborhood in Seattle. When he was off-duty, he was a real carouser." In
meetings on Capitol Hill, Bolima would talk with great feeling about his
people and their traditional ties to the land. "It was very effective with
Congress," Whitesell said. "They were just in awe of him. He was amazing
to watch in action." Bolima was equally effective behind the scenes, Whitesell
said. "We had so many crises where work we had done for year was about
to go down the drain. Sterling would come up with a brilliant strategy. But
he kept his cards very close to the vest."

Gambel and Bolima maintained an arm's-length relationship with the
national conservation groups during the intense political negotiations of
the Alaska lands campaign. Gambel recalled: "The Sierra Club tried to
make a deal with us: We'd support their agenda in other parts of the country
like Yellowstone, and in return they would support protection for Admiralty
Island. We told them, 'We're not environmentalists, we're not
preservationists, we're here for one reason and one reason only.' We told
them our fight hadn't been for only forty years but from time immemorial.
It had been going on for ten thousand years."

4

THE BIG SQUEEZE

Glenn and Alex Reid left their family farm near Great Falls, Montana, in the early 1940s to try their hand at logging the great forests around Petersburg, Alaska. Once they got established, they sent for their relatives. All six Reid brothers eventually came to Southeast Alaska, some to log, some to try their hand at dairy farming. Glenn Reid served in the Aleutians in World War II. During the war he and Alex married sisters who had grown up in a rustic logging camp a quarter-mile from the Reids' own base of operations. After the war, the two young couples formed a partnership, Reid Brothers Logging Co., and moved to a little floathouse fifty miles by water from Petersburg. In the spring of 1946 they began cutting trees and hauling them to water by Caterpillar tractor. By 1948 they had built a network of logging roads on southwest Kupreanof Island and were hauling logs to water by truck.

The life of an independent logger in Southeast Alaska was an itinerant and precarious existence. The independent or "purchase" loggers were the Paul Bunyans of the North, braving rain, mud, tides and ferocious brown bears to wrest a living from the Alaska rain forest. Their floating camps were the most isolated in North America. In their heyday, between the end of the war and the early 1970s, when the pulp companies ran them out, more than one hundred independents operated in Southeast.

The Reids ran a typical operation. They bid on small Forest Service timber sales earmarked for independent purchasers. They hired crews to fall and buck the trees, haul them to saltwater and bind them into rafts for towing to distant mills. Then they towed their floating camp to the next inlet, the next timber sale. Like most early logging camps, theirs was a self-sufficient community that supplied its own water and electricity, fed its loggers at a communal cookhouse and sheltered them in rough bunkhouses.

Being an independent was a risky business. Seldom did the Reids have a guaranteed buyer when they bid on a sale, and the early years were lean.

But over time they earned reputations as skilled loggers and astute, honest businessmen. In the course of two decades, through hard work, sacrifice and business acumen, Reid Brothers Logging became a successful enterprise. In its early years Reid Brothers sold its logs to a company named Columbia Lumber, which operated small mills in Juneau, Sitka and Whittier. In 1953, the Reids sold their first raft of spruce logs to Ketchikan Pulp Co., the new player in Southeast.

Joe Penttila, a green-eyed Finn, arrived in Petersburg in 1956 with an appetite for hard work. He logged for Reid Brothers and two other outfits before starting his own business. In the beginning nearly all of his timber went to a sawmill at Wrangell. Later, when he got into truck logging, he sold chips to the new Alaska Lumber Co. pulp mill in Sitka. The pulp companies provided a ready market for the lower-grade logs that were unsuitable as sawtimber, and that made up roughly half the commercial timber on the Tongass.

The era of the independents was robust while it lasted. It also took an environmental toll. In those early years there were few brakes on logging. Stream buffers were nonexistent, and primitive roads built over gravel failed frequently, dumping sediment into rivers. By the early 1960s, when logging to supply the pulp mills began picking up steam, nearly all of the accessible coastal areas and sheltered coves in the Alaska Panhandle had been cut.

The pulp mills attracted larger logging operations, and higher-volume harvesting methods supplanted the logging techniques of the 1940s and 1950s. The Forest Service began auctioning bigger sales that required expensive trucks and cable yarding systems and constructing miles of logging roads. Many small-scale loggers, unable to afford the investment, left the business. But Reid Brothers succeeded in assembling the capital, equipment and personnel to compete in this new game.

A NO-WIN SITUATION

Once both pulp mills were operating, the deck was stacked against the independents. One of the first blows came when the mills changed the method by which they calculated how they would pay the independents for federal timber. Until 1960, independents were paid by the cubic foot. Under this system, the loggers got a fair price for old-growth logs that were not of sawtimber quality but could be chipped and fed to the pulp mills. Then, in 1960, the mills started using the Puget Sound Scaling Bureau system, which measured sawmill-grade timber in board feet. That system was advantageous to the pulp mills, because they paid little or nothing for pulp-grade logs, even though they used them to fuel their mills. But it put the independents in an untenable position, because the Forest Service required them to fall, buck, yard, truck, raft and remove all the trees in a sale unit, defective or not. "We couldn't make any money on these logs," Glenn Reid said. "We had to fall everything. But it caused loggers to leave a lot of stuff in the woods. Then we were accused of being sloppy. All the companies went broke."

Glenn Reid was president of the Alaska Loggers Association during this change. "In the summer of 1964," he recalls, "we got some big pulp logs, and we held a demonstration on the beach at Ketchikan. We were trying to show that we were getting robbed. By evening I was no longer president of the Alaska Loggers Association." Soon after, the pulp mills took control of the association, silencing an independent voice in Southeast Alaska's timber industry.

The pulp mills wielded so much political power that even top Forest Service managers were intimidated by them. Joe Penttila recalls that in 1960 a popular Petersburg district ranger, Jack Bennett, who had publicly criticized the pulp mills, was directed by his bosses not to attend a big meeting of the Pacific Logging Congress in Ketchikan. The order came after Art Brooks, Ketchikan Pulp's timber manager, let it be known he did not want to see Bennett at the meeting.

To prevent the independents from selling logs to potential new mill operators, or to the few remaining independent sawmills in Southeast Alaska, the pulp companies reduced the loggers to economic bondage by paying below-market prices and then loaning them just enough money to allow them to keep producing logs. By deliberately depressing the market, they made it impossible for the independents to show a profit.

Both mills also held the loggers hostage through harsh borrowing terms. "You could go to Alaska Lumber and Pulp and say you needed a new tower," Penttila recalled. "Towers cost $90,000 to $120,000 apiece. They would let you have the tower, but you owed your soul to the company store." Alaska Lumber and Pulp managers insisted that the independents sell exclusively to ALP, resorting to threats when necessary: "If you sold to a small mill," Penttila said, "the company would say, 'They can have all your logs.'" But the small sawmills had no use for pulp logs, and they could not afford to buy them and resell them to the pulp mills, which either refused to buy them or refused to pay a competitive price.

In 1964 Puget Sound Pulp and Timber, which held a half-ownership in the Ketchikan pulp mill, merged with Portland-based timber giant Georgia-Pacific Corporation, and G-P took over operation of the Ketchikan mill. Soon after, both pulp mills' parent companies ratcheted up their campaign to drive the independents out. Like dominoes, the small mills and purchase loggers of Southeast began to fall. The mills were acquired or shut down. The purchase loggers were replaced with contract loggers, who logged timber owned by the pulp mills. The contract loggers kept the pulp mills supplied with logs. But because they were selling services, not logs, they couldn't provide timber to the remaining independent sawmills or to potential new entrants into the Southeast Alaska timber industry.

In the mid-1960s, Wrangell Lumber Co., an independent logger, contracted to sell timber to Mitkof Lumber Co., a small sawmill in Petersburg. Soon after, ALP bought Wrangell Lumber Co. and entered into a formal log supply agreement with Mitkof Lumber, effectively placing the Petersburg sawmill under its control. In 1967 Ketchikan Pulp Co. bought Ketchikan Spruce Mill, a fixture on the Ketchikan waterfront, eliminating another market for the independents.

At about that time the city of Petersburg asked the Forest Service to put up a large timber sale to encourage the establishment of a veneer mill in the town. The Forest Service complied by auctioning the largest independent timber sale ever offered in Southeast. But Mitkof-Wrangell, now a front for ALP, outbid two smaller companies and won the sale. It was the first of many instances in which pulp company fronts masquerading as independents bid premium prices for Tongass timber—a tactic calculated to tighten the pulp companies' control of the timber industry in Southeast. The tactic also helped eliminate the purchase loggers' source of supply. They could not hope to outbid the pulp mills for the most desirable timber because they would have to sell their pulp logs to those same mills. The losses the pulp companies incurred on such sales were more than offset by the low stumpage rates they paid for millions of board feet of timber under their long-term contracts.

In an effort to encourage the establishment of independent sawmills and veneer plants in Southeast Alaska, the Forest Service had earmarked as much as one-third of its timber sale program for independent purchasers. When agency officials began suspecting that the pulp companies were using fronts to acquire these sales, on top of the hundreds of millions of board feet guaranteed to them annually under their long-term contracts, they asked the U.S. Department of Justice to investigate the companies for possible violations of antitrust laws. But the Justice Department took no action, the Forest Service failed to act on its own to end the fraud, and the pulp companies' quiet campaign to eliminate competition in the Southeast Alaska timber industry continued.

By the late 1960s, many independents had fallen by the wayside. Some owners had gone broke; others had suffered nervous breakdowns. Most didn't understand what was happening to them. "They were out in their isolated camps," Martha Reid recalls. "The only time we all got together was at the Alaska Loggers' Association meetings." Even then, she said, the talk was of new logging equipment, not the squeeze on timber prices. "The pulp mills would tell us not to talk about prices because that would be antitrust!"

DIVIDING THE TERRITORY

The pulp mills scrupulously honored an unwritten agreement that Alaska Pulp would bid only on timber sales from the north end of the Tongass, Ketchikan Pulp only on sales in the south. From 1959 to 1975, Alaska Pulp and Ketchikan Pulp almost never bid against each other on a timber sale. In 1971, when Forest Service timber appraiser Ron Galdabini went to work for the Alaska Region, he quickly figured out that something fishy was going on. "Once I got to Juneau and got a chance to see all the sales on the forest, things didn't make sense," he said. "KPC was towing logs past other mills to its own mill. It was obvious that the pulp mills had divided up the territory. But when I asked questions, all I got was a lot of rationalizations." It was also obvious to him that nearly all the high bidders on Tongass timber sales were fronts for the pulp mills, and that new players couldn't get a foothold. "When the plywood mills moved in and tried to get established, the pulp mills would bid them out," he said. "The plywoods never did manage to break into the market."

K.J. Metcalf worked in the Alaska Region of the Forest Service from 1962 to 1982, long enough to see the pulp mills extend their monopoly throughout the Tongass. He says both the Forest Service and the Department of Justice turned a blind eye to blatant evidence of collusive bidding. "The Forest Service sold to front companies. The Forest Service knew these were front companies. They had no equipment, no workers. The Justice Department knew the Forest Service had knowingly sold sales to these companies and was part of the collusion."

HANGING ON

In 1968 the Reid brothers split their business and divided their assets. Alex and Mary Reid, bowing to the inevitable, formed a new company to do contract logging exclusively for Ketchikan Pulp. Glenn and Martha Reid kept the name Reid Brothers Logging Co. and continued to go it alone. In 1969 Reid Brothers contracted with Japanese-owned Alaska Prince Timber Co. to sell timber to its sawmill at Metlakatla on Annette Island, a Tsimshian Indian reservation near Ketchikan. "The Indians at Metlakatla had a fair amount of timber," Ron Galdabini said. "They wanted primary processing to create jobs. The Japanese said, 'Let us export logs from your land and we'll buy federal timber for your mill.'" Reid Brothers made a profit on the deal and contracted to sell Alaska Prince more timber. In 1970 the Reids went into debt to buy more equipment, including two rubber-tired skidders and a boom boat.

The Reids' stubborn persistence caught the attention of Harry Merlo, a flamboyant and ruthless Georgia-Pacific executive. Merlo had cut his teeth in the timber industry, running a logging-camp store at the age of thirteen. He had a reputation within G-P's executive echelon as a "jungle fighter." In 1970 a team from G-P headquarters in Portland was dispatched to Ketchikan. The days of Reid Brothers and the other surviving independents in Southeast Alaska were numbered. Soon after, Ketchikan Pulp bought Alaska Prince, eliminating Reid Brothers' best customer and one of the last independent mills in Southeast Alaska.

The Reids were working harder than ever, but despite a strong market, they weren't making it. Glenn Reid was asking himself, "How are they going to get me?" The answer wasn't long in coming. In 1972 Reid Brothers bid on a big sale called Muddy River 3, and contracted to sell the logs to Ketchikan Pulp. Glenn Reid needed to borrow about $200,000 to cover the cost of road-building and logging equipment and pay off old debts before he could begin logging the sale. When he tried to negotiate with KPC for the startup money, company officials informed him that in order to borrow the money, he would have to sign over the logging rights he had won at auction, wiping out any profit he might realize and turning him into nothing more than a logger-for-hire. With no other market for the timber, Glenn Reid had run out of options. He reluctantly signed over his stumpage rights.

At KPC's insistence, Reid agreed to deliver timber to the company for a firm $64 per thousand board feet, a price that left no margin for profit. Then, in 1973, lumber prices increased substantially. If Reid had retained his stumpage rights, he would have been entitled to a portion of the price increase and might have been able to make a profit on the job. But under his deal with KPC, the $64 rate was not subject to renegotiation. Instead, KPC pocketed the profits.

After a quarter-century in the logging business, for the first time Glenn Reid was unable to pay his bills. In September of 1973, KPC's timber manager, Don Finney, terminated the company's contract with Reid Brothers Logging. Glenn Reid shut down operations at Muddy River and started looking for a lawyer.

MERLO'S STAMP

As the last of the independents went under, big changes were taking place in the ownership and management of Ketchikan Pulp Co. In 1972, as partial settlement of a federal antitrust suit, Georgia-Pacific Corporation spun off its half-ownership of the Ketchikan pulp mill and its Samoa pulp mill on California's Humboldt Bay to a newly created company, Louisiana-Pacific Corporation. It was a shrewd move; both pulp mills depended heavily on public lands for raw materials, which left them vulnerable to changes in federal forest policy. Georgia-Pacific held onto its private lands. Three years later Louisiana-Pacific Corporation bought FMC's share of Ketchikan Pulp Co., and Ketchikan Pulp became a wholly owned subsidiary of Louisiana-Pacific.

Merlo became president and chief executive officer of Louisiana-Pacific. He quickly set about living up to his jungle fighter image. He embarked on a buying binge, acquiring eleven mills in 1973, and tripling L-P's sales over the next six years. Maintenance and worker safety at Ketchikan Pulp began to suffer almost immediately as Merlo sought to squeeze more profits out of the plant. KPC's profits jumped 165 percent between the first half of 1972 and the first half of 1973, and company bookkeepers forecast that the company's cash buildup would skyrocket from $768,000 to nearly $17.6 million in the twelve months ending June 30, 1974.

During the week of September 10, 1973—the same week KPC shut down Reid Brothers' logging operations—Louisiana-Pacific executives met to discuss what to do about KPC's enormous profitability. The strategy they settled on was to hide their profits in a corporate shell game that would take Forest Service investigators years to figure out.

Chemical engineer Roland Stanton had been with Ketchikan Pulp since the beginning. Hired in the 1950s to develop and refine KPC's pulp manufacturing process, by the mid-1970s he had worked his way up to technical director and was a member of the mill's top management team. In May of 1975 Stanton attended a meeting of mill supervisors. When an overhead projector flashed the mill's latest financial report on the wall, he noticed immediately that the cost of raw material for the pulp mill had jumped 70 percent, erasing all profits. He asked KPC's general manager, Martin Pihl, "Why did the price of wood shoot up?" That question cost him his job.

Years later, in an article and a followup interview, Stanton described what happened next: "Harry Merlo had decreed that all units of the company would pay the same price for wood. The sawmills got the good $200 logs for $100, and the pulp mill got the $60 junk for the same $100 figure. In this one stroke Harry had transferred about $8 million in revenue from the pulp mill to the sawmills." Stanton couldn't keep his mouth shut. He remarked, "No one else in the business keeps books this way. It won't be much fun to be a pulp mill supervisor anymore, since they will be forever chewing on us to make a profit." His comment was met with dead silence. A few days later he was called to a closed-door meeting. "The first thing they told me was, 'We want you to resign.' I asked why, and the answer was, 'You are not a team player.'" Stanton asked his bosses what would happen if he didn't resign. He was told he would be demoted and lose his office. He said he could live with that. A week later, mill managers came to him to negotiate a settlement.

Stanton felt insulted. "I had spent twenty-two years as an idea man, constantly coming up with new ideas to make more pulp, better pulp and cheaper pulp. In the five years directly before, I had solved the greatest single problem of the industry as it tightened up for pollution control— how to solve the problem of calcium buildup in pulp production and make money doing it. To my colleagues in the industry I was a hero. To KPC I must have been a threat."

"It took a long time for me to put my comment about 'not much fun in the pulp business' into context," Stanton said. "Apparently, I blew Harry's cover. What he wanted to do was to get the pulp mill closed and expand the sawmills. However, the fifty-year contract with the U.S. Forest Service required the operation of a pulp mill." He speculated that Merlo hoped the government would release KPC from its contract if the pulp mill consistently lost money,

Both pulp mills had other reasons to conceal the enormous profits they were reaping from their federal timber contracts and their monopoly control of the Tongass timber sale program. Windfall profits might arouse the curiosity of the Internal Revenue Service. And skyrocketing profits might prompt the Forest Service to increase the bargain rate the pulp companies were paying for Tongass timber.

GETTING EVEN

Glenn and Martha Reid were determined to sue the pulp companies for restraint of trade. But most Alaska lawyers they contacted didn't believe their story, and the rest either worked for the pulp mills or weren't competent to mount a major antitrust case. "Antitrust suits are a funny thing," Glenn Reid said. "They aren't meant for the little guy." The search for competent legal representation ate up two years.

In 1974, when the Reids finally were referred to Culp, Dwyer, Guterson & Grader, a top-flight Seattle law firm, they got some bad news: Even in the unlikely event that they prevailed against the pulp companies, the statute of limitations might allow them to collect only four years' damages.

William Dwyer, a founding partner of Culp Dwyer, and his colleagues, Jerry McNaul, Richard Yarmuth and Peter Vial, could see the contours of a major antitrust case in the story the Alaska loggers told them. But they investigated carefully before they agreed to represent them. Reid Brothers and the other independents were Davids to the pulp company Goliaths. The case would not be a money-maker for years, if ever. Still, they believed it was winnable. They finally agreed to represent the Reids on a contingent-fee basis. "It looked like a just cause," Dwyer recalled. "Glenn Reid was a man of honor. He was confronted by some kind of big economic force he didn't fully understand. He and Martha were determined that their creditors would be paid every cent they were owed. They didn't want to declare bankruptcy. They stood personally behind their little company. This was the real fun of practicing law, when you had a good cause, good people and a lot at risk. It creates a great deal of camaraderie among lawyers and between lawyers and clients."

On March 13, 1975, Reid Brothers Logging brought suit against Ketchikan Pulp Co. and Alaska Lumber and Pulp under the Sherman Act, alleging that the companies had engaged in collusion and conspiracy to drive independent loggers out of Southeast Alaska. By the time the suit was filed, no true independents were left in Southeast Alaska. However, the pulp mills gave their contract loggers a price increase immediately after. One logger told Reid the lawsuit had put him in the black.

The pulp companies retained the best legal representation money could buy. Ketchikan Pulp hired the prestigious San Francisco law firm of Morrison & Forrester, which put a platoon of lawyers on the case and leased nearly an entire floor of a downtown Seattle hotel for the duration of the trial. Both companies also hired high-priced Seattle lawyers.

In October of 1976, eight months after the Reids filed their suit, Alaska Regional Forester John Sandor asked the U.S. Justice Department to investigate the two pulp mills for possible restraint of trade. In December the Justice Department's Antitrust Division reported that after an "extensive" investigation it had closed the case because of insufficient evidence. The following year the Forest Service instituted a small business timber sale program on the Tongass. Under the program, independent mills and logging companies previously locked out of the region would be offered a price break on federal timber to encourage new entries into the Southeast Alaska timber industry.

In 1977, and again in 1978, U.S. Department of Agriculture auditors reviewed the Tongass timber sale program at Sandor's request. In 1978 the regional forester asked auditors to transmit evidence on timber sale bidding patterns to the Agriculture Department's Office of the Inspector General for investigation. But again these investigations produced no indictments., and Sandor chose to take no action on his own.

A CLOSE CALL

The attorneys at Culp Dwyer had to start from scratch. They began by casting a wide net in their search for internal pulp company documents that might prove collusion. "We would request documents regarding areas of operation, for example, or U.S. Forest Service timber sales, or their business with small logging companies," Dwyer said.

During the six years it took to prepare for trial, the lawyers examined hundreds of thousands of pages of documents. McNaul and Vial visited Alaska countless times to gather information and take depositions.

On the night of February 16, 1976, much of this work was nearly lost when a fire broke out at the Ketchikan Spruce Mills office and warehouse on the Ketchikan docks, where Ketchikan Pulp Co. had stored many boxes of subpoenaed KPC documents. Fire inspectors discovered that the main valve to the building's sprinkler system had been shut off and an alarm system disabled shortly before the fire. Cleanup crews were about to bulldoze the boxes of soaked documents when nephews of Glenn and Martha Reid rushed to the docks to rescue them. No one was ever arrested in the arson fire.

Peter Vial flew to Ketchikan, and he and Jerry McNaul spent weeks sorting through the moldering papers. Some had to be frozen to preserve them. But the hard work paid off when they uncovered incriminating memos that would ultimately prove that the pulp companies had pursued a calculated and deceptive strategy of bid-rigging, collusion, and conspiracy to drive all competitors out of Southeast Alaska.

The Reids and Joe Penttila spent a couple of winters in Seattle, going through hundreds of boxes of documents and shaking their heads over evidence of collusion they discovered in pulp company files. They were amazed, amused, and occasionally angered at what they found. Pulp company officials had put everything in writing and had saved all of it. "I can see why they tried to burn their paperwork," Penttila said.

A VAST CONSPIRACY

The scale of the conspiracy, as revealed in internal communications and depositions from pulp company officials, independent loggers and small mill operators, was breathtaking. Between 1960 and 1974 the pulp mills had driven at least ninety-nine independent logging contractors out of business, eliminating an industry that had operated for decades in Southeast Alaska. Between them, the companies had acquired ownership or control of seven mills—Alaska Prince, Ketchikan Spruce Mill, and Alaska Timber Corp., all acquired by KPC; and Wrangell Lumber Co., Schnabel Lumber Co., Alaska Wood Products, and Mitkof Lumber Co., all acquired by ALP. By 1976, no truly viable independent mills were left in Southeast Alaska.

Not only had the pulp companies consolidated monopoly control of the Tongass; they had also eliminated a reality check on the true cost of logging and lumber and pulp production in Southeast Alaska. With the field to themselves, the pulp companies could hide their own costs and profits from the Internal Revenue Service and from Forest Service appraisers who might use the information to increase the price they paid for federal timber.

The Reids' attorneys uncovered ample evidence that the pulp companies had deliberately divided up the Tongass, leaving nothing for the independents. One smoking gun was a January 14, 1974, memo from KPC timber manager Don Finney to his boss, KPC vice president D.L. Murdey, suggesting that "it would be most beneficial to ALP and ourselves to realign the operations so that KPC had the West Coast." Finney went on to explain his thinking: "(I)t is obvious that any increased program must come from other than the South Tongass. This means that future sales will geographically be better positioned for ALP than for KPC. It makes sense for us to work out this fact now, so that we control the S. Tongass and at least those sales that will logically feed into Sumner Straits, Duncan Canal and Wrangell Narrows and let ALP have those feeding into Kake, Frederick Sound and points north."

Revealingly, Finney's memo concluded that the proposed realignment "would also strengthen both of us in a competitive position for any outside interest (U.S. Ply or whoever) who tries to compete for sales with us at a later date." The word "realign" was the give-away, said Forest Service timber appraiser Ron Galdabini. "'Realign' means there was previous alignment. That one word cost Don Finney his job."

The lawyers also uncovered copious evidence of "collusive communication" and joint projects between the pulp companies. They found records revealing that the companies had sold valuable cedar logs to each other and had used a dual invoicing system to conceal the true price from the Forest Service in order to keep cedar stumpage values low. Other records showed that the companies had agreed to share, and to avoid bidding on, timber from the best Sitka spruce stands in the region. Over the years the companies, which shared the same lawyers and accountants, had exchanged information on every aspect of their operations, including the prices they paid for logs, log production figures, and the threats posed by the possible entry of new mill competitors into the market.

Between 1966 and 1975 the companies bid on 166 national forest timber sales. Over that period, they bid against each other only three times. Neither did either company buy logs from a contractor who was selling logs to the other. Both knew well that this refusal to compete for timber had the effect of artificially depressing log prices. That was the point. As KPC timber manager Art Brooks acknowledged in a 1969 memo: "(W)e are deterred from establishing a realistic log price by our fear that it will be reflected in Forest Service stumpage rates."

A STRATEGY LAID BARE

Amazingly, mill managers had put even their detailed strategies for squeezing small mills and independent loggers out of the market in writing. These memos allowed the Reids' lawyers to reconstruct the steps by which KPC had denied Alaska Prince a timber supply and forced the Alaska Native-owned company to sell out, eliminating Reid Brothers' primary customer.

In fact, they learned that KPC had tried to thwart establishment of the sawmill in the first place. When timber manager Art Brooks learned in 1968 that the Oji Paper Company in Tokyo had agreed to finance a sawmill on Annette Island, he wrote to the company to try to dissuade it from going ahead. The Japanese disregarded Brooks' letter and began constructing the mill, which prompted Brooks to warn his bosses in a memo: "Once in the area they no doubt plan simply to outbid everyone for enough logs to supply the mill, which they can probably do, unless a combination effort by the local groups run them out." After the mill began operating, Brooks reported to Georgia-Pacific executives: "Alaska Prince is beginning to cause us trouble among the so-called independent loggers by going around and offering them $70 for spruce sawlogs and $60 for sawlog hemlock."

To extinguish this competition, KPC called in its loans to independent loggers. Brooks pointed out to Alaska Prince "the futility of going around and offering the people logging for us more money for logs when we have them either under contract or have security agreements which permit us to seize their logs, if necessary."

KPC also plotted to deny Alaska Prince raw materials. At one Forest Service timber auction, a KPC front bid nearly three times the Forest Service minimum bid against Alaska Prince. At another auction, the company instructed its timber manager to outbid Alaska Prince "regardless of cost" and "at any price." Similarly, the Reids' legal team traced Alaska Lumber and Pulp's strategy of predatory bidding against Dant & Russell, which owned a small mill in Haines in the early 1970s. ALP bid up the stumpage on one sale from $17.10 to $63.72 per thousand board feet, nearly four times the minimum bid. On a second sale, ALP offered twice the minimum bid. Soon after, the Dant & Russell mill closed for good.

The story was repeated, with variations, in Ketchikan Pulp's acquisition of Ketchikan Spruce Mills, which had operated on the Ketchikan waterfront since 1903; in Alaska Lumber and Pulp's acquisition of Schnabel Lumber Co.'s sawmill in Haines; and in the pulp companies' acquistion of four other mills in the 1960s and early 1970s. Records the Reids' lawyers obtained during discovery proved that both pulp companies used bidding fronts, and that KPC in particular used fronts whose ownership could not be traced, that it purchased timber sales with non-traceable cashier's checks, and that it gave out false information to federal agencies. Alaska Lumber and Pulp never purchased timber or logs in its own name. Although all decisions on timber procurement were handled by ALP executives in Sitka, sales were bid on and purchased in the name of Wrangell Lumber Company or by one of the contract loggers or small mills ALP controlled.

Each part of the pulp companies' strategy reinforced the other parts. Acquiring small mills or driving them out of business eliminated competition for the purchase of logs and logging services. That made it easier for the pulp companies to control independent loggers by ensnaring them in debt and ultimately eliminating them from the field. And that extended the pulp mills' monopoly power, making it impossible for other mills to compete in Southeast Alaska. Glenn and Martha Reid had been caught in a game larger and far more elaborate than anything they had imagined.

PREPARING FOR TRIAL

The Reid Brothers case was initially assigned to U.S. District Judge Morell Sharp, who consolidated four other suits against the pulp mills, two filed by independent loggers and two by operators of small sawmills, into a single case for purposes of discovery and pretrial motions.

Lawyers for the pulp companies pursued a stonewall defense, conceding nothing. Massive discovery was necessary. In 1978 they filed a voluminous set of motions, including a motion to strike the Reid Brothers' demand for a jury trial and eleven motions for summary judgement. Judge Sharp denied all but one of those motions. As an appeals court panel would later note, the pulp mills "resisted on every issue, filed motion after motion seeking to prevent the case from going to trial, and refused to concede facts even in the face of overwhelming evidence."

The pulp mills' delay tactics were part of a larger strategy. On the other side of the country, a seven-year Alaska wilderness campaign was hurtling toward resolution, and the fate of the pulp mills' long-term contracts might hinge on the trial's outcome. "Delay in allowing the antitrust cases to go to trial was extremely important to the pulp mills' political strategy," said John Sisk, a Southeast Alaska Conservation Council grassroots organizer in the 1980s. "A big factor was to make sure nothing happened in the district court before the Alaska National Interest Land and Conservation Act passed. If the verdict had happened any sooner, before the end of 1980, it would have been a completely different Alaska Lands Act."

Judge Sharp died during the long process of preparing for trial, and the case was reassigned to U.S. District Judge Barbara Rothstein, a relative newcomer to the federal bench. Because the docket was clogged with cases, the Reids reluctantly agreed to waive a jury trial in order to get a trial date in 1980. By the spring of 1980, when Rothstein set a trial date, the Reid Brothers case had been pending for five years.

The trial finally began on August 4 and continued for forty-one days. Nearly six years of meticulous preparation by the lawyers at Culp Dwyer paid off at trial. The internal memos they had acquired during discovery painted a devastating picture of monopolistic and coercive behavior that left little to the imagination. In all, 60 persons testified in person or by deposition; 1,291 exhibits were admitted into evidence; and more than 6,000 pages of trial testimony were transcribed.

At trial, attorneys for the pulp companies argued that each part of the alleged conspiracy must be considered separately from every other part, and that Reid Brothers Logging could not show it had incurred damages from those separate acts. But Dwyer countered that the various parts of the strategy had been designed to work together, and had done so, to devastating effect.

At the end of the trial, Judge Rothstein instructed both sides to submit extensive post-trial briefs and proposed findings. Glenn and Martha Reid and their friends and associates went home to Alaska to await the verdict.

5

Opening Up the Country

In 1978, when Forest Service engineer Ron Skillings arrived in Southeast Alaska, the timber market was hot and the logging was frenetic, especially on Prince of Wales Island. The Tongass National Forest was still wide open; aside from a few research natural areas and buffer zones around bald eagle nests, almost no land had been set aside for permanent protection.

Engineers scrambled to survey and lay out logging roads opening up intact watersheds. Loggers lived in floating camps or primitive cabins. Forest Service employees made do with knock-down prefab houses and camper trailers that could be lowered by crane into remote sites. Road-building equipment was brought in by barge because most of the logging shows were in isolated areas unconnected to the existing road system.

Out in the woods, it was every man for himself. "It was survival of the fittest," Skillings recalled. "We had 350 Forest Service employees that we just threw out in the field. We didn't have an interconnecting road system. We didn't have places for people to sleep. We had survey teams working ten days in a row in a tent. At the time I came in 1978 there was a 45 percent turnover every year on the Ketchikan area. I replaced an engineer who lasted nine months. When I arrived, my boss said, 'I don't have time to brief you. Go out to this place on the map and meet with so and so and they'll tell you what to do.'"

In about 1980 the Forest Service established a ranger station at Thorne Bay on the east coast of Prince of Wales Island, site of a permanent logging camp and the largest log-sorting yard in the world. It built offices and houses for its permanent employees. "That's when Thorne Bay went from the world's largest logging camp to a community where people could house their families," Skillings said. Even after Thorne Bay was incorporated in 1982, the Forest Service was for all practical purposes the camp's municipal government.

A decommissioned logging road on national forest land near Flicker Ridge in the extreme northwest corner of Prince of Wales Island. Photo by Trygve Steen.

Road-building techniques in Southeast Alaska were still primitive. Crews used front-scooping shovels or caterpillar tractors to push tracks into the soggy wilderness. "Because the ground was so soft and there was so much muskeg, the common practice was to take the road down to bedrock and sidecast the materials," Skillings says. "We would end up with a berm on one side and brush on the other." Culvert washouts and road failures were common on saturated ground. Road-building often triggered mass land movements on unstable mountainsides. "This is a young country," Skillings observed. "It's still trying to find its angle of repose."

Eventually, after a federal auditor came to look at logging roads on the Tongass, road-building techniques improved. The Alaska Region hired more engineers like Skillings. Instead of digging down to bedrock, engineers began laying out roads on top of soil and organic material, thereby reducing the number of roadcuts and fills. "We started letting roads follow the natural terrain," Skillings said. "It was lighter on the land."

A LONG-TERM STRATEGY

Beyond bringing timber out of the woods, the Forest Service road-building program had a larger purpose, articulated in the agency's 1964 Multiple Use Management Guide for the Alaska Region: to open up the backcountry and connect the isolated communities of the Alaska Panhandle. The 1964 plan envisioned a system of "forest highways" that would link Southeast communities to each other and to the recently established Alaska Marine Highway ferry system. Ferry routes, the plan said, would provide "a major trunkline system for tying together the existing links of Forest highway and Forest development roads into an integrated road system serving the needs of the National Forests." But the Forest Service must do its part as well, the plan stressed: "The development of potential recreation sites, a continuing and expanding timber harvest, and distribution of hunting and fishing pressures all require a vastly expanded system of roads. To date, high road construction costs and limited road funds have permitted only a token effort in this direction."

Ron Skillings bought into that vision. "We spent $150,000 per mile on our roads," he said. "We looked at our roads and bridges as a long-term investment. The Forest Service had to look at 'How do we manage the land over the long haul?' We needed to build a permanent infrastructure." After Forest Service logging roads had served their original purpose, the Federal Highway Administration upgraded many to two-lane roads and turned them over to the state for maintenance. Those roads opened up the island and brought new permanent residents to small settlements like Craig and Thorne Bay. Skillings took pride in that. "We have very active communities down there today," he said in 1997. "People have established a lifestyle because of the road system." Ironically, the road system also made it possible for Alaskans and visitors to see firsthand the clearcuts, landslides and trashed streams left in the wake of national forest logging on Prince of Wales Island.

The Forest Service spelled out the details of its inter-island road plan in a 1968 article in the *Juneau Empire,* which extolled the benefits that would come with the opening up of the Southeast Alaska wilderness to hunters, fishermen and tourists. New roads "will pass through fishing and hunting areas now visited only by bear and deer and an occasional adventurous man." Routes would wind "along serene rivers, through open meadows frequented by deer, past lakes dimpled by leaping trout, and ponds that give life to the yellow water lily." A road north of Ketchikan would extend all the way to the Naha River ,"where fabulous fishing for lunker steelhead, rainbow and cutthroat trout is now enjoyed by people who have boats, or who can afford to fly into one of the lakes on the Naha chain." A logging road would extend the full length of Admiralty Island's west coast. A road connection to Wrangell would cross the grass flats of Dry Island "where myriad of ducks and geese provide outstanding hunting," and connect with a proposed highway up the great Stikine River through the Coast Range, intersecting with the Alaska Highway in British Columbia.

The Alaska Conservation Society printed large sections of the story in its newsletter, ending with the cryptic comment: "What is one man's (or agency's) dream is another man's nightmare."

TAKING INVENTORY

In the 1970s the Forest Service still lacked a reliable inventory of the forests, fish, wildlife and other resources of the Tongass National Forest. When Ron Dippold transferred to the Tongass in 1974, his assignment was to conduct that inventory. The best information at the time came from the 1948 U.S. Navy aerial photos, taken on overflights that covered the entire Tongass, from Yakutat to Hydaburg. The Navy photos, and maps the U.S. Geological Survey had produced from those photos, had allowed the Forest Service and other agencies to fill in some of the blanks on the Southeast Alaska map, locating major salmon streams and other geographical reference points and providing navigational landmarks for pilots.

The Forest Service had attempted an inventory in the 1950s, mainly to estimate timber volume. "It was very humbling to realize how far off those early projections were," Dippold said. Growth projections had been based on crude tree measurements because so little second growth existed. "It was hard in the early days to find young trees and measure growth. You had to look for windthrow or old Russian cuts." Research plots were established up and down the Tongass, but many plots were logged before they yielded meaningful data.

Dippold's job was to map tree types and ages, rates of tree growth, wildlife populations and other data on the entire national forest, which at the time encompassed 15.2 million acres. It was a daunting assignment. "One of the mystiques of the Tongass is that it scares you with its size," he said. The methodology available to Dippold's team was limited by the technology of the times. "We punched holes in aerial photos and predicted what was there: rocks, ice, the size of trees." Then came the real challenge: field-checking a sampling of those points on the ground.

Bushwhacking across the untracked Alaska rainforest, with its enormous fallen logs, its soggy muskeg bogs, its mud and its inclement weather, was a slow, exhausting and dangerous undertaking. "Each point took about a day," Dippold said. "We would start in late April and try to cover as many points as we could, using float planes. We had to go in from a known point. If we could land on a lake and walk in in eight to ten hours, we'd do it that way. We did use helicopters where necessary. There were times we stayed on the beach. But if you're overnighting, you're hauling gear."

Yet even with all that hard work, in retrospect Dippold acknowledged that the field checks were not reliable enough to allow sweeping judgments about the ages and types of forest that grew on the Tongass. "They weren't site-specific enough. What was true for one small area of Prince of Wales Island was inaccurately extrapolated to cover the entire island." Over-optimistic projections of timber volume in the 1970s inventory would come back to haunt forest managers in the 1990s.

Dippold's team also conducted archeological inventories prior to logging. "At Hidden Falls on Baranof Island we found what looked like a midden," he said. "That stopped all work. It was a major find. Archeologists found enough shells and wood and bone to do some carbon dating." The Hidden Falls discovery pushed back the date at which anthropologists could document human occupation of the Alaska Panhandle to 9,500 years before the present.

EARLY PLANNING

Updated forest inventories were essential as the Alaska Region confronted new federal laws and regulations in the 1970s. The 1969 National Environmental Policy Act required all federal agencies to conduct site-specific assessments of the environmental impacts of major actions. The 1976 National Forest Management Act required all national forests to prepare detailed multiple-use management plans. Both laws required extensive public involvement. On the Tongass, these laws threatened business as it had been practiced since the signing of the long-term contracts in the 1950s.

In those first decades, the pulp companies had essentially run the show, writing their own five-year logging plans and administering their own timber sales. In effect, the Forest Service had worked for the pulp companies. Many

Tongass managers believed that the pulp mill contracts trumped even laws passed by Congress. These managers viewed the new federal mandates as impediments to their overriding mission: moving timber from the forest to the hungry maw of the mills.

NEPA's immediate effect in Alaska was to delay the flow of timber. As the Tongass and Chugach national forests geared up to put the machinery of environmental documentation and public involvement in place, timber sales were temporarily delayed. In his history of the Forest Service in Alaska, Forest Service historian Lawrence Rakestraw reflected the view that NEPA was mainly a means of harassing federal agencies: "The National Environmental Policy Act lent itself to litigation and was as deadly, and occasionally as random, in its operation as was the old Allen Pepperbox in the hands of the frontiersman." But public involvement did prompt the Forest Service to redesign some timber sales to make them more environmentally acceptable, and some agency officials welcomed NEPA despite its red tape.

Alaska Regional Forester Charlie Yates took the first halting step toward modern forest planning on the Tongass even before NMFA, when in the early 1970s he directed his planning staff to develop an overall forest management plan. The result, a seven-hundred-page document called the Draft Tongass National Forest Land Use Plan (TNFLUP), released in 1975, divided the Tongass into discrete geographic units. The unwieldly plan tried to have it both ways, directing that each unit be studied for possible wilderness designations—and simultaneously that each unit containing commercial timber be made available for timber harvest. "The effort was very transparent," said K.J. Metcalf, a Forest Service planner assigned to coordinate public involvement after the plan's release. "The rationale was that there might be some acreage in each of the units that would be suitable for wilderness, but not at the expense of timber harvest."

Metcalf told planner Bill Overdorff that people would find the document so massive and confusing that they wouldn't understand it. As he recalls, Overdorff replied, "Good. Every time the public understands what we are doing they cause us trouble."

The plan's blatant timber emphasis outraged commercial fishing interests. One fishing group warned Yates that if he adopted the approach outlined in the draft plan, fishermen would see the Forest Service in court. Guy Martin, Alaska's commissioner of natural resources, formed a task force to stop Yates from acting on the draft. One of the options the task force considered was to take the Forest Service to court as "unfit land managers."

Buried within the huge document were two sentences laying out the agency's concept of an inter-island highway linking the communities of Southeast. "The reference was very obtuse and I couldn't see how that was being honest with the public," Metcalf said. But when he tried to get the road plan put out for public comment, Joe Zylinski, the head of planning, told him that people concerned about the inter-island system would find the two-sentence reference.

Metcalf then wrote a memo to Bob Rehfeld, the assistant regional forester in charge of planning, stating, "It's obvious that the inter-island system will have far-reaching impacts on the land, resources, and communities involved, even greater impacts perhaps than the long-term timber sales." Because the proposed system would be highly controversial, Metcalf said, the Forest Service should be prepared to explain when and how the decision to build the road system had been reached and what other transportation alternatives had been considered. He also urged planners to seek broad public comment. "We are starting from a position that the inter-island system is a good and wanted system," he wrote. "This basic assumption may or may not be correct." Years later, Metcalf learned that Rehfield had considered his memo so dangerous that he had hidden it away in a drawer rather than place it in a file where it might be read by a member of the public or an employee of another agency.

Safety in the turbulent skies above Southeast Alaska became another argument for an expanded road system after a tragic plane crash took the lives of twelve passengers flying over the Tongass on August 25, 1978. The accident prompted the Forest Service to adopt a new policy aimed at reducing flying time by making more of the forest accessible by road.

TENAKEE FIGHTS BACK

The Forest Service master plan for an inter-island road system escaped the attention of most Southeast Alaska residents. But it did not escape the residents of Tenakee Springs, a community perched on stilts between mountains and saltwater near the mouth of Tenakee Inlet. A wide dirt road leads from Tenakee's picturesque harbor into town, which is three blocks long, and ends at the community bathhouse. The public toilet sits at the end of a pier; the outgoing tide supplies the plumbing. Wood houses cling to forested hillsides. A snug bakery doubles as community center and art gallery. Traffic is limited to walkers and cyclists. There are no cars. Tenakee likes it that way.

The town has always drawn spiritual seekers and rogues. Before the arrival of white settlers a Tlingit band wintered there, attracted by its hot springs, which the Tlingit believed to have medicinal value. "Winter place," "copper shield" and "where the great waters meet" are some of the meanings linked to the settlement's Tlingit name. Tenakee historian Vicki Wisenbaugh writes that the main spring was "an uncovered, steaming fissure barely above high tide . . . The clear hot water reflected the gray of Southeast skies. Bubbles rose from deep inside the earth to break on the surface, and rain hammered the pool to dimple it like pewter. It was a place of magic for the imaginative, and comfort for the sick and tired."

In the 1880s miners blasted the pool of the largest spring and built a log bathhouse to provide privacy. Tenakee became an affordable resort for miners, loggers and fishermen to wait out the winter. Fish, shellfish, venison, ducks, geese and grouse were plentiful. Tenakee's remote location also attracted bootleggers, gamblers, and prostitutes. There was infrequent mail service, and no law in the early years. The first local "government" was the Bath House Committee, created at the behest of the Forest Service. A school was established in 1917, and a U.S. marshal was assigned to the town. Canneries opened to process salmon, but most of them closed by the late 1950s, and the population dwindled. In 1970, the census recorded eighty-six residents. Incorporation did not come until 1971.

The Forest Service's road plan called for linking Sitka with Hoonah via roads and ferry crossings over Peril Strait and Tenakee Inlet to open East Chichagof Island and North Baranof Island to logging, hunting and motorized recreation. But Tenakee Springs stood squarely in the path of this vision. Tenakee liked its isolation. Its residents had voted repeatedly to continue the town's ban on motorized vehicles. They did not welcome the prospect of ferries delivering hunters from Juneau to Hoonah and across Chichagof Island on logging roads into their back yard.

The standoff between the Forest Service and Tenakee began in the 1970s, and was not resolved until 1990. The intervening years saw the heaviest logging and road-building in the history of Southeast Alaska, both on the Tongass and on Native corporation lands. Logging reached Tenakee's front yard in the early 1970s, when loggers began cutting trees on the south side of Tenakee Inlet, at Corner Bay, to supply the Alaska Pulp Corp. mill at Sitka. Clearcuts and logging roads also began encroaching from the north end of Chichagof Island. In 1973 the Forest Service began building a road into the Indian River drainage, just east of Tenakee Springs. The agency announced that the Indian River Road would eventually be connected to Game Creek Road, which ran south from Hoonah, so that timber cut on Chichagof could be trucked to a log-sorting yard on Tenakee Inlet.

The plan threatened to transform Tenakee forever. "There would have been strongly increased hunting pressure from the north end, and also pressure to extend the road from the mouth of Indian River into town," said John Wisenbaugh, who moved from Ohio to nearby Corner Bay to log in 1973 and stayed on in Tenakee to become a commercial fisherman and serve as mayor. Fortunately, he said, Tenakee Springs had a couple of aces up its sleeve. For one thing, Alaska Pulp Corporation needed the town's permission to build a log dump and transfer facility offshore on Tenakee Inlet. For another, the town was due a grant of state land under provisions of the Alaska Statehood Act. Tenakee played these cards shrewdly.

In 1977, a three-way agreement was reached between the town, the state of Alaska and Alaska Lumber and Pulp. Tenakee Springs agreed to issue the permit for the log dump. In exchange, Alaska Pulp promised not to connect the Indian River Road to any other road system, including Tenakee's. To protect its flanks, Tenakee selected 4,500 acres of state land on both sides of the town, reaching along the shore of the inlet and to the top of the mountain behind town. Its land selection included six-tenths of an acre that the Forest Service needed to complete its road link across Chichagof Island.

The logging of the Indian River watershed began in 1978 and continued for four years. In all, the Forest Service carved more than fifteen miles of road into the upper Indian River watershed. But Tenakee's tactic prevented the agency from completing its road connection, and kept clearcutting out of the lower end of Indian Creek. It was enough to throw a monkeywrench into the Forest Service's grand plan. So the Forest Service declared war on Tenakee Springs. The agency sued for title to the city land that blocked its road link. Tenakee in turn sued to stop the road, and in 1987 won an injunction temporarily halting the road connection.

The citizens of Tenakee spent a good share of their meager town budget paying lawyers to fight the road connection. They got help from influential friends in Juneau, who formed Friends of Tenakee and raised money to help pay the town's legal bills. Bitterness on both sides ran deep. In the end, Congress would decide Tenakee's fate.

THE AREA GUIDE

In 1976, John Sandor succeeded Charlie Yates as Alaska regional forester. He arrived with marching orders from Forest Service headquarters in Washington, D.C., to placate the state of Alaska and commercial fishing groups over Yates' much-reviled 1975 Tongass plan. Work had already begun on a new plan, a Southeast Alaska Area Guide, which was to set formal, institutional policies for management of the Tongass.

K.J. Metcalf was named to lead the team that would develop the area guide. He threw himself into the assignment, and took people from all walks of life—environmentalists, fishermen, labor representatives, miners, Alaska Natives, timber company officials, community leaders— out to look at logging operations on the Tongass. It wasn't always pretty. At one logging operation near Sitka, he recalls standing in what he thought was a stream. It turned out to be a road. "We saw it warts and all," Metcalf said. "We asked, What do we need to do to correct bad logging practices?"

In early 1977 the Forest Service unveiled its Southeast Alaska Area Guide. Among other policies, it stated that all salmon streams would be protected from the adverse effects of logging. Both Sandor and Alaska Governor Jay Hammond wrote cover letters endorsing the guide as a blueprint for the way logging should be done. Then, said Metcalf, Sandor put the guide on a shelf and continued to manage the Tongass the way the pulp mills wanted.

"Sandor clearly used us," Metcalf said. "He took away the policies in the area guide. He totally dismantled it. " Metcalf was particularly bitter because his team had done its best to convince the public and skeptical state officials to stick with the process, promising that enlightened management would result. "My belief is that Sandor's strategy was that through the area guide, attention would be diverted away from the amount of logging, the state and the public would become willing partners in the process, and time would be on the side of the Forest Service," he said.

Rai Behnert also served on the team that developed the area guide. He believes Sandor saw it as a way to air conflicts and set a new direction for the Tongass, but later found his ability to effect change limited by the power of the pulp companies and their political allies in Congress.

Passage of the National Forest Management Act brought some improvements in federal forest practices, including a 100-acre limit on the size of clearcuts. After its passage, Sandor moved quickly to adopt a new Tongass Land Management Plan. There was good reason to act expeditiously.

Congress was considering a massive Alaska Lands Act that would establish wilderness areas, national parks and national wildlife refuges across the state. With a new management plan on the books, Sandor hoped to preempt designation of large portions of the Tongass as wilderness.

The driving force behind management of the Tongass—to fulfill the requirements of the long-term contracts—had not changed. For that reason, it was important that the new plan support a logging level high enough to keep the pulp mills supplied. The agency also was in the throes of adopting a new five-year logging plan for Alaska Pulp Corp.'s Sitka mill, which called for opening vast unroaded watersheds on the north end of the Tongass to road-building and logging.

The basic math of the Tongass timber program was straightforward: 300 million board feet annually for the two pulp companies, 100 million board feet for independent operators. But Rai Behnert and other planners objected to letting the long-term contracts dictate the terms of the plan process. Behnert recalls: "Our planning team went to John Sandor in 1977 and said, 'Look, these contracts really tie our hands. We need to be able to manage the forest for what people want. We want the freedom to explore all alternatives. If we can't do that, we might as well shut it down.' Sandor said, 'Go ahead, and we'll deal with the long-term contracts later.'"

Planners divided the entire Tongass National Forest into 867 watersheds, which the agency, in tortured bureaucratese, dubbed "value comparison units," or VCUs,. These averaged roughly 17,500 acres in size. "We set up five task forces and instructed them to look at the units in terms of their timber, wildlife, fish, wilderness, recreation and minerals values," Behnert said. The teams gathered what little data was available and rated each VCU on a scale of zero to five for each value studied. Then, using early computer software, they assigned varying land use designations to each of the 867 watersheds.

Although the technology was primitive, the methodology was ahead of its time; it was one of the earliest examples of planning by watershed in the national forest system.

The twelve-member interdisciplinary team came up with several alternative harvest levels. Five members favored an alternative that allowed a timber harvest of 3.9 billion board feet per decade. This alternative, the team wrote, "provides the best balance in the use of the forest's prime amenity and commodity values." But the team ultimately recommended an alternative that allowed a harvest of 4.1 billion board feet per decade, on grounds it would provide more opportunities for growth and development in Southeast Alaska.

Behnert was proud of his team's work. "We did a plan for an area the size of West Virginia, in two years, using existing information and aerial surveys," he said. But Sandor rejected the team's recommendation. When the draft plan was released, it carried the industry's number: 5.2 billion board feet per decade.

Fishermen and conservationists threatened to sue if the Forest Service didn't lower its timber sale projections in the final plan. There was dissension within the ranks of the Forest Service as well; the agency's own economists warned that market demand did not justify such a high timber target. Even Native corporations objected; they said that if the Forest Service flooded the market with cheap federal timber, they would be unable to sell their own pulp logs to the mills at a fair market price.

In the end, Forest Service Chief John McGuire and his boss, U.S. Agriculture Secretary Bob Bergland, overruled Sandor. McGuire directed Sandor to ramp down the timber volume in the final plan to a maximum of 4.5 billion board feet per decade. When the Alaska congressional delegation threatened to legislate 5.2 billion board feet, Bergland stood firm, retorting that such a bill "would constitute a congressional mandate to overcut the Forest."

The Tongass Land Management Plan, signed in 1979, became the first national forest plan formally adopted under the National Forest Management Act. And it did institute some reforms. It established standards for culverts and roads. It required loggers to leave narrow coastal "shelter strips" to provide deer and other game access to beaches. It required better control of soil erosion and more protection for scenery—though loggers protested that scenery regulations requiring narrower roadways increased their chance of being injured by falling trees. Another thing the plan did, Behnert said, "was to put a cap on the Southeast timber industry's growth." Slowly, the Forest Service was wresting control of the Tongass from the pulp companies.

THE SCHOEN-WALLMO REPORT

By the late 1970s, a few Alaska game biologists could see that logging was on a collision course with maintaining healthy populations of Sitka black-tailed deer in Southeast Alaska. The long-term implications were potentially huge.

Deer hunting in Southeast Alaska is more than sport. Deer taken in the fall get families through the lean winter months until the return of spring salmon runs. Deer fill a crucial niche in the forest ecosystem as well, providing the main prey base for the Alexander Archipelago wolf and a significant food source for the brown bear, both of which keep deer populations under control. Deer populations fluctuate with weather cycles, but over the long term, in undisturbed forests, they maintain a natural equilibrium.

The unlogged Alaska rain forest is a banquet of dwarf dogwood and five-leaf bramble for deer. Its thick canopy and open interior forest offer life-saving shelter from heavy winter snows. But by the mid-1970s an impenetrable second-growth forest, virtually useless

A dense stand of 75-year-old second-growth timber near Hollis, Prince of Wales Island, in 1988. Photo by Jack Gustafson.

to deer, had grown up in heavily clearcut areas of the Tongass National Forest. Because this second-growth forest lets in almost no light, its floor is barren and devoid of deer browse—in ecological terms, a desert. Its spindly trees block deer passage. Its sparse canopy offers little cover during harsh Alaska winters. Yet until the late 1970s, almost no serious attempt had been made to document the connection between clearcut logging and deer use in the Alaska rainforest.

John Schoen moved to Alaska with a Ph.D. in wildlife ecology in 1977 to work for the Alaska Department of Fish and Game. Before long, he transferred to Juneau and became the first state research wildlife biologist based in Southeast Alaska. He soon struck up a professional relationship with Olof C. "Charlie" Wallmo, a Forest Service research biologist. He became acquainted with other prominent biologists as well, including Starker Leopold and Reginald Barrett, who had conducted the Admiralty Island wildlife habitat study for U.S. Plywood Champion in the early 1970s.

In 1977 Wallmo and Schoen kicked off a research project of their own to determine how logging was affecting Sitka black-tailed deer. The design of the study was elegantly simple. They identified twenty pairs of study sites on Admiralty and Chichagof Islands, each consisting of a recent clearcut or second-growth stand and a nearby unlogged stand of old-growth trees. Then they established "pellet group transects" through the stands to count fecal deposits and track deer use. They did one count in the fall of 1977, to measure deer use the previous spring, summer and early fall, and another in the spring of 1978, to measure deer use over the winter. The results were striking. They found five times more use of old-growth forests by deer in spring, summer and fall, and seven times more use of old-growth forests in winter. "It was so black and white that there was no question what was going on," Schoen said. The difference was particularly clear in winter, when deer avoided clearcuts covered with snow.

In 1979, Schoen and state wildlife biologist Matthew Kirchhoff followed up with radio telemetry studies of the deer's home range. They found that the animals would not wander far; their average range was only two hundred acres. That meant deer in heavily logged areas might perish in large numbers during severe winters. Even in the clearcuts they found less deer use that they had expected. "The conventional wisdom when we started was that clearcuts were good for deer," Schoen said. But few researchers had looked critically at the habitat values of old-growth forests, because in the Pacific Northwest, where the majority of forest research had taken place, few large tracts of old-growth forest survived.

Sitka black-tailed deer seeks shelter and forage in old-growth forest stand, Southeast Alaska. Photo by John Schoen.

It was risky to extrapolate from research in the Northwest anyway, Schoen said, because logged-over land in the Alaska rainforest was far less hospitable to deer. "It takes 200 to 300 years to develop the ecological conditions of old growth in Southeast Alaska. With 100-year logging rotations, it never comes back. Our conclusion was that old-growth is not renewable on a 100-year or even a 200-year rotation. If you convert old growth to clearcuts and second growth you'll see a dramatic decline in deer."

Schoen and Wallmo published their findings in an Alaska Department of Fish and Game newspaper, and in June of 1978 they presented their study at a Juneau conference on timber management and deer in Southeast Alaska. Conservationists understood its implications immediately.

The scientists decided to submit their paper to the Forest Service's Pacific Northwest Research Station for publication. Before they did, they asked three respected academic foresters, including Starker Leopold, to review it. Schoen recalls, "They all said, 'This is a great paper. You need to get this out as soon as possible!'" As a courtesy, Donald Schmiege, the director of the Forest Service's Juneau Research Station, gave a copy of the study to Regional Forester John Sandor. Sandor "went ballistic and gave it to his timber managers," Schoen said. "They were furious. They said it was premature, and they criticized our methodology." Next, timber industry officials got their hands it. The upshot was that Sandor asked Schmiege not to publish the deer study.

Word got back to Wallmo, who confronted his Forest Service bosses. At that point, Don McKnight, the research chief at Alaska Fish and Game, entered the fray. He wrote to Schmiege warning that if the Forest Service refused to publish the Schoen-Wallmo study, he would submit it for publication in a peer-reviewed wildlife journal without Wallmo's name on it, and Wallmo would explain in a footnote why his name had been removed. Confronted with that embarrassing prospect, Sandor gave up on trying to squelch the study. It was published in the journal *Forest Science* in 1980, under both authors' names.

Schoen went on to study the habitat preferences of brown bears. Kirchhoff and other biologists began studying the Alexander Archipelago wolf, which is endemic to Southeast Alaska. They documented that the wolf depends on an abundant prey base of Sitka black-tailed deer, and that wildlife poaching increases as logging roads penetrate wilderness. They hypothesized that as deer numbers declined, and as the hunting of wolves increased, the wolf itself would face long-term survival threats.

Gradually, wildlife biologists began to build a case for the vital role old-growth forests play in sustaining wildlife populations in Southeast Alaska. "This started to change the way people looked at old growth," Schoen said. "Before, old growth had been regarded as sterile habitat. After we made the point that old growth had important wildlife values, that all changed."

6

THE BACKROOM DEAL

In the beginning, the campaign that would produce the most sweeping wilderness legislation in U.S. history and dictate the terms of logging on the Tongass National Forest for a decade had nothing to do with Tongass trees.

The Alaska Native Claims Settlement Act of 1971 had given the Secretary of the Interior two years to select up to eighty million acres of Alaska wilderness worthy of protection "in the national interest." Congress had given itself until December of 1978 to protect those lands permanently as national parks, national forests, national wildlife refuges and wild and scenic rivers. In the meantime, they had been withdrawn from state and Alaska Native land selections and all other forms of appropriation.

There was much at stake in wild Alaska: wildlife havens of global significance in the Yukon Delta; world-class salmon runs on the Kenai Peninsula; wildlands bordering Mt. McKinley National Park and Denali, North America's highest peak; more than twelve million acres of ice fields and volcanic mountains in the Wrangell-St. Elias Range; the North American portal to the submerged Bering Land Bridge on the Seward Peninsula. Only a few of those places faced imminent development. But the threat of long-term exploitation was real.

Much of Alaska held buried treasure in the form of mineral deposits or petroleum reserves. The most dramatic example was the Coastal Plain of the Arctic National Wildlife Range, established by Congress in 1960. Oil companies were eager to conduct exploratory drilling beneath the tundra of the Coastal Plain. They believed they would discover oil reserves to rival the black gold at Prudhoe Bay. Early in the Alaska lands campaign, environmentalists made a strategic decision to seek wilderness designation for the Coastal Plain, a vast summer nursery for tens of thousands of migrating caribou and millions of migratory birds.

It fell to Rogers C.B. Morton, President Nixon's Interior secretary, to make the first cut. On December 18, 1971, immediately after Nixon signed ANCSA, Morton set a two-year deadline for the Forest Service, National Park Service, Fish and Wildlife Service and Bureau of Outdoor Recreation to submit plans for the management of up to eighty million acres of unreserved federal land in Alaska. These became known as the "d-2 lands," for the section of ANCSA that authorized their withdrawal. The Park Service and Fish and Wildlife Service had just three months to propose a second list of "d-1 lands" to be withdrawn from mineral development and state selection because of their value as future transportation corridors, or for other public purposes.

The Interior secretary's directives triggered several months of frenetic activity by federal land managers. The BLM, which had jurisdiction over Alaska's 290 million acres of unreserved land, never had been given the resources to conduct reliable inventories of fish, wildlife, vegetation or geological features. Much was unknown. Teams were formed to conduct field studies; task forces were appointed to make recommendations. Morton understood the historical importance of the process he had set in motion. He told his staff that, in Alaska, "We must do it right the first time."

The federal agencies competed vigorously for control of wild Alaska. Each prepared its own recommendations for land designations and jurisdictional boundaries. The Forest Service was no exception. Because Alaska's two national forests, the Tongass and the Chugach, had been "reserved" as units of the national forest system early in the century, they were not available for d-2 land selections. However, the agency saw a chance to vastly expand its presence in Alaska. It set up a planning team, which recommended expansions of the Chugach and Tongass national forests and the establishment of eight new national forests covering huge expanses of the Alaska Interior.

MAPS ON THE FLOOR

Conservation groups had been preparing for an Alaska lands campaign since 1966, when Interior Secretary Stewart Udall froze all transfers of public land pending the resolution of Native land claims. It was clear to them then that Congress ultimately would divvy up all of Alaska like an enormous ice-cream cake. They vowed to win permanent protection for as much of the nation's northern wilderness as they could get.

Udall's directive gave birth to the Maps on the Floor Society, a series of strategy sessions held in the home of an Anchorage environmentalist, Mark Ganopole. Between 1969 and 1971 a core group of conservationists with detailed field knowledge of the Alaska wilderness met regularly with state and federal resource specialists in Ganopole's living room to draft and map a conservationists' statewide lands proposal. The Maps on the Floor Society also worked closely with federal land managers to influence the outcome of the federal planning process.

At a Washington, D.C. wilderness conference in late 1971, the national groups urged the Alaskans to get their proposal into final form. Over the Christmas holiday Ganopole's group prepared a detailed overlay map highlighting twenty-six areas for protection, including the Brooks Range, the Coastal Plain, the Yukon Delta and the Wrangell-St. Elias Range. The Alaskans agreed that these areas represented the most critical wildlife habitat and the most significant ecosystems in Alaska.

In March of 1972, with preliminary recommendations from the federal agencies in hand, Morton withdrew 45 million acres of d-1 lands. Then he jumped the gun by also withdrawing 83.4 million acres of d-2 lands. As icing on the cake, Morton remarked that he believed even more Alaska wilderness should be protected. Taken together, his withdrawals encompassed all the major sites on the conservationists' wish list.

Yet on closer examination, conservation leaders were disappointed with the details of Morton's proposal. They especially disliked his plan to designate three new national forests encompassing more than eighteen million acres, including taiga forest in the Interior and lands flanking the proposed Wrangell-St. Elias National Park. These lands, they said, must not be turned over to the Forest Service to be roaded, logged and mined.

Morton got flak from the other side too. Alaska Governor William Egan, the Alaska congressional delegation, the state's business leaders, and the pro-business *Anchorage Times* all denounced his proposal as preservationist overkill. The state eventually sued in an effort to reverse this preemption of its land-selection process and won some concessions, including a reduction in the size of the proposed Gates of the Arctic National Park.

In 1973 U.S. Senator Henry "Scoop" Jackson of Washington introduced a bill setting aside 83.4 million acres of Alaska—Morton's exact recommendation—as national interest lands. He also introduced a second bill, drafted by the Sierra Club, which called for setting aside 106 million acres. Neither bill included land selections in the Tongass National Forest. Neither bill went anywhere.

Between 1974 and 1978 several other members of Congress also introduced Alaska lands bills. Rep. Morris Udall, an Arizona Democrat, favored a strongly preservationist bill. Rep. John Dingell, a Michigan Democrat, had an avid interest in establishing Alaska wildlife refuges. Alaska's Rep. Don Young and Sen. Ted Stevens introduced bills calling for minimal levels of protection for Alaska wildlands. In 1975 U.S. Rep. John Seiberling of Ohio and two other members of the House Interior Committee visited Alaska to view the d-2 lands and discuss their future with Alaska Natives, conservationists and politicians. The trip made Seiberling an advocate for the strongest possible Alaska lands bill.

With the election of President Jimmy Carter in 1976, the torch at Interior was passed from Rogers Morton to Cecil Andrus. The Forest Service deeply resented Andrus, who made no secret of his environmentalist sympathies; Forest Service historian Rakestraw wrote that Andrus "had a bulldozer approach to matters and was therefore harder to bargain with."

AN IMPOSSIBLE TASK

In Southeast Alaska, conservationists were trying to figure out how to get a seat at the table. Fate handed Ted Whitesell a supporting role in this political drama. As a biology undergraduate at the University of Colorado in Boulder, Whitesell had helped organize a student group to study Colorado's national forest primitive areas and develop wilderness recommendations. Whitesell and his pal Pete Brabeck had fantasized about homesteading in Alaska. But after graduation, Whitesell agreed to stay in Colorado to help a struggling wilderness advocacy group get on its feet. Brabeck headed for Alaska alone.

On March 7, 1975, forty conservationists from throughout Southeast met in Sitka to adopt the Southeast Alaska Conservation Council's Tongass wilderness proposal. The meeting had been arranged hastily by Rich Gordon, a dedicated conservationist and naturalist. Its timing was critical; the Forest Service had just released its controversial 1975 Tongass plan, which proposed designating Granite Fiords, Tracy Arm, King Salmon Capes, Petersburg Creek and Russell Fiords as wilderness study areas. These areas were notable for the fact that they encompassed mainly rocks and ice and had almost no commercially valuable forest. Conservationists had only six weeks to respond with their own proposal.

At the meeting, they agreed to move beyond their modest 1970 wilderness proposal. Instead, they came up with a list of forty-five areas that deserved protection from logging. They proposed the designation of nine wilderness areas, eighteen roadless recreation areas, twenty protected watersheds, and one wild river, the Situk. They also called for deferral of logging along shorelines bordering popular anchorages , in watersheds surrounding Forest Service recreation cabins, and in other watersheds "determined to be of major value for recreation, wildlife, and fisheries."

"Our basic thinking is that we did not wish to be constrained by the narrow Forest Service approach, but wished to emphasize a positive program, including human wildland experience values as well as logging," Rich Gordon wrote in a letter seeking broader feedback following the meeting. Some groups worried that SEACC was asking for too much, so Gordon also included an option that omitted fourteen of the areas.

When Pete Brabeck heard about the "forty-five areas" proposal, he looked up Jack Hession, the Sierra Club's Alaska representative. Sierra Club President Ed Wayburn had given Hession $1,500 to support wilderness advocacy in Southeast Alaska. Brabeck thought the wilderness campaign model he and Whitesell had developed for Colorado would work well in Southeast. He persuaded Hession to hire Whitesell and Gordon Rodda, another Colorado buddy, to undertake a crash survey of Tongass wilderness. Brabeck also offered to share his own experience in the politics of wilderness preservation with Rich Gordon, who in turn introduced Brabeck to Southeast Alaska.

Whitesell and Rodda jumped at the chance to work on Alaska wilderness issues. Their assignment was to gather information on the forty-five areas and produce all the data SEACC would need to mount a credible wilderness campaign. They would have $1,500 and two months over the summer of 1975 to get the job done. Given the size of the Alaska Panhandle and the expense and logistics of getting into the backcountry, it was clearly an impossible task. Whitesell was unfazed. "They flew us up, the plane landed in Ketchikan, and Gordon and I rushed out to the runway and jumped up and down and said, 'Hey, we're in Alaska!'"

Once in Juneau, the two realized that there wasn't time or money to visit each of the forty-five areas, so they traveled to the places they could get to by ferry, and interviewed Forest Service officials, fish and wildlife biologists and local conservationists. Whitesell and Rodda did find time to take a trip across Admiralty Island with Hession and Gordon. "That was a trip I'll never forget, coming out at Mitchell Bay at night in a canoe," Whitesell recalled. "There was a beautiful full moon and the loons were crying." The two also kayaked around lushly forested Long Island and Dall Island at the southernmost tip of the Tongass, and Whitesell photographed totem poles near the beach. It was a poignant trip. Whitesell had no doubt that the islands' unprotected stands of massive spruce, cedar and hemlock soon would be logged.

REFINING THE LIST

The summer ended; Whitesell stayed on in Alaska to write his report. SEACC had no money to pay him but made sure he had a roof over his head. Rich Gordon helped by writing detailed boundary and ecological descriptions for each of the forty-five areas, some of which were scheduled for imminent logging. Both knew they had a rare opportunity to protect an irreplaceable natural legacy if they did their job well.

"It took a visionary like Rich Gordon to flesh out the areas," Whitesell said. "Whereas in a lot of places in the Lower 48 wilderness proposals were last-ditch efforts, in Alaska we always had the slogan, and it was more than a slogan, that this was the last chance to do it right."

Yet on closer study Whitesell and Gordon found SEACC's forty-five-area proposal too timid. Several important areas had been omitted, the areas proposed for protection were too small, and the level of protection proposed was in many cases inadequate. SEACC had proposed administrative designations instead of permanent protection for many areas—designations which the Forest Service could easily withdraw. "Gordon and I felt this was a grave mistake," Whitesell said. "We decided that we would try to convince them to be stronger. We tried to do it with some sensitivity, understanding that they had jobs and families. Basically our argument was, 'The Forest Service will love your proposals.'"

Once Whitesell, Gordon and other SEACC volunteers had done the fine-tuning, the next challenge was to build grassroots support for the SEACC plan. Whitesell believed SEACC needed to broaden its base, to reach beyond its middle-class founders and recruit fishermen and loggers, hunters and outfitters. He agreed to help organize whatever grass roots were out there. In Craig, he struck up a friendship with a logger named Al Dennis, who had been driven out of business by Ketchikan Pulp. Dennis hated conservation groups, but he hated the pulp mills more. "Al helped me understand relations between small loggers and big business," Whitesell said. "We got along great." Whitesell met a horse logger in Wrangell, and fishermen up and down the Panhandle.

Kay Greenough was living on the edge in 1976—teaching preschool in Juneau, climbing mountains, kayaking, and staying in a beach cabin with no running water. She needed a job. SEACC needed a director but had no money. She agreed to share the job with another young activist, Ron Hawk. Greenough and Hawk became a formidable tag team for wilderness. Greenough traveled to several communities during hearings on the draft Tongass plan. Often she was the only environmentalist present at field hearings packed with hostile timber workers. Still, she was surprised by what she heard. "There were people in every community who had seen the devastation and wanted to protect areas around their town."

BELTWAY 101

Greenough and Whitesell went to Washington, D.C. for hearings on the National Forest Management Act in 1976 and badgered people about the need to get rid of the long-term pulp mill contracts. "It was the first time SEACC had made an appearance inside the Beltway," Whitesell recalled. "We were a thorn in the side of the national conservation groups." Brock

The Kasaan Peninsula, seen here from the east coast of Prince of Wales Island, one of the first places to be logged under the Ketchikan Pulp Co. long-term contract. Photo by Trygve Steen.

Evans, vice president of the National Audubon Society, took Whitesell aside and lectured him about his appearance. But Whitesell was unpersuaded. "I was in my rubber boots, my plaid shirt. My hair was long and I wore it in a ponytail. I thought it gave me credibility." His appearance also gave him a strategic advantage. "Not only do you come off as a grass-roots activist, but they don't assume you're very sophisticated. They're more open, not so wary."

The Alaskans set about learning how to play the Beltway game. "Our main objective, first and foremost, was to get rid of the fifty-year contracts," Whitesell said. "We told Brock, 'We've got to get rid of these.' He said, "You're right, but this bill is being passed in a crisis atmosphere. We're going to have to be in a defensive posture.' We were very upset. We knew we couldn't change anything until we got rid of those contracts."

As the upstarts from Southeast Alaska pressed their case, revelations from the Tongass were causing the national groups to rethink strategy. By the mid-1970s, clearcutting on the national forest had taken such a toll on salmon streams that the state of Alaska was beginning to complain. In 1977 the Alaska Department of Fish and Game listed the Kadashan watershed as one of Southeast's most productive salmon streams, and once again urged the Forest Service to abstain from logging there, a request the agency declined.

The Forest Service's draft Tongass plan, released in 1978, also served as a wake-up call. The plan proposed designation of seventeen wilderness areas totaling 5.4 million acres. However, four of its five alternatives also proposed clearcutting Admiralty Island and West Chichagof Island—areas that both President Carter and the House Interior Committee had endorsed for protection—and other unique and pristine wildlands, including Misty Fiords and the Yakutat Forelands. Perhaps its most shocking feature was its revelation that 65 percent of all watersheds on the Tongass containing commercial timber had been logged, or soon would be. The Alaska Conservation Society lacked money to finance a legal challenge of the Tongass plan. The Sierra Club came to the rescue, joining with SEACC to challenge the final plan in court.

In 1977, seven national conservation groups formed the Alaska Coalition to join forces for the Alaska lands campaign. With the member groups' combined funding and political clout, the coalition swiftly became a key player. That year, hearings were held on House Resolution 39, a strong Alaska lands bill co-sponsored by Seiberling and Udall. SEACC lobbied the Alaska Coalition to include some Tongass wilderness in its Alaska lands proposal. At a minimum, SEACC wanted to see Admiralty Island and West Chichagof Island protected.

Ted Whitesell spent a year in Anchorage with Jack Hession, educating him about the Southeast Alaska rainforest. "This was a great opportunity to get the SEACC forty-five areas into the legislation being drafted by John Seiberling," Whitesell said. "But it was a hard sell, even with the Alaska Conservation Society. They said, 'The Tongass is a different situation.' Being opportunists, we asked, 'How can we buy into this argument?' President Carter had made Alaska his highest environmental priority. We decided to take matters into our own hands."

However, even some SEACC members had deep reservations about combining their own wilderness campaign with the fight for the d-2 lands. Only after Whitesell made a persuasive plea at a SEACC meeting in Juneau did the organization agree to throw in with the Alaska Coalition. Initially, H.R. 39 included only areas from Glacier Bay north. But at a meeting on the East Coast, after receiving a hand-delivered memo from Rich Gordon, the national groups agreed to add five areas in Southeast Alaska—West Chichagof-Yakobi, Admiralty Island, Misty Fiords, the Yakutat Forelands, and the Stikine-LeConte area south of Petersburg.

AMERICA SPEAKS

At field hearings across the nation, Americans from all walks of life spoke up to support protection for Alaska wilderness. In part, the groundswell was a testament to the lobbying and organizational skills of the Alaska Coalition. But something unique to the American psyche also was on display at these hearings—a wistful desire to hold onto the last American frontier. Ordinary people who might never set foot in Alaska said it was important to preserve a vast unspoiled wilderness where natural forces could play out undisturbed by human activity.

"In days past, our national and state governments sanctioned the spirit of manifest destiny," Michael Grady, an Evanston, Ill., businessman, testified at a hearing in Chicago on May 7, 1977. "It was a noble obligation—to subdue, tame, and harness the hostile environment 'to better serve man. . . .' At this stage in our country's development our political leaders and decision makers should see through the selfish concerns and unrealistic thinking of those who wish to tame our remaining wilderness."

In Atlanta, Carolyn Carr of Auburn, Alabama, said Alaska must not meet the fate that had befallen the South and the Eastern Seaboard. "Those of us here in the great public-land desert of the eastern United States know better than anyone what happens when the public domain is frittered away," she said.

In Denver, Kenneth McClaugherty, a young Texas musician who was nearly blind, said he had learned about Alaska through recorded books. "Beauty is all around if we would search for it," he said. "If we were to lose those values of wilderness I spiritually would lose something, even though I have never been there."

In Alaska, more than a thousand speakers had their say at five public hearings and twenty town meetings. Even in Alaska, about half the citizens who spoke favored H.R. 39's strong protections for Alaska wilderness.

As national support for a strong Alaska Lands Act built, however, so did tensions between SEACC's leaders and the Alaska Coalition. Ron Hawk was SEACC's first Washington, D.C., lobbyist. Hawk and Kay Greenough staked out an uncompromising position on protection for the Tongass. Leonard Steinberg, who became SEACC's executive director in 1978, recalled the volatile climate: "Ron could be an extremely charming person but he could also have a tongue of fire. He could even call the top leaders on the carpet. (National conservation leaders) Tim Mahoney, Chuck Clusen and Doug Scott—they all hated him. They would come up with a plan for lobbying ANILCA, and Ron and Kay would show up in town and say, 'We're going to talk to whoever we want to and we're not going to play by your rules.' They were uncontrollable. Kay and Ron felt so strongly about what they were doing, and in some ways were so unwilling to compromise, that they made enemies not only in D.C. but in Southeast Alaska."

In late 1978 Hawk and Greenough resigned, and so did half the board. Board president Larry Edwards and long-time members Lee Schmidt and Don Muller managed to hold the organization together. They replaced Hawk and Greenough with the 24-year-old Steinberg, who had been in Alaska only two years.

Meanwhile, in Washington, D.C., Paul Peyton, who succeeded Hawk as SEACC's lobbyist, was trying to maintain some kind of working relationship with the national groups. "Paul had a tough job," Steinberg said. "He was alone. He needed the help of the large organizations. They didn't entirely trust him, but they saw him as easier to deal with than Kay and Ron. Paul couldn't win. He got blamed by some people in Southeast if he worked with the national conservation groups. A number of people at home felt it was his job to be eyes and ears in Washington and to let everyone know how Congress was going to screw us."

CARTER STEPS INTO THE BREACH

On May 18, 1978, H.R. 39 was sent to the House floor. U.S. Rep. Don Young of Alaska introduced an amendment to delete 4.5 million acres from protective designations and make that land available for state selection. His amendment failed, and the bill passed on a vote of 277 to 31. But it faced an insurmountable roadblock in the Senate, where Alaska's two Republican senators, Mike Gravel and Ted Stevens, fought it with every means available to them. Gravel threatened a filibuster, and the session ended without a Senate vote on an Alaska lands bill.

Congress had given itself until December of 1978 to pass an Alaska Lands Act. Supporters of H.R. 39 feared failure to meet that deadline might reopen Alaska wildlands to state land selections. President Carter and Interior Secretary Cecil Andrus took matters into their own hands. On November 16, Andrus used his emergency authority under the Federal Land Policy and Management Act to withdraw 110 million acres from mining and state selection for a period of three years. On December 1, President Carter held a news conference to announce that he was using his powers under the Antiquities Act of 1906 to establish seventeen national monuments totaling nearly 56 million acres in Alaska. Both Admiralty Island and Misty Fords became Forest Service national monuments by presidential fiat.

Carter's bold act won praise from Alaska Coalition Chairman Chuck Clusen. "By moving quickly and decisively to ensure that our last great wilderness frontier will be preserved, President Carter joins Theodore Roosevelt as one of the greatest conservation presidents in our nation's history," Clusen declared. The pressure was now on Congress to pass its own Alaska Lands Act. SEACC turned up the heat in its campaign-within-a-campaign.

Back in Juneau, Kay Greenough and Ron Hawk founded SEACC Expeditions, a nonprofit corporation, to support SEACC and introduce influential people to the wonders of Southeast Alaska. They knew the Tongass was best experienced by boat, so they contacted philanthropists Larry Rockefeller and Michael McIntosh and persuaded them to contribute the use of a former minesweeper, the *Observer*, which McIntosh had purchased and retrofitted as a luxury tour boat. "I was the naturalist on board," Greenough recalled. "We would hike in the afternoon, lecture in the morning. The first trip, in 1979, was a huge success. Everyone who has ever come here has been blown away by this place. We didn't make any money, but we introduced lots of people to the Tongass National Forest."

RAISING THE STAKES

In 1979, Rep. Morris Udall introduced a new and even stronger version of H.R. 39 that carried the names of nearly a hundred sponsors. It added proposals for a Copper River wildlife refuge and wilderness designation for 85 million acres of new and existing parks and refuges, including large sections of the newly designated Admiralty Island and Misty Fiords national monuments.

The Alaska Coalition, which by now included fifty-three organizations, had grown in sophistication and influence. But the state of Alaska, armed with a hefty appropriation from the Alaska Legislature, had geared up to fight a strong Alaska lands act, and the timber industry was working closely with U.S. Senator Ted Stevens and the rest of the Alaska delegation to minimize wilderness set-asides, especially on the Tongass.

The Udall bill survived an assault in the House, but the Senate Energy and Natural Resources Committee, which held jurisdiction over Alaska lands, stalled until October and finally passed a much weaker bill. The Alaska Coalition denounced the Senate bill, and Senate Majority Leader Robert Byrd of West Virginia decided to delay bringing the Alaska lands issue to a vote in the Senate until early 1980.

In 1980, the Senate again played a game of delay. Sen. Henry "Scoop" Jackson, chairman of the Senate Interior Committee, wanted to bring an Alaska lands bill to a vote by March. But in early February the Alaska senators, Stevens and Gravel, brokered a highly unusual behind-the-scenes deal with the majority leader. Byrd agreed to pull the bill from the calendar for five months. In exchange, the Alaskans promised not to filibuster when it did come up for a vote. The Alaska Coalition's main Senate allies, Paul Tsongas of Massachusetts and John Durkin of New Hampshire, were powerless to challenge the deal. They had little clout and were not yet fully up to speed on Alaska land issues. "The Senate was a way different situation from the House side," SEACC lobbyist Paul Peyton said. "The Senate leadership was a lot less willing to let things blow up. We had enough votes to fix some major problems on the Senate side, but we couldn't get it to the floor."

During the interim, conservationists marshaled support. In June, they persuaded the Senate to consider five amendments that strengthened the bill, adding more areas and increasing protection for wildlife habitat. The amendments passed by a 3-to-2 ratio, surprising both Jackson and Stevens. Stevens took to the floor of the Senate and vowed to delay a vote on the Alaska lands act by attaching no fewer than 232 amendments and tying up the bill for the rest of the session. Jackson then yanked the bill from the floor, and the action on Alaska lands moved behind closed doors.

THE DOUBLE-CROSS

Senator Byrd, a master at the art of legislative horse-trading, wanted badly to see an Alaska lands bill passed in 1980. He summoned Stevens, Udall and a few others into a closed session. When the bill re-emerged, on August 4, it included two new sections. One left the door open to future oil and gas development in the Arctic National Wildlife Refuge by excluding part of the Coastal Plain from wilderness protection. The other, Section 705, directed the U.S. Treasury to make available to the Forest Service "at least $40,000,000 annually or as much as the Secretary of Agriculture finds is necessary to maintain the timber supply from the Tongass National Forest to dependent industry at a rate of four billion five hundred million board foot measure per decade." Section 705 stipulated that the money would come from oil, gas, coal and timber receipts and would be exempt from review by Congress in its annual appropriations process. The Senate bill also dropped the proposed Duncan Canal, Karta, Rocky Pass, and Yakutat Forelands wilderness areas, all of which had been in the House bill; reduced the size of the West Chichagof wilderness area; and deleted 149,000 acres within Misty Fiords National Monument to open the way for development of a borax mine.

Alaska timber interests had fought hard to exempt the $40 million Tongass Timber Supply Fund from congressional review. They knew there was a chance the pulp mills would lose the Reid Brothers antitrust case, which had gone to trial in Seattle on August 4. If the pulp mills were found guilty of violating anti-trust laws, Congress might look askance on granting them special favors.

Conservationists were blindsided. Not one of them had been allowed into the backroom negotiations that produced Section 705.

On August 19, the Senate passed the rewritten bill by a vote of 78-14. Jackson and Stevens announced that this would be the Senate's final word on Alaska lands. There would be no conference. If the House wanted a bill in 1980, it would have to accept the Senate's rewrite as the final version.

Section 705 was an act of sheer chutzpah by Stevens, demonstrating his willingness to play hardball on matters involving Alaska. "There are very few things Stevens fought as hard as he fought wilderness for the Tongass," SEACC lobbyist Paul Peyton said.

Because there was no floor debate on Section 705, there was no clear record of legislative intent. Instead, the Tongass timber supply provision became a kind of Rorschach Test for all the vying interests. The pulp companies insisted that the guaranteed $40 million annual appropriation was a "wilderness compromise" intended to hold them harmless and guarantee their timber supply despite the new Tongass wilderness withdrawals. Conservationists argued that the purpose of the money was to allow the Forest Service to prepare more "marginal" timber sales, thereby curtailing the high-grading of the most productive forests on the Tongass and preserving the best wildlife habitat.

The Forest Service greeted the Tongass Timber Supply Fund as a guarantor of the funding it needed to implement the new Tongass Land Management Plan and meet its timber sale target of 4.5 billion board feet per decade. In truth, said agency planner Rai Behnert, the Tongass wilderness withdrawals in ANILCA had little effect on the Forest Service's ability to meet its contractual obligation to sell timber, because with the exception of Admiralty Island, most of the new wilderness consisted of rocks, ice, muskeg, and timber of marginal value. "What we found, coming out of ANILCA, was that it didn't throw a great big rock into the plan," Behnert said.

The Congressional Research Service, in a 1987 report on Section 705 of ANILCA, concluded that "the one common thread of concern to Members . . . was that jobs in the timber industry would not be lost due to a decrease in the available timber as a result of wilderness designations, while at the same time other resource values would be protected."

To SEACC staff members, one thing was painfully clear: Section 705, with its legislated timber target and guaranteed subsidy, handed the Forest Service a blank check to cut timber.

The last stages of the Alaska lands campaign played out against the backdrop of the 1980 presidential campaign. By the fall of 1980, polls showed President Jimmy Carter trailing Ronald Reagan, the charismatic former California governor, who had demonstrated his conservation ethic with the quip, "If you've seen one redwood, you've seen them all." Carter stood ready to sign a strong Alaska lands bill. But he might soon be a lame duck. The national conservation groups knew that what one president had protected by executive order, another could undo. They weren't about to risk losing protection for Denali and the Arctic National Wildlife Refuge for the sake of Tongass trees. For Alaska lands, it was now or never.

On election eve, Nov. 3, 1980, Ed Wayburn hosted a strategy meeting of national conservation leaders at his home in San Francisco. The next day Reagan was elected in a landslide and the Republicans won control of the Senate. Wayburn sent word to Udall: "Make your peace with the Senate." On Nov. 12, 1980, after a seven-year battle, Udall introduced the Senate substitute bill on the House floor, and it passed on a voice vote.

An Act of Desperation

Back in Juneau, Kay Greenough and Ron Hawk despaired. As the price of allowing sweeping protection for Alaska wildlands, Stevens had won language that removed almost every barrier to logging on the Tongass. Without authority from the SEACC board, the two flew to Washington to try to persuade the national conservation groups to withdraw their support for ANILCA. It was a futile move. Greenough returned to Juneau and took to her bed. "I was sick," she said. "I lay on my couch for two weeks. It was like giving the pulp mills a wheelbarrow to cart the money away. I finally got over it and decided to get on with my life."

Leonard Steinberg was one of the few who supported this desperate effort to derail ANILCA—in retrospect. "That trip Kay and Ron took was extremely important in making both congressional leaders and national conservation leaders feel bad enough about what they had done to pave the way for the Tongass Timber Reform Act" ten years later, Steinberg said. "It was their ranting and raving that paved the way."

Not everyone saw it that way. Paul Peyton was disappointed and bitter. He knew some at SEACC blamed him for the debacle. He considered that grossly unfair. "The House had the choice to start over with another bill, but there was zero chance such a bill could pass the new GOP-controlled

Senate," he said. "Yet there were people who wanted to go that route." In the unlikely event that SEACC had succeeded in killing ANILCA, he added, "our credibility with the nationals would have been shot. And the very first thing the industry would have gone for was Admiralty Island."

Peyton left town exhausted and dead broke. "I did not attend the signing," he said. "I voted with my feet. I was pissed off enough that I quit and wouldn't have anything to do with SEACC for two years." He later made up with SEACC and served on the board for fourteen years.

Some in Southeast accused the Alaska Coalition of trading away the Tongass for Admiralty Island. But Ed Wayburn denied that a deal was cut to save Admiralty. And he defended the decision to embrace the Alaska Lands Act, warts and all. "When Congress is closing down, people on the firing line in Washington, D.C. sometimes have to make decisions they don't like," he said. "ANILCA remains the largest conservation act ever passed by Congress. We had violent opposition from the Alaska delegation. Senator Stevens called it the biggest disappointment of his life." Indeed, signaling his continuing opposition, Stevens gave a speech soon after the bill's passage vowing to return with a bill that would "fix" the act.

On December 2, 1980, as one of his last acts in office, President Carter sat at his Oval Office desk, flanked by four Democratic congressmen, and signed the Alaska National Interest Land and Conservation Act. With a flourish of his pen he conferred protection on 104.3 million acres of Alaska. In Southeast, the bill established the 900,000-acre Admiralty Island National Monument and the 2.1 million-acre Misty Fiords National Monument, permanently removing 3 million acres of the Tongass from development. In all, 5.4 million acres of the Tongass became designated wilderness.

"ANILCA on the whole was an incredible triumph far beyond my 'realistic' fondest dreams," said Rich Gordon, who had worked behind the scenes with congressional staff members to save as much acreage as possible. "The mainland Alaska portion was splendid." Though Gordon was disappointed that the act failed to protect more lowland old-growth forest on the Tongass, "given the gigantic improvement I lived through between 1966 and 1980, my intellect told me our Tongass achievement was significant, despite its limitations.," he said. What his gut told him, however, was another matter. "I was sufficiently dispirited that I passed up the Carter signing and went off to hike in the Blue Ridge Mountains."

Unfinished business

ANILCA contained important language guaranteeing Alaska's "rural residents" the right to a subsistence harvest of fish and game. This subsistence guarantee, which conflicted with the Alaska Constitution, would provoke lawsuits and heated debate over management of Alaska's fish and game harvests. It would also become a contentious issue for the Forest Service as Alaska Natives saw their traditional hunting grounds clearcut in the 1980s and 1990s.

ANILCA also contained language allowing Angoon's Native corporation, Kootznoowoo Inc., to exchange land on Admiralty Island for land on Prince of Wales Island, where the corporation would soon begin clearcutting for maximum profit. A delegation from Angoon traveled to Washington, D.C., and presented President Carter with a dog salmon vest in a White House ceremony celebrating the victory.

Logging by Shee-Atika Corporation along Lake Kathleen, Admiralty Island. Photo by James R. Mackovjak.

But in fact, ANILCA would prove a mixed blessing for Angoon. ANILCA also authorized Shee-Atika, Sitka's Native corporation, to select timberland on Admiralty. A shocking seven-mile-long clearcut eventually scarred the traditional hunting grounds of the Angoon Tlingit and greeted cruise ship passengers traveling through Chatham Strait. The bad blood between Sitka and Angoon persists to this day.

TRANSITION TIME

Back in Juneau, Leonard Steinberg , SEACC's director, accepted an invitation from Ted Whitesell to travel in Central America. He knew it was time to pack his bags. "We hadn't accomplished what we'd hoped for, and things were likely to get worse. The impacts of the Native land selections were also coming up. We knew that there would be a lot of logging on the national forests and that all of this new Native logging would be starting up too. Whatever was going to happen was going to be a new thing. It seemed like a logical place to make a transition."

In January 1981, Ronald Reagan was sworn in as president. Soon after, he appointed James Watt, a charming, nefarious pro-development lawyer from Colorado, to become his secretary of Interior. John B. Crowell, vice president and legal counsel for Louisiana-Pacific Corporation, was tapped to become the assistant secretary of agriculture in charge of the Forest Service. All the pieces were now in place for a shocking rainforest raid.

Photo on opposite page: Logging by Klukwan Corporation on Long Island in the extreme south end of the Alexander Archipelago. Photo by Jack Gustafson.

PART II

1980 TO 1990

"The trouble with political bargains is that they mirror current relative power better than current human needs, ecologic realities or the always-discounted future."

—Robert B. Weeden, *Messages from Earth: Nature and the Human Prospect in Alaska*

7

PICKING UP THE PIECES

im Stratton drove off the ferry into Juneau on a cold January day in 1981, his 1966 Ford Custom 500 four-door sedan packed to the rafters. No one was there to meet him. When he arrived at his office, the only welcome the new executive director of the Southeast Alaska Conservation Council found was a note from a volunteer offering him a place to crash.

The office had an abandoned feel. "No one had been in since late November," he said. "There were two brown paper bags on the floor. Someone had been collecting the mail and depositing the checks. There was a note on the telephone from (SEACC board member) Kay Greenough, saying 'Don't talk to the press!' We had just lost a major lawsuit challenging logging on state land in Chilkat Valley. Not only that, the judge had ordered SEACC to pay $25,000 in attorney fees."

Stratton knew nothing about the case. He went next door to talk to lawyers at the Sierra Club Legal Defense Fund. They told him, "Don't worry about the $25,000, we'll appeal it." His mood soon brightened. "I was in Alaska. I was on Cloud Nine. It was like a dream come true."

With passage of the Alaska National Interest Land and Conservation Act, SEACC had fallen apart. The acrimony ran deep. Southeast activists were furious with the national conservation groups for what they regarded as a sell-out of the Tongass. The nationals were equally frustrated with SEACC. Sierra Club strategist Tim Mahoney had named his cat SEACC, with the cryptic explanation: "You feed the cat, try to do everything for it, but then the cat attacks you."

From Central America, Leonard Steinberg had sent Stratton a note, hand-written in pencil on two sheets of legal paper, offering the names of some contacts who could provide information and advising him to read the files. Beyond that, the 24-year-old Stratton was on his own.

STRATTON TAKES CHARGE

When all the finger-pointing was done, the dispirited forest activists of Southeast Alaska were left with a profound sense of doom in the weeks following the signing of ANILCA. Stratton walked into this slough of despond with more enthusiasm than experience. Like Ted Whitesell, he had landed in Southeast Alaska through a series of coincidences. In 1977, while working on a degree in recreation management at the University of Oregon, he had taken a course at the Survival Center, a student environmental organization. Drawn to environmental activism, Stratton spent time hiking in the Cascades and soon took a job at the Survival Center. He started hanging out with the tree huggers at the Oregon Wilderness Coalition. After he graduated in 1979 he joined the coalition's executive committee, coordinating fund-raising, and selling Birkenstocks on the side.

Stratton visited Alaska in 1979 and fell in love with a woman from Anchorage. Back in Oregon, he pined for her and looked for a way to move north. One day he saw a notice posted on the Oregon Wilderness Coalition bulletin board: "Wanted: executive director of SEACC." He decided to apply, not really expecting to get the job. But his application was delivered to the wrong address, and by the time he found out, the application deadline had passed. He called Marilyn Conley, a member of the SEACC board, to plead for an extension. His resume finally showed up in Sitka on the day the board was planning to make its choice. The list of candidates had been narrowed to two. The board decided to interview him as well. "They called and said, 'If you pay half your way to Sitka and Juneau, we'll interview you,'" Stratton recalled. By then, he had done his homework. "I knew what the issues were. I knew they had big trees up there." He also knew someone who ran rafting trips down the Stikine River and kayaked in Misty Fiords.

Larry Edwards met Stratton's plane in Sitka and escorted him to a SEACC board potluck supper. Stratton looked around and realized for the first time that he might actually have a chance to land the position. "I launched into my sales pitch, explaining why I was the right person for the job. In the middle of the interview the sun came out and I saw the view of water and rock, and I said, 'Excuse me for a minute, can we take a break so I can look at this view?'"

A week after his trip he got the call. He had the job—and, with the passage of ANILCA, a challenge he hadn't bargained for. Expectations were low. "The board was split," Stratton said. "The people who didn't support me gave me six months."

His new job came with a salary of $1,200 a month and no staff. Eventually the board let him hire a secretary. His first task was to raise money. During the Alaska lands campaign, SEACC had survived on grants from the McIntosh Foundation and the Kendall Foundation. "The amount of income coming into the organization had been substantial," Stratton said. But with passage of ANILCA, that money had dried up. Now SEACC, like Stratton, was on its own.

To develop clout, SEACC also needed members. "SEACC was not a membership organization. It was a coalition of existing local groups. So the first thing I did was to create a membership organization." That generated some revenue from dues. It also began to give SEACC the influence that only a group with dues-paying members can wield. SEACC needed a voice as well. Stratton hired an editor on contract to publish SEACC's dormant newsletter, *Ravencall*. Working with the board on these tasks was a hard sell. "Nobody wanted to talk to me. The board members said, 'We're burned out.' They said, 'We want you to do good work, report to us, don't get bad press.' There were no board committees, no policies. The board rubber-stamped my proposals and played no role in decision-making."

Public apathy was another challenge. "Every member of the Alaska political establishment believed it was over," said John Sisk, who would become Stratton's grassroots organizer. "The Tongass issue was over. The rest belonged to the timber companies. George Ishiyama, the head of Alaska Pulp Corp., and Harry Merlo, the president of Louisiana-Pacific, believed the Forest Service's job from then on out would be to help the pulp mills by supplying them with timber."

The pulp companies were actually better off as a result of ANILCA. West Chichagof Island, in Alaska Pulp's supply area, was now protected as wilderness, but most of it was too rugged to log anyway, and in exchange Alaska Pulp had gained access to more productive land on Kuiu Island. The new Misty Fiords National Monument, in the Ketchikan Pulp timber supply area, was mostly sheer rock cliffs and ice.

For SEACC, the work of a decade was toast. SEACC's forty-five areas proposal had been largely ignored in the Forest Service's 1979 Tongass Land Management Plan. "The Tongass was completely off the radar screen" of the national groups, Sisk said. "They had gotten whipped on the Tongass. And the implication was that they were part of the deal. They didn't want to amend ANILCA. They didn't want to give Ted Stevens a chance to reopen it."

Frank Murkowski, a gruff, combative banker, who had served as Alaska's commissioner of economic development and had developed close ties with the Alaska timber industry, had been elected to the U.S. Senate from Alaska in the 1980 Republican sweep. Don Young, Alaska's lone U.S. representative, was a popular maverick, a former schoolteacher in the remote outpost of Fort Yukon who had worked his way up the political ladder from the city council to mayor and on to the Alaska House and Senate before his election to Congress in 1973. A self-styled Alaska chauvinist (and California native), Young played to the crowd back home by denouncing federal agencies and baiting environmentalists, whom he dismissed as "a waffle-stomping, Harvard-graduating, intellectual bunch of idiots." This GOP troika— Stevens, Murkowski and Young—made up the Alaska delegation at the dawn of the Reagan era. For Southeast Alaska's dispirited environmentalists, prospects couldn't have looked grimmer. As for the Forest Service, its attitude was that Congress had spoken. The fate of the Tongass was resolved.

KADASHAN

In his first two years at SEACC Stratton was preoccupied with fighting a borax mine in the newly designated Misty Fiords National Monument. But a timber sale in the Kadashan watershed on Chichagof Island got SEACC back into the forest. The Kadashan was the only intact large watershed remaining in Tenakee Inlet. With its abundant runs of pink and chum salmon and its large populations of brown bear and Sitka black-tailed deer, it had been on SEACC's list of must-save roadless areas from the beginning. In the spring of 1983 Kadashan popped up on the Forest Service's own radar screen as an area scheduled for eventual logging under Alaska Pulp's long-term contract. The plan called for building an eleven-mile-long road into the watershed in the late 1980s.

The state of Alaska had been trying to keep logging and road-building out of the Kadashan for more than twenty years. When the Forest Service's plan became public, Alaska Fish and Game Commissioner Don Collinsworth asked Regional Forester John Sandor to postpone logging and road-building there until at least 1990 to protect the river's important fisheries. United Fishermen of Alaska asked the Forest Service to "indefinitely defer timber harvest" and "discontinue any plans or preparation for road construction" in the Kadashan. The town of Tenakee Springs passed a resolution opposing the Forest Service's road-building plan. Sandor denied all entreaties and proceeded with plans to begin road construction in the spring of 1984.

Joe Mehrkens, a Forest Service economist who was sympathetic to environmentalists, had been feeding Stratton information on the wasteful economics of the Tongass timber sale program. Stratton believed Kadashan was the case that could drive home the message of waste and environmental destruction. However, to save the Kadashan, SEACC would have to sue. The McIntosh Foundation put up $5,000 for legal expenses. But Stratton needed a lawyer, and the Sierra Club Legal Defense Fund, which was busy fighting Shee-Atika land selections on Admiralty Island, declined to take the case. Other national groups wouldn't touch it. Stratton picked up the phone and called Steve Kallick.

Stratton and Kallick had met in the summer of 1982 while Kallick, a law student at Northwestern School of Law in Portland, was serving a legal internship in Juneau. The two boyish redheaded hippies had hit it off immediately. Kallick was the son of a doctor who practiced in a blue-collar Chicago neighborhood and drove his family out west every summer. He had inherited his dad's wanderlust. At seventeen, he and a friend made a trip to Alaska and spent four months driving everywhere they could get to by road, financing the trip by selling pot to Alaskans they met on their journey. During their wanderings they saw the big tree country of British Columbia's Cassiar region and the headwaters of the Stikine River, the Northern Yukon and Prudhoe Bay. Sometime during that drug-enhanced summer, maybe while he was playing poker with pipeline workers in Fairbanks, Kallick had a moment of clarity.

"The scene in Fairbanks in 1975 was intense, as close to the Wild West as most people of my generation ever get," Kallick recalled. "I knew that if I stayed there my life would be a life of gambling and pot." He went home, earned a degree in rhetoric at the University of Illinois, tried his hand at newspaper reporting, and ended up applying to law school at the last possible moment in the spring of 1980. "I put everything in my Volkswagen bus and drove west. Somehow I knew even then that I was headed for Alaska."

In 1982 he accepted an internship with the Sierra Club Legal Defense Fund, and spent the summer fighting Shee-Atika's logging plans on Admiralty Island. During that summer he was dispatched to Angoon to sign up plaintiffs in the case. It was there that he met Sterling Bolima, Angoon's leading strategist in the fight to save Admiralty. Bolima had come up with the idea of enlisting every adult resident of the village as a named plaintiff in the case against Shee-Atika. When Kallick arrived, he was unnerved to realize that he was the only white person in town.

For the first two days, Kallick said, not one Angoon resident entered his small makeshift office. "Sterling kept saying, 'Don't worry, it will be all right. They're waiting for the elders.' On the third day Sterling got on his CB radio and said, 'I think it's time for the elders.' In a few minutes this bus came over filled with Tlingit elders. They stood in front of my table and did a war dance for fifteen minutes." Kallick asked a young Tlingit what was going on. "We're going to war with Shee-Atika," he was told. Of 300 people present in Angoon that day, 230 signed up as plaintiffs in the case.

It was the highlight of Kallick's summer. He returned to Oregon to finish law school, and after graduation accepted a job with the Columbia Inter-Tribal Fish Commission in Portland. He was happy with his job, and happily involved in a relationship with his college sweetheart, when Stratton called to offer him a job.

Kallick said he would not consider moving to Alaska unless Stratton could guarantee him twelve months' work. Stratton told him, "I only have six months' worth, but come anyway." In truth, Stratton had only the grant from the McIntosh Foundation and no guarantee of more. But he knew that once Kallick got to Juneau, there would be plenty for him to do.

It was with deep ambivalence that Kallick agreed to leave his job and girlfriend and return to Alaska. "I knew I was trading off something very secure and very good for something that was financially uncertain. I remember driving north in my Volkswagen bus feeling this combination of excitement and dread."

He arrived in Juneau on Dec. 18, 1983. He found Stratton running a one-man show. "He was like this guy breathing on a wet fire. He was like a used-car salesman. No one took him seriously." But Stratton's dogged perseverance was catching. When Kallick learned that his new boss had only $5,000 to pay him, he got the Juneau office of the Sierra Club Legal Defense Fund to hire him as a special projects attorney. Then he got the Alaska Conservation Foundation to give him a grant, so he could develop a multiple-year legal strategy for protecting the Tongass.

Kadashan was Kallick's first case. He believed the Forest Service was vulnerable under the National Environmental Policy Act because the agency had failed to analyze in detail the impact of opening the valley to logging. In an environmental impact statement covering three million acres, there was only a single paragraph about the Kadashan. Kallick knew NEPA; one of his college professors had helped write the implementing regulations. "I knew this was not legal," he said. "It was not site-specific enough." Juneau lawyer Rich Burnam, a member of the SEACC board, filed the suit as the attorney of record because Kallick was not yet a member of the Alaska Bar. But Kallick conducted all the legal research and wrote all the briefs. In his research, he uncovered a study by state wildlife biologist John Schoen on the brown bears of Chichagof Island. He knew immediately that he had found the key to a winning case.

Schoen had put radio collars on six brown bears so he could monitor their movements. He had concluded that as many as 25 brown bears inhabited the Kadashan watershed. He told Kallick he believed the Kadashan had the highest density of brown bears in Southeast Alaska. Schoen picks up the story. "I was contacted by SEACC and asked to give a deposition in a suit they had brought to stop the road. Steve Kallick interviewed me. Don McKnight (Schoen's boss) sat in on the deposition. I suggested that if they built a road in that watershed it would have a severe impact on bears." Kallick got an affidavit from another brown bear biologist, Jack Lentfer, as well. "It was an enormous issue the Forest Service had not even considered," he said. "I really focused on the bear. You need to focus on a simple story."

The suit was filed Feb. 1, 1984. SEACC asked U.S. District Judge James Von der Heyt for a temporary restraining order to halt road-building in the watershed. Already, the Forest Service had pushed the road seven miles up the Kadashan Valley. At the hearing, in March, the judge acknowledged the evidence but said Alaska Pulp's contract trumped NEPA. It was the same argument the Forest Service and the timber industry had been making for ten years. Kallick appealed. A long and ominous silence followed.

A TEST

In April of 1994, while awaiting the ruling, Kallick went to Kadashan with Jim Stratton and John Sisk, SEACC's newly hired grassroots coordinator. Kallick had never visited Southeast Alaska's backcountry. He ignored advice to invest in rubber boots and a full suit of rubber rain gear. It was a decision he quickly regretted. "We went in a skiff. It was raining hard. I had leather boots and GoreTex rain gear." The temperature was 45 degrees.

The three went as far up the estuary as they could by skiff, then dropped anchor and waded the rest of the way through thigh-high water to a cabin maintained by the Alaska Department of Fish and Game. Kallick was cold and drenched. He could feel the warmth leaving his body and knew he was on the verge of hypothermia. Once they got to the cabin, Kallick encountered another reality of the Alaska wilderness. "We wandered out in the trees and there were bears everywhere. There was bear scat still warm on the ground. It was the full-on bear experience. It was intense. I was freezing to death and scared." He knew he was being tested. Was he tough enough to survive in Southeast Alaska?

On his last night at Kadashan the weather cleared and a run of herring came into the mouth of the river to spawn. In the morning the rocks glistened white with their eggs, as if snow had fallen overnight. "It was absolutely gorgeous," Kallick said. "I'd passed the test. I knew at that point that I was going to go back and win that case."

Sure enough, in April, the clerk for the 9th Circuit called Kallick with a single question: How soon could the Forest Service resume road-building in the Kadashan? Kallick responded that the Forest Service was loading road-building equipment onto barges as they spoke. A week later the 9th Circuit issued a one-line injunction blocking any further road construction in the Kadashan until the case was resolved.

For John Schoen, the repercussions were immediate. His affidavit provoked a call from Alaska Regional Forester John Sandor to Alaska Governor Bill Sheffield. "Sandor was so irate he wanted Sheffield to fire me," Schoen said. Sheffield called his commissioner of fish and game, Don Collinsworth, who called in several other fish and game officials, then summoned Schoen to a meeting. "It didn't start out cordial," Schoen said. "They wanted to know what the hell I had done. I said, 'Here's my deposition.' They read it, and they said, 'There's nothing wrong with this. It's the truth.'"

The Kadashan injunction was a turning point, not only for SEACC but for the Forest Service. Said Stratton: "It cracked the Forest Service's armor of invulnerability." In June, he told the story of the Kadashan road to a congressional subcommittee reviewing the implementation of the Alaska Lands Act to illustrate the kinds of projects that were being paid for out of the Tongass Timber Supply Fund. "For over twenty years the state of Alaska, commercial fishing groups, professional biologist associations, the local community of Tenakee Springs and conservationists have fought to protect Kadashan from road building and timber harvest," he said. "We had been successful until just a couple of weeks ago, when construction began on a road that is planned to slice along the length of the Kadashan River." The road, he said, was being paid for out of the Timber Supply Fund.

ON A ROLL

There were plenty of other tasks to occupy Kallick's time while he waited to argue the Kadashan case at trial. He filed a successful appeal of the Chugach National Forest management plan. He represented Tenakee Springs in one of several suits to block the Forest Service road connection. And he took the Forest Service to court over the Chuck River timber sale near Petersburg. In that case, merely filing the lawsuit was enough. "The Forest Service administratively decided not to pursue the sale because the entire commercial fishing industry was opposed, the city of Petersburg was opposed, and then the state of Alaska came out against it," Stratton said. "You had the Forest Service being told that not every timber sale was acceptable." SEACC was on a roll.

The Forest Service was still trying to find a company to build a pulp mill near Juneau. As a sign of good faith, the agency started building a road to Berner's Bay, a wildly popular kayaking area in Juneau's back yard. Ultimately, the Forest Service planned to build twenty-seven miles of logging road at Berner's Bay and open the area to clearcutting. Juneau had been shielded from the impact of industrial logging. Most of its residents bitterly opposed the project. And Kallick had a personal stake in stopping it. He was penniless and living in a shack. But he had won a sea kayak in a raffle, and he still had his Volkswagen van. Berner's Bay was the only place he could afford to go kayaking.

In May of 1985, as the Forest Service prepared to auction the first independent timber sale at Berner's Bay, a dozen Juneau environmentalists held a goodbye campout there. Someone asked, "Isn't there something we could do about this?" Kallick said he might be able to stop it with a lawsuit using the same NEPA argument that had halted the Kadashan road. But he needed money.

"People started volunteering to do things," Kallick said. "It was a great rallying point. Within a week we had a meeting, with 350 people packed into a church. And we blistered them." By September SEACC had persuaded a court to enjoin the road at Berner's Bay. "It galvanized Juneau," Kallick said. "It devastated the regional forester, John Sandor. It brought the whole Tongass issue home to Juneau. The Forest Service knew its whole timber program was illegal if we won that case."

NOURISHING THE ROOTS

Jim Stratton was convinced that untapped support for saving the Tongass lurked in the small communities of Southeast. Since 1983, he had tried to persuade the SEACC board to let him hire a grassroots organizer. But the board had deep reservations. SEACC was heavily involved in fighting mines on Admiralty Island and at Misty Fiords. Some members believed what SEACC needed most was a person to write administrative appeals. Some doubted there were many grassroots conservationists to organize in Southeast. But Stratton finally prevailed. His first choice for the job declined, but she told her sister, who told her boyfriend, a young Colorado activist named John Sisk. It must have been destiny.

Sisk grew up in New Mexico, and after college he worked for the Colorado Division of Wildlife and the Colorado Open Space Council. He did some rural community organizing, analyzed some national forest plans, and campaigned to save some wild and scenic rivers. He also fought U.S. Interior Secretary James Watt's efforts to open up wilderness areas in the Rocky Mountains to oil and gas leasing. In Colorado, his constituency included ski resort owners, ranchers, and wilderness outfitters and guides. "We had everybody," Sisk recalls. "It was a great organizing strategy."

Sisk had wanted to visit Alaska since seeing the film "Admiralty Island: Fortress of the Bears." When the offer from Stratton came, he didn't hesitate. "I thought, 'Somebody is going to pay me to come to Southeast Alaska, travel to all the communities and meet some of the most interesting people I've ever met? Yeah, I think I can spend a year or two at that.'"

Stratton offered him $14,000 a year. In fact, he only had enough money in the bank to pay Sisk for one month. "When I got up here," Sisk says, "I realized things were really tenuous at SEACC." Sisk's hiring was so controversial that in 1984 the SEACC board tried to fire him, and Kallick as well. But Stratton stood by his new hires. And Sisk, like Kallick, soon proved his worth.

Ted Whitesell had done some early grassroots organizing, but John Sisk had to start fresh. People were disoriented and demoralized; SEACC came close to folding again soon after he arrived. Sisk was committed to a new approach. "I was free of the intimidation and polarization of the ANILCA battle," he recalled. "I just walked in."

He traveled the length of the Alaska Panhandle, from Ketchikan to Yakutat, by ferry, floatplane and skiff. He found environmentally minded citizens—newcomers and oldtimers alike—in every community. What they had in common was that they hated what the Forest Service was doing on the Tongass. "My objective was to answer a question, and not one that SEACC had given me," he said. "The question was, Do working people in Southeast Alaska who actually live in the forest have things in common that amount to some kind of conservation spirit? And if so, what is it? Because if that wasn't there, it was pointless."

Sisk had no objection to logging. But he objected to pulp mill monopolies and the long-term contracts. He suspected that most people felt that way. "The situation was so ridiculous. I just couldn't imagine that the average Alaskan was content with the pulp mills owning everything." He went to Prince of Wales Island in his new Helly Hansen rain gear, carrying the names of a couple of contacts. One, passed on to him by Whitesell, was retired logger Al Dennis, who lived in Craig. Dennis took Sisk out in his boat for a tour of old logging shows and introduced him to the mayor of

Craig. Sisk saw the brutal logging by Native corporations at Sunny Hay Mountain and around Klawock Lake. It was shocking, but no more so than the logging taking place on the Tongass at that time. Near Hollis, on national forest land, thousands of contiguous acres had been cut. Loggers had laid bare entire watersheds down to the streambanks.

Sisk also visited Sylvia Geraghty, who owned a small store and fueling station on a tiny island off the west coast of Prince of Wales Island.

Sylvia Geraghty provided powerful testimony on behalf of rural residents of Southeast Alaska at early congresional hearings on Tongass reform. Photo by Trygve Steen.

Geraghty's customers were loggers and commercial fishermen. She had written Stratton a couple of letters saying, in effect, 'I'm really nervous about getting involved with environmentalists, but I'm very concerned about what's happening here."

The logistics of traveling to remote places were daunting, but that was part of the fun. "It was very difficult to get around the west coast of Prince of Wales Island," Sisk recalls. "It was out there on the edge of the known world. People who lived there depended on just their gumption and their own stick-to-it-iveness."

WHERE THE HERRING SPAWN

In his meetings with rural Alaskans, Sisk talked fish and wildlife, not logging. It was a political decision. "My goal was to find a common denominator in people who believed in standing forests. But there was a big corporate presence, a big Forest Service presence, and a big political presence to make sure there was no opposition to the timber industry. I met two kinds of people: people who worked for Louisiana-Pacific, and people who didn't. The people who didn't hated what L-P was doing. The people who did just didn't want to talk about it." His goal was not only to sign up SEACC members but to empower people to take action on their own. "I'm not a real advocate of a legalistic approach," Sisk said. "I think appeals and lawsuits are disempowering. Once it's in court, defendants can't talk about it. The role of citizens then becomes to raise money to pay the lawyers. I just wanted people to talk to each other, to know they were not alone, to understand the Forest Service. People on the west coast of Prince of Wales didn't know there was a Reid Brothers case, didn't know there was an alternative to becoming Oregon."

Local Forest Service officials were less than welcoming. "The biologists were always thrilled to see me," Sisk said. "The timber beasts just stared at me." Sisk held town meetings and asked people to tell him about the places that were important to them. He wanted to know where they gathered shellfish and spruce roots, where the herring spawned, where the deer found winter cover. He wanted to know where they hunted, trapped, fished and crabbed. "I wasn't interested in bashing the timber industry," he said. "I didn't run into very many people who wanted to shut down the industry, but I ran into a lot of people who wanted to change it."

He spent a lot of time in the logging communities of Craig, Hollis, Klawock and Thorne Bay on Prince of Wales Island. "I stood out like a sore thumb because my jeans weren't torn off at the bottom and I wasn't wearing a hickory shirt," he said. He also hung out in Ketchikan and Petersburg and Wrangell. "Wrangell is tough if you're an environmentalist," he said. "It's hardscrabble. I held a meeting there to organize. The timber industry showed up to disrupt it. We were the first environmentalists to come there—what else were they going to do? It felt like one of those old westerns. After it was over, some of the guys who had been harassing me came up and we were joking, and we actually got along pretty well." In fact, Sisk liked the feel of Wrangell. It reminded him of home. "It was more the Alaska I expected to find when I moved up here—just a working town in the forest," he said. "I was shocked when I saw Juneau and what it had become with all the oil money. Juneau is more like Boulder. The rest of Southeast is like western Colorado."

Away from Juneau, Sisk found the soul of Southeast Alaska. He found people who were making a life in the wild. "The constituency I was focusing on was not a national wilderness campaign," Sisk said. "It was a constituency that owns chainsaws and uses them, but that needs the Forest Service for other things. They need the fish and the wildlife. These people were completely disenfranchised. Commercial fishermen felt their economic well-being was being jeopardized. They felt a commercial timber industry was appropriate, but it wasn't right to subsidize one industry by jeopardizing another one. They wanted stream buffers, and they wanted to protect high-productivity watersheds like the Kadashan and Chuck River."

Sisk provided a reality check at a critical time in SEACC's evolution. "Part of my job was to organize a constituency for SEACC," he said. "Part of it was to sensitize SEACC to the needs of this constituency. Over time it became obvious that the issue wasn't wilderness but, 'How do we live here?'"

8

COVERUP

It was April Fool's Day, 1981, when Forest Service timber appraiser Ron Galdabini was summoned to a meeting with his boss, Dale Heigh, director of timber management for the Alaska Region. Heigh's own supervisors were in a tizzy. On March 5, U.S. District Judge Barbara Rothstein had ruled in favor of Reid Brothers Logging Co. in its antitrust suit against Ketchikan Pulp Company and Alaska Lumber and Pulp. Heigh told Galdabini, "We've got to do something about this."

Rothstein's initial ruling, in March, had garnered only a brief Associated Press story in the *Anchorage Daily News*. But a few weeks later, when she issued findings of fact describing collusion, conspiracy and outright lying on the part of the pulp companies, and awarded Reid Brothers triple damages totaling nearly $1.5 million, people began paying attention. Rothstein found that the plaintiffs had proved their antitrust allegation against the pulp mills. "The Court believes that the proof in this case has overwhelmingly established that the defendant mills, both KPC and ALP, conspired to restrain trade and to monopolize the timber industry in Southeast Alaska," she wrote. "The Court feels that the evidence establishes that the two mills achieved monopoly power and exercised this power."

Rothstein's written findings repeated much of the evidence recapped by Reid Brothers attorney William Dwyer in his brilliant and devastating post-trial brief. The pulp companies, she declared, had conspired "to restrict and eliminate competition in all phases of the timber industry in Southeast Alaska; to refrain concertedly from competing against others for timber or logs; to keep would-be competitors out of Southeast Alaska by cutting off their timber supplies through preclusive bidding and other means; to eliminate mill competition by acquiring ownership or control of the sawmills in Southeast Alaska, while expanding their own operations; to control and manipulate the log supply to the few surviving mills; to pay artificially low prices to independent loggers for logs and logging services; to eliminate purchase loggers from the field; and to attain and exercise monopoly power, i.e., the power to set prices and exclude competition in the timber industry in Southeast Alaska . . . (E)ach part of the defendants' combination and conspiracy interlocked with every other part, and was aimed at the same goal of restricting and eliminating competition in the timber industry of Southeast Alaska."

Glenn and Martha Reid celebrated victory in Petersburg, though they would not see the money for years. Lawyers for the pulp companies immediately appealed Rothstein's ruling to the 9th U.S. Circuit Court of Appeals. They argued that Reid Brothers Logging had failed to prove it had been damaged by a conspiracy intended to drive it out of business. In the plaintiffs' appellate brief, Dwyer wrote: "This is a case in which a relatively small private enforcement action exposed a massive conspiracy and monopolization which had operated successfully for many years . . ." Then he proceeded to lay out the evidence in seventy-five pages of precise and damning prose.

Until the verdict, the Forest Service had all but ignored the five-year-old Reid Brothers case. In late summer of 1980, soon after the trial got underway in U.S. District Court in Seattle, a Small Business Administration official had called Heigh and advised him to get somebody down to Seattle because some "pretty interesting stuff" was coming out. By the time the Forest Service dispatched observers to Seattle, however, most of the factual material had already been presented.

Rothstein's findings reflected no credit on the Forest Service. In fact, they plunged the agency into crisis mode. If the evidence was so overwhelming, how could the agency have looked the other way all those years? Alaska Regional Forester John Sandor acted quickly to control the damage. He announced a three-month suspension of all timber sales. He asked the Small Business Administration to recertify all companies that claimed eligibility for benefits under the forest's small- business preference program, in an effort to ferret out pulp company fronts. And he announced that he would appoint a review team, consisting of a forester, an accountant and a lawyer, to examine all the testimony and evidence in the Reid Brothers trial and recommend what actions the Forest Service ought to take. That's where Ron Galdabini came in.

Galdabini, a 19-year Forest Service veteran, was a logical choice for the team. "I'd been in the battle since 1971," he said. "I had seven years of cost-collecting experience." But when Heigh asked him whether he was interested in the job, Galdabini said no. "Why not?" Heigh inquired. "Because nothing will ever happen," Galdabini responded. "Nothing will come of it."

Galdabini's cynicism was well-founded. Before his transfer to Alaska, he had observed and reported collusive bidding practices and apparent timber trespass by several Oregon timber companies on the Detroit Ranger District in the Willamette National Forest, but the concerns he raised had been brushed aside by his superiors. He doubted things would be different on the Tongass. (Eventually the Department of Justice had brought bid-rigging charges against two of the Oregon companies Galdabini investigated, and in 1975 a federal court had convicted the companies of collusive bidding on five national forest timber sales in the early 1970s. Because of the statute of limitations, however, their alleged bid-rigging on nearly a hundred other sales had gone unpunished.)

Galdabini finally was persuaded to take the job. "They didn't have anyone else who had the extensive knowledge of the inner workings of the pulp mills as they related to the timber appraisal process," he said. The other members of the review team were Paul Marz, a Forest Service timber appraisal cost accountant, and Jim Kauble, a lawyer in the Natural Resources Division of the Office of General Counsel. Kauble's job was to research applicable laws, including the statute of limitations, to determine whether the Forest Services was entitled to damages as a result of the pulp companies' antitrust activities. Marz was in charge of determining the true costs and values to be used in calculating lost revenue to the federal treasury. The toughest job the team had was to put together a case the Department of Justice would be willing to prosecute.

The trial had generated eleven thousand pages of depositions, memos and other court records. The trial transcript alone filled two file-drawer-sized boxes. The review team traveled to Seattle to wade through the exhibits and depositions, which were kept under lock and key at the federal courthouse. Reid Brothers attorney Peter Vial tried to point team members toward some of the 300,000 documents not entered into evidence, but attorneys for the pulp mills protested. Environmentalists were eager to get their hands on the review team's findings. "Everyone wanted to see what we were finding, but we had to keep our own review confidential," he said.

The Forest Service review panel conducted its review of the Reid Brothers court documents expeditiously and reported back to Regional Forester Sandor in June of 1981 with a slate of recommendations, with a time frame for action on each one. Should the Forest Service consider debarring either company—prohibiting it from purchasing federal timber—that needed to happen quickly, Galdabini said. "You wouldn't want someone who is engaging in collusive bidding to keep buying timber."

Galdabini, Kauble and Marx lugged two full sets of case files to Washington, D.C. and had a roundtable discussion with Forest Service Chief Max Peterson about their findings. Sandor and his superiors implemented some recommendations, like changing to sealed bids on timber sales to deter bid-rigging, right away. Sandor also announced that the Forest Service would begin offering small timber sales, five million board feet or less in volume, to increase opportunities for small-scale timber purchasers in Southeast Alaska. But for Galdabini, the job that started on that fateful April 1, 1981, was turning into an ordeal that he would come to regard as a huge April Fool's joke. "This was supposed to be a three-month assignment," he said. "I didn't get rid of it until 1986."

SETTING A FAIR PRICE

The search of trial documents began to answer questions that had puzzled Galdabini for years, and it raised new suspicions as well. Internal memos and letters showed that the pulp companies had conspired to keep down stumpage rates—the price they paid for federal timber—by driving competitors out of Southeast Alaska, divvying up the Tongass between them, and hiding their profits through bookkeeping sleight-of-hand.

The companies had two motives for hiding their profits. One was to avoid paying higher state and federal corporate income taxes. The other was to avoid paying a higher stumpage rate for federal timber. Internal memos from the mid-1970s revealed that Louisiana-Pacific Corporation, and Georgia-Pacific Corp., its parent company until 1972, appeared obsessed with controlling stumpage rates in Southeast Alaska. "They were more worried about letting the Forest Service get hold of their internal accounting practices than they were about the repercussions of the IRS obtaining their financial records," Galdabini said

Secret memos indicated that from the beginning, Alaska Pulp Corporation had sought to hide its profits and avoid paying U.S. corporate income taxes. In 1972 Georgia-Pacific Vice President Harry Merlo and KPC timber manager Art Brooks went to Tokyo, where Merlo offered to buy Alaska Lumber and Pulp from the Japanese, an offer firmly rejected by

APC executives. Afterward Merlo sent a memo to his bosses laying out the situation he had found in Tokyo. "The owners of APC have never really paid a fair price for their dissolving pulp, so the true financial picture of Alaska Pulp Company reflects this subsidizing," he wrote. Brooks explained in a separate memo: "(T)he Japanese operations are going to be manipulated so that any profit therefrom is taken in Japan and there will be little or no taxes paid to the State of Alaska or the Federal Government."

Galdabini had direct experience with the pulp companies' attempts to conceal their financial records from the Forest Service. The Alaska Region was trying to put a new timber appraisal system in place, and he and other accountants had spent years battling KPC and APC for the financial information the agency needed to implement the new system. Tongass timber managers had long suspected that the pulp companies were taking advantage of the existing system. That system based stumpage rates on the value of logs before processing, rather than on the actual market value of the "finished product"—a bundle of lumber or a ton of pulp. A big part of Galdabini's job in the early 1970s was to find out the true cost of every part of the process of producing pulp as well as the value of the finished product, in order to arrive at the "fair market value" of Tongass timber. It was a task the Forest Service had never before attempted. However, not only was this effort responsible government policy; it was the law. The 1897 Organic Act, which established the national forest system, specified that "timber shall not be sold at less than fair market value."

Getting accurate sales and cost figures was key. On national forests, the minimum stumpage rate—the lowest bid the Forest Service will consider for timber at auction—is calculated by a complex formula that figures in the costs a purchaser incurs in producing a finished product, and builds in a profit and risk estimate for the purchaser as well. However, calculating those costs and end-product prices had proved almost impossible on the Tongass. The reason was that on the Tongass, there was no such thing as an arm's-length transaction. Prices were not set by the market. They were set by the pulp mills' parent companies, and often bore no resemblance to true market price.

"If you're in an open market, where there is real competition, the stumpage rate will be bid up to whatever the market will bear," Galdabini explained. "But in Alaska there was no real competition for the majority of timber volume being appraised. The long-term contracts did not have that competitive force to assure a true market value to the government, so it was doubly important that the minimum bid appraisal, and the data on which it was based, be correct."

On the Tongass the only parties engaged in true competitive bidding had been the independent purchase loggers and a few small mills. By the early 1970s the pulp mills' successful campaign to drive them out of business had eliminated that reality check.

As he dug through the boxes of depositions and pulp company memos, Galdabini found detailed documentation of the myriad ways in which both companies had concealed their profits. Minutes of internal meetings revealed that Louisiana-Pacific "found every way possible to draw money out of Ketchikan Pulp" so KPC would appear unprofitable on paper, even though in the 1970s it was making money hand over fist, Galdabini said. For instance, L-P sold KPC caustic soda and chlorine, two chemicals essential to the production of dissolving pulp, for as much as double L-P's cost. L-P also billed KPC handsomely for management and research and development services.

The effort to disguise Ketchikan Pulp's rosy financial picture was both aided and complicated by the fact that until 1976, the company had been jointly owned by Louisiana-Pacific and Chicago-based FMC. That meant bookkeepers had to divide the profits transferred out of Ketchikan Pulp between its two parent companies. KPC sold about 80 percent of its pulp to FMC, at a substantial cash discount. KPC paid both of its parent companies millions of dollars in fees and commissions, which KPC deducted as "expenses" but which really amounted to draws against the pulp mill's profits. Even after those withdrawals, however, Galdabini found that KPC's Alaska operations remained highly profitable.

THE GREEN DOOR

Getting accurate cost information from Alaska Pulp Corporation, the Japanese-owned parent company of Alaska Lumber and Pulp, was even more complicated. Because APC was integrated into the complex Japanese economy, it had countless ways to hide its profits. For instance, as a requirement of doing business in Japan, buyers and sellers in business transactions customarily bought stock in each other's companies. This practice created a series of interlocking relationships that presented Forest Service appraisers with an impenetrable maze. When he started trying to trace those relationships, Galdabini said, there was no point at which the buying and selling of a product met the Forest Service's definition of an arm's-length transaction. "It just evolved into the massive Japanese economy and the Japanese Industrial Bank."

Both in Tokyo and in Alaska, the shell game was elaborate. Alaska Lumber and Pulp and its sawmills, Wrangell Lumber Company and Alaska Wood Products, functioned as suppliers to ALP's parent company, Alaska Pulp Corporation. APC's Tokyo executives determined the price they would pay for ALP logs, lumber and pulp products. APC bought all the pulp produced by ALP at its Sitka mill and set the price. APC also purchased all the lumber products produced by the two sawmills, then resold the pulp and lumber products to APC shareholders, who used the products or resold them to customers in Japan. In the 1970s, records of ALP sales and costs stopped at the point at which the company's products were loaded aboard ships in Alaska. "We nicknamed this point 'the green door,'" Galdabini said. "We could not go beyond the green door."

Galdabini wanted to know what the parent corporation was selling its product for, but APC refused to disclose the monetary value of its transactions in Japan. "We thought if we could just open that green door, we could find out the answers. In 1978, the Forest Service was allowed to look behind the green door. But behind the green door was a red door, and behind the red door was a blue door."

Complicating the task further was the need to observe Japanese business protocol. "You couldn't be as point-blank in discussions with them as you could with L-P. They were foreign nationals. They were a lot more polite in their business transactions. Some didn't speak English well." Galdabini would ask a question like, "Do you have a set of books that lists your costs?' " An animated discussion would ensue—in Japanese. Finally the company's English-speaking U.S. representative would answer, "No."

One of the review team's recommendations was that the Forest Service send a team to Tokyo for an in-depth inspection of APC's cost and sales records. Galdabini was scheduled to go, but he was removed from the team at the request of ALP officials. However, he gave a detailed list of questions to Paul Marz, who did make the trip. The team returned with extensive documentation of APC's financial practices, which it described in a document entitled "Validation Report on Alaska Pulp Company, Ltd." The team concluded that data collected from ALP and its subsidiaries in Southeast Alaska was not reliable for the purpose of establishing stumpage rates for Tongass timber. "Alaska Pulp Co. does no business without a shareholder company being involved somewhere in the transaction," it wrote. The Validation Report remained under wraps until 1989, when environmentalists obtained it and released it to congressional committees and the press.

Eventually, the Forest Service did obtain the information it needed to establish realistic stumpage values. However, much of Galdabini's hard work in trying to uncover the profits the companies had realized from manufacturing pulp and lumber in Southeast Alaska was for naught. In 1982, when a timber industry recession hit Alaska, the Forest Service granted the pulp companies emergency rate reductions. "All these cases I had investigated to a standstill got resolved in compromise agreements during rate redetermination negotiations," Galdabini said. KPC's rate dropped from $73.15 to $3.09 per 1,000 board feet in 1982. The following year APC's rate dropped from $43.88 to $1.48 per 1,000 board feet. Those rates meant the Forest Service was virtually giving away old-growth Sitka spruce and hemlock to the pulp mills. Even after the market began to improve in 1987, these bargain-basement rates were locked in until pulp mill stumpage rates came up for periodic rate adjustments in 1988 and 1989.

DECLINING TO PROSECUTE

When Ronald Reagan became president in January of 1981 the politics of the federal timber sale program changed overnight. Reagan's choice of Louisiana-Pacific executive John B. Crowell to oversee the Forest Service drew fire from environmentalists and fierce opposition from Democratic leaders. Though Crowell insisted he had played no role in the matters under litigation in the Reid Brothers case, many said that putting Crowell in charge of the Forest Service was like setting the fox loose in the chicken coop.

During Crowell's Senate confirmation hearings, Galdabini was given another urgent assignment. "We had to drop everything and go down to Washington and go through all the court documents (in the Reid Brothers anti-trust case) to look for Crowell's name," he said. They did find at least ten references to Crowell in the court record. Nonetheless, Crowell was duly confirmed by the U.S. Senate.

On Dec. 17, 1982, the Agriculture Department formally submitted the Forest Service case against the pulp companies to U.S. Attorney General William French Smith and the U.S. Department of Justice for possible civil and criminal prosecution. James Perry of the Office of General Counsel admitted that the government's case was based almost entirely on the pulp companies' violations of antitrust laws. But he also presented a case for collecting civil damages, based on the argument that the companies had breached their long-term contracts by failing to report accurately their costs and other financial data to the Forest Service. Perry said the companies might have cheated the federal government out of millions of dollars, though the statute of limitations prevented the Justice Department from collecting damages for events that had occurred before 1978. "If damages are determined to be of sufficient magnitude, cancellation of these contracts on the basis of material breach may be justified," Perry wrote. Those four explosive words, "cancellation of these contracts," sent shock waves through the Alaska pulp industry and the Alaska congressional delegation.

Three months later, Perry's letter was answered by Jane Rastani of the Justice Department's Commercial Litigation Branch. Rastani posed scores of questions about when the alleged illegal activities had occurred and demanded extensive documentation of every alleged cost to the federal treasury. Galdabini was ordered to stop everything else and respond to the memo with a detailed analysis of how much money the government had lost on each and every Tongass timber sale bought by the pulp companies since 1978. "We had to document everything," he said. "I had to come up with estimates. I had to develop new stumpage rates for each tree species in each sale." Galdabini even had to develop his own spread sheet to do the complicated calculations. Despite that Herculean effort, he admits that his calculation of damages was, in his words, "an educated wild-ass guess."

Galdabini estimated that the Federal Treasury had lost about $64 million as a result of pulp company anti-trust activities. A more complete damage assessment prepared by an outside consultant pegged total damages at between $76.5 million and $81.5 million, and said a large portion of that loss had occurred after the filing of the Reid Brothers case in 1976. No one knows how much money the Forest Service actually lost due to pulp company bid-rigging and collusion over two decades. In a way, Galdabini says, the actual figure is irrelevant. "Everything these companies did reduced stumpage. And we never did collect a dime of damages, primarily because the statute of limitations had run out. "

During the review of potential damages, Galdabini discovered that the Forest Service had erroneously allowed both pulp mills to earn millions of dollars in "ineffective purchaser road credits"—credits against the cost of federal timber for roads never built—and to distribute these credits throughout their operations. "That really woke people up," Galdabini said. Ketchikan Pulp settled its debt to the government in 1986, with a $1 million cash payment and an upward adjustment in its stumpage rate. In exchange, KPC got to "bank" purchaser road credits that it could not use when timber rates were low and use them later to offset the cost of federal timber when rates increased. Alaska Pulp chose a different course. It contested the antitrust claim and filed an $83 million counterclaim against the Forest Service, contending that the agency had failed to meet its contractual obligation to provide the company with "economic timber."

THE PAYOFF

On March 1, 1983, a federal appeals court panel reviewing the Reid Brothers case upheld Judge Rothstein's ruling in the strongest terms. "The alleged conspiracy aimed its tentacles at the timberland of the Tongass National Forest in southeast Alaska," visiting U.S. Circuit Judge Elbert Parr Tuttle wrote. Tuttle, who had presided over landmark civil rights cases in the Deep South, directed some of his harshest words at the pulp companies for the way they had treated the independent loggers: "By calculating payments to loggers on the basis of the loggers' costs rather than the value of the logs, ALP and KPC created a network of 'captive' loggers heavily indebted to the defendants. With a drop of the executioner's sword, the defendants could

At his home in Petersburg, retired independent logger Glenn Reid reviews papers from his successful antitrust suit against the Alaska pulp companies. March 1997. Photo by Kathie Durbin.

cut off a logger's financing, force the logger out of business, and acquire the company or its assets." The pulp mill companies appealed the ruling to the U.S. Supreme Court. On October 17, 1983, the high court declined to hear the case.

When the payoff finally came--$10 million in damages, to be divided among the Reids and three other companies--Glenn and Martha Reid reacted with equanimity. "We weren't sure we were going to win," Glenn Reid told the *Petersburg Pilot*, his hometown newspaper. "But we were sure they were guilty." The award put him back where he should have been before the pulp mills drove him out of business, he said. The judicial system "gets there if you stay around long enough." Still, the Reids had hoped for more. "We were hoping to do something for the general public as well as for ourselves," Martha Reid said. "I think it made people look twice at what was happening and made the companies more careful." Yet the long-term contracts remained in effect, she said, and there was no sign the government intended to take action to recover damages from the mills. William Dwyer, the Reids' lead lawyer at trial, was gratified by the outcome. "The whole thing took a long time, but the results were worth it," he said, "and the plaintiffs lived to see the award."

However, the rulings had no discernible effect on the Reagan Justice Department, which already had decided not to bring charges against the companies but instead to sweep the whole messy business under the rug. On January 4, 1983, Helmut Furth, a Justice Department antitrust lawyer, had notified Agriculture Department lawyers that the Antitrust Section would initiate neither criminal nor civil action against the pulp mills. "We have not found evidence of antitrust violations, occurring within the past five years, of a character sufficient to support a criminal prosecution under the antitrust laws," Furth wrote. "With regard to a possible civil action seeking injunctive relief, we have concluded that, despite evidence of past antitrust violations by the two companies, there is at this time no realistic prospect of obtaining effective and meaningful injunctive relief. Most of the questionable conduct occurred in the 1960s and early 1970s, and contributed marginally, if at all, to the dominance of the Southeast Alaska timber market enjoyed by these two companies . . ." He added that the Justice Department had concluded that it would be unable to show a financial loss to the government between 1979 and 1982, the only period for which it could claim damages under the statute of limitations.

On April 11, 1983, Robert W. Ogren, chief of the Department of Justice Fraud Section, notified Agriculture Department lawyers that his office too had decided against taking action against the Alaska pulp companies: "In light of the extensive civil litigation, the date of the alleged transactions (pre-March 1975), and the declination by the Antitrust Division after an extensive review, we are declining to consider the matter for further criminal investigation or prosecution purposes." In May, the Forest Service asked the Department of Justice to reopen its antitrust investigation so it could review actions of the pulp companies after 1975, including suspected bid boycotts and preclusive bidding. The Justice Department declined.

And there the matter would have ended, but for a feisty Democratic congressman from Oregon named Jim Weaver.

"A LONG HISTORY OF CHICANERY"

Weaver was a maverick—a homebuilder elected on a labor platform, a wilderness advocate sympathetic to the plight of loggers and mill workers in Oregon's timber-dependent Fourth Congressional District. Weaver had no love for the moneyed timber interests of the Pacific Northwest, but he understood that one of his jobs was to bring home the bacon—in his case, a stable supply of federal timber—to his constituents. However, he also represented Eugene, home to the University of Oregon and a hotbed of environmental activism. After his election to Congress in 1974, he quickly made a name as a partisan Democrat of the old school, blaming GOP policies of "high interest, unemployment and budget cuts" for plywood mill closures in his district. So strident was Weaver that after just four months in office, he was targeted by arch-conservative political operative Paul Weyrich for a $2 million reelection challenge in 1976.

But Weaver was popular back home and won reelection. In his second term, he chaired two House subcommittees with jurisdiction over the Forest Service. When he heard about the Reid Brothers antitrust ruling, he was livid. How was it, he wanted to know, that a private law firm could bring a successful civil case against the pulp mills for egregious antitrust violations while the U.S. Department of Justice stood on the sidelines, taking no action to hold the mills criminally liable? Bern Johnson, one of Weaver's staff assistants, recalls that his boss started asking, "Why didn't the Forest Service bring this lawsuit?"

In 1981 Weaver turned Johnson and another staff assistant, Greg Skillman, loose on the case. They turned up the report of the three-man Forest Service review team, which the agency had refused to give to Congress. The never-released report described numerous instances of possible criminal violations by the pulp mills, including the submission of false logging invoices and false statements regarding the use of bidding fronts. For instance, it revealed that Ketchikan Pulp Company had used duplicate invoices in the sale of cedar logs to Wrangell Lumber Co. in an attempt to keep the true value of the logs from the Forest Service. But these findings, as well as the review team's recommendations to the Internal Revenue Service and the Department of Justice for follow-up investigations, had been deep-sixed by the Justice Department.

Weaver's staff also obtained Forest Service documents revealing that the agency was losing roughly 97 cents for every dollar it spent on timber sales in Southeast Alaska. Ketchikan Pulp Co. was paying $3.09 per 1,000 board feet for timber comparable to timber that was selling for $150 per 1,000 board feet in the Pacific Northwest. Alaska Pulp Corporation was paying $1.48 per 1,000 board feet for the same high-value timber. The Forest Service was practically giving away trees from the Alaska rainforest. And outside Southeast Alaska, hardly anybody knew it.

Getting information out of the Forest Service was like pulling teeth, Johnson said. "For months we went back and forth with the Forest Service, using Weaver's subpoena powers. The Forest Service would gradually release information, piece by piece, saying, 'Don't release this to the media, it's confidential, the matter is under investigation.'" Ron Galdabini was one of the few Forest Service officials who did talk to Weaver's staff, but only with the approval of the Office of General Counsel.

Weaver scheduled a subcommittee hearing to gather testimony on timber industry practices in the Tongass. A few days before the hearing, his staff released internal documents to the *Washington Post* and the *New York Times* purporting to show that neither the Agriculture Department nor the Justice Department had followed up on the Forest Service review team's recommendations, and that no attempt had been made to recover the cost to the federal treasury of the pulp mills' antitrust activities over two decades.

Privately, Weaver was convinced that was no coincidence. He had bitterly fought John Crowell's confirmation. But his staff had turned up no solid evidence that Crowell had used his Agriculture Department position to squelch criminal indictments against the mills. Nonetheless, Weaver told the press: "If the documents we have now had been available at the time of his confirmation, it is likely he would not have been confirmed."

The newspapers ran the story of the alleged coverup in their June 12, 1983, Sunday editions. In a story headlined "Probe Says Two Big Firms Buy U.S. Timber at Toothpick Prices," *Washington Post* reporter Ward Sinclair wrote: "The U.S. Forest Service has lost millions of dollars in income from two timber companies found guilty of an antitrust conspiracy in Alaska, but the Department of Justice has declined to prosecute them, according to a House investigation." Estimates of revenue lost to the U.S. Treasury "range from $63 million to $81 million," Sinclair wrote. Philip Shabecoff of the *New York Times* reported that the Department of Justice had failed to investigate antitrust activities alleged to have occurred after the Reid case was filed, even though Weaver's staff believed the two companies "continue to benefit by virtue of their past illegal activities and may still be engaged in them."

Weaver told the press that the documents assembled by his staff showed "a long history of chicanery in the Tongass National Forest by these companies and virtually nothing being done by the Forest Service or the Department of Justice to stop it." Jerry Griffith, Louisiana-Pacific's spokesman in Portland, responded that Ketchikan Pulp Co. had followed "the letter of the contract," and accused Weaver of conducting a "malicious" assault on the company. "This has become a very pregnant political cow to milk by some of our little friends back there, principally Mr. Weaver among them," he said.

Eight years after Glenn and Martha Reid filed their lawsuit, the scam perpetrated by the Alaska pulp companies finally was national news.

Weaver's June 29 hearing was a one-man show. He grilled Forest Service Chief Max Peterson, Alaska Regional Forester John Sandor and members of the Forest Service review team for hours. Peterson vigorously objected to Weaver's assertion that the Forest Service had sat idly by while the pulp mills consolidated their monopoly control of the Tongass National Forest. He detailed the agency's efforts, dating from 1968, to get the Department of Justice and the Department of Agriculture's Office of Inspector General to investigate the pulp mills for possible illegal restraint of trade. But the chief did not explain why the Forest Service had failed to conduct its own thorough investigation of the pulp mills or pursue administrative remedies on its own.

Rep. Don Young of Alaska, a member of the subcommittee, was apoplectic that Weaver had conducted his investigation in secret and had notified him of the hearing only a few days in advance. And he was furious at Weaver for releasing internal Forest Service documents to the national news media. "This unauthorized release of information clearly places in jeopardy any objective review of the material by the Government," Young fumed.

The issue lay dormant following the hearing, but the release of the review team's report, and the national publicity Weaver's hearing generated, did not go to waste. Soon after, the Wilderness Society published its own report on the pulp companies' antitrust activities. "The Wilderness Society had the resources to publicize the work that we did to expose the mess on the Tongass," Johnson said. "The Wilderness Society helped keep the issue alive so the agencies could not go back to ignoring it."

The pulp companies' antitrust convictions would become a potent weapon in the Tongass reform campaign to come. Yet though the companies sustained political damage, neither was ever prosecuted for criminal or civil violations of federal antitrust laws.

To Dwyer, the government's failure to bring civil or criminal charges against the mills was a lasting disappointment. "Even in that setting, and with that administration, we thought the evidence and the findings were so compelling that something would happen to remedy the situation in Southeast Alaska," he said years later.

The Reids too were bitterly disappointed. In 1985 they wrote to James Michener, who was researching a book on Alaska, and urged him to include their story: "We naively thought we could be an instrument of change. We thought our lawsuit and subsequent investigations would cause the mills to behave in a more humane way. Our lawsuit was as a pinprick to an elephant. Nothing has changed. The U.S. Forest Service and the Justice Department are impotent because the experts the mills hire are more experienced than the government they face."

9

TIMBER MINING

I n 1980, Southeast Alaska's thirteen Native corporations began logging the prime timber conveyed to them from the Tongass National Forest under the Alaska Native Claims Settlement Act. An era of timber mining even more destructive than the logging on the Tongass commenced on Native corporation lands.

As state-chartered corporations, the fledgling enterprises were charged with paying dividends to their shareholders. About 15,500 Alaska Natives held shares in Sealaska Inc., the regional corporation. Of those, 8,950 deemed eligible on the day the law took effect also held shares in a village or urban corporation. Under ANCSA, Native corporation land was exempt from state and local property taxes for twenty years, and stock in Native corporations could not be sold for twenty years. After 1991, however, the land would be subject to taxation, and the stock would become freely transferable. This left a short window of time in which the corporations could convert their natural resource assets to cash and create a stable source of dividends for their shareholders.

A CASH CROP

In Southeast, Native corporations held title to an asset that was easily convertible to cash—an estimated eleven billion board feet of commercially valuable timber in standing old-growth forests transferred from the Tongass National Forest. Generating dividends would require them to liquidate this standing timber and invest the proceeds in more lucrative enterprises. The forest had provided sustenance to countless generations of Tlingit and Haida. It had taught them the natural order of things. It had informed their spiritual beliefs and inspired their traditional ceremonies. Now, according to the provisions of ANSCA, it must be leveled and exported to the highest bidder.

Village leaders in Angoon and Klukwan negotiated special deals that allowed them to select lands distant from their villages. They were able to live surrounded by intact forests while loggers labored far away to produce their dividend checks. But in Hoonah, Hydaburg and Kake, where Native corporations selected land close to their villages, the severing of ancestral bonds to the land would prove traumatic.

For the inexperienced directors of the new corporations, assembling the capital and other resources to begin logging was a huge undertaking. Before they could harvest, they had to borrow money, buy equipment, hire experienced timber managers, build roads, establish log dumps, and secure markets for their timber. Finding markets was the easy part; Japan, and later China and Korea, were willing to pay a premium for large unprocessed hemlock and spruce logs, and the Native corporations were not bound by federal rules that required at least minimal processing of federal timber in Southeast Alaska. They were free to export, and export they did.

ANCSA required that for twelve years after the bill's passage, lands selected by the Native corporations must be managed according to federal principles of sustained yield and environmental protection "no less stringent than such management practices on adjacent national forest lands." That language never was enforced. Native corporation lands were wide open for the worst sort of timber mining. The amount of land the corporations in Southeast owned—some 550,000 acres, of which 88 percent held commercial grade timber—was minuscule in comparison to the 16.7-million-acre Tongass National Forest. But it was the best of the best. And, unconstrained by state or federal regulations, the corporations proceeded to log it at breakneck

A felled Sitka spruce on Klukwan Corporation land, Long Island, where the largest trees in Southeast Alaska grew. Photo by Jack Gustafson.

speed. In 1980 they harvested 70 million board feet from 3,500 acres. By 1984 the harvest, spurred by a strong market for softwood logs, had nearly tripled to 202 million board feet, rivaling the 249 million board feet of timber cut from the Tongass that year.

Ironically, the logging did not generate many jobs for Alaska Natives. The corporations hired outsiders to run their timber operations, and many loggers were imported from Oregon and Washington. Nor did the logging produce jobs processing the timber; nearly all of it was exported as raw logs.

BEARING WITNESS

Don Cornelius went to work as a game biologist for the Alaska Department of Fish and Game in 1969. Because he was not an avid hunter, Cornelius didn't really fit into the culture of the agency. In the early 1980s he found his niche when he was transferred to the department's newly created habitat division, which among many other responsibilities was charged with reviewing logging along salmon streams. His transfer to Ketchikan coincided with the beginning of logging by the Native corporations. His territory included all of southern Southeast Alaska—Prince of Wales, Heceta, Long, Dall, Revillagigedo, Suemez and Tuxekan islands, as well as the mainland. It encompassed lands selected by seven Native corporations as well as entire watersheds within the Tongass National Forest that had been logged since the mid-1950s under the Forest Service's long-term contract with Ketchikan Pulp Co.

Cornelius spent nearly four years in Ketchikan, trying to keep up with the frantic pace of Native corporation logging on Prince of Wales and adjacent islands. One of his main jobs was to review the forest practice notifications landowners were required to file with the state before logging, then follow up with field checks of their logging practices on the ground. From the beginning it was a no-win situation. The corporations, eager to recoup their investments in equipment and personnel, held themselves to almost no environmental standards. Their logging roads triggered horrific landslides. Their loggers left few trees to buffer streams. Their clearcuts went on for miles. And Cornelius was nearly powerless to stop or even slow the destruction.

The only tool habitat biologists had to protect salmon in the early 1980s was a requirement that loggers cut trees along salmon streams so that they fell away from stream banks rather than into the streams. "The industry would send us a rough map, sometimes just a circle on a white sheet of paper," Cornelius said. "If there was a salmon stream we would always require an inspection." But the pace of logging was so rapid that biologists sometimes found themselves flagging salmon streams as trees fell all around them.

The Klawock River, which flows west to the Pacific Ocean from Klawock Lake on Prince of Wales Island, was particularly vulnerable. It supported some of the finest wild salmon runs in Southeast Alaska, runs that in good years totaled more than 500,000 red, pink, chum and silver salmon. However, the lake's natural temperature was warm for salmon, and even slight increases in water temperature threatened survival of the abundant runs. Nevertheless, between 1981 and 1985, two Native corporations clearcut more than fifteen thousand acres in the mountains above Klawock Lake, including shade trees along feeder streams that helped to keep the water cool.

By 1985, Sealaska clearcuts surrounding Big Salt, a long saltwater lagoon southeast of Klawock village, had laid bare more than nine hundred acres of steep-sloped drainages and ridge tops, creating a lunar landscape. That

Land along the shores of Klawock Lake, logged by Klawock Corporation in 1985. as it looked in 1996. Photo by Jack Gustafson.

year six major logging projects got underway on Prince of Wales Island, including several in the middle of drainages that supported important salmon runs.

The Department of Fish and Game kept a catalog of anadromous fish streams. "Biologists would go along shorelines, identify streams and mark the upper limits of where salmon were present," Cornelius said. When he first went to work for the habitat division, its policy was that if the mouth of a stream was catalogued, the entire stream was automatically protected. "Protected" was a misnomer, however. Loggers were not required to leave unlogged buffers along salmon streams. "If we were lucky," Cornelius said, "they would leave the unmerchantable trees."

Even this weak rule was vulnerable to political pressure, however, as Cornelius learned the hard way. One day in the early 1980s, he was out in the field near Craig, on Prince of Wales Island, when a forester for Sealaska suggested they take a look at a nearby logging operation. When they got there they discovered that Sealaska's logging contractor, Seley Corporation, had felled all the trees on both sides of a small creek with salmon in it. "The stream was under piles of logs and they were yarding timber across it while salmon were spawning," Cornelius said. "I went to the phone and called enforcement." Cornelius recommended that Sealaska be prosecuted for violations of state fish protection laws. Sealaska and the logging contractor eventually paid a $10,000 fine. But soon after this incident, a new interpretation of the stream protection rule came down from the director of the department's habitat division: henceforth, it would apply only to the sections of salmon streams actually marked and listed in the catalog. "Vast areas were uncatalogued," Cornelius said. "There was no legal protection for those stream stretches."

There was no clout at all for wildlife. Cornelius watched helplessly as irreplaceable habitat on Prince of Wales Island surrounding the communities of Klawock, Craig and Hydaburg fell to the chainsaw. Clearcuts on Native corporation land frequently exceeded 100 acres. Many exceeded 900 acres, or the equivalent of 1.4 square miles. Initially Cornelius did make comments on how logging projects might affect deer, bear, and other game. That stopped, he said, after Rick Harris, a vice president at Sealaska, complained to higher-ups in the division. Harris said that under the Alaska Forest Practices Act, biologists had no authority to comment about impacts to wildlife. Ultimately a compromise was reached that allowed biologists to write separate letters to the corporations. "We were so overloaded that writing one more letter to people like Harris, who wouldn't pay any attention anyway, was more than we could handle," Cornelius said. "The shareholders who needed to see them never would, so the wildlife comments stopped."

CUMULATIVE EFFECTS

In 1984, Cornelius was transferred to Petersburg, where his turf included the holdings of Kake's Native corporation, on Kupreanof Island, and Juneau's Goldbelt Corporation, on the mainland at Hobart Bay. Jack Gustafson, who had first been employed by Alaska Fish and Game in 1970, and who had lived and worked throughout Alaska, took his place in Ketchikan. He left his bags packed the first week. "It didn't take me long to figure out that things were different here," he said.

What shocked Gustafson was the cumulative impact of a quarter-century of intensive logging on both public and private lands in southern Southeast Alaska. "The extensiveness of it was a real jolt—the loss of wildlife habitat and of the commercially important forest lands, the cutting from one property line or drainage to the next," he said. Although by the mid-1980s the Forest Service generally limited the size of its clearcuts to 100 acres, it permitted adjacent units to be logged as soon as clearcuts "greened up" with naturally regenerated seedlings, causing cumulative loss of wildlife habitat in some watersheds that was comparable to the loss on Native corporation land.

In fact, Gustafson found some of the early logging on the Tongass more egregious, because drainages were cut with so little regard for the impact on salmon. Damage to the Harris River watershed near Hollis, one of the first watersheds logged under Ketchikan Pulp's long-term contract, was so extreme that the state closed the river to commercial fishing for decades.

In 1985, Gustafson agreed to talk to Hal Bernton, a reporter for the *Anchorage Daily News,* about the impact of Native corporation logging. "There is a lot of habitat degradation going on," he told Bernton. He said he spent most of his time trying to ensure that debris from logging operations did not block salmon passage. "We're just trying to work with the Native corporations to minimize things as much as we can." But the pace of logging was overwhelming, and sometimes units were clearcut before state fish and game biologists could get out to see them. Gustafson said that when he showed up to inspect one Kootznoowoo Inc. logging operation, the stream he had come to inspect was already buried under ten feet of toppled trees.

Bernton's series on Native corporation logging, published in August of 1985, painted a devastating picture. Two years later, Gustafson talked to Bernton again, telling him that Native corporation logging was causing "rather widespread damage to fish and wildlife habitat in this part of Alaska. " This time, repercussions were not long in coming. Robert Loescher, a politically influential Sealaska Corporation executive, contacted Bruce Baker, director of the department's habitat division, who wrote a memo to his bosses stressing "the need for us to be diligent yet at the same time politically astute in our conduct regarding private timber harvests." Bernton got hold of Baker's memo and published it too. Gustafson soon found himself on more than one political hit list.

Don Cornelius found himself on the same lists. But the two embattled biologists won allies among commercial fishermen. Gustafson had taken hundreds of photographs documenting damage to streams and watersheds and had put together a slide show, which he showed to fishing organizations on request. "Jack was a real pusher, a politically astute biologist," Cornelius said. "He had photographs of all these horror stories." At meetings between Native corporation officials and state regulators, Gustafson's photographs had a way of silencing dissent.

PREVENTABLE LANDSLIDES

In Cornelius's new territory, the effects of logging varied by area. The country around Kake, in the northwest corner of Kupreanof Island, was rolling terrain with few steep slopes except in the deep notches carved by salmon streams. Loggers initially left more trees in these notches, but many of them later blew down in fierce windstorms. However, Hobart Bay, on the mainland, was quite steep, consisting of glacially formed valleys and unstable soils. At Hobart Bay, after one rainstorm, Cornelius went out to inspect a Goldbelt Corporation logging show and found eighteen landslides on land recently logged by the Juneau-based Native corporation. On another occasion, he went out with a state forest practices forester, Jim McAllister. to inspect a logging operation at Salt Chuck Creek, a coho salmon stream at Hobart Bay. After getting a look at the steep, unstable mountainside where the logging road was to be built, Cornelius suggested, "Maybe you ought to just get down off this slope." As he recalls, McAllister just laughed. Loggers proceeded to push the road across the slope and hit a sandbank. The sand washed into the creek. "They tried to keep me from seeing it, even refusing to stop at the site," Cornelius said. "It was a constant source of sedimentation. They never did stabilize it. That quarter-mile road ended up costing $250,000, paid for by the Forest Service no less."

Yet another time, in a test of the Alaska Forest Practices Act, Cornelius joined forces with the state's departments of Environmental Conservation and Natural Resources to try to stop a road across an extremely steep hillside directly above a branch of the West Fork of the Chuck River, one of the top salmon streams in Southeast Alaska. "We all agreed it was going to slide," he said. After considerable posturing between the agencies and Goldbelt Corporation, the state agencies agreed to ask a Forest Service research scientist, Doug Swanston, to look at the road and abide by his findings. "Swanston wrote a report saying if they did full bench construction, no sidecasting, and took all these heroic steps, it would minimize the chance of a slide," Cornelius said. "We were obligated to follow his recommendation. Then it did slide, twice."

CHALLENGING SHEE-ATIKA

In 1980, with the inclusion of special language in the Alaska Lands Act, Shee-Atika Inc., Sitka's Native corporation, won its fight to select lands on Admiralty Island But the Sierra Club and the village of Angoon managed to stave off the logging for several years. They went to court to challenge Shee-Atika's plan to construct a log dump in Cube Cove, home to some of the richest crab beds in Southeast Alaska. The lawsuit was finally dropped after some members of Congress accused the Sierra Club of trying to drive the corporation into bankruptcy with its legal maneuvers.

Sierra Club lawyers also worked through a federal mediator, and at one point even asked the Trust for Public Land to purchase an easement covering Shee-Atika's 23,000-acre land selection, which covered a six-mile stretch of Admiralty Island's west coast and extended up three major river drainages. The logging of Shee-Atika's land on Admiralty began in 1986. By then, however, the corporation was near bankruptcy, and looking for a way to stem its losses.

"THE LAND ITSELF IS AT RISK"

Alarm over how the Alaska Native Claims Settlement Act was affecting traditional ways of life in Native villages first surfaced in the Arctic. In 1983, the Inuit Circumpolar Conference, an international organization of Eskimos from Alaska, Canada, and Greenland, appointed Thomas Berger, a retired British Columbia Supreme Court judge, to review ANCSA's effects on Alaska Natives. Between 1983 and 1985 Berger visited sixty Indian, Eskimo and Aleut villages in Alaska. He listened—simply listened—to the people. He compiled his findings in a 1985 book, *Village Journey: the Report of the Alaska Native Review Commission.* Berger's book documented a cultural tragedy of historic dimensions unfolding.

"For most village corporations, the story is a sad one," he wrote. "Undercapitalized, without corporate experience, with virtually no business prospects, the corporations were at the mercy of the lawyers, advisers, and consultants who flocked to the villages like scavengers. Now the money is largely gone, and the land itself is at risk."

In Berger's view, ANCSA was the nation's "domestic application of economic development theories previously only applied to the Third World." He concluded that the law's drafters had fully expected the Native way of life to disappear. To prevent that, he recommended the "retribalization" of Native lands under tribal governments that would restore traditional uses. He also proposed changes in the law to assure that the lands conveyed to Alaska Natives would remain in Native ownership forever. In 1987 Congress did amend the law to extend the ban on transfer of stock past 1991.

At meetings in Southeast Alaska, Native speakers told Berger they feared ANCSA had cost them their freedom to hunt, fish and gather plants in traditional and customary places. "We surrendered our aboriginal rights of hunting and fishing in 1971," Lonnie Strong Hotch testified at Klukwan. "Now we depend on state and federal laws. These have brought restrictions. I'm worried that we won't be able to fish in our river here. Soon they'll say, 'The Natives don't need fish.'" In Sitka, Nelson Frank explained the deep meaning of "subsistence" to Native people. "The relationship between the Native population and the resources of the land and the sea is so close that an entire culture is reflected," he said.

In Craig, Antoinnette Helmer attempted to describe how concepts of wealth differed in Native and non-Native cultures: "Profit to non-Natives means money. Profit to Natives means a good life derived from the land

and sea, that's what we are all about, that's what this land claims was all about. Living off the land and sea is not only traditional, but owing to the scarcity of cash income, it is required for our families to survive . . . The land we hold in trust is our wealth. It is the only wealth we could possibly pass on to our children. Good old Mother Earth with all her bounty and rich culture we have developed from her treasures is our wealth. Without our homelands, we become true paupers."

These poignant words hinted at the reality of the transformation that ANCSA had brought. For many Alaska Natives, it was a form of cultural genocide, inflicted ironically by their own hand.

WINNING BY LOSING

Most Native corporations had borrowed heavily for equipment and personnel to get into the logging business, using their land as collateral. In 1984, just as logging on Native corporation lands reached a crescendo, the bottom fell out of the softwood timber market. Suddenly there was a timber glut. A timber industry depression followed, the worst since the 1930s. Mills closed up and down the West Coast. Timber purchasers sought release from their contracts to buy public timber. But even as the depression deepened, most Southeast Native corporations stepped up their rate of cutting in a frantic effort to pay off their debts.

By 1985 most Native corporations were buried in debt. That year Hydaburg-based Haida Corp. filed for protection from its creditors after it failed to log its lands fast enough to meet payments on $4.3 million in loans. Goldbelt of Juneau canceled a timber sale after it calculated that it couldn't get enough money for timber it had already cut to pay off its debts, including two loans totaling $11.5 million from the Federal Land Bank of Spokane. Shee-Atika, which had fought so hard to hold on to its land selections on Admiralty, offered to trade its lands or to refrain from logging in return for $3.1 million in cash from Congress. But in the depressed market of the mid-1980s, there were no takers.

Sealaska Chief Executive Officer Byron Mallott questioned the strategy of stepping up logging at a time when the timber market had hit rock-bottom. "We have to ask ourselves, Does it make sense to cut down every bloody stick of timber in order to retire debt?" he said. Mallot expressed the hope that bankers would renegotiate loans, and that Congress would help bail out the village corporations.

In 1986, U.S. Sen. Ted Stevens of Alaska stepped up to the plate. During the early 1980s, the Internal Revenue Service had allowed money-losing corporations to sell their net operating losses to profitable corporations looking for tax write-offs. Congress moved to close that loophole in the massive 1986 Tax Reform Act. But in a House-Senate conference committee, Stevens inserted language allowing Alaska Native corporations, and only Alaska Native corporations, to sell their net operating losses to profitable companies and pocket some of the tax savings.

Stevens defended the sweetheart deal as "a social justice concept, not a tax justice concept"—an infusion of capital that "would allow many Native corporations to put their houses in order." He pointed out that because Native corporations were prohibited by ANCSA from selling stock before 1992, they had no other way to raise cash to offset their operating losses.

Overnight, the Native corporations of Southeast Alaska had something of value to sell. Their unprofitable logging operations had become a prized commodity. "In essence, it's a new ANCSA," Richard Rosston, an Anchorage attorney who helped to negotiate many of the tax loss deals, told the *Anchorage Daily News* "The first ANCSA was designed to give them a start in life. This is designed to give them a second chance."

The tax break allowed a money-losing Native corporation to buy a small amount of equity in a profitable corporation, thereby permitting the profitable enterprise to deduct the Native corporation's net losses from its own year-end profits. A percentage of the tax savings the deal earned for the profitable corporation might then be turned back to the money-losing Native corporation. Stevens estimated that the loophole would cost the federal treasury no more than $50 million—an estimate that proved far off the mark.

Dozens of large corporations in the Lower 48, including General Motors and Marriott, moved quickly to take advantage of the tax break. Anchorage accountants and tax attorneys rushed to put together deals in the weeks before lower corporate income tax rates set by the 1986 Tax Reform Act went into effect. The Net Operating Losses loophole was rife with opportunities for abuse, and lawyers and accountants soon found them. In Southeast Alaska, for instance, a number of corporations totted up not only their actual losses—those resulting, for instance, from failed investments in logging equipment—but also "soft losses," paper losses that resulted when they sold their timber during the mid-1980s timber depression for far less than it had been appraised for at the time it was acquired.

Some Native corporations devalued their timber, sold it at a loss to partially owned subsidiaries created for that purpose, sold their resulting tax losses to profitable corporations, then reaped windfall profits when their subsidiaries cut the undervalued timber. One Ketchikan accountant calculated the difference between initial timber appraisals and actual sale prices for Native corporation timber at more than $1 billion. Sealaska used its calculation of its "soft losses" to sell $60 million in net operating losses to a New York investment firm and pocket more than $20 million in cash.

The IRS took particular notice of the activities of Shee-Atika Inc. According to an account in the *Anchorage Daily News*, the IRS found in an exhaustive audit that the Sitka-based corporation had sold its timber on Admiralty Island at a bargain-basement price to Atikon, a joint venture company in which it held a 49 percent interest. Shee-Atika had then claimed a huge loss on the sale, and sold that net operating loss to Quaker Oats Co. Corporate documents claimed that in selling its timber to Atikon in 1987 for just $10 million, Shee-Atika had lost more than $155 million. Yet ten months before the sale, Shee-Atika executive Roger Snippen had valued the timber at $70 million—and timber markets had improved in the interim. The IRS initially challenged many such sales, but ended up settling most of the challenges for a tiny fraction of their value.

By effectively rewarding the Native corporations for losing money on their timber operations, the Net Operating Losses loophole spurred accelerated logging on corporate lands. In 1989, Native corporations in Southeast Alaska cut 613 million board feet of timber, far outpacing the 445 million board feet cut from the Tongass National Forest that year. According to the University of Alaska's Institute for Social and Economic Research, by 1990, when Congress finally closed the tax loophole, documented timber-based net operating losses by Alaska Native corporation had cost the U.S. Treasury more than $716 million.

The Net Operating Losses loophole bailed out many Native corporations in Southeast Alaska, saving them from bankruptcy and allowing them to pay dividends to their shareholders for the first time. But no annual dividend check could ever make up for what had been lost.

RETHINKING ANCSA

By 1990, only Sealaska, which had reduced its rate of logging during the timber recession, still had plenty of uncut timber. The end of logging was now in sight for the village corporations. As Forest Service research economist Gunnar Knapp wrote in a 1992 report: "No village corporation has attempted to follow a sustained yield approach in its timber harvesting. Most village corporations will have harvested all their merchantable timber within twenty years from when they began harvest, about one-eighth the time needed to produce marketable volumes of timber on second-growth stands in southeast Alaska." But from an economic view, Knapp added, the accelerated rate of logging made economic sense: "Individual village corporations had to cut timber at a much faster rate than is possible under sustained yield management to harvest enough volume to cover the high fixed costs of timber harvesting."

Nonetheless, Alaska's political leaders knew something had to be done to correct the flaws in ANCSA. In 1990, President George Bush and Alaska Governor Wally Hickel set up a federal-state commission to study the role of tribal governments in Alaska. The commission recommended a renewed and enlarged role for Alaska tribal governments in management of the ANCSA lands.

It would take more than recommendations from government commissions to resolve the fundamental contradictions set in motion by ANCSA, however. Years of legal and legislative battles would follow as state, federal and Native interests debated the meaning of "subsistence," the concept of "Indian country," and the relationship between Native corporations and traditional tribal governments in Alaska.

10

UNION BUSTING

The pulp mills were supposed to provide steady, family-wage jobs in Southeast Alaska. In the early years, they did that and more. Loggers and millworkers from the Pacific Northwest and elsewhere headed to the Alaska Panhandle, attracted by promises of good pay and fantasies of unlimited fishing and hunting opportunities. Gil Smith started work at the Ketchikan Pulp Co. mill in 1964. He said the early years were happy years. "From 1964 to 1976 it was as good a place to work as any you'd find." Like many KPC workers, he fell in love with Southeast Alaska, and put down roots in Ketchikan. "I had no urge to live anywhere else," he said.

But Smith and other longtime employees said things started to go sour in 1976, when Portland-based Louisiana-Pacific Corporation became the sole owner of Ketchikan Pulp Co. "From that time on, the company was run from Portland," Smith said. "When the final say is a thousand miles away, it doesn't work."

Over more than forty years at the mill, Charlie Stout held a variety of jobs—in the finishing room, the digester lineup, the machine shop. He witnessed disturbing changes in management. Like Smith, he blamed Harry Merlo, the Georgia-Pacific executive who became the president and chief executive officer of Louisiana-Pacific in 1976, and who was to run the company for two decades with an iron hand. "Harry Merlo had a different philosophy," Stout said. "It was slash and burn."

John Wolon's uncle got him a job at the Ketchikan mill right out of high school in 1976. Wolon got active in the Association of Western Pulp and Paper Workers local and later became a union trustee. He recalls his uncle telling him that until L-P took over, "it was a real different place, like a family."

MAINTENANCE BY CRISIS

One of the first things to suffer under L-P sole ownership was maintenance. Until 1977, the Ketchikan pulp mill had been run on a strict maintenance schedule. But Merlo's strategy was to cut maintenance costs to the bone. Mill managers were ordered to stop doing regular twice-a-year maintenance shutdowns. The corrosive acids used in the production of dissolving pulp are hard on pipes and machinery, but L-P chose not to replace worn-out equipment—a decision that would have serious effects on worker health in future years. "When Harry Merlo was getting $1,500 a ton for pulp, he wasn't investing in the mill," Smith said. "The profits were being drained out of that mill."

Production jumped immediately after L-P consolidated control. "We broke all production records in 1977," Stout recalled. "Up until then you never went over a certain speed. You ran only eight of the nine digesters at a time. One was down for maintenance at all times. When L-P took over, it was 'Run it till it blows.' They'd stick a rag in the hole in the magnesium oxide slurry line and seal it with tape. It fell apart, and then you'd have to replace the iron pipe. We went from scheduled maintenance to what we affectionately called maintenance by crisis."

KPC pulp mill and sawmill complex at Ward Cove, March 1997. Photo by Kathie Durbin.

In 1984 Merlo eliminated the mill's painting crew. "Southeast Alaska is tough on steel," Stout said. "It used to be the painting crew started at one end of the mill and painted everything until it got to the other end." But that routine maintenance work came to an end. "Things didn't get sandblasted when they should have," he said. That hastened the end of the mill's lifespan.

In Sitka too, the early years were good years for most pulp mill workers. Pay and benefits were generous. As in Ketchikan, workers even enjoyed the use of company-paid rental cars on their paid vacations. Japanese mill managers cultivated an amicable relationship with labor unions, the town of Sitka and the Shee-Atika Native corporation. But all of that changed in 1983, when office workers arrived one morning to find the mill manager in tears. The Japanese supervisors, accused of indulging the unions and failing to control labor and production costs, had been fired and summoned home to Tokyo. George Ishiyama, an American recruited by the major shareholders and banks that controlled Alaska Pulp Corporation, had taken charge. To cut operating costs, Ishiyama reduced the ranks of pulp mill management and then, declaring that mill wages in Sitka were 25 percent higher than comparable wages worldwide, he went after labor costs, seeking and getting wage concessions from the United Paperworkers International local.

BREAKING THE UNIONS

When the world pulp market went into a downward spiral in 1984, Louisiana-Pacific announced that it was considering closing the Ketchikan mill. At the time the 384 members of the Association of Western Pulp and Paper Workers local in Ketchikan local were negotiating with L-P on a new contract. Strike talk was in the air. But when the rumors of a possible mill closure began circulating, union leaders shelved their strike plan and began a different line of negotiations with L-P: The company would lay everyone off, allowing workers to draw unemployment benefits. And the union would attempt a worker buyout of the mill. "We worked out a wage and benefit reduction agreement with L-P," recalled Paul Lamm, who helped negotiate the deal for the pulp workers' union. "In exchange, over a period of several years, ownership would pass from L-P to the workers. All the unions agreed to this. The Forest Service was going to give the workers a reduction in stumpage rates."

But once it appeared that the worker buyout might actually fly, Harry Merlo pulled the plug. In June of 1984 Merlo announced that L-P was terminating negotiations to sell 56 percent of its interest to workers. Instead, he said, the company would work "to improve the competitiveness of these facilities under sole L-P ownership." Then he closed the mill for three months for repairs. Workers called it a lockout. The union never recovered, and from that day forward workers at Ketchikan Pulp worked without a contract.

When they returned after the six-month shutdown, they found Merlo had slashed pay and benefits. AWPPW went to court to terminate its pension plan and allow its members to cash in their pension benefits, since there was no longer a contract to enforce terms of the plan. But KPC fought termination of the pension plan. When an arbitrator ruled for the union, the company appealed to a federal court, which ruled in its favor. "They held it over our heads," Lamm said. "They wanted full control."

After the lock-out, things just got worse. Returning workers discovered that wages for journeyman mechanics had been slashed from $19.50 to $12 an hour, effective immediately. Insurance benefits had been reduced. The union safety committee had been disbanded. The profit-sharing plan the company instituted didn't make up for the lost wages, and workers said profits were not distributed fairly. "We lost 70 percent of our fringe benefits, our rental car benefits, our plane fare benefits," Charlie Stout said.

Workers in Ketchikan were not the only ones struggling under Merlo's regime. In 1983, Merlo broke ranks with other large timber companies and refused to settle with one of L-P's major unions, International Woodworkers of America. The following year, as the worldwide timber depression deepened, the National Labor Relations Board gave L-P the go-ahead to hold union decertification elections at eleven L-P mills and log yards. Breaking the unions was an integral part of Merlo's cost-cutting campaign, as he freely acknowledged. In a June 1984 interview with the *Seattle Post-Intelligencer,* Merlo complained that he was forced to pay workers at L-P's union mills $11 to $16 an hour plus benefits, while workers at L-P's non-union plants in the Great Lakes region got $6.50 an hour.

Ketchikan workers were hit harder than most by Merlo's cutthroat labor relations strategy, because the town was one of the West's most expensive places to live. As KPC workers matched up their shrunken paychecks against the high cost of rent and grocery bills, the grim reality of their situation hit home.

Paul Lamm returned to KPC in 1984 after taking three years off to work in construction. He found things had changed drastically. To get a week's paid vacation, he now had to work a full year. Two weeks' vacation didn't come for five years. Still, he chose to stay on as a pipefitter-welder, he said, because working at the pulp mill "was still the best full-time employment in Ketchikan."

But many of the new workers hired by KPC after the strike didn't stick around long. And those who did stay didn't feel the same connection to organized labor as the old-timers. "After 1984 the attitude was 'Work as directed or get the hell out,' " Charlie Stout said. "When they hired journeymen mechanics for $12 an hour, they got $12-an-hour mechanics. The younger generation said, 'Why should I join a union? What have unions done for me?' "

STRIKE IN SITKA

In 1986, four hundred members of the United Paperworkers International local struck Alaska Pulp Co.'s Sitka mill. The strike was bitter and divisive. APC waited only ten days to hire permanent replacement workers, then launched a campaign to break the union. When the strike finally ended ten months later with the decertification of the union, striking workers were called back only to entry-level jobs. The strike changed the way Sitka viewed the company.

Florian Sever, a millwright and union organizer at the Sitka mill, was incensed at the treatment he and his fellow workers had received at the hands of Alaska Pulp's new management team. APC had persuaded his union to accept wage and benefit rollbacks during the crash in pulp markets so it could stay competitive. But the company had then reneged on a promise to compensate workers for their sacrifice when business improved. He decided Congress ought to know. In 1987, he testified at a congressional hearing on reform of the Tongass timber sale program. His message was that Alaska Pulp had broken faith with its workers, as well as with the U.S. government, and was no longer entitled to special favors or multi-million-dollar subsidies. Sever's testimony would cost him his job, his financial security and his peace of mind.

A TOUGH MARKET

The Alaska pulp mills had reason to seek wage concessions. Their competitive position in the global market had never been strong. It had weakened further in the mid-1970s, with the opening of the huge South African Sappi Saiccor Ltd. Mill, which used fast-growing plantation pine and had access to cheap labor and transportation. Sappi Saiccor could produce the same kind of dissolving pulp the Sitka and Ketchikan mills produced for 20 percent less.

Even the generous subsidies Congress provided were not enough to keep the Alaska pulp industry robust as market conditions continued to deteriorate in the 1980s. The demand for dissolving pulp lessened as nylon, polyester, and other petroleum-based products began to replace rayon as fabrics favored by consumers. The expense of transporting logs hundreds of miles by water from forest to factory boosted the mills' raw material costs and further eroded their ability to compete.

To improve its position, APC asked for and got local government tax breaks—though the mill had never shown a paper profit, never paid a dime of income tax, and never paid a tax on its sale of logs. The city of Sitka agreed to cut the mill's property tax assessment by 40 percent.

FADED DREAMS

By 1987 the number of timber-related jobs in Southeast Alaska had dwindled from 2,700 to 1,800, in part because of the downturn in the pulp market, in part because several small mills had closed. By then, for many workers, the dream of an idyllic life in Southeast had faded. Workers drawn north by the opportunity to fish, hunt and camp in the wilderness found they could not afford to enjoy their wild surroundings. The Forest Service spent lavishly to prepare timber sales; it spent almost nothing on trails, campgrounds and canoe routes. Until 1990, Prince of Wales Island did not have a single developed campground. And few workers could afford to travel by float plane to the remote camping cabins the Forest Service maintained for tourists.

Many workers became disenchanted over the mills' disregard for environmental compliance and their cynical attitude toward the regulatory agencies, the Alaska Department of Environmental Conservation and the U.S. Environmental Protection Agency. "DEC and EPA would levy fines and KPC would pay them," Charlie Stout said. "It was extortion, is what it was. It was, 'This is your protection money.'"

Paul Lamm blames the regulators as much as the companies. "The agencies encouraged it. You paid the fine and no problem. KPC just paid them and kept on polluting."

The most visible pollution was in Ward Cove. For many years, the cove ran red with the lignin or "red liquor" produced during the process of cooking wood chips. "The mill used to dump the stuff directly into the cove," said Gil Smith. "We used to take our boats out in Ward Cove and the wake of our boats was red with this red liquor." Still, most millworkers regarded the despoiling of Ward Cove as an acceptable tradeoff for family-wage jobs. "You have to balance the need for an industry against two square miles," Smith said.

When it came to their own health and safety, however, millworkers were less sanguine. Before 1984, Lamm said, Ketchikan Pulp's safety record never ranked below fourth or fifth among the forty-five pulp mills in the Pacific Northwest. But from the mid-1980s until the mill closed in 1997, it consistently ranked forty-fourth or forty-fifth—in the cellar. Sulfuric acid leaks inside the mill, a chronic problem, regularly sent workers to the hospital. On the job, workers constantly chewed Tums and Mylanta. "If you worked around the acid digester you would be exposed," said Gil Smith. "You would get it into your mouth and nose and you would swallow it. It would give you indigestion." Occasionally the leaks escaped the mill and wafted downwind. Neighbors complained of being gassed in their own homes. Some ended up in the hospital emergency room.

The cause of the chronic leaks became public only in the mid-1990s, after an investigation ordered by the federal Occupational Safety and Health Administration found that titanium pipes in the mill had corroded over decades of reacting with hydrogen sulfide gas, a product of the breakdown of sulfur dioxide inside the pipes. When the temperature changed suddenly, the hydrogen sulfide gas expanded rapidly, creating small explosions inside the pipes.

Asbestos exposure was another continuing problem. Ketchikan Pulp Co. was cited repeatedly by OSHA for exposing its workers to asbestos. In a 1988 settlement, OSHA ordered the company to label all asbestos-containing material and to either encapsulate or remove all friable asbestos at the mill within four years. But according to an OSHA report, though the company made an effort to comply, many of the labels fell off.

The 1988 settlement also specified that only KPC employees who were state-certified in asbestos abatement would be allowed to handle asbestos-containing materials.

The extent to which KPC had ignored the OSHA order became apparent five years later. In September of 1993, Bruce Romine and his supervisor, Russ Davis, were working on one of the mill's power boilers at the mill during a maintenance shutdown. When they came out of the powerhouse they noticed that their coveralls were covered with asbestos. "There were chunks of the original asbestos lying all around," Romine said. One of his supervisors "took a power hose and blew it all over the place. The area was totally contaminated." That night Jim Eakes, the mill's hazardous materials supervisor, tried to get pipefitters to go into the powerhouse and clean up the mess. They refused. "Eakes tried to get Davis to persuade the workers that it was safe," Romine recalled. He told OSHA investigators that when workers complained to KPC's asbestos coordinator about the inadequacy of the asbestos cleanup effort, they were told, "You guys are all expendable anyway."

In 1994, the Alaska Department of Labor fined Ketchikan Pulp $49,000 for two "willful" violations of Alaska's occupational health and safety standards regarding exposure to asbestos. The state noted that it had cited KPC for asbestos violations numerous times over a ten-year period. Alaska Assistant Attorney General Robert Royce prosecuted the case. Testimony at a hearing revealed that at one point 187 bags of asbestos had been left outside on the ground at the KPC mill, exposing at least 180 workers.

Carelessness caused accidents at both mills. Charlie Stout remembers one incident at the Ketchikan mill: "They put raw acid into the chips and it immediately exploded and sent seven people to the hospital." In September of 1989, a worker operating the bander-strapper machine at KPC's new Ward Cove sawmill was crushed to death when a gate crashed down on him while he checked a bundle of timber. A state inspector said the mill had no operative sounding device to warn workers when the gate was about to fall. Alaska Pulp's safety record was blemished that year as well, when a twenty-eight-year-old husband and father of two in Sitka was crushed to death by a giant pulp roller as he tried to change a roll of finished pulp.

THE LOGGER'S LIFE

Loggers were a different breed. The isolated life of the Alaska logging camps appealed to many families and single men. There were two kinds of logging camps in Southeast Alaska. At semi-permanent communities like Alaska Pulp's Rowan Bay camp on Kuiu Island, families could live out the dream of a frontier lifestyle that had once been commonplace in the Pacific Northwest. In more remote areas were the all-male floating camps, where men lived and worked most of the year, moving from inlet to inlet as units became available for cutting, and sending their wages home to families they barely knew.

In 1989, Mark and Kathy McCann and their two children were living in a shabby but cozy mobile home on blocks at the muddy Rowan Bay camp. Mark McCann worked six days a week cutting timber for Alaska Pulp. Kathy had a part-time job as a teacher's aide at the camp's twenty-three-student school next door. They had moved to Alaska from the logging town of Forks, Washington, where Mark McCann cut big Douglas-firs for ITT-Rayonier. Forks was getting too big for them, Kathy McCann said. "Down south there's so much exposure to drugs. The school system here is so much better."

Southeast Alaska suited them. On weekends they fished for halibut, went clamming or took their Great Pyrenees, Bogart, out to roll in the muskeg. They put up a hundred pints of halibut each summer. Their groceries arrived twice a month by floatplane from Petersburg, except when fog or rain kept the plane grounded. The McCanns weren't particularly political, but they didn't appreciate attacks on their livelihood. "If you're a cutter, you're an outdoorsman," Mark McCann said. "I'm more of an ecologist than these guys hammering spikes into trees."

"KEGGING UP"

Ron Phillips relished life in the all-male floating camps. Six days a week, nine hours a day, from February to November, he cut trees from the slopes surrounding whatever inlet the Silver Bay Logging Co. camp happened to be anchored in at the time. A lean, hard-muscled man, he liked the camaraderie of being part of a tight-knit crew "kegging up" in a place so remote from the outside world. He grew to love the cold, the rain, the

Logger Ron Phillips has a family in Oregon but spends most of each year at remote floating logging camps in Southeast Alaska. Photo by Kathie Durbin.

wind, the snow. "When the wind blows, it keeps my adrenaline up," he said after a long wet day in the woods at Appleton Cove in 1996.

Phillips' father got him his first job in the Alaska woods in 1971, the year he graduated from high school in Myrtle Point, Oregon. He eventually married, had a family, and sent most of his $4,000-a-month paycheck back to Myrtle Point to support his wife and six kids. But he saw them only a couple of times a year and over the winter shutdown.

In the floating camps, life was stripped down to its essentials: eat, sleep, work. In the camps, Phillips left the tumult of the outside world behind. The long winter nights invited reflection. In time, he gave up hunting and fishing. "Why take something if you don't need it?" he said. "Why molest the fish?" He had taken a two-year break from logging, he said, "because I didn't believe in clear-cutting and tearing up the land." But he had also seen the Alaska land green up after logging. "In two years it's a green carpet. All the spruce and hemlock are coming up as thick as grass."

At the age of forty-two, Phillips considered himself something of an anachronism. He had spent twenty-six years logging, most of that in the Alaska woods. He had no illusions about the future. Neither did he have any intention of quitting. "It's a dying trade. But it's what my grandfather and my father did."

11

CONFRONTING THE BEAST

The Alaska Lands Act handed the Tongass National Forest a bloated budget and an inflated, legislated timber sale target at a time when serious environmental concerns were beginning to surface over the long-term impact of clearcutting the Alaska rainforest.

Research by John Schoen, Charlie Wallmo and other biologists had clearly documented the close association between Sitka black-tailed deer and intact old-growth forests. Yet from the beginning of the long-term contracts in the 1950s, the Forest Service had concentrated its timber offerings in the most productive low-elevation stands on the Tongass. Those stands, where the timber volume exceeded 30,000 board feet per acre, accounted for only 13 percent of the commercial forest land on the Tongass. Yet a 1983 Forest Service report revealed that nearly all of these high-volume stands outside protected wilderness had been liquidated in less than thirty years. In contrast, half the available medium-volume stands (those containing twenty to thirty thousand board feet per acre) had been logged, and only a quarter of low-volume stands (those containing less than twenty thousand board feet of timber per acre) had been harvested. This "high-grading" of the rainforest carried potentially severe consequences for wildlife in Southeast Alaska.

The Forest Service's own 1979 Tongass Land Management Plan had recognized the problem of high-grading, and had addressed it by setting a schedule for harvesting more marginal, so-called "uneconomic" timber. Much of this marginal timber grew at higher elevations. It cost the agency more money to lay out timber sales and build roads in the high country. Often it cost more than the timber was worth. Some members of Congress held that subsidizing this marginal logging was the main purpose of the Tongass Timber Supply Fund. Rep. Morris Udall, chairman of the House Interior Committee, declared on the floor of the House in 1980 that the subsidy was intended to "encourage retention of old growth" and "maximize protection for environmentally sensitive areas."

Clearcuts on a steep slope near Red Bay, North Prince of Wales Island. Photo by Trygve Steen.

But that argument didn't carry much weight with the Forest Service. In 1981, Tongass managers began a frenzied campaign to meet their ten-year timber target of 4.5 billion board feet, which they regarded as a fixed and unalterable congressional mandate. All else took a back seat to putting up their annual quota of 450 million board feet. Old-growth retention was not a priority. In fact, Alaska Regional Forester John Sandor approved a new rule during this period that encouraged removal of the most valuable trees by allowing loggers to leave more low-volume timber in the woods.

With an open-ended subsidy from the federal treasury, the agency spent $123 million between 1981 and 1986 to build 303 miles of logging road, 21 bridges and 13 log transfer stations, in the process sullying countless salmon streams and violating its own wildlife habitat guidelines. Many of these roads penetrated pristine watersheds; between 1979 and 1984, the Forest Service built roads through 94 of the 351 unroaded watersheds earmarked for timber harvest under its 1979 plan. During this same period, contractors for the pulp companies built an additional 456 miles of logging roads. A report later commissioned by Congress concluded: "By building roads through 27 percent of the available roadless areas within five years, at a time when many of the timber sales were not necessary to meet demand . . . the Forest Service policy was both a waste of taxpayer money and an insult to responsible resource management."

Salmon were now paying the price for the poor road-building practices of thirty years. Log culverts build under logging roads were rotting, and organic fill dumped on top of the culverts was collapsing, blocking small rearing streams used by migrating salmon. Logging roads were failing and spilling soil into spawning streams. On Prince of Wales Island, the expanding road system invited the overhunting and poaching of deer and the overharvest of wolves by trappers.

In 1984, a nationwide timber recession took hold, and many Tongass timber sales drew no bids at auction. Yet still the road-building continued under the Forest Service's "pre-roading" program. A number of these expensive and environmentally damaging logging roads became roads to nowhere.

FIELD REPORTS

Jim Stratton saw that the Southeast Alaska Conservation Council must inform the public about the voracious timber machine the Tongass timber provisions of the Alaska Lands Act had unleashed. He had no money for a public education campaign. Fortuitously, some conservationists had foreseen the need for ongoing support of Alaska wilderness even before the act's passage. In 1979 Celia Hunter, founder of the Alaska Conservation Society, and Denny Wilcher, founder of Sierra Club Books, had established the Alaska Conservation Foundation to raise money and award grants to Alaska environmental groups.

Stratton got a grant from the foundation and hired Joseph Cone, a writer for Oregon State University's Sea Grant program, to document the carnage on the Tongass. "We wanted to define the problem for people, and we wanted to define it in the words of Forest Service employees," Stratton said. He dispatched Cone to interview Forest Service workers in the field.

Working on contract for SEACC, Cone traveled the length of the Tongass asking Forest Service field specialists how the timber target was affecting their ability to protect fish, wildlife and other resources. Most of those he interviewed said the pace of logging was unsustainable. A few let him use their names.

"We're cutting the best timber and having a harder and harder time meeting the cut," wildlife biologist Kurt Becker told Cone. "That's a real problem in the Wrangell area. Our district ranger is quite open about it . . . He gets his marching orders to cut trees, and if he doesn't he'll be walking down the road kicking a can." As a consequence, Becker said, "We're overharvesting. Take a look at Zarembo Island, which is probably the highest yield on our district. It's about 70 percent cutover, with just a phenomenal volume (approximately 500 million board feet) that's come off it in the last twenty years, yet we keep having to go back in . . . to meet the district cut."

Wildlife biologist Vivian Kee said the Forest Service had chosen to ignore the cumulative impacts of logging on the landscape. "We're not adequately addressing the effects of multiple entries; we're not combining it with the impacts of adjacent land owners like the Native corporation timber sales," she said. "In several areas we're planning right up against the Native areas where they're also doing timber sales."

Forestry technician Cynthia Croxton said pressure to get out the cut was overriding the best judgment of professionals in the field. "On the four major sales I worked in laying out," she said, "there were always marginal area where we found ourselves saying, We shouldn't really be going near this wildlife corridor, or we shouldn't be cutting on this slope, or we shouldn't be anywhere near this stream. But the cut was all-important."

SEACC published this powerful testimony in an eighty-seven-page "Tongass Accountability Report." Stratton knew it would help make the case for reform of the Tongass timber sale program—if he could get the message out.

In 1983, Stratton accompanied Denny Wilcher on a trip to Boston and New York to meet the directors of a few conservation foundations. He was the first grass-roots activist from Southeast Alaska to be invited on such a trip. Stratton delivered his spiel about the importance of the Tongass National Forest and the Arctic National Wildlife Refuge and presented his slide show to the moneyed ranks of the conservation movement. "They were all very interested," Stratton said. "They asked very good questions."

The following year, Wilcher called Stratton and offered him a job. The timing was propitious; Stratton's girlfriend had informed him that she would not spend another winter in rainy Juneau. Stratton felt he had accomplished a lot. "I had taken SEACC from two paper bags inside the door and no membership to a membership group that had put together a pretty good coalition. The problem had been defined. It made sense at this point to move the issue to the national arena. I didn't have those contacts." It was time for Stratton to move on.

SEACC needed a strong, seasoned, charismatic leader who could hold the coalition together in Southeast Alaska and play the insider political game in Washington, D.C. as well. When Bart Koehler got the call he was ready.

THE BUCKAROO

Koehler was born in Portchester, New York, on April 21, 1948. He grew up reading James Fenimore Cooper and admiring the conservation deeds of Teddy Roosevelt. When he finally made his pilgrimage west, the raw wilderness of the Rocky Mountains spoke to his soul. When he learned in his 20s that he had been born on John Muir's birthday, and on the exact date of Aldo Leopold's death, he figured that his path had been defined in the stars and in the blood.

In 1971 Koehler enrolled in a graduate program in natural resource management at the University of Wyoming and threw himself into a wilderness inventory of the Medicine Bow National Forest so exhaustive that it put the Forest Service's efforts to shame. In the early 1970s, as a Denver-based field officer for the Wilderness Society, Koehler found his place in an emerging male subculture within the western conservation movement. He and his compadres worked hard, drank hard and projected a swaggering machismo. They had a strong gut feeling for the wild, and were willing to work impossible hours at starvation wages to save as much of it as they could. They called themselves the Buckaroos.

Koehler had a manic streak, and his wild drunken outbursts were notorious. A doctor eventually diagnosed a biochemical deficiency. But Koehler's passion and energy drew hundreds of young volunteers into the campaign to save some incomparable Rocky Mountain wildlands. He also put in an apprenticeship on Capitol Hill, where two of the best veteran Wilderness Society lobbyists showed him the ropes. Things began to sour for Koehler in 1979, after a patrician, old-line conservationist, William Turnage, became executive director of the Wilderness Society. Turnage called field representatives like Koehler "the wild Indians" of the movement and insisted they come back on "the reservation." Koehler was not convinced Turnage had the fire in the belly to take on the powerful logging, mining, livestock, and oil and gas interests arrayed against western wilderness protection. On April 21, 1979, his 32nd birthday, he quit. As Susan Zakin describes the incident in her book *Coyotes and Town Dogs* , he sent Turnage a telegram saying, "I'm leaving the reservation. Your blankets are thin and your meat is rotten."

The other Buckaroos were experiencing similar epiphanies. In 1980 five of them took a road trip across Mexico's Pinacate Desert. In legends spun later from those blurred days and nights, this became the genesis of Earth First!, a collective of eco-anarchists who would soon part ways with traditional conservationists to confront environmental destruction head-on through symbolic protests, road blockades, tree-sitting, monkey-wrenching and other forms of mischief.

Koehler spent four ribald years with the Earth First! road show, singing and playing his guitar and building a cult following of sorts as "Johnny Sagebrush." In the middle of this traveling carnival, he returned to Wyoming to lead a coalition pushing for a strong Wyoming Wilderness Act. He also battled Getty Oil, successfully blocking a road through critical elk calving grounds on the Bridger-Teton National Forest that later became part of the Gros Ventre Wilderness.

The Wyoming wilderness campaign was winding down in the spring of 1984, and Koehler was considering what he might do next, when a friend told him about the SEACC opening. He dashed off a hand-written note to the SEACC board on Sierra Club stationery with his resume attached.

Koehler had set foot in Alaska only once, and briefly. During his college years, he and two buddies had made it to Ketchikan by ferry to win a bet. However, he had studied up on Alaska as a lobbyist for the Wilderness Society during the Alaska lands campaign.

He was in Chico, California, on April 21, his birthday, playing an Earth First! rally for the Tuolomne River, when he got a call from a SEACC board member, who interviewed him by phone. In May he spent a week in Juneau, basking in an unusual stretch of warm, sunny weather. SEACC board members asked him about his wild past. "I was straight with them," Koehler said. He told them he was taking lithium to control his manic episodes and had cleaned up his act. He knew intuitively that coming to Alaska was the right thing. "It was a clean slate. It was a fresh start. I didn't have to keep looking over my shoulder." It seemed the right thing to the SEACC board as well. Koehler got the job.

ONE BIG WESTERN

The situation in 1984 was undeniably grim. The Forest Service had a legislated timber target, and as much money as it wanted to sell timber. The pulp mills had their long-term contracts and the Alaska congressional delegation firmly in their pockets. Koehler had a staff of two, an annual budget of $100,000, and nowhere near that in the bank. "I knew it was bad," he said. "A rational person would have said, 'You're never going to change this.'" He tried to keep things in perspective by pretending that the situation on the Tongass was one big western movie. On his office wall he taped a photo of Teddy Roosevelt riding a white horse. Beneath it he copied a quote from the Rough Rider: "Fighting for the right is the noblest sport the world affords."

Jim Stratton had left the Tongass Accountability Project unfinished. Koehler grabbed hold of it and expanded it. The full report, finally printed in the winter of 1985, laid out the story of waste and destruction on the Tongass in great detail, and in terms anyone could understand. SEACC now had an organizing tool it could use to launch a national campaign.

Stratton and John Sisk had rebuilt SEACC into a coalition of eight groups representing close to a thousand activists who volunteered countless hours to keeping tabs on the Forest Service. Hundreds of them were willing to write a letter at a moment's notice. Stratton was mindful of the need to keep these activists engaged. From Anchorage, he remained closely involved in the Tongass campaign. One of the first Alaska Conservation Foundation projects he funded was Sisk's "Citizens' Guide to the Tongass National Forest," which offered detailed information on how to appeal and litigate timber sales.

Yet trying to reform the Forest Service from inside Alaska was proving a hopeless task. To Tongass managers, the annual timber target of 450 million board feet was regarded as the Holy Grail. Nothing else mattered. They feared retribution from the Alaska delegation and lawsuits from the pulp companies if they failed to meet it. Reform would have to come from Congress, and pressure for reform would have to come from outside Alaska. It would require working around the Alaska delegation and taking the story of the Tongass to the nation. But how to start?

As it happened, the Alaska Lands Act itself held the answer. It required the Forest Service to report to Congress on the status of the Tongass National Forest by Dec. 2, 1985, and to consult with various interest groups, including

SEACC, the timber industry, commercial fishing groups and the state of Alaska, in preparing the report. In May of 1984 Stratton wrote to Regional Forester John Sandor demanding that he conduct a full analysis of how achieving the timber sale target had affected fish, wildlife, recreation and other resources. Stratton also castigated Sandor for diverting $1.25 million of the $1.5 million Congress had budgeted for the review to the Tongass road program

GETTING IT ON THE RECORD

On June 22, 1984, a week before Koehler officially took over as SEACC director, Rep. John Seiberling convened the House Interior Subcommittee on Public Lands and National Parks to review implementation of the Alaska Lands Act. Stratton testified with Koehler at his side. He told the committee the Forest Service was misspending its $40 million-plus annual appropriation. The fund's purpose, he said, "is clearly defined as protection of old growth by subsidizing the harvest of lower volume marginal lands. This isn't happening on the Tongass." He also accused the Forest Service of willfully misinterpreting the timber target of 4.5 billion board feet per decade. Tongass managers, he said, had "turned a funding provision into an inflexible mandate to cut the forest regardless of the impact on fish and wildlife habitat or what the market demands."

Koehler and Stratton vowed to push for reform during revision of the Tongass Land Management Plan. But they asked Congress to do its part by demanding a full Forest Service review of the need for a timber sale program of 4.5 billion board per decade, and pointed out that the Tongass had not sold enough timber in the previous three years to meet that target. They also asked Congress to order the Forest Service to analyze the environmental impact of stepped-up logging on the Tongass, and to involve the public in preparing its review. "In the past we have been continually frustrated by the lack of cooperation and consultation on the part of the Forest Service," Stratton said. "We sincerely hope that this situation improves as we approach the deadline for the report to Congress."

The hearing attracted little attention outside Alaska. However, it created a formal record and established most of the major themes of the campaign to come.

SEACC followed up with "Last Stand for the Tongass," a well-written and thoroughly documented sixty-page report to Congress on the status of

The Forest Service's infamous "campground in a clearcut" at Staney Creek, Prince of Wales Island, 1988. Photo by Jack Gustafson.

management on the Tongass. The report, written largely by Bart Koehler and Steve Kallick, and edited by Julie Koehler, Bart's wife, was published in January of 1986. "Last Stand" introduced readers to the situation on the Tongass with photographs, charts, and compelling prose: "Over one hundred years ago, John Muir explored Southeast Alaska in a Tlingit Indian canoe and described the grandeur of the Tongass as an 'endless rhythm and beauty.' Today that endless rhythm and beauty is threatened with destruction. The Tongass is not only our largest, but also our most mismanaged and most abused national forest. This abuse has reached crisis proportions in the last six years. The source of this abuse is a U.S. Forest Service timber management program intended to liquidate virtually all the unprotected old-growth forest on the Tongass within the next century . . . ."

The report laid out the money-losing economics and environmental impacts of the Tongass timber sale program, described the pulp mills' antitrust activities, and explained the threats logging posed to other commercial sectors, including commercial fishing, tourism and Native corporation logging enterprises. It concluded: "It is not too late to stop the destruction of this land. Congress has the power to turn this troubled national forest around; to help build a lasting stable economy for all the people of Southeast Alaska; to end waste, fraud, and abuse of public money and resources; to bring balanced multiple-use management to the Tongass; and to ensure maintenance of those uniquely Alaskan qualities that make up life on the last frontier."

A BEACHHEAD

John Sisk, SEACC's grassroots organizer, believed a fullblown congressional oversight hearing would offer the best forum for exposing the excesses of the Tongass timber program. In 1986, Koehler dispatched Sisk to Washington, D.C. to establish a beachhead and garner that hearing. Sisk, accompanied by Kallick, paid a visit to Roy Jones, chief of staff for the House Interior Committee and a formidable gatekeeper. As Kallick recalls, they did not get a welcoming reception. "Jones told Sisk, 'Get the hell out of Washington, D.C. We made a deal with Ted Stevens. We know what's going on up there. We don't want you here.' " Afterward, Kallick asked Sisk, "'What shall we do? Is it over?" Sisk didn't waver. "We're going to get our hearing," he vowed.

Help soon came. Joe Sebastian, a fisherman in Point Baker and a SEACC board member, called Sisk one day and asked what he could do to help. Sisk said, "Come on back." Sebastian and his girlfriend Joan Kautzer took a train across the country in March of 1986 and stayed in the nation's capital for six weeks. Sisk instructed them on the basics of lobbying, and they were on their own. Over six months they visited two hundred congressional offices to tell their story. "People really cared, even if their bosses were friends of (Alaska Rep.) Don Young," Sebastian said. "They would say, 'I'd like to go there someday, and when I do I hope these places will still be there.'"

Sebastian and Kautzer lived a life beyond the imagining of most Capitol Hill denizens. They spent their summers fishing on their small boat and their winters holed up in a homemade house made of salvaged beach logs. They lived on the salmon they caught in Sumner Strait and the deer they killed on North Prince of Wales Island. In fact, they had brought jars of home-canned salmon and venison as gifts for members of Congress. "It was really a deep cultural event," Kallick recalled. "They were giving them the most precious gift they could imagine. They were saying, 'This is the American dream, to live off the land.'"

Not everyone understood the symbolic significance of these gifts, however. One day Kautzer and Sebastian met with Rep. Sam Gejdenson, a conservative Democrat from Connecticut. When they set the fruits of their labors on his desk, Gejdenson recoiled, and demanded to know, "What's that?" A member of Gejdenson's staff later took the Alaskans aside and said, "I think you really grossed the congressman out."

Sisk got help from other grassroots activists, but the Alaskans got the cold shoulder from most of the national conservation groups. The attitude of the embattled nationals during the Reagan years was, "Wait until there's a new president." But the SEACC lobbyists didn't have time to wait. "We met with Tim Mahoney of the Sierra Club," Joe Sebastian said. "He told us, 'It just really does my heart good to see you guys working on this issue, but you don't have a chance.'" An exception was Steve Richardson of the Wilderness Society, who helped them get their hearing.

One of the biggest hurdles they faced was the power of Sen. Ted Stevens, who had engineered the Tongass Timber Supply Fund in the first place. As a member of the Senate Appropriations Committee, Alaska's senior senator was a force to be reckoned with. "People did not want to buck Stevens," Sebastian said. "Ted was vindictive."

AN OVERSIGHT HEARING

Yet against all odds, SEACC prevailed. On May 8 and 9, 1986, the House Interior Subcommittee on Public Lands held an oversight hearing on management of the Tongass timber program. U.S. Rep. John Seiberling, who had read "Last Stand for the Tongass," chaired the sessions.

Sisk and Koehler knew the hearing offered the perfect opportunity to introduce Congress to the faces of Southeast Alaska—to people like Joe Sebastian and Joan Kautzer. Koehler in particular was eager to bring SEACC board members and grassroots activists to Washington. He was a familiar face on the Hill from his tenure as a lobbyist for the Wilderness Society, and his years with Earth First! had gained him a certain notoriety. He knew SEACC's members could speak for the Tongass better than he, an outsider and a hired gun, could ever hope to.

On the hearing's first day SEACC presented the committee with resolutions passed by fourteen small Southeast communities opposing the Tongass timber target and the $40 million subsidy. Timber industry supporters presented their own pro-timber resolutions from Juneau, Sitka, Ketchikan, Petersburg, Wrangell and Metlakatla. What they didn't say was that testimony before the Sitka and Petersburg assemblies on their resolutions had been evenly split for and against, and that everyone in Juneau had testified in opposition to the fixed timber target.

During his testimony, Joe Sebastian questioned whether the pulp mills deserved the preferential treatment they continued to receive under the long-term contracts. "Louisiana-Pacific, Ketchikan and Alaska Pulp Co., after driving many small loggers in southeast Alaska out of business, deserve to have their fifty-year timber contracts broken by Congress as an act of faith to show the honest people of America that fraud and monopolistic attempts to dominate public resources will not be tolerated or sanctioned by further subsidies or giveaways," he said.

Forest Service Chief Max Peterson, presented with new reports showing that the Tongass timber sale program was losing $60 million a year, squirmed and finally admitted, "We knew the Tongass wouldn't make money, but we didn't think things would be this bad."

Koehler knew the hearing was going well when, halfway through the first afternoon, Mark Trautwein, a member of Rep. Morris Udall's staff, pulled him aside and asked him, "Can you bring a few of the people who are testifying over to talk to Mo?" Udall, chairman of the House Interior Committee, "needed to feel good about going ahead," Koehler said. Udall spoke with some of the grassroots activists. At the end, he told them, "I think you've got some valid concerns." After that meeting, the dynamic in the House changed.

In July, Rep. Bob Mrazek, a freshman Democrat from New York, introduced a Tongass Timber Reform Act that proposed to cancel the legislated timber target and the automatic $40 million annual appropriation. "Mrazek had nothing going for him, wasn't even on the Interior Committee, but he was hungry," said SEACC lobbyist Scott Highleyman. "He wanted a bill and was willing to work to get co-sponsors." Mrazek's bill clearly was a long shot, but to the Alaska delegation, it was also a shot across the bow.

THE PAYOFF

Meanwhile, in Anchorage, Denny Wilcher was trying to persuade leaders of the ten major national conservation groups to tour Alaska. The trip was overdue, but the nationals, known as the Group of 10, were too busy trying to fend off the Reagan administration's attacks on the environment to pay much attention to Alaska.

"Everyone had put so much work into ANILCA," Stratton recalled. "Carter had signed the law, but then Reagan got elected. After 1980 all the implementation was handed back to Alaska environmentalists. The nationals were totally obsessed with fighting (Interior Secretary) James Watt." Even in Alaska conservationists were otherwise engaged as they fought to keep hunting out of the new national parks and oil and gas exploration out of the Arctic National Wildlife Refuge.

In July of 1986 the Group of 10 did come to Alaska, accompanied by two influential East Coast funders, Donald Ross of the Rockefeller Family Fund and Bob Allen of the Kendall Foundation. Stratton, who organized the trip, had the weather gods on his side that week. "From Anchorage we flew them to Fairbanks and the North Slope, where we met with ARCO," he recalled. "Then the weather cleared for the first time in two weeks. We put them in two planes and flew them over the Coastal Plain." The visiting bigwigs saw muskoxen and tens of thousands of snow geese.

In Juneau, the visitors boarded two floatplanes for a tour of Chichagof Island and the southern Tongass. The Forest Service led the tour, but allowed SEACC to provide the narration. Koehler pointed out the clearcuts from a speaker phone at the front of one plane, with all the Group of 10 on board. Again the weather was stunning. The visitors picnicked on the Tongass, and returned sunburned to Juneau for a potluck supper and party.

Stratton had stressed the importance of the meeting to SEACC's staff, board and member groups, telling them, "We're going to have the Group of 10 for a couple of hours. You need to tell them what you need from the national groups." Koehler had prepared a campaign plan and a detailed legislative strategy describing how the conservation movement could get Congress to repeal the timber target. Donald Ross picked up a copy. A couple of weeks later, he called Stratton and asked, "Is this real? Is it doable? Give us a budget. What will this cost?" Stratton called Koehler, and they put together a budget of $60,000.

Ross recalls that the Group of 10 seemed far more interested in protecting the Arctic Refuge from drilling than in saving the Alaska rain forest from logging. He knew ample resources would be available to take on the oil companies. "The issue that captured my attention was the Tongass," he said. "There was such an opportunity there." He agreed to give SEACC $60,000 in seed money for a national Tongass campaign. Other funders— the MacIntosh Foundation, the Compton Foundation and the Tortuga Fund—soon agreed to kick in money as well. In all, about $500,000 eventually was pledged for a five-year campaign. It was a fortune for a shoestring organization that had come close to folding only recently.

Koehler rounded up two talented young environmental lobbyists, Jay Nelson and Scott Highleyman, to carry the campaign to Washington, D.C. Both had lobbied environmental bills in the Alaska Legislature. "Bart came to us and said, 'I want to hire one of you,'" Highleyman recalls. "We told him, 'You have to hire both of us.' We were used to working as a team." Koehler agreed to pay them $40,000, which they split 50-50.

Donald Ross hired Art Mackwell, a retired corporate lobbyist and former newspaperman who also happened to be his neighbor in Washington, D.C., to help out as senior advisor to the campaign. "We paid him roundtrip airfare and gave him a computer," Ross recalled. "He went up to Juneau and spent a few days getting acquainted with activists. He really hit it off with these guys." Ross thought Mackwell could show the amateur lobbyists the ropes in Washington. But after meeting Nelson, Highleyman, Koehler and the rest of the SEACC staff, Mackwell reported back to Ross: "Are you kidding? These guys are naturals."

Ross believed Koehler's years as a Wilderness Society lobbyist would give the SEACC campaign credibility and clout. "Bart came out of Washington and was known to people here," he said. "They respected him. Bart is a guy who is very tough. He wasn't going to be intimidated."

The challenge, as Ross saw it, was to mount a campaign that projected the passion, sincerity, and commitment that only people who are truly connected to a place can convey. If SEACC could do that, he figured saving the Tongass would be an easy sell. "It doesn't take much, when you're a congressman from Kansas and you've never heard of the Tongass, to get you to vote for trees."

12

SMOKED SALMON AND ALASKAN BEER

In Washington, Jay Nelson and Scott Highleyman rented a three-bedroom flat near the Anacostia River on Capitol Hill, which they named Safe House, and set up an office in a cubicle at National Audubon Society headquarters. In early 1987 they began laying the groundwork for a national Tongass reform campaign. Their marching orders from Bart Koehler had been direct: get the special Tongass timber target and subsidy—the 4.5 billion and $40 million—repealed. Get the Forest Service to manage the Tongass the same way it managed every other national forest. Within months, however, those orders changed. "Bart called one day and said he was upping the ante," Highleyman said. "We were going for ending the long-term contracts and adding wilderness."

Their first challenge, however, was to get someone—anyone—to pay attention. Every conservation group inside the Beltway told the Alaskan upstarts that they didn't have a chance. Highleyman made the rounds of congressional offices trying to drum up interest in the Tongass. What he got, mostly, was blank looks. "There was no awareness at all," he said. "Paul Tsongas had just been elected to the U.S. Senate, and people called it the Tsongas National Forest." The one exception was Rep. Bob Mrazek. In March, the Democratic freshman from New York reintroduced his Tongass Timber Reform Act. Before long a bumper sticker was spotted on the floating outhouse at the end of the dock in the Southeast Alaska fishing village of Pelican proclaiming, "I'm Proud of My Congressman Bob Mrazek."

U.S. Sen. William Proxmire, a Wisconsin Democrat, agreed to sponsor a Tongass reform bill in the Senate. Highleyman regarded Proxmire's support as a mixed blessing, however. The creator of the Golden Fleece Awards, which highlighted wasteful government spending, "was regarded as a gadfly," he said.

Highleyman and Nelson were advised to concentrate their efforts on the Senate campaign. "If we couldn't win the House we were dead anyway,"

Highleyman said. "The Senate had a tradition of squashing bills on public lands and wilderness." They divided the Senate into those who would support them no matter what, those who would oppose them no matter what, and those who were on the fence. The fence-sitters would be their targets. They thanked their supporters with gifts of smoked salmon and Alaskan beer.

SERENDIPITY

Hoping to win a hearing on Mrazek's bill, the SEACC lobbyists called on Rep. Morris Udall, who had been a friend to Alaska conservation during the Alaska Lands campaign. But Udall's aide, Mark Trautwein, told them he would not schedule an oversight hearing unless another committee member requested it.

Luck was on their side the day they visited Rep. Sam Gejdenson. The Connecticut Democrat was between staff assistants; a temporary staffer, Dan Adamson, was filling in for a week. They briefed him on the Tongass. "He loved the issue, he knew the issue," Highleyman said. "He got all excited and said he would talk to Gejdenson about it."

Luck struck again as they walked with Adamson toward the elevator and ran into Jill Lancelot of the National Taxpayers Union. "Dan introduced us and we went and had coffee together," Highleyman said. "We talked about trees for the price of a cheeseburger. She totally got into it. She was one of our best allies from then on." Lancelot and the Taxpayers Union got the Mrazek bill most of its Republican sponsors. "When *we'd* talk about the waste of money, people would look at us cross-eyed," Steve Kallick said. "When *they* talked about it, people listened."

As soon as John Schiebel, Gejdenson's new staff assistant, came on board, Nelson and Highleyman gave him their pitch. He agreed to schedule the hearing. "Udall and his staff couldn't believe it," Highleyman said. "Every week we went back and we'd accomplished what they said we had to do, and every week they'd tell us there was another wall to jump over. It was like a mythical quest."

Seiberling, the Interior Committee's Alaska lands specialist, had retired at the end of 1986. Udall was suffering from the early stages of Parkinson's Disease and needed someone with enough vigor to take on the troublesome Alaska delegation. Rep. George Miller, a mustached, rough-and-tumble liberal Democrat from California, was his choice. However, Miller was more interested in fighting oil drilling in the Arctic National Wildlife Refuge than in saving rain forests.

Coincidentally, in 1987 Miller hired Jeff Petrich, a former Alaska legislative aide, who knew the situation on the Tongass. Petrich lobbied hard to persuade his boss to get involved in the Tongass mess. Miller finally relented. He would become one of the most passionate congressional advocates for Tongass reform.

As Nelson and Highleyman prepared for the hearing on the Mrazek bill, they got some unexpected help from the Forest Service. The agency reported that it had a six-year backlog of unsold timber sales on the Tongass and that its Tongass timber sale program was losing $60 million a year. The report also revealed that pulp mill employment had plummeted during the 1980s recession, yet the Forest Service still maintained a work force of nearly 700 government employees in Alaska—approximately one bureaucrat for every two timber workers. The Tongass Timber Supply Fund had become a Forest Service full-employment program.

OVERSIGHT

Gejdenson chaired the two-day hearing before the House Interior Subcommittee on Energy and Environment on May 19 and May 21. SEACC's lobbyists had corralled several national conservation groups to testify in favor of the Mrazek bill, which had managed to attract ninety-four co-sponsors. The two pulp companies did not testify on their own behalf. Instead, Don Finney of Ketchikan Pulp Co. and George Woodbury of Alaska Pulp Corp. testified against the Mrazek bill for the Alaska Loggers Association. There was testimony as well from scientists, state officials, and residents of several Southeast Alaska communities.

Sylvia Geraghty, a fourth-generation Alaskan, spoke in favor of the Mrazek bill. Geraghty operated a rustic lodge and marine supply store on remote Tokeen Island off the west coast of Prince of Wales Island. She had founded a small group called Alaskans for Responsible Resource Management. She spoke, she said, on behalf of its members—small-scale logging contractors, tree thinners, commercial fishermen, trappers, and others who depended on the Tongass for their livelihood.

"We are certainly not opposed to logging on the Tongass," Geraghty said. "A number of our members earn a full or part-time living from logging or from other industries associated with logging. However, we are opposed to the monopolistic, arbitrary industry we have now, and the way in which the Forest Service manages the Tongass National Forest for the primary use of that industry. The Forest Service tells us they must continue on the same shameful course because they have two valid contracts . . . and they can do nothing else. I feel that they have forgotten that their primary and most important contract is with the people of the United States."

Retired Forest Service planner K.J. Metcalf testified that during his twenty years on the Tongass he had watched responsible forest management fall victim to the tyranny of the long-term contracts time after time. He described his involvement in development of the Southeast Alaska Area Guide in the 1970s. "This was to be the model for managing the Tongass," he said. "It was a promise of public and other agency involvement, of using the best scientific information in making decisions, and above all, a promise of honesty and trust with the public. Those promises were not honored. I was deceived into thinking a new era of management was at hand. I, in turn, deceived other people with promises of change. I publicly apologize to them."

On the hearing's second day, Gejdenson grilled Jim Clark, an attorney for the Alaska Loggers' Association and Alaska Pulp Corporation. He wanted to known why APC had sued the Forest Service for $83 million in damages for alleged breach of contract. Clark explained that the timber the Forest Service had made available between 1981 and 1986 was less valuable timber than APC was entitled to under its contract. But Gejdenson had done his homework. He retorted: "The fact that the Forest Service spends . . . $100 a thousand board feet to give you timber at $2 a (thousand) board (feet)? That's not enough?"

In November, Proxmire's bill got a hearing before the Senate Energy Subcommittee on Energy and Natural Resources. The Wisconsin senator stressed the high cost of the Tongass timber sale program, calling it "an insult to U.S. taxpayers who paid $36,000 last year for each Tongass timber job." In a highly unusual alliance, the National Taxpayers Union joined national conservation groups in offering a statement of support for the Proxmire bill.

Former Forest Service economist Joseph Mehrkens provided key testimony. Mehrkens, who had recently left the Alaska Region to work for the Wilderness Society, said the Tongass Timber Supply Fund had failed to maintain economic stability in Southeast Alaska during the timber industry recession of the mid-1980s. The Forest Service was now spending nearly twice as much to sell timber as before the fund's establishment in 1980, he said, yet Tongass timber harvests were down by half from pre-1980 levels, and the number of jobs dependent on Tongass timber sales was down by one-third from average levels in the 1970s. These economic arguments got lawmakers' attention. Momentum for reform was building. SEACC was ready to raise the stakes.

On December 10, the House Interior Subcommittee on Energy and the Environment held a hearing on a new Mrazek bill, the Tongass Timber Contract Modification Act, which proposed to terminate both pulp mills' long-term contracts. Timber-dependent communities and pulp industry executives outnumbered conservationists at the hearing as they mobilized to counter this new threat.

THE MILLER BILL

By early 1988, Rep. George Miller was on board the Tongass reform train. And it was picking up speed. Early in the year, at Rep. Morris Udall's request, Miller, Bart Koehler and other supporters of reform sat down with Rep. Don Young of Alaska and timber industry representatives to try to negotiate a deal acceptable to all sides. It was a fruitless exercise; after six weeks of talks, the timber industry representatives walked out. Still, Miller and Young pledged publicly to continue efforts to reach a compromise acceptable to the Alaska delegation before Tongass reform legislation reached the House floor.

Commercial fisherman Joe Sebastian used his boat as a message board in 1989 during the campaign to reform the timber sale program on the Tongass National Forest. Photo by Jack Gustafson.

In March, Miller unveiled a new bill that amended and strengthened Mrazek's original Tongass reform bill. It called for repealing the timber target and subsidy, modifying (but not canceling) the long-term contracts, and imposing a five-year moratorium on timber sales in nineteen areas of critical fish and wildlife habitat on the Tongass. Under the Miller bill, the timber program would be funded annually through the normal congressional appropriations review process. The timber sale level would be determined not by fiat, but by market demand under a true multiple use management plan. And the Forest Service would be directed to renegotiate the fifty-year contracts, to comply with modern forest management practices and bring a better economic return to the U.S. Treasury.

THE FACES OF SOUTHEAST ALASKA

On May 25 and 26, the House Agriculture Subcommittee on Forests, Family Farms, and Energy held hearings on the Miller bill. These hearings offered some of the most dramatic and heartfelt testimony from Southeast Alaska yet heard on Capitol Hill.

During their first year in Washington, Jay Nelson and Scott Highleyman had testified before congressional committees as grassroots activists. "But after a year we knew too much," Highleyman said. "We knew how the committees worked. We weren't outsiders anymore, didn't sound like outsiders. We started putting grassroots lobbyists up there to testify instead. Alaska had an amazing group of people. Some of these people had given everything for thirty years. We were taking our direction from them."

Ernestine Hanlon, a Tlingit basketweaver from Hoonah, came to Washington and impressed everyone with her quiet dignity. "I went with her once to the Smithsonian Museum to see a Tlingit basket collection," Highleyman said. "They let her in to handle the baskets. She was looking at artifacts from her village with patterns she didn't know anything about. She got angry because the baskets were falling apart. The Smithsonian was failing to protect her heritage."

At the May hearing, Hanlon began by introducing herself, her village, and her traditional way of life. "I am Tlingit from the Raven tribe and the Dogsalmon clan from Hoonah, Alaska. I am a traditional Tlingit spruce root basket weaver and Chilkat blanket weaver. . . ." The word "subsistence," she said, was not a word in the Tlingit language. "It is our life, like breathing and sleeping.

Subsistence, to me, is more than food on the table. It is spruce roots, grass and dyes for my baskets. It is mountain goat and yellow cedar bark for my Chilkat blankets. It is medicine to heal. My people believe that every living thing has a spirit. When I harvest spruce roots for my baskets, I thank the trees. I tell them I will not waste the roots. I will make something. Every time I am in the woods harvesting my roots, I feel the spirits of my grandparents, and those trees remember them, when many generations before, they also came to the trees and showed them the respect and gratefulness."

Until the late 1970s, Hanlon said, the forests surrounding Hoonah had been intact. "We did not have far to go to get our deer and berries, and the herring spawned right in front of Hoonah. Up the bay we trolled for salmon." But logging on the Tongass National Forest over the previous decade had changed everything, she said. "People who come back home after ten years are very surprised how rapid our village has changed. We have miles of roads, lots of cars. Logging is all around us . . . ." Deer were scarce, and the herring no longer spawned in front of the village now that a log dump had been placed there. Yet the Forest Service showed no concern for the plight of her village, she said. Eighteen timber sales near Hoonah were in the planning stages or already being logged.

Supporters of Tongass reform did not have a monopoly on powerful and moving testimony. Helen Finney, the wife of Ketchikan Pulp Co timber manager Don Finney, described an era before the pulp mills came, and tried to explain what the arrival of the timber industry had meant to Southeast Alaska. "I was born and raised in Alaska, as my father left the farm in Iowa to take the gospel north sixty-five years ago," Finney said. "I remember the depression years of the 1930's just vaguely. We were poor but everybody was poor . . . . We were dependent upon the fishing and the fishing was seasonal and cyclical. And the money just didn't last until spring." She described the construction boom in Sitka during World War II, and the collapse of prosperity in the postwar period when the construction was done. "(T)he fishing was in a downward spiral, and people were desperate for some way to pay their bills. Every night, as the saying went, the Chamber of Commerce members were on their knees praying for miracles to put more life back into Southeast Alaska."

For her neighbors and friends, the arrival of Alaska Pulp Corporation answered those prayers, Finney said. "I, who always knew I wanted to stay in Alaska, found a forester to marry, and that's how it happened that I was sitting on the beach when the first loggers came to a place called Hollis." She landed, she said, "in a small amphibian plane with a baby and two duffel bags of household gear. The tide was high. It had been raining, and there was no place clear to go ashore."

Finney recalled her ten years in the Alaska wilderness. "All the years that I sat in the living room and listened to the loggers, the cruisers, the Forest Service, the industry, which was new, and they didn't have all the rules, they didn't know all of the ways to make it work, I never heard them do anything but worry about making it work and keeping jobs for the people." She wept every night for three months after her husband was transferred to Ketchikan. Finney concluded: "I ask you please don't lose sight of these individuals who make their living from the resource, pay their dollars into the integrated and fragile infrastructure that makes up our Southeast Alaska economy."

By the end of two days of testimony, lawmakers had seen the human faces of the Tongass. And those who listened carefully had gained a deeper understanding of the controversy before them.

"FOREST SERVICE FOLLIES"

As the various reform bills worked their way through the congressional maze, the Tongass National Forest was getting some very bad press. In March of 1988 *Sports Illustrated* published a merciless story on the Tongass timber sale program by writer John Skow. "Forest Service Follies" described the agency's proposal to log a beautiful wildlife sanctuary on the Tongass called Lisianski Inlet. Skow wrote: "The Forest Service's record in Southeast Alaska and the damage it is still trying to do there are so bizarre that an observer draws back periodically and shakes his head to clear the fog. You don't have to be an environmentalist—just a taxpayer—to ask why the Forest Service is doing this. Where is the gain?"

Udall took note of the *Sports Illustrated* article during an Interior Committee markup session on the Miller bill in May. He also read from a 1986 *Reader's Digest* piece, "Time to Ax This Timber Boondoggle," and quoted from a 1987 *New York Times* editorial on the Tongass timber subsidies: "Here's a federal plan so wrongheaded it's likely to provoke profanity from any fair-minded person."

As if to reinforce the message, the General Accounting Office released a report in 1988 revealing that between 1981 and 1986 the Forest Service had spent $257 million preparing timber sales, of which half had gone begging. The report contained other juicy revelations. Awash in money, the Forest Service had constructed elaborate facilities for itself: a $6.4 million complex on Prince of Wales Island that included an employee ball field decked with sod shipped by barge from Seattle, and a work center at a remote bay on Chichagof Island equipped with a weight room, sauna and cable television. The GAO report attracted a media feeding frenzy. Newspapers and magazines across the nation sent reporters to the Tongass to see the clearcuts, the boondoggles and the roads to nowhere.

LABOR WINS ONE

Alaska Pulp Corporation's labor record also came under fire in 1988. United Paperworkers International Local 962, which struck the Sitka mill in 1986, had voted to disband the following year after the company hired strikebreakers and forced a decertification election that broke the union. After the strike ended, union organizer Florian Sever, who had testified before Congress about the company's poor labor record, asked for his job back. When the company refused to reinstate him, Sever filed a complaint with the National Labor Relations Board. Frank Roppel, Alaska Pulp's executive vice president and general manager, denied that the company's refusal to rehire Sever was retaliatory. But Roppel readily acknowledged that after Sever's attacks on APC, including a never-published letter Sever had written to the *Sitka Sentinel,* he did not want him back on the payroll.

The National Labor Relations Board concluded after an investigation that Sever's congressional testimony had cost him his job. The board ordered Alaska Pulp to take him back. And it went further: It declared that APC was guilty of unfair labor practices against more than two hundred striking workers, and it ordered the company to set aside $10 million to compensate the workers for back pay. The company immediately appealed the ruling, and managed to keep the issue tied up in court for more than a decade. In May of 1999, more than 100 former Alaska Pulp workers, including Sever, still were waiting to be compensated for the back pay due them.

The National Labor Relations Board ruling caught the attention of syndicated columnist Jack Anderson, who wrote a column about what had happened to Florian Sever when he exercised his First Amendment rights. The ruling also caught the eye of Rep. Sam Gejdenson, who chaired the House Subcommittee on General Oversight and Investigations. Gejdenson was so incensed by this apparent assault on the right of free speech that he launched his own investigation of Alaska Pulp's labor record. On June 30, 1988, his subcommittee held a special public inquiry into Sever's termination. "This country can't allow members of Congress or the president to fire people, to ruin people's lives, who speak out against the policies of this government, and it is darned sure that we can't allow corporations to have that power either," Gejdenson said. His committee asked the U.S. Department of Justice to prosecute Alaska Pulp Corporation for criminal violations of the National Labor Relations Act. But the Justice Department declined to bring charges.

Florian Sever returned to work in 1990. He was given a rough time by the strike-breakers who were now his co-workers. Things got even rougher after he filed a suit in the Alaska state court system seeking civil damages from Alaska Pulp. He lost that case, and APC retaliated by seeking more than $900,000 in reimbursement for legal fees. The judge in the case eventually ordered Sever to pay $90,000. "APC tried to take my house and force me into bankruptcy," Sever said. He finally agreed to pay the $90,000 out of the $165,000 in back pay plus interest the company still owed him—if and when he and his fellow strikers ever saw the money.

MOMENTUM MOUNTS

Press exposure of these issues did nothing to shore up the image of the pulp companies or to enhance their bargaining position with Congress. Instead, it helped drive more members of Congress into the Tongass reform camp. On July 27, the House of Representatives approved Miller's bill on a lopsided vote of 361-47.

By now the Alaska delegation understood that the reform campaign was something to be taken seriously. "It hit Don Young first," Scott Highleyman said. "He was the ranking Republican on House Interior. He had to sit through all of this. We were bringing in the best people—real people, not polished, with just terrific testimony." Young snubbed these constituents when they stopped by his office to pay him courtesy calls during their visits to Washington. He also walked out of the first Tongass oversight hearing after the timber companies testified, turning a deaf ear to more than a dozen Alaskans who were waiting to give testimony.

In the summer of 1988, Congress came to Southeast Alaska. A House delegation led by Udall, Miller, Mrazek, and Gejdenson visited Sitka and

Juneau by ferry to conduct a field inspection of the Tongass, tour the Sitka pulp mill and hear from local residents. SEACC made sure it had at least a hundred supporters on hand in each city to greet the fact-finding delegation and that it had friends on the ferry as well. The lawmakers flew to Pelican for a town meeting, and the entire village turned out to meet them. Koehler says Udall told him it was the first time he had ever been welcomed in Alaska, "and the first time anyone had waved at him with a full hand instead of one finger." In each town the congressmen heard from Forest Service and pulp mill representatives as well as environmentalists. Conspicuously absent from the tour of his home state was Rep. Don Young.

ROAD SHOW

Lobbying Congress on Capitol Hill was only half of SEACC's job. The other half was winning supporters and editorial endorsements for Tongass reform across the nation. Highleyman and Nelson criss-crossed the country in 1987 and 1988, targeting key states and congressional delegations, telling the Tongass story and asking for letters and editorials in favor of reform at every stop. "We worked as a tag team," Highleyman said. One of them would stay in D.C., the other would hit the road. "We would go for three weeks to each state. We had put together a great slide show, and we would show it to anyone who would listen. It was an easy issue to sell. Jay and I got to be like shoe salesmen. We could get people fired into a frenzy."

The main objective of these road shows was to generate letters to key senators asking them to co-sponsor a Tongass reform bill. "We would give our pitch, get people worked up, then start passing out different kinds of paper, different kinds of pens, and a fact sheet, and we'd ask them to write their letter right then," Highleyman said. "No one likes to write letters like that. They'd rather ask questions. We never took questions. We got an average of three hundred letters in every state we went to."

To make these sudden outpourings of constituent mail from Kansas and Louisiana appear to be something other than the result of an orchestrated letter-writing campaign, the SEACC lobbyists used different kinds of envelopes and different kinds of stamps and sent the letters out a few at a time. "We didn't fool too many staff people," Highleyman said. "We'd go back and they'd say, 'You've been busy.' But it didn't matter. Three hundred hand-written letters were impossible to ignore, especially if you were undecided."

Nelson and Highleyman also organized a media campaign targeting editorial writers. "We refused to talk to reporters," Highleyman said. "That got us nothing. But we found editorial writers incredibly receptive." They distributed reprints of the *Sports Illustrated* and *Reader's Digest* articles and talked about how the Tongass timber program was hemorrhaging federal dollars. The response was amazing. In Kansas alone, six newspapers published editorials calling for Tongass reform. The number of supportive editorials eventually reached one hundred. The Alaska delegation was demonized and on the defensive. "It was an extraordinary thing," said Highleyman, "to roll your own delegation."

THE SHAPE OF REFORM

In 1989, during the first six months of the 101st Congress, four separate Tongass bills were introduced, and six House and Senate hearings were held to receive testimony on them. It was clear by now that Congress would pass some kind of Tongass reform legislation. The question was how far that legislation would go, and whether the long-term contracts would survive.

In February, Miller introduced a new reform bill, the strongest yet. It called for canceling the long-term contracts and replacing them with standard short-term timber sales; eliminating the timber quotas and subsidies; and protecting 1.8 million acres of Alaska rain forest as wilderness in twenty-three separate units. The areas proposed for protection had been identified by community leaders, commercial fishermen, Native corporations, the state of Alaska, and conservationists. Most were considered critical fish and wildlife habitat. The list included the contested watersheds of the Chuck, Kadashan, Lisianski, Nutkwa and Karta rivers, which conservationists had fought to protect for more than a decade. In the Interior Committee, the bill was amended to require 100-foot stream buffers along both sides of salmon streams. "Everyone says bills always get weaker as they go through the process," Highleyman observed. "Ours got stronger."

On March 14, the House Interior Committee held a hearing on the Miller bill, which had quickly attracted 152 sponsors. The following day, the House Agriculture Committee held a hearing on a weaker bill, favored by Rep. Don Young, which proposed a flexible timber supply goal, elimination of the $40 million subsidy and renegotiation of the fifty-year contracts, but still offered wilderness protection for the twenty-three areas.

*Picketing at Forest
Service Headquarters in
Ketchikan in 1989.
Photo by Jack
Gustafson.*

At that hearing, SEACC attorney Steve Kallick argued that as long as the contracts remained in effect, laws governing management of other national forests would not apply on the Tongass. "Despite two decades of legislation designed to protect our national forests and manage them for a variety of other uses in addition to timber production, the Tongass National Forest remains first and foremost a pulp timber allotment—managed more like a private plantation than a public reserve," Kallick said. "The fifty-year contracts control Forest Service management and all other uses of the Tongass to an unwarranted and unwise degree; they set up exclusive fiefdoms for the contract holders, and assure the majority of Tongass timber is sold without benefit of competitive bid; and they form the root of the timber-based management that threatens other competing uses of our forest today."

Meanwhile, things were moving fast in the U.S. Senate. In February, Sen. Tim Wirth, a Colorado Democrat, introduced his own strong Tongass reform bill. The Wirth bill differed from the new Miller bill in only one particular: to win broad support, Wirth proposed a temporary logging moratorium, rather than permanent protection, for the twenty-three wilderness areas.

Sen. Frank Murkowski of Alaska introduced his own Tongass reform bill early in the session, a two-page document calling for repeal of the automatic $40 million subsidy, and little else. On February 28, Sen. Dale Bumpers, an Arkansas Democrat, held a hearing on both the Wirth and Murkowski bills before his Senate Energy Subcommittee on Public Lands, National Parks and Forests.

A month later, in the predawn hours of March 24, the *Exxon Valdez* ran aground on Bligh Reef, and North Slope oil from ruptured tanks began flowing into Prince William Sound. The environmental catastrophe that unfolded over the following weeks and months riveted the world's attention as 10.8 million gallons of crude oil sullied more than 1,200 miles of pristine coastline, poisoning the food chain, coating thousands of seabirds and otters, and disrupting the subsistence food gathering of Alaska Natives in the sound and beyond. Heartbreaking photographs of dying sea otters and paeans to the beauty of Prince William Sound before the spill sent a disturbing message about the fragility of the nation's last great wilderness—and the failure of the systems humans had put in place to protect it.

It is impossible to know how the *Exxon Valdez* disaster affected the votes of members of Congress as the Tongass reform campaign gained momentum in 1989. But it is reasonable to assume that many who wanted to express their outrage over the tragedy in Prince William Sound saw a vote for a strong Tongass reform bill as a way to make a statement about the nation's commitment to protect Alaska.

THE LOUISIANA CONNECTION

Senate Energy Committee Chairman Bennett Johnston, a Democrat from the oil state of Louisiana, wanted to see a Tongass reform bill pass in the 101st Congress, and he wanted it done with minimal dissension. He called in Murkowski and Wirth and asked their help in crafting a compromise. What Johnston had in mind was a bill based on a proposal advanced by Alaska Governor Steve Cowper and the Southeast Conference, a coalition of community and business leaders from Southeast Alaska.

The Southeast Conference proposal called for reducing the $40 million annual subsidy to $15 million, directing the Forest Service to renegotiate the long-term contracts, establishing an annual automatic $20 million appropriation for regional economic diversification, protecting twelve key fish and wildlife areas from commercial logging, and making the 4.5 billion board feet timber target a ceiling rather than a floor. It was a far cry from Wirth's bill, but it was a starting point on the road to agreement.

In April, the Senate Energy Committee held field hearings in Sitka and Ketchikan on both the Wirth and Murkowski bills. Murkowski tried to stack the speaker panels with pulp mill supporters, but Johnston's office intervened, and in the end all interests were well represented. Commercial fishermen, wildlife biologists, wilderness outfitters, mayors of small communities and Alaska Natives spoke forcefully in favor of the Wirth bill with its tough management reforms and protections for key fish and wildlife areas. Sig Mathisen of Petersburg Vessel Owners was one of them. "My entire life has been spent in the waters of Southeast Alaska," he said "I am very aware of the fisherman's need to steward this resource and to protect the fragile natural salmon incubator that is the Tongass National Forest."

Murkowski seemed to take the testimony of these constituents to heart. He promised to heed their calls for protection of the Lisianski River watershed and the Yakutat Forelands and the cancellation of the road link between Hoonah and Tenakee.

A few pulp mill workers risked their jobs to speak out publicly for reform. "KPC's callous exploitation of the Tongass is compounded by their callous exploitation of the work force," declared Wayne Weihing, an employee of Ketchikan Pulp. "As pulp mill employees, we've seen our wages cut, medical benefits reduced, and have been forced with the threat of termination to work under unsafe working conditions." Like Florian Sever, Weihing made the argument that his employer no longer deserved the special treatment conferred by its fifty-year contract.

Only pulp company officials and a few millworkers and loggers stood up for Murkowski's bill. One was Martin Pihl, president and general manager of Ketchikan Pulp Co. and a twenty-seven-year employee of the company. Pihl traced the history and purpose of the long-term contracts. He described the investments the company had made in Southeast Alaska, including the recent construction of a new sawmill at Ward Cove, and the stability the mill had brought to Ketchikan during the timber recession. "Without our pulp mill greatly aggravated unemployment would have occurred in our region during the period 1981 through 1985, when our local timber industry faced the most severe and prolonged recession in its history," he said.

Pihl also delivered a threat: If Congress canceled KPC's long-term contract, the company would close the Ketchikan mill and sue the government under the Due Process Clause of the Fifth Amendment, which requires the government to pay "just compensation" when it takes private property. If the company prevailed, American taxpayers would pay a high price to compensate KPC, Pihl said—beginning with the full value of the mill and all foregone profits that would have been realized during the remaining nineteen years of the contract.

LINING UP VOTES

No doubt the Senate took this threat seriously. But the biggest roadblock the Wirth bill faced was a possible filibuster by Stevens and Murkowski. It takes sixty-one votes to end a filibuster in the U.S. Senate. To withstand that threat, the bill's supporters needed to line up as many co-sponsors as possible. By mid-1989 they had only twenty, and felt they had hit a wall. The SEACC team turned the campaign into a contest and mounted a full-court press. Koehler agreed to lobby conservative western senators he knew from his years in Wyoming. Nelson and Highleyman competed to see who could sign up the most co-sponsors. Once the list reached thirty names, others who wanted political cover piled on. The bill ended up with fifty-three sponsors.

One reason Tongass reform was making progress in the Senate was that so many Southeast Alaska communities were now calling for change. "We worked hard to get resolutions out of the far-flung communities," Koehler said. "When we went to visit senators, they asked, 'Why aren't Stevens and Murkowski doing something?' We said, 'They never will. Here are all these communities that can't get their U.S. senators to listen to them.'"

Back in the House, the maneuvering continued. On May 31, the House Interior Committee marked up the Miller bill. At the last minute Don Young of Alaska and Jerry Huckaby of Louisiana introduced a substitute bill calling for what amounted to cosmetic changes in the Tongass timber sale program. The committee rejected the Young-Huckaby ploy on a 24-16 vote, then passed Miller's bill 23-15. But Miller's bill had to survive one more hurdle before it reached the House floor. On June 21 it was taken up by the House Agriculture Committee, which added weakening amendments that made it conform more closely to its own bill. This set the stage for a floor fight when Tongass reform finally reached the full House.

PEOPLE OF THE TONGASS

John Skow's article had so infuriated the pulp companies that they helped underwrite a book, *People of the Tongass: Alaska Forestry Under Attack*, a history and defense of the Tongass timber program. The book was the brainchild of Ron Arnold, executive director of the Center for the Defense of Free Enterprise, a right-wing think tank in Bellevue, Washington. Arnold had been trying for some time to recruit writers to tell the story of the timber industry in Southeast Alaska. In 1986, he gave a pitch to a group of Alaska loggers. Someone suggested K.A. Soderberg and Jackie Du Rette. The two loggers' wives agreed to write the book for free. In its blurb, they promised that *People of the Tongass* would unmask the "lies, slander, and devious tactics environmentalists have used in a deliberate effort to destroy the timber industry in Alaska," and introduce readers to people from all walks of life in Southeast Alaska who supported the forest industry. "The message is compelling: decades of logging has not harmed the Tongass in any measurable way!" Soderberg and DuRette declared.

All three members of the Alaska delegation contributed introductions. A Tongass Book Fund, organized by logger John Schnabel of Haines, raised $60,000 to get the book edited, typeset and published. The Free Enterprise Press printed 10,000 copies. *People of the Tongass* came out in February of 1989, as the Tongass timber reform campaign was reaching critical mass. Schnabel drove all over Alaska in his pickup truck trying to get bookstores to sell it at a discount or on consignment.

But *People of the Tongass* was no match for the revelations of waste and environmental destruction now coming out of Washington and Juneau.

THE PRICE OF A CHEESEBURGER

On May 29, 1989, the *New York Times* published a page-one story by staff writer Timothy Egan with a Sitka dateline. "Here in the emerald panhandle of southeastern Alaska, where rain is measured in feet and the legacy of Russian America can still be seen in onion-domed churches, the Forest Service sells five-hundred-year-old trees for the price of a cheeseburger," Egan wrote. The notion of ancient trees owned by all Americans going for the price of a cheeseburger, first coined by Rep. Bob Mrazek, seemed to crystallize the issue for the public and many members of Congress. Even those who had no aversion to clearcutting had a hard time defending the selling off of the nation's largest rainforest for the price of a Big Mac.

The Forest Service and Alaska Pulp Corporation tried to neutralize the economic argument by announcing in September of 1989 that they had negotiated significant changes in APC's fifty-year contract. But the changes only highlighted the sweet deal both pulp companies had enjoyed for so long. Ketchikan Pulp had agreed to a rate increase the previous year, but APC was still paying just $2 per 1,000 board feet for old-growth trees. The Forest Service would now have the authority to raise as well as lower the price it charged for timber to reflect changing markets, and could do so whenever market conditions justified it. Another change transferred authority to designate cutting areas from APC to the Forest Service. Nowhere else in the national forest system had timber purchasers been allowed to call the shots on where they would log.

OUT OF COMPLIANCE

By 1989, the pulp mills' abysmal pollution records had become serious political liabilities. To draw attention to the issue, Rep. Miller asked the state of Alaska for a summary of both mills' records of compliance with state and federal environmental laws. Dennis Kelso of the Alaska Department of Conservation responded with a devastating status report.

Alaska Pulp Corp.'s Sitka pulp mill was out of compliance with both state and federal clean air standards and operating without an air discharge permit under a court-imposed consent decree. In March, a state superior court judge had denied the state's motion to hold the mill in contempt of court for failing to improve the performance of its power boilers. The state had already fined Alaska Pulp for exceeding opacity standards in the consent decree. "Air pollution in Sitka's air shed receives significant numbers of citizen complaints," Kelso wrote. But he added that his financially strapped agency was unable to document violations because it lacked an ambient air monitoring network. Alaska Pulp also was in violation of its federal water pollution discharge permit; two solid waste disposal permits, one covering industrial wastes and asbestos, the other wood waste dredge spoils; and state hazardous waste disposal regulations.

Ketchikan Pulp Co.'s record was equally dismal. The Ketchikan mill was operating in violation of its state and federal air discharge permits and its federal water pollution discharge permit. "Ward Cove, the mill's receiving water, has experienced serious water quality violations and documented fish kills," Kelso wrote. "Water quality concerns have triggered a joint ADEC/EPA water quality study." In 1986 the EPA had included language in Ketchikan Pulp's water pollution discharge permit requiring the mill to achieve compliance with the Clean Water Act by the end of 1987. Yet three years later, KPC still had not met the deadline. In October of 1988, the EPA had filed a complaint with the Department of Justice citing KPC for more than 500 violations of its permit since 1985.

It was hard for the pulp mills to argue that they deserved special treatment from Congress, given their flouting of state and federal environmental laws.

VICTORY FOR TENAKEE

Molly Kemp left her home near Tenakee Springs in 1989 and went to Washington, D.C. to lobby on behalf of her community's way of life. Kemp, a native of northern Michigan, had lived in Southeast Alaska since 1976. With her neighbors, she had spent more than a decade fighting to keep the Forest Service road system at bay. But by 1989, it seemed that the fight had been lost. Congress was Tenakee Springs' last hope.

Things had gone from bad to worse since the Forest Service sued for title to the tiny parcel of land that blocked its road link between Hoonah and Tenakee. In 1988 the Forest Service had begun condemnation proceedings to acquire the town's strategically vital parcel. Adding insult to injury, it proposed to pay the town all of $100 in compensation. In 1989 a federal judge had ruled in favor of the Forest Service in the Tenakee Springs lawsuit.

When Kemp arrived in Washington, veteran lobbyists showed her the ropes. She found sympathetic ears on Capitol Hill. Two of those ears belonged to Eni F.H. Faleomavaega, the delegate from American Samoa, who took to the House floor to defend Tenakee Springs. "Although far apart in both miles and latitudes, the people I represent in American Samoa and the people of Southeast Alaska have something in common," he said. "We both are proud people with unique lifestyles; we have alive and rich native cultures; and we are closely tied to our environments—counting on the sea and our lush rain forests to sustain us economically and spiritually."

In March, Kemp wrote a letter to the mayor and city council back home telling them that things were looking up. House sponsors of the Tongass reform bill were willing to include language prohibiting the Forest Service road connection. The Forest Service's bullying posture toward a bunch of spirited individualists trying to protect their town was backfiring. "As you all know, the Forest Service condemnation of the city right-of way marked the end of our ability to resist a road connection in the courts," she wrote. "What you may not realize is just how bad it makes the Forest Service look back here."

In April, at the Senate field hearing in Sitka, Murkowski was confronted with impassioned testimony from residents of Tenakee Springs. To everyone's surprise, he responded: "I certainly have no objections to the community expressing its wishes against not having a road and would totally support that." Murkowski said he would not fight reform bill language prohibiting the road connection. It was a sweet end to a long and bitter battle.

ALMOST THERE

On July 13, backers of the two House reform bills fought it out on the House floor. Don Young, who favored the Agriculture Committee version, declared that the Miller bill "crushes the American dream." Miller, who led debate on the House floor, attacked the cozy relationship between the Forest Service and the pulp companies, declaring: "The timber companies keep the bureaucrats employed and the bureaucrats keep the timber companies wallowing in federal subsidies." The House defeated the Agriculture Committee substitute 269-144 and then passed the Miller bill on a lopsided 356-60 vote.

The bill had everything SEACC had worked for: cancellation of the $40 million and the 4.5 billion, termination of the contracts, one-hundred-foot buffer strips for salmon streams, and permanent protection for 1.8 million acres of Tongass wilderness. SEACC's work in the House was nearly done.

But Wirth's companion bill stalled in the Senate after Miller and Murkowski failed to reach agreement on a compromise in a House-Senate conference committee before Congress adjourned. The main sticking point was Murkowski's refusal to protect "core areas" of critical wildlife habitat. The gang at SEACC was undeterred. There was always next year.

By the fall of 1989, the campaign to save the Tongass had become an international cause—and a source of embarrassment to the United States abroad. In September, William Reilly, administrator of the U.S. Environmental Protection Agency, returned from a trip to Brazil and announced at a news conference that it had been "difficult" for him to argue against the destruction of the Amazon rainforest. The Brazilian environmental minister had thrown his argument back at him, asking, "But what about Tongass?"

13

First Victory

J
ack Gustafson and Don Cornelius spent the last three days of August 1989 taking a tour of national forest lands on North Prince of Wales Island. The two Alaska state habitat biologists wanted to inspect areas logged since 1984 under the Ketchikan Pulp Co. long-term contract, as well as areas slated for logging in the next five-year cycle. What they saw shocked and angered them: salmon spawning streams logged to the banks or buffered only by skimpy alders. Steep, unstable banks sliding into streams. Gravel deposits from a bridge-removal project blocking fish passage. As they continued their tour, they came upon many logged units and units marked for logging that had been designated "old growth retention" areas under a wildlife protection agreement between the Forest Service and the Alaska Department of Fish and Game.

Some of what they saw was inexplicable: a 150-foot buffer zone around a muskeg bog had been cut, and the unmerchantable bull pines left lying on the ground. One of the last stands of old forest in a large, heavily logged drainage, a stand used by bear and deer, was on the chopping block. Another stand surrounding two blown-down eagle nest trees on an exposed headland had been cut, leaving the eagles with no nearby replacement nest trees.

In many areas, Gustafson and Cornelius found evidence of recent "salvage logging," spurred by a new Forest Service policy that allowed export of unprocessed logs cut in salvage sales. Numerous healthy large conifers in old-growth retention areas had been removed without state review. A five-acre rock pit had been plunked down in the middle of one retention area. Others were bisected by roads and 200-foot cleared rights-of-way.

They were particularly incensed to find that a fifty-acre stand of old growth, strategically located between Sarkar Lake and saltwater on west Prince of Wales Island, had been destroyed. "This tract provided old-growth habitat values and, most significantly, a wildlife migration corridor through this area," they wrote in a report to Frank Rue, director of the habitat division of Alaska Fish and Game. "What remains are two fragmented tracts of old growth which clearly have reduced wildlife values, and are in turn subject to more wind throw. Had the state been given the opportunity to review the environmental assessment for this activity, we would have objected strenuously . . . . Clearly, something must be done to change the direction of the Forest Service before retention is irreparably altered beyond recognition and purpose."

The state biologists followed up with a scathing letter to Ketchikan Area Forest Supervisor Mike Lunn, describing numerous instances in which the agency had allowed loggers to cut stream buffers and destroy critical wildlife habitat without consulting with the state or doing its own required environmental documentation. "The extent of this cutting is significant, and creates serious consequences to both wildlife and the effectiveness of the planning process," they wrote. Lunn never answered their letter. But the habitat biologists' report from the field made waves inside the agency, as well as on Capitol Hill.

On its heels came another report from fisheries biologists who said more than 25,000 salmon had died in August during a rare Southeast Alaska drought. The fish died before spawning, apparently suffocating in warm water. Six of the eight fish kills had occurred on Prince of Wales Island, and five of those six had occurred on national forest land. In each case, the surrounding watershed had been heavily logged. Most of the deaths had occurred in streams where no buffers had been left to provide cooling shade. Ten thousand salmon had perished in Staney Creek, where nearly 90 percent of streamside trees in the watershed had been removed. Lunn responded that the Forest Service had banned the type of streamside logging done at Staney Creek twenty years earlier. But biologists pointed to at least four streams on Prince of Wales where logging had damaged salmon spawning streams just that spring and summer.

Jack Gustafson had spent most of his time between 1985 and 1988 trying to control damage from Native corporation logging. Only recently had he found the time to focus on damaged national forest land. In December of 1988 he had visited a large landslide at Rush Creek, on the heavily logged Thorne Bay Ranger District. Both state and Forest Service resource specialists had warned the district ranger there not to proceed with roading and logging the steep, unstable drainage because of the risk to fish habitat. Disregarding the warnings, the ranger had approved the operation. Sure enough, a torrent of soil, mud, root wads, logs, limbs, and road materials had tumbled into Rush Creek.

To supply timber to Ketchikan Pulp during the 1989-94 period, the Forest Service planned to enter the Salmon Bay Lake watershed on northeast Prince of Wales Island. But state and federal resource specialists feared that logging in the watershed would trigger a mass soil movement similar to the one at Rush Creek. They warned Alaska Regional Forester Michael Barton that four units in the Salmon Bay Lake drainage posed "an unacceptable risk" to the watershed's million-dollar fishery, which produced nearly 200,000 coho, pink and sockeye salmon in good years.

SAVING SALMON BAY

Alan Stein was still working as a gillnetter in Southeast Alaska, and he had not stopped fighting the Forest Service to win protection for salmon streams. In 1988 he began digging through his files from his 1975 lawsuit against the Forest Service and found numerous memos citing abuses to salmon streams during logging. He made the rounds of state and federal fisheries agencies, gathering more documentation. When he asked a National Marine Fisheries Service biologist whether there was evidence that the impact of old-growth logging next to salmon streams was "irreparable," the biologist said yes—but he refused to sign an affidavit saying so without his supervisor's approval. Stein persuaded the supervisor to take the heat. At that point he believed he had what he needed—evidence of irreparable damage to a resource—to win an injunction against the Forest Service and halt logging at Salmon Bay.

Stein took the affidavit and his boxes of documents to Steve Kallick, SEACC's attorney, and asked him to file a lawsuit challenging the Ketchikan Pulp Co. five-year logging plan. But SEACC was consumed with the national Tongass timber reform campaign. Kallick told him, "We're too busy." Next he paid a visit to the Sierra Club Legal Defense Fund, where he told staff attorney Eric Jorgensen, "I have a winning lawsuit here. You have to file this." But the boxes gathered dust in Jorgensen's office for two months.

When the Forest Service finally released its four-volume 1989-1994 Ketchikan Pulp Co. operating plan, Stein spent three days and three nights reading it from cover to cover. When he finished, he was more convinced than ever that he had a winning case. He asked Bart Koehler for help, but Koehler told him he expected to get stream buffers included in the Tongass Timber Reform Act. He suggested Stein go see Buck Lindekugel.

Robert "Buck" Lindekugel had landed in Juneau through a bizarre twist of fate. In 1980, after graduating from Seattle University with a political science degree, he had moved to Craig, Alaska, to make his living as a commercial fisherman. Working as a cook and deck hand on a purse seiner, Lindekugel spent hours watching the sea otters, orcas and humpback whales that cavorted in the protected waters of Southeast Alaska. To him, it all felt like primeval wilderness. "Craig was untouched then," he said. "You could travel a long way without seeing the logging." But he did see other things that bothered him, like plastic and aluminum garbage routinely tossed overboard by fishermen.

Lindekugel decided to return to school and get a degree in environmental science. But fate had other plans. On Easter Sunday 1982, while hiking along the coast south of Bellingham, Washington, he fell from high rocks and landed on his head. When doctors operated, they found massive swelling in his brain and had to drill a hole to relieve the pressure. "I woke up two weeks later and I had lost my identity," Lindekugel said. "I was someone else, not me. After a while I chose not to rely on memories. I developed a new persona."

He assumed his college nickname, Buck, and worked framing houses while taking massive doses of an anti-seizure medication. Then, out of the blue, he decided to go to law school. It was the only thing that seemed to make sense. To his amazement, Lewis and Clark College's Northwestern School of Law in Portland accepted him. From the first day, he had a single goal: "To come to Alaska to practice natural resources law. That was what drove me." With a law degree in his briefcase, Lindekugel moved to Juneau to study for the Alaska Bar. When he finally opened his one-man law office, in the spring of 1989, he was flat broke.

Stein was his first client. He lugged his boxes up three fights of stairs in a Juneau office building nearly as old as the Gold Rush. There he found a long-haired, bushy-bearded guy wearing a cowboy hat and a halibut earring. He said, "I must have come to the wrong office. I'm looking for an attorney named Lindekugel." Buck smiled. "No, that's me. Come in."

Stein showed Lindekugel his evidence and his affidavit. He told him, "I want to sue the Forest Service to get buffers on all the streams and save Salmon Bay. Will you take the case?" Lindekugel thought it over. He said, "I'll need $3,000 and you'll need to get an organization incorporated. Can you do that?" Stein went down to the Juneau docks and raised $3,000 from fishermen in one day. Within a few weeks he had organized commercial fishermen and fish processing companies under the banner of the Salmon Bay Protective Society.

Lindekugel filed the suit in July of 1989. In August, U.S. District Judge James Von der Heydt issued an injunction blocking all logging within a hundred feet on both sides of salmon streams in the Ketchikan Pulp supply area—a full year before the Tongass Timber Reform Act, requiring stream buffers across the Tongass, became law.

The state of Alaska, taking its cue from the Salmon Bay ruling, decided it had better do something to protect salmon on state and private land. In May of 1990, after two years of negotiations involving commercial fishing groups, timber interests and conservationists, Alaska Governor Steve Cowper signed an amendment to the state's Forest Practices Act establishing sixty-six-foot no-cut buffers along both sides of major salmon streams. The amendment was supposed to prevent "significant adverse effects of logging on fish habitat and water quality" on state and private land. But Native corporations, the parties most affected by the new rule, made full use of a loophole that allowed them to request "variances" in enforcement of the stream buffers.

Don Cornelius was one of the state habitat biologists charged with enforcing the new rule. It was, he said, a pointless exercise. "The corporations asked for variances that would allow them to cut virtually every large tree in the buffer." This "variances in the buffer" scam made a mockery of the concept of stream buffers. And Cornelius's efforts to enforce the buffers made him a highly visible target.

When he went to inspect a site, "The logging company would have tied ribbons on all the trees they wanted to cut, right down to the stream bank," Cornelius said. "Sometimes there would be as many as five hundred or even a thousand trees the corporation wanted to cut in the buffer. I would take the ribbons off. Things got hot." Eventually, the Department of Fish and Game eliminated his position and Cornelius left the agency. Soon after, he began a new career as a writer, photographer, and shipboard naturalist on the Alaska Marine Highway.

READY TO DEAL

Back in Washington, D.C., Scott Highleyman smelled victory early in 1990. "At a certain point you know a bill is going to pass. There was a sense of inevitability. It was fun to be a part of." Jay Nelson had left the campaign by then. But once the victory train was moving, there was no keeping Bart Koehler away. In January of 1990, with the concurrence of the SEACC board, Bart and Julie Koehler moved to Washington for the duration to work for the best Tongass reform bill possible. Steve Kallick, who had divided his time between Juneau and Washington since 1987, wanted to be where the action was too. He quit his SEACC job and moved to Washington to work as a citizen lobbyist. Buck Lindekugel, fresh from his victory in the Salmon Bay lawsuit, replaced Kallick as SEACC's staff attorney.

Highleyman admired Koehler's forceful presence and his pragmatic, cut-to-the-quick lobbying style. Koehler's charisma and strength of character had held the Tongass reform coalition together. But he was annoyed to have Koehler suddenly looking over his shoulder. "I had been impressed early on that he was remarkably willing to delegate. In the end, you couldn't keep him away. He was just a nervous ninny."

Koehler's talents were most evident behind the scenes, Highleyman said. "He was terrific in negotiations, the best negotiator I've ever seen." Highleyman and Kallick were in the room when Koehler negotiated with Rep. Don Young's staff over wilderness area set-asides in the Tongass reform bill. They watched in awe as Koehler cut to a discussion of the areas SEACC would not compromise away.

Sen. Bennett Johnston was the key to putting a deal together in the Senate. One day in January, Johnston's staff called the SEACC office and asked for a meeting. "Johnston wanted to know, 'Would we cut a deal, or were we complete ideologues?'" Highleyman said.

Koehler wore his lucky plaid short-sleeved shirt and his brown "howling coyote" tie, not loose as usual but tightly knotted, to the meeting, an acknowledgment that serious business was on the table. He respected the Louisiana senator as a man who knew how to get things done. "Johnston was like Joe Montana," Koehler said. "He had the ability to march down the field in a two-minute drill, throwing touchdowns. Tim Wirth was pushing his bill hard. The Alaska delegation was threatening a fight on the floor of the Senate." It was time to resolve this thing.

Highleyman recalled a brief, bizarre exchange between Johnston and Koehler during the meeting over wilderness areas set aside in the Miller bill. "Johnston said, 'Do you really need all that?' Bart said, 'No, of course not. We just put all that in so we could take some out.' Johnston looked up from his desk and you could see him thinking, 'This is someone I can play poker with.' He said he was so frustrated with conservation groups that refused to negotiate. The meeting broke up two minutes later, and the two staff people came over and shook our hands like we were the Israelis and the Palestinians. Nothing had been negotiated." But on another level, everything had been decided. Johnson knew SEACC was ready to deal.

Koehler puts a slightly different spin on that crucial meeting: "Bennett needed to figure out if we were serious about getting legislation passed. He just wanted a signal that we weren't going in there saying all or nothing. I was under strict orders from our board to get the strongest bill possible."

With Koehler running the campaign, Highleyman saw no reason to stick around. He told Koehler, "This is your show and you can finish it." SEACC took note of his efforts in its *Ravencall* newsletter, noting that since 1987 Highleyman had "left piles of shoe leather on the marbled halls of Congress, consumed hundreds of double cheeseburgers . . . initiated tens of volunteers in the ways of the Capitol, learned to use an umbrella, shared living quarters with other staff volunteers and witnesses, and spent countless late nights in SEACC's office, all in search of that elusive goal known as Tongass reform."

THE JOHNSTON SUBSTITUTE

Soon after his meeting with the SEACC lobbyists, Johnston unveiled a compromise Tongass reform bill. This "Johnston substitute" contained most of the reforms in the House-approved bill, but it did not cancel the long-term contracts with the pulp mills, and it protected most, not all, of the twenty-three proposed wilderness areas. "It was a bill Johnston perceived as tough but reasonable, something that would pass out of the U.S. Senate," Koehler said. Johnston's committee held a brief hearing on the Miller bill in February. On March 7, Johnston held a second hearing to consider his own bill. It was to be the last hearing held in Congress on Tongass timber reform.

By then, Alaska Governor Cowper and the Southeast Conference had signed on to the "Johnston substitute." The Senate Energy Committee passed the bill and sent it to the Senate floor, where on June 13 it swept to passage on a 99-0 vote. Touchdown.

There was a story behind the unanimous vote, of course. To force the Alaska senators to support the Johnston bill, Sen. Tim Wirth and Sen. Wyche Fowler of Georgia had bluffed a floor fight, threatening to bring a bill to the Senate floor that would lock up an additional 1.3 million acres of Tongass wilderness. The bluff worked perfectly. Faced with the prospect of losing more acres to wilderness, the Alaska senators wrote a formal letter to

Johnston in which they agreed to support his bill. Once they were on board, the way was clear to schedule the Senate vote.

Pulp mill executives and Forest Service administrators could smell the changing tide. Seeking to influence the reform legislation, the Forest Service unveiled a new, hastily written draft Tongass Land Management Plan that called for dramatically increased protection of old-growth forests. The agency and Alaska Pulp Corporation also jointly announced final agreement on a hefty increase in the price the company would pay for Tongass timber. "No matter what happens now, the price of a cheeseburger has gone up," quipped George Woodbury, APC's vice president for timber operations.

A House-Senate conference committee was appointed in August to resolve differences between the Miller and Johnston bills. But it did not begin deliberating until October. The House floor fight had made Miller uneasy. He did not want to go to conference with his bill until he was sure he had a working majority among the committee's House members. It was a serious concern; House members from the Interior and Agriculture committees were evenly divided between those supporting the Miller bill and those favoring the weaker Agriculture Committee version. "We could have ended up with a bill that looked a lot more like the Senate version," Koehler said. At the last minute, House Speaker Tom Foley came to the rescue. He appointed Bob Mrazek to the conference committee. That gave Miller a working majority.

"A BALANCED BILL"

In September, the SEACC board met in Hoonah. Koehler flew out from Washington to report on the status of negotiations. He told the board, "We can win this. Here's where we need to go. We won't get everything." The board told Koehler to do the best he could. SEACC was pinning its hopes on the House-Senate conference committee to strengthen the Senate bill.

In Southeast Alaska, grassroots activists were edgy and anxious. To channel their energy, SEACC lobbyists launched Operation Meltdown. They urged SEACC members to call the front desks of Stevens, Murkowski and Young on October 9 and October 10 and demand that the Tongass bill be sent to the conference committee immediately. Hundreds did. Johnston's Senate compromise went to conference on October 11.

The bill that emerged from the committee forfeited permanent protection for several prized areas, including East Kuiu Island, portions of Upper Hoonah Sound and Upper Tenakee Inlet. But it still protected far more land than the Senate compromise. The conference bill set aside 300,000 acres as wilderness, and it barred logging and most road-building on another 722,482 acres, which the Forest Service was to manage to retain its "wildland character" in perpetuity. It protected 100-foot stream buffers on both sides of fish-bearing streams. It repealed the legislated timber target and the $40 million annual subsidy, though it added language directing the Forest Service to "seek to meet" market demand for Tongass timber. But it let the long-term contracts stand.

On October 24 the U.S. Senate adopted the conference report. Johnston praised it as a balanced bill. "It protects the centuries-old trees in an ecosystem replicated nowhere in North America. It protects key fisheries and wildlife habitat," he said. "And, importantly, the conference agreement retains a viable, healthy timber industry."

Alaska's senators tried to put the best possible face on what was clearly a devastating political defeat. Sen. Murkowski found some things in the bill to praise, including language directing the Forest Service to work with the Small Business Administration to help small timber operators buy timber. "The important thing is that the mill operations will remain viable," he said. The House-Senate compromise went too far, Murkowski insisted. "However, with its passage will come an end to the many divisive issues involved in the debate over Tongass reform," he added. "Many of my constituents look forward to this dark cloud passing. I call on all Alaskans to put their differences aside with the passage of this legislation and to work in harmony to produce a diversified and healthy economy in southeast Alaska."

Sen. Stevens delivered a bitter speech, reviewing what he described as a nineteen-year campaign by environmentalists to place as much of the Tongass as possible off-limits to logging. Then he read a fax he had received earlier that day from Bart Koehler that said: "Ted, it surely sounds like Alaskans are ready and willing to put this issue to rest." Grudgingly, Stevens agreed. "I have been assured on all sides that this action will put this issue to rest; that there will be no more requests for wilderness in the Tongass," he said. "After nineteen years, we deserve a little peace. And after nineteen years, I guess it is time to seek peace."

There was no such note of statesmanship from Rep. Don Young when the conference bill came before the House two days later. "I can assure those on the other side of the aisle that have taken jobs away from Alaskans . . . they had better not come back at me again," he said. "I may be only one, but they had better not come back at me again. They had better leave my people alone and leave my state alone."

Rep. Morris Udall added a note of dignity to the proceedings. He recalled the day, nearly ten years earlier, when he had stood on the floor of the House and asked his colleagues to pass the Alaska Lands Act despite "grave misgivings" about its Tongass provisions. "At the time I said that the greatest failing of the Senate Alaska lands bill was, without question, its treatment of the Tongass National Forest in Southeast Alaska," Udall said. "The wilderness designations were easy ones for the most part, limited to treeless, rocks and ice areas. The mandate that the Forest Service provide 4.5 billion board feet of timber per decade to two pulp mills was, I said, a mandate to overcut the nation's last temperate rainforest. And the provision of an annual, off-budget flow of at least $40 million, ostensibly for intensive management of marginal forest lands, was an open invitation to misuse of public funds. That day, I said that I 'shed a tear' for southeast Alaska and its magnificent forest, and that the House would never rest until we had gotten it right, once and for all. Today . . . I can wipe away that tear and rejoice in the fulfillment of the promise made that day."

Rep. George Miller heaped praise on SEACC during the floor debate, even thanking Bart Koehler by name. "Quite simply, Mr. Speaker, we would not be here on the House floor today without SEACC," he said. "Fighting a seemingly unwinnable battle against powerful timber interests and the entrenched bureaucracy of the Forest Service, this remarkable coalition of small communities, fishermen, and other concerned Alaskans has prevailed."

A MILLION ACRES OF RAIN FOREST

At 4:44 p.m. Eastern Standard Time on November 28, 1990, with no fanfare, President George Bush signed the Tongass Timber Reform Act. For SEACC, a small regional conservation group that had built a successful national campaign on passion and commitment, it was a stunning achievement. As Scott Highleyman put it: "Four years after we showed up, we walked out of there with a million acres of rain forest."

In February of 1991 Bart Koehler left SEACC. For the next few months he and Julie rested up on Admiralty Island and visited some of the areas they had helped to protect. By September they were out of money, and Bart Koehler was chomping at the bit to get involved in another conservation campaign. He accepted a job with the Greater Yellowstone Coalition and the two moved to Montana, leaving the misty isles of Southeast Alaska in safe keeping, or so they thought.

PART III

AFTER 1990

". . . at some point it is no longer useful to make decisions according to a policy designated to meet perceived needs of a bygone time."

—Robert B. Weeden, *Messages from Earth: Nature and the Human Prospect in Alaska*

Photo above: Adult male northern goshawk (Accipiter gentilis), Juneau, Alaska, July, 1992. Photo by Craig Flatten.

14

Science Unmuzzled

E uphoria over passage of the 1990 Tongass Timber Reform Act was short-lived. Reality soon reasserted itself. The pulp companies' long-term contracts had survived. And though the legislated timber target was gone, in its place the Forest Service had a mandate to "seek to provide" enough timber to meet market demand. U.S. Senator Ted Stevens made it his business to see that Tongass managers did just that.

In 1991, as the market demand for pulp and lumber picked up, the Tongass sold 406 million board feet of timber, more than it had sold in any year since 1987. In 1992 Tongass timber sales reached a five-year high of 437 million board feet. Meanwhile, Alaska Regional Forester Michael Barton proposed a Tongass plan revision with an annual timber sale level of 418 million board feet—only slightly less than the legislated target Congress had just repudiated. It was a discouraging denouement to the six-year Tongass reform campaign.

THE VPOP COMMITTEE

By the 1990s, 900,000 acres of the most productive Alaska rainforest had been leveled. About half this acreage was on the Tongass National Forest, half on Native corporation land. Alaska wildlife biologists could now point to a body of research on the habitat requirements of Sitka black-tailed deer and brown bears to back up their warning that continued loss of this original forest threatened the web of life in Southeast Alaska. But for Tongass managers, fish and wildlife concerns continued to take a back seat to timber production.

At the urging of federal and state wildlife biologists, the 1979 Tongass Land Management Plan had included modest old-growth retention areas across the forest. But because planners had not mapped the areas, the provision was virtually meaningless. And because the plan had been formally adopted before rules implementing the 1976 National Forest Management Act were in place, Tongass managers largely escaped the implications of one of its key implementing rules, the "viable populations" rule. This rule said that activities on national forests must not threaten the survival of viable populations of native vertebrate species or reduce their distribution throughout their natural range.

Preparation of a new management plan for the Tongass was underway in 1990 as strong Tongass reform legislation was working its way through Congress. In Juneau, Alaska Regional Forester Michael Barton was looking for a way to head off Senate passage of a strong reform bill similar to the Miller bill passed by the House in 1989. In April, Barton took the unprecedented step of sending Congress a remarkable blueprint for wildlife viability on the Tongass—two months before it was released to the public. The draft environmental impact statement called for setting aside permanently at least 24 percent of unprotected old-growth forests on the Tongass, in well-distributed tracts between 5,000 and 10,000 acres in size, in order to maintain habitat for native vertebrate species. At the direction of Barton's lead planner, Steve Brink, a three-man committee had drafted the standard in just three days; it had sailed through environmental review in a few weeks. Cole Crocker-Bedford, a wildlife biologist tapped to serve on the committee, was amazed; he had heard that the Tongass was managed to produce timber, but the new plan had the strongest wildlife protection measures he had ever seen.

A special printing of the draft plan was done for Congress. Only later did it become apparent that Barton's planners had not changed the timber yield numbers to reflect the withdrawal of large tracts from the timber base. The message to Congress was clear: It was possible to preserve wildlife habitat aplenty and sell more than 400 million board feet of timber annually at the same time. And it was apparently persuasive; in October of 1990, a House-Senate conference committee had approved a Tongass reform bill that protected significantly less land than the 1989 House version—and significantly less than Barton's draft plan.

At that point the regional forester needed to find a way to abandon his wildlife-friendly alternative. He asked Steve Brink to appoint a committee to review the scientific literature on wildlife species associated with old-growth forests and develop a conservation plan. This panel of federal and state biologists, known as the Interagency Viable Populations Committee, or VPOP for short, would be the first ever to attempt a comprehensive evaluation of the impact of logging on multiple wildlife species in Southeast Alaska. Preparation of the survey of existing research was an on-again, off-again process that took more than a year to complete. It was complicated by the fact that with the exception of the brown bear and the Sitka black-tailed deer, little was known about wildlife species associated with the Alaska rainforest.

State deer biologist Matthew Kirchhoff, a member of the VPOP Committee, recalls an early brainstorming session. Scientists listed the factors that might put a species at risk: low population size, low reproductive potential, specialized habitat requirements, or a large range. They applied these criteria to all vertebrate species found on the Tongass, then ranked the species in order of vulnerability, eventually settling on nine species of concern. Each member of the committee prepared a status report on one of the species. Kirchhoff chose the Alexander Archipelago wolf, a small, dark subspecies of the gray wolf, found only on some islands of the archipelago and on the narrow Southeast Alaska mainland. Crocker-Bedford chose the rarely seen Queen Charlotte goshawk. John Schoen chose the brown bear. Other biologists gathered what little research had been done on the marten, river otter, mountain goat, northern flying squirrel, boreal owl, and great blue heron, all denizens of the Alaska rain forest.

The VPOP panelists were given a great deal of autonomy in developing the conservation plan. They found the work stimulating, even liberating. But some of them wondered whether their report would ever see the light of day. Although they began without preconceived notions about where their work would lead, Kirchhoff said he soon realized that their findings "were painting the Forest Service into a corner." Their surveys revealed that a number of key species, including the wolf, the goshawk and the brown bear, faced long-term risks if the Forest Service did not alter its logging plans.

THE QUEEN CHARLOTTE GOSHAWK

While based in northern Arizona, Forest Service biologist Cole Crocker-Bedford had researched the effects of logging on the northern goshawk. After his transfer to Alaska in 1989, he initiated the first habitat and population analysis for the Queen Charlotte goshawk, a northern goshawk subspecies. He concluded that the goshawk naturally occurred at low densities and had never been widely distributed in Southeast Alaska, but that extensive logging of its preferred old-growth forest habitat had pushed the fierce raptor to the brink.

Baseline data on the bird were virtually nonexistent. But Crocker-Bedford estimated based on its loss of habitat that the number of Queen Charlotte goshawks in Southeast Alaska had declined by as much as 30 percent from pre-logging levels, and that only 200 to 500 goshawks survived in the region. Like the northern spotted owl, the Queen Charlotte goshawk appeared to be closely associated with old-growth forests. "Home ranges include stands of large trees for nesting, for goshawk flight space beneath the canopy, and for greater abundance and accessibility of some prey," he wrote. The closed canopy of the old-growth rain forest provided the goshawk with cover from predators.

Crocker-Bedford recommended that the Forest Service set aside large and small habitat reserves for goshawks across the Tongass. Large reserves should be big enough to support eight breeding goshawk pairs, and should be located no more than twenty miles apart, he said. Small reserves should support two goshawk pairs and should be no more than eight miles apart. He also recommended protecting each known goshawk nest site outside the reserve system with a 1,600-acre buffer, where logging could not occur. He proposed managing the mostly pristine Cleveland Peninsula in the South Tongass as a vast reserve, where all logging would be banned. And he called for converting the Tongass logging program to a three-hundred-year rotation. By any measure, it was a bold slate of recommendations. On the Tongass, it was doomed from the start.

Biologist Craig Flatten holds a juvenile Queen Charlotte goshawk, the first captured and banded in Southeast Alaska, near Sarkar Lakes, Prince of Wales Island, in 1992. Photo by Jack Gustafson.

THE BROWN BEAR

Brown bears, Admiralty Island. Photo by John Schoen.

Southeast Alaska's Admiralty, Baranof and Chichagof islands harbor the highest densities of brown bears in the world. The brown bear or grizzly requires large areas of undisturbed habitat. VPOP Committee members John Schoen and Kimberly Titus concluded as a result of their VPOP survey that the risk the grizzlies of Southeast faced was not extinction but extirpation from areas that had been heavily roaded and logged.

Brown bear populations were highest on Admiralty Island, where as many as 1,700 bears roamed freely within the 900,000-acre national monument. The bear's prospects were more dismal on northeast Chichagof Island, where a network of logging roads and huge clearcuts had opened formerly pristine forests to hunters in trucks and recreational vehicles. The biologists warned that 250 bears eventually would be extirpated on northeast Chichagof "given continued high human-induced mortality rates." They proposed setting aside 40,000-acre habitat reserves twenty miles apart across the brown bear's range, each encompassing high-volume old-growth forests and at least one salmon spawning stream. They also urged the Forest Service to begin a program of road closures, and to restrict public access to cutting units on the national forest.

THE ALEXANDER ARCHIPELAGO WOLF

With the Alexander Archipelago wolf, logging activity posed threats of two types. The wolf population in Southeast Alaska was believed to be stable at about 690 wolves in 85 packs. Wolves are not particular about where they live as long as they can find abundant food. But logging had eliminated large blocks of habitat for the wolf's principal prey, the Sitka black-tailed deer. Studies that Matt Kirchhoff reviewed in his VPOP survey revealed that the average adult wolf in Southeast Alaska consumes twenty-six deer each year. Because the deer depend on intact old-growth forests for winter forage and cover, the wolf's fate was inextricably linked to the fate of the forest, he concluded.

The second threat to the wolf arose from the extensive system of logging roads, especially on Prince of Wales Island and Kupreanof Island. "Formerly pristine drainages are being accessed by a rapidly expanding road system," Kirchhoff wrote. "Direct mortality can be expected as roads bring man into increasing contact with wolves . . . ." And the forecast was for a vastly expanded road system in the

Alexander Archipelago wolf peering out from forest. Photo by David Person.

future. "The planned road network for the fifty-year sale area for the Ketchikan Pulp company, for example, will be 2.5 miles per square mile, roughly 2.5 times greater than the threshold wolves reportedly tolerate," he noted.

Rescuing the wolf from extirpation, Kirchhoff concluded, would require maintaining habitat to support an abundant, well-distributed and stable population of Sitka black-tailed deer, and closing roads and beaches to reduce pressure from hunters and trappers.

A UNIFIED PLAN

Once biologists had completed their research surveys, they faced the task of merging their findings and recommendations into a single conservation plan that would cover all nine species. To stem the loss of habitat for the Queen Charlotte goshawk, brown bear, and marten, the species most closely associated with old-growth forests, and to protect breeding populations of these forest-dwelling species across large landscapes, the biologists proposed setting aside reserves called habitat conservation areas, or HCAs. Initially they recommended large reserves of up to 80,000 acres, each including at least 20,000 acres of high-volume forest and 40,000 acres of productive forest, and smaller reserves of up to 30,000 acres, each including at least 8,000 acres of high-volume forest and 16,000 acres of productive forest. They attempted to incorporate as many existing wilderness and roadless areas as possible into their strategy, but inevitably some reserves overlapped areas where Tongass managers planned to offer timber sales under the long-term contracts.

The VPOP committee stressed that its recommendations represented the minimum action needed to protect viable populations of native vertebrate species in Southeast Alaska, and would not guarantee abundant populations for subsistence hunting or wildlife viewing.

"Toward the end, when we were writing this up, the decision was whether or not to produce a map," Kirchhoff said. VPOP members believed a map was key to making their plan understandable to the public and policy-makers. Tongass planner Steve Brink opposed mapping the reserves, but in the end a map was produced and included with the report. "It was a pivotal decision," Kirchhoff said. "When people see places on the ground where logging cannot occur, they get excited. Putting it on a map makes it tangible."

A WARNING IGNORED

The VPOP Committee submitted its draft report, "A Strategy for Maintaining Well-Distributed, Viable Populations of Wildlife Associated with Old-Growth Forests in Southeast Alaska," to Steve Brink in February of 1991. It should have been a wake-up call. The scientists warned that unless the pace of logging slowed, and soon, several species could eventually disappear from large areas of the Tongass. The natural fragmentation of the forest on islands and along narrow river corridors, the high-grading of the most biologically productive forests, and the management of commercial forest lands on a continuous 100-year logging rotation all contributed to the long-term risk, they wrote: "Where logging does occur it is typically concentrated in the rare, highly productive old-growth stands at low elevations. In general, these same stands are the most valuable for wildlife; their loss results in disproportionate impacts on certain species."

Logging rotations were too short to allow second-growth trees to attain old-growth characteristics, the scientists said, resulting in "an essentially permanent change from the natural steady-state forest condition." The discontinuous distribution of wildlife habitat presented a unique challenge to Forest Service management, they said, because many subspecies endemic to the Alaska rain forest were found on only a few islands. The wolf, for instance, was abundant on Prince of Wales Island but absent from Admiralty, Baranof and Chichagof.

The VPOP Committee stressed that on the Tongass, there was still time to do the right thing for wildlife: "Because a relatively small percentage of the landscape has been modified, land managers in southeast Alaska still have an opportunity to maintain biological diversity through application of the principles of conservation biology . . . on a large geographic scale. However, if management actions are not taken soon to ensure the maintenance of biological diversity, future management options will be foreclosed."

A high-level internal Forest Service steering committee reviewed the draft VPOP report. In October of 1991 its members released a critique praising the VPOP Committee's work and recommending that it be incorporated into the new Tongass Land Management Plan. One reviewer pronounced the conservation strategy "state-of-the-art." But the rave review was hidden even from members of the VPOP Committee. That same month Regional Forester Barton unveiled a draft plan that ignored the VPOP Committee's work. The plan's preferred "Alternative P" called for an annual timber sale level of 418 million board feet. In contrast to the June 1990 version, this new plan proposed no retention of old-growth forest stands for wildlife habitat; in fact, it criticized the strategy of setting aside large habitat conservation areas for old-growth species. Barton's plan was a slap in the face to the VPOP team. Cole Crocker-Bedford resigned in protest.

As if that weren't enough, Alaska Governor Wally Hickel jumped into the fray, calling on the Forest Service to raise the annual timber sale level to 521 million board feet. For some state biologists, it was the last straw. David Anderson of the Alaska Department of Fish and Game wrote: "I am not going to ask how 521 million board feet can be reconciled with a commitment to recognize and maintain subsistence, recreational, and commercial uses of fish and wildlife . . . We know the answer—it can't."

The VPOP scientists realized Tongass managers had no intention of taking their report seriously. In the winter of 1991-92 they rewrote their recommendations, cutting the large habitat reserves from 80,000 acres to 40,000 acres, about the size of an average river drainage. Crocker-Bedford, who argued against cutting the HCAs in half, maintains that in doing so, the committee was bowing to political pressure. But Kirchhoff and VPOP Chairman Lowell Suring insist that they were merely acknowledging reality on the ground. When they tried to map reserves of 80,000 acres, Kirchhoff said, "it became apparent that many pristine areas of Southeast didn't meet minimum requirements for size and forest composition. How could we defensibly say this was the minimum needed when it wasn't available, and never had been, over much of the Tongass?"

Steve Brink, a road engineer by training and a timber beast by reputation, conducted the final review of the revised VPOP recommendations. He concluded that logging was unlikely to harm the goshawk because sufficient habitat had been set aside in wilderness areas and other reserves. Then he sat on the report. The Forest Service was not eager to get caught in the crossfire between science and commerce in Southeast Alaska, nor to incur the wrath of the Alaska congressional delegation.

THE SCOOP

On December 27, 1992—twenty-two months after the VPOP scientists submitted their initial report—Bridget Schulte, a reporter for States News Service, broke the story of the squelched VPOP Committee report. "U.S. Forest Service officials have suppressed a report from their own biologists warning that several species of wildlife could disappear from parts of Alaska's Tongass National Forest unless more old-growth timber stands are protected from logging," she wrote. The Forest Service had turned over the report only after Schulte submitted a federal Freedom of Information Act request.

Schulte reported that the VPOP committee, fearing its report would be dismissed for political reasons, had cut the size of its proposed habitat conservation areas in half. She quoted Steve Brink, who said the committee "went a little farther than I asked." In his experience, Brink told her, wildlife could survive in logged-over areas. "Humans will live in northeast Washington behind the Capitol and survive and even reproduce, but that isn't their preferred habitat," he said. "They'd much rather live in Georgetown. Wildlife are much the same way."

The story was front-page news in Alaska. Democratic House leaders, incensed by the appearance of suppressed science, attached language to a 1993 Forest Service appropriations bill ordering an independent peer review of wildlife conservation practices on the Tongass. Yet even the furor over the quashed report did not derail the Tongass plan, or modify its timber sale emphasis. On the contrary. By February of 1993, a record of decision adopting a new Tongass plan with an annual timber sale level of 430 million board feet was ready for Barton's signature.

But in January, with the inauguration of President Bill Clinton, the federal government had come under new management. A group of leading conservation biologists wrote to Vice President Al Gore, asking him to support the work of the Alaska biologists. Soon after, the Clinton administration quietly shelved Barton's plan. Steve Brink was eventually transferred out of Alaska.

The Alaska delegation now faced the challenge of keeping the lid on a growing body of scientific data that argued for sharply reduced logging on the Tongass. In the fall of 1993, Stevens showed he was up to the task when he inserted language in an appropriations bill that prohibited the Forest Service from implementing tough new stream protection standards in Alaska. The so-called PACFISH standards, developed by a panel of leading fisheries biologists, called for 300-foot-wide buffers along both sides of major fish-bearing streams on national forest land. The PACFISH standards were incorporated into management plans for national forests in Washington, Oregon and California. But in Alaska the 100-foot-wide buffers legislated in the Tongass Timber Reform Act, now considered inadequate, remained the standard for protection of even the most important salmon streams.

PEER REVIEW

In March of 1994 the peer review team appointed at the direction of Congress—eighteen biologists with impeccable credentials, from across the United States and Canada—released its report. The rigorous critique held the work of the VPOP Committee to exacting standards and found it wanting. Reviewers said the committee's recommendations, while well-intentioned, were too conservative. The proposed habitat reserves were too small and too far apart to support viable populations of goshawks, brown bears and other sensitive species across the Tongass in the long term.

Biologists who reviewed the proposed habitat reserves for breeding populations of Queen Charlotte goshawks were especially critical. They said much larger reserves would be required to assure the survival of the goshawk, which they concluded would soon win federal protection as an endangered species. This finding was particularly gratifying to Crocker-Bedford. But because the natural fragmentation of the forest required young goshawks to fly long distances to disperse, even very large reserves might not rescue the bird, the reviewers said. Tongass managers must change the way they managed the land between the reserves. They must let trees grow longer between logging cycles, quit high-grading, and leave intact forests alone. "Do not further fragment existing large blocks of high volume old growth," they wrote. "Do not differentially cut low altitude, high volume old growth." After the peer review became public, there was no turning back.

HEAVY ARTILLERY

In Boulder, Colorado, far from the political intrigue of Alaska forest politics, Jasper Carlton saw an opportunity. As the director of the Biodiversity Legal Foundation, Carlton made it his business to stay abreast of research on sensitive species. The foundation's self-appointed mission was to sue on behalf of biodiversity, using the heavy artillery of the federal Endangered Species Act to protect wildlife, plants and imperiled habitat. Since its inception in 1989, the foundation's two staff attorneys and a cadre of lawyers willing to do pro bono work for wildlife had racked up a formidable record of legal victories. Carlton was not intimidated by the political power of the Alaska delegation. "Alaska is part of the United States, and the Tongass has not received a de facto exemption from the Endangered Species Act," he said.

In the fall of 1992 Carlton called a friend, Eric Holle, who had a degree in biology and had recently moved from Boulder to Haines, Alaska. He asked Holle what he knew about the Alexander Archipelago wolf. Not much, said Holle, who was working for the state of Alaska as a seasonal fisheries technician and volunteering with the local Lynn Canal Conservation Council in his spare time. "Jasper said he had some concerns about the Alexander Archipelago wolf and he needed an Alaska person to look into it," Holle recalled. "He asked me to work on a status review. I said I hadn't done anything like that, but I would be willing to make a stab at it."

Holle called Matthew Kirchhoff, who put him in touch with David Person, a doctoral candidate at the University of Alaska at Fairbanks. Person, who was conducting ongoing wolf research on Prince of Wales Island, was "absolutely the primary source," Holle said. "But he had not addressed long-term viability. He and Matt both felt there was spotty information, that to make a strong case would take several years of research." Holle nonetheless proceeded to write a detailed description of the Alexander Archipelago wolf—its status, its range, its dependence on abundant Sitka black-tailed deer, its vulnerability to hunters and trappers in areas with high road densities, and its long-term prospects under the existing Tongass management regime.

As a courtesy, he paid a visit to the SEACC office in Juneau to notify staff members about the pending wolf-listing petition. "I wanted to see where their primary areas of concern were, and whether those overlapped with habitat for the wolf," Holle said. To his surprise, SEACC's board and staff reacted with hostility. "They beat up on me. They said, 'You should not do this, we are going to get hit, our people who live in these communities are going to get hit.'"

Holle persevered. He wrote most of the biological text for the petition. Carlton added legal language and forwarded the petition to Eric Glitzenstein, a Washington, D.C. lawyer with expertise on the Endangered Species Act. And that is how it came to pass that in December of 1993 Eric Holle and the Biodiversity Legal Foundation petitioned the U.S. Fish and Wildlife Service to list the Alexander Archipelago wolf as a threatened species under the Endangered Species Act.

The petition conceded that wolf numbers were not in decline, but said the best scientific analysis projected that "problems will manifest themselves twenty to thirty years after logging with declines in both deer and wolf populations." Citing language in the VPOP report, it concluded, "Planned timber harvests on the Tongass National Forest place viable populations of wolves in 'serious jeopardy . . . and substantial and irreversible declines are anticipated' in some areas." The petition sent a shock wave through the Alaska Region office of the Forest Service that reverberated all the way to Washington, D.C.

THE SPOTTED OWL OF THE TONGASS

Meanwhile, in Tucson, Arizona, Kieran Suckling of the Southwest Biodiversity Project was studying up on the Queen Charlotte goshawk. In May of 1994 he petitioned the U.S. Fish and Wildlife Service to list the goshawk—and sent an even bigger tremor rippling through the Forest Service. The Biodiversity Project had a longstanding interest in protecting the northern goshawk, a raptor that favors the rapidly diminishing old-growth forests of the Southwest. In 1991 the project had petitioned the service to list the species throughout its range—except in Alaska. The agency had denied the petition. Years of litigation had ensued.

Both goshawk petitions were inspired by Cole Crocker-Bedford's research. Crocker-Bedford had paid a high price for his research on the northern goshawk in Arizona's Kaibab National Forest. When the Biodiversity Project started citing his findings in litigation, officials in the Forest Service's Southwest regional office applied heavy-handed pressure to silence him. Crocker-Bedford eventually accepted a transfer to the Tongass, where he continued his research, focusing on the Queen Charlotte goshawk.

The Forest Service in Alaska had been aware that the rare raptor might be in trouble since 1986, when a working group proposed designating it as a "sensitive" species. In 1989, state habitat biologist Jack Gustafson had warned his supervisors in writing that logging plans in effect on the Tongass might jeopardize the goshawk's viability. Gustafson wasn't even sure the bird was breeding on the Tongass, because until 1989 there were no breeding records. The goshawk appeared to know its adversary, though; one had recently attacked a logging crew.

In 1990, Crocker-Bedford wrote a paper suggesting that logging posed a risk to the goshawk. Soon after, Ketchikan Area Supervisor Mike Lunn warned his superiors that if they did not take action immediately to protect its habitat, the bird could become the spotted owl of the Tongass. The Alaska Department of Fish and Game and an interagency wildlife committee urged a "sensitive" listing. Still the Forest Service resisted. The agency's director of timber management warned that "the goshawk may be such a rare species in Southeast Alaska that its designation as a sensitive species would lead to numerous inappropriate land management prescriptions."

Gustafson drafted a petition for the Alaska Department of Fish and Game asking the U.S. Fish and Wildlife Service to list the goshawk as a threatened species. Tongass managers persuaded the state agency not to file the petition, promising to review the "sensitive species" listing and establish a temporary protection plan for the goshawk.

Crocker-Bedford's work with the VPOP Committee caught Kieran Suckling's attention in Tucson. "We had not done anything in Alaska, and had no intention to," he said. "But we decided we needed to put our northern goshawk work on hold because the Queen Charlotte goshawk was so imperiled. I decided I needed to go to Alaska, so I took all my goshawk files and went to Ketchikan on the ferry. I wrote most of the listing petition living out of my backpack."

Suckling talked to the Alaska Rainforest Campaign in Anchorage and to Buck Lindekugel at SEACC. Like Eric Holle, he got the cold shoulder. "I said, 'We're going to file this petition. We'd like you to join.' That is when the ice curtain began to fall. Buck said, 'We don't want another spotted owl up here.' My response was, 'Why not? Someone is coming up and offering you a tool that could protect a tremendous amount of land. You would think people would be interested.' "

Matters came to a head at a March 1994 environmental law conference in Eugene, Oregon, shortly before the goshawk listing petition was filed. During the conference, there was an informal pow-wow over the proposed listing. "It got ugly," Suckling said. "No one denied that the goshawk was imperiled. There was a question about do we have enough evidence. But there was also the fear of it . . . . I was taken aback that the leadership to make this happen was not coming from the mainstream environmental organizations."

Negotiations ultimately broke down. "It became apparent they were not going to go for this," Suckling said. He told the Alaskans: "Look, if I know a species is going extinct, I have a moral responsibility to do this. We're going to file, with or without you." Larry Edwards offered to put up $1,000 of his own money to help pay for the listing campaign, and Don Muller signed on as a petitioner.

CAVES AND KARST

Wildlife concerns were not the only emerging resource protection issues on the Tongass. In the late 1980s, recreational cavers brought forth compelling new evidence that logging posed a continuing threat to fragile karst formations and world-class caves in Southeast Alaska.

In the summer of 1987 Kevin and Carlene Allred, veteran cavers who had taken up recreational caving while living in Utah, traveled by ferry from their home in Haines to Prince of Wales Island. They hoped to locate some of the caves they had read about in geologists' reports. When they looked at Forest Service aerial photographs of the island, they recognized not only several individual caves but an entire landscape of limestone and marble formations, known as a karst landscape. "We had never seen anything like it," Kevin Allred said. "We were ecstatic." The Tongass was virgin territory for cave exploration. They were discoverers on the shore of a new world.

They headed for Whale Pass, on the island's northeast corner, where they found large sinkholes created by the collapse of cave ceilings, including one gaping hole a hundred feet wide and a hundred feet deep. "We rappelled down and took turns surfing the cave," Allred said. "It wasn't long before we had the longest cave in Alaska." They named their discovery Starlight Cave. At the bottom, they found a pair of vise grips, apparently dropped by a logger, which they used to repair their car's leaky gas line. Later on that trip they explored El Capitan Cave, which was much larger than Starlight Cave. The caves were beautiful, but the Allreds were shocked by the stumps and denuded hills that surrounded them.

The story of how these karst formations came to be, and how they got to Southeast Alaska, is a fascinating tale. They originated 400 million years ago as the shells and skeletons of marine creatures, which settled on the ocean floor south of the equator. In time, clay, silt and gravels buried these "carbonate" deposits, exerted pressure and turned them to stone. Over millennia, spreading ocean plates carried them to Southeast Alaska, where they folded, fractured, and finally rose above sea level when Ice Age glaciers retreated. Limestone outcrops have been found in Southeast Alaska at elevations above 3,900 feet. Once the formations rose above the surface of the sea, weathering processes formed sinkholes, caves and other karst features. Geologists believe that because of the high rainfall and unique geology of Southeast Alaska, karst and caves developed wherever carbonates were found.

Stumps grow from karst near Flicker Ridge, in the extreme northwest corner of Prince of Wales Island. Photo by Trygve Steen.

A TREASURE DEFILED

Loggers, locals and timber sale administrators had known of the presence of caves on the Tongass for years. As early as 1949, a U.S. Geological Service employee, Robert J. Hackman, published an article in the *National Speleological Society Bulletin* describing the small caves and other karst features he had found in Southeast Alaska. He concluded: "The few caves I have attempted to describe are probably but a fraction of the ones that exist, and I am sure future investigations in these parts will turn up some rich cave material." Jokes circulated among loggers about caves that held the bones of timber fallers still gripping their chainsaws.

But until Allred brought his discovery to the attention of the Forest Service, the agency had ignored these geological oddities. Timber sale planners had done nothing to protect cave openings, to learn more about the rare karst formation, or to study the impact of logging on fragile cave features. On the contrary, the agency targeted karstlands for logging, because it was on these lands, where trees drew nutrients from highly soluble limestone, that the tallest and most commercially valuable trees grew. A 1996 study published by the Forest Service's Pacific Northwest Research Station found that two-thirds of the commercial forest land on known karst landscapes on central Prince of Wales Island had been harvested by 1993.

It was not unusual for the boundaries of clearcuts to follow the demarcation line between non-carbonate bedrock and karst. On one side would be muskeg and stunted bull pines, on the other a stump farm, all that remained of the original towering forest. And beneath the ground, unseen by the loggers and timber sale administrators, would be ruined caves. Loggers filled sinkholes with slash and logging debris. Logging plugged cave entrances with silt. The removal of vegetative cover changed the hydrology of caves, damaging cave structures such as stalactites and stalagmites. At a site called Thrush Cave, silt that fell through cracks in the carbonate bedrock after logging dissolved portions of a rare and spectacular white calcite formation on the walls and ceiling, a formation known as moonmilk.

Allred had no expectation that he could persuade Forest Service officials to do anything to preserve the caves. "To them, anything esthetic didn't seem to mean much," he said. "It was hard to explain to them why they should protect something that isn't there, because that's what caves are, a void." But in 1988, providentially, Congress passed the Cave Resource

Protection Act, requiring at least minimal protection for karst and cave features. And as news of the Tongass caves spread, speleologists and recreational caving groups appealed to the Forest Service to protect these features before logging, since it was nearly impossible to find caves in the impenetrable thicket of second growth forests.

"A VAST UNEXPLORED KARST REGION"

In 1990 the Forest Service hired geologist James F. Baichtal to serve as liaison between the Tongass National Forest and developers of a proposed molybdenum mine in Misty Fiords National Monument. After that project was abandoned, someone told him about "a few caves" on the northern half of Prince of Wales Island he might like to inspect. On aerial photos, Baichtal, like Allred, saw evidence of hundreds of deep sinkholes, fissures and caves. "What had been thought by some to be a few caves was part of a vast unexplored karst region," he wrote later.

The Tongass Cave Project of the National Speleological Society and volunteer cavers from around the world agreed to cooperate with Baichtal and the Forest Service on mapping, inventorying and exploring karstlands and caves. They organized expeditions to remote islands. They discovered that more than 800 square miles of the Tongass is underlain with limestone and marble karst formations, and that the Ketchikan Area alone encompasses 480 square miles of karstlands, mostly on the Thorne Bay Ranger District, the most heavily logged district in the South Tongass.

Caves were not confined to the South Tongass, however. Molly Kemp of Tenakee Springs spent several years searching for caves on Chichagof Island. She found a marble arch high enough for a skiff to pass through. Forest technician Mary Dalton, surveying on Northwest Baranof Island, discovered the distinctive karst formations in several areas. In all, cavers, some working alone, some with the Forest Service, discovered more than five hundred caves in the decade after Kevin Allred reported on his first cave finds. With Forest Service funding, they began exploring about three hundred of them.

Many caves held the bones of ancient mammals. A 44,500-year-old marmot tooth was found in one cave; others have yielded the skeletons of black and brown bears, one dating to 39,000 years ago.

More than thirty caves and rock shelters in the South Tongass have produced significant archeological finds. In 1996, near Labouchere Bay on northwest Prince of Wales Island, an explorer found the jaw and hip of a

9,800-year-old man, the oldest human bones ever recovered in Alaska. Archeologists say the discovery provides the first definitive evidence supporting the Pacific Rim Hypothesis—the theory that humans migrated by boat from Asia to North America along the coast of Alaska at the end of the last Ice Age. "Southeast Alaska," says Forest Service archeologist Mark McCallum, "holds the potential for rewriting the history of the world." No one knows what other clues to human prehistory have been lost due to the wanton destruction of Tongass caves.

Kevin Allred and Pete Smith of Whale Pass, founding members of the Tongass Cave Project, developed an uneasy working relationship with the Forest Service in an effort to get stronger cave and karst protection rules. At first, the agency proposed only minimal forested buffers of about 100 feet around cave entrances. But some of those buffers blew down in strong winds, damaging the caves. Continuing pressure from professional and recreational cavers finally forced the agency to develop a plan to protect entire karst ecosystems as part of its 1997 Tongass Land Management Plan.

Smith says the plan the agency came up with, which provides varying levels of protection for caves depending on their perceived significance, is too little, too late. "This is the only place on earth, with the possible exception of Tasmania," he says, "where you have a temperate rain forest sitting on top of karst."

The most famous of the caves is El Capitan, accessible via a steep climb up wooden stairs flanked by trees growing directly from karst. With over eleven thousand feet of mapped passage, El Cap remains the longest known cave in Alaska. Nearly one thousand feet of the cave are open to the public in summer, offering views of deep pits and pools containing rare cave invertebrates.

Pete Smith considers the Forest Service's limited public access program a double-edged sword. "It gets people interested in caves," he says. But he is unconvinced that the Forest Service will protect the rarest and most fragile cave formations, and the project no longer shares information about new caves with the agency. "The Tongass Cave Project," Smith says, "has always been of the opinion that the best way to protect caves is to keep them secret."

NEW MARCHING ORDERS

All of these developments—wolves, goshawks, caves—demanded a fresh look at the Tongass. It was against this backdrop that Phil Janik, assistant director of wildlife and fisheries in the Forest Service's Washington, D.C., office, accepted a daunting new assignment. In April of 1994, he was dispatched to Juneau by Jack Ward Thomas, the new chief of the Forest Service, to succeed Michael Barton as Alaska regional forester. To environmentalists, Janik's appointment seemed an auspicious development. Barton had taken orders from the pulp mills and the Alaska delegation. Janik had risen through the ranks as a biologist, serving as director of fish and wildlife for the Alaska Region in the 1980s. He might answer to a higher authority.

That higher authority turned out to be the federal Endangered Species Act. One month after Janik arrived, the Southwest Center for Biological Diversity and nine other organizations and individuals petitioned the U.S. Fish and Wildlife Service to list the Queen Charlotte goshawk as an endangered species.

That same month, the Juneau field office of the Fish and Wildlife Service issued its required ninety-day finding on the Alexander Archipelago wolf petition. The federal biologists concluded that there was sufficient evidence that the wolf "may be threatened" for the agency to proceed with a full twelve-month status review, the prelude to a formal listing.

The scientists estimated the total wolf population in Southeast Alaska at about one thousand, and said populations presently appeared "stable at low to moderate levels." In fact, they said, wolf numbers might actually grow with continued mild winters and increased deer forage in new clearcuts. But they added, "As the second growth canopy closes and the understory becomes devoid of forage, the deer population will decline." And they predicted that as deer became scarcer, wolf numbers would begin to plummet.

Noting that the definition of a threatened species is one which "is likely to become endangered within the foreseeable future throughout all or a significant portion of its range," the biologists said the wolf clearly qualified. "Because the effects of timber harvest are far-reaching (i.e., more than 250 years into the future), the interpretation of 'foreseeable' plays an important role in the evaluation of the status of the Alexander Archipelago wolf . . . . The conversion of old growth forest into managed stands in southeast Alaska, which began on an industrial scale approximately 30 years ago, is expected to begin resulting in dramatic adverse effects on deer and wolf populations in ten to thirty years."

Phil Janik's marching orders from Chief Thomas were clear: get a scientifically credible, legally defensible Tongass National Forest land management plan written, and get it out on the street. The goshawk and wolf petitions added urgency to the challenge. Janik knew a fundamental shakeup in the timber-driven culture of the Tongass would be required. The new plan couldn't be just an inside job; Janik had to enlist outsiders if he wanted it to be credible and survive inevitable legal attacks.

Two months after he arrived, Janik sent out a call for help to Charles Philpot, director of the Forest Service's Pacific Northwest Research Station. He asked Philpot to help him rehabilitate the discredited Tongass planning process by collaborating with the Alaska Office on a revised Tongass plan. Philpot agreed to the unusual request.

An uneasy merger

It was an unlikely collaboration for a couple of reasons. The research branch of the Forest Service had never before been closely involved in preparing a national forest management plan. Moreover, within the agency, the Alaska Region was widely regarded as a timber shop, where scientific research findings got lip service at best.

Fred Everest, a Forest Service research fish biologist based in Juneau, agreed to serve as policy coordinator for the new TLMP team. Assembling the team was a challenge, he said. "It was a tough recruit. It was a two-year effort, it meant uprooting a family, and it was controversial and political." Research scientists were skeptical that the effort to write a scientifically credible plan would be worth their while. But Everest eventually persuaded five other research scientists to join the team. Janik dismissed the VPOP Committee, telling its members, "We've got all the information we need." Then he informed his timber managers that he would be deferring sales within the committee's proposed habitat conservation areas until a final plan was adopted.

The new regional forester identified five issues the new Tongass plan must address: wildlife viability, fish habitat, caves and karst, alternatives to clearcutting, and social and economic issues. The job of the research scientists would be to assemble the best available information on those issues. The role of the full team would be to take that information and apply it to the alternatives under consideration. However, the preferred alternative would be chosen by the three area supervisors on the Tongass. This odd division was intended to separate the "pure science" underlying the plan from management decisions requiring tradeoffs between science and politics. It was a recipe for compromise, and Everest said the partnership between research and management was uneasy. "There were a lot of problems initially in merging the science culture and the culture of the Tongass National Forest."

The wolf and goshawk listing petitions had upped the ante. In the fall of 1994 Janik announced that he would implement the VPOP committee's habitat conservation areas on a temporary basis. Alaska's U.S. senators, Ted Stevens and Frank Murkowski, swiftly gave him a lesson in the hardball world of Alaska environmental politics. They introduced a measure slapping a one-year moratorium on any federal agency action that restricted "recreational, subsistence or commercial use of any land under the control of a federal agency." It was a none-too-subtle ploy to prevent Janik from adopting the VPOP report as official agency policy. Though it failed on the Senate floor, it sent the intended message: science would not call the shots on the Tongass if the Alaska delegation had anything to say about it.

In December of 1994, Janik signed an unusual memorandum of understanding with the U.S. Fish and Wildlife Service and the Alaska Department of Fish and Game. It committed all three agencies to work together to conserve habitat and prevent the listing of species under the Endangered Species Act. From that day forward, these frequent adversaries would be closely involved in developing the new Tongass plan.

15

TOXIC BEHAVIOR

Williiam Kevin James, a chemical engineer at Ketchikan Pulp Co., contacted the U.S. Environmental Protection Agency in October of 1991 with information he could no longer keep to himself. While working in the pulp mill laboratory, he had observed company officials tampering with sampling devices and had witnessed direct discharges of untreated pulp mill waste into the waters of Ward Cove. James knew both of those activities violated Ketchikan Pulp's water pollution permit, issued under the federal Clean Water Act. His disclosures to EPA criminal investigators set in motion a three-year investigation involving a small platoon of EPA and FBI agents—an investigation that would hasten the end for the Ketchikan mill.

That same year, in August, the *Anchorage Times* published an exhaustive series that contained shocking revelations about pollution caused by the Alaska Pulp Corp. pulp mill in Sitka. The following March, longtime Sitka environmental activist Larry Edwards filed a class action lawsuit against Alaska Pulp on behalf of waterfront property owners in Sitka, alleging that the mill had recklessly polluted the community of Sitka and had damaged property values and the quality of life for affected landowners, himself included. Edwards and his lawyers offered reams of supporting materials documenting hundreds of violations of the mill's federal water pollution permit and state water quality rules. Edwards sought not only payment of damages to property owners but also changes in operation of the mill, including conversion to a "closed-loop" pulping process that would reduce discharges to Silver Bay from 40 million gallons per day to zero.

For both pulp mills, a day of reckoning had arrived.

RELUCTANT ENFORCEMENT

For decades, Alaska's political leaders, state and federal regulators, mill managers and most residents of Sitka and Ketchikan had looked the other way when it came to pulp mill pollution. The events of the early 1990s forced them at last to confront the trail of environmental abuses the pulp industry had perpetrated on the communities of Sitka and Ketchikan.

There had been problems from the beginning. In the early years of pulp mill operations in Southeast Alaska there was no federal Clean Water Act, and the mills were not required to treat their wastes before discharging them into public waterways. Throughout the 1960s, both the Ketchikan and Sitka mills discharged lignins, resins, wood sugars, bark and chemicals into Alaska waters. The tainted and decomposing wood wastes formed thick mats on the bottoms of Ward Cove and Silver Bay that robbed the water of oxygen. Ocean currents carried suspended toxins far from discharge pipes.

In 1971, the year before Congress passed the Clean Water Act, giving the federal government authority to regulate industrial and sewage discharges into the nation's waters, Ketchikan Pulp Co. built a primary wastewater treatment plant to reduce settleable solids in its effluent and recover and burn more bark, wood and pulp fibers. Yet its discharges into Ward Cove continued to be problematic.

In 1974 the Environmental Protection Agency issued the first National Pollution Discharge Elimination System (NPDES) permits to the Alaska pulp mills. Unlike most states, Alaska had declined to administer the NPDES program itself, preferring to leave that political hot potato to the federal government. Alaska did, however, assume responsibility for enforcing the 1970 Clean Air Act, which set emission limits for all major pollution sources in an effort to improve the quality of ambient air—the air that people actually breathe.

It took until 1977 for the EPA to establish limits on pulp mill discharges into waterways. Danforth Bodien, the EPA's expert on pulp mill pollution, who had written the Alaska mills' permits, also wrote the new national standards. Both mills immediately applied for waivers from the standards. From the outset, Bodien said, both KPC and APC "fought everything, legally and administratively."

The mills also fought regulation politically, using economic blackmail to win support for exemptions from the new laws. In 1979, the EPA scheduled a hearing in Ketchikan on the company's discharges into Ward

Cove and into air near the mill. One week before the hearing, Ketchikan Pulp announced that if the EPA required it to install scrubbers, air filters and treatment ponds to control pollution, it would be forced to close its doors, shattering Ketchikan's economy. KPC ultimately gave in to prevent the EPA from disclosing financial information it had been required to provide to the agency to support its hardship claim. But KPC repeated its threat numerous times over the next two decades as it resisted investing in equipment necessary to protect public health and the environment. These threats struck fear in the hearts of its workers and Ketchikan's business community.

A HISTORY OF NONCOMPLIANCE

As the EPA official responsible for enforcing the pulp mills' NPDES permits, Bodien had the opportunity to observe how the pulp companies operated in a regulatory environment. "Initially Ketchikan Pulp and Alaska Pulp were very close," he said. "They always did things in concert. They had the same lawyer. They were like one entity. They both appealed everything."

Gradually, the companies took different paths. Alaska Pulp vigorously contested pollution fines and kept polluting. Ketchikan Pulp Co. paid its fines and kept polluting. KPC was more willing to invest in pollution control measures, however, Bodien said. "They fought the terms of their permits, but Ketchikan was always the first to give in and say, 'Okay, we'll do it.'"

The Ketchikan mill was older, but it was better maintained, at least in the early years. "Traditionally they had more engineers and did more engineering," Bodien said. "Initially APC hired a lot of engineers, but then they cut back on staff. Eventually they ran with a skeleton staff of technical and professional people. Half the offices were empty. The mill had holes in the floors, holes in the walls."

In 1984 the U.S. Senate reauthorized and strengthened the Clean Water Act. The new law imposed more stringent restrictions on oxygen-robbing waste discharges to waterways and required improved secondary waste water treatment and incineration of the sludge produced in the pulp manufacturing process. Pulp company officials predicted that compliance would cost each mill $30 million.

The Alaska congressional delegation pressured EPA to grant the mills waivers from the new regulations. The EPA denied the waivers. "The Alaska pulp mills said the Clean Water Act guidelines didn't apply to them because they were fundamentally different," Bodien said. "They claimed that doing business in Alaska was different from doing business anywhere else, because they had to pay more for land, transportation, chemicals, and labor. We did an extensive study of their claims and rejected them. The upshot was that their wood was real cheap. When we looked at costs, we found they weren't fundamentally different."

In 1985 the EPA granted Ketchikan Pulp a new water pollution discharge permit on condition that the company build a new water treatment plant. Soon after, on July 1, the mill closed "indefinitely" in the midst of an attempted worker buyout. In October, U.S. Sen. Ted Stevens took to the Senate floor and claimed that without taxpayer subsidies for the new treatment plant, the pulp mill never would reopen. The Ketchikan mill did reopen, and began a three-year wastewater reduction program. Nonetheless, by the 1980s the bottom of Ward Cove was a dead zone. One biological study found that the number of bottom-dwelling species had declined from forty to two. Only two species of pollution-resistant worms survived.

Things were hardly better in Sitka. Before the mill came, the waters of Silver Bay, an important commercial salmon-fishing area, were achingly pure. But in 1965, just six years after the mill began operating, a U.S. Department of the Interior study concluded that parts of Silver Bay near the mill were so polluted that certain bottom fish and vital elements of the food chain had little chance for survival. In 1982 biologists from the U.S. Fish and Wildlife Service undertook a survey of mussels in Silver Bay. Once plentiful, after twenty-three years of pulp mill discharges, they had vanished from waters within a two-mile radius of the mill.

In 1986, after lengthy negotiations, Alaska Pulp Corp. reached a settlement with EPA over violations of its NPDES permit. Within a month after the settlement was announced, APC had violated the terms of its permit again.

THE DIOXIN DEBACLE

The despoiling of Silver Bay with mill effluent was not APC's only environmental legacy. Chronic air pollution from the pulp mill plagued residents of Sitka. For twenty-five years, until the mill installed electrostatic precipitators, dioxin-tainted fly ash went up the stacks. Prevailing winds carried mill emissions into the town. Contaminated fly ash was even dumped directly into Silver Bay. How this happened, and how the company tried to cover it up, is worth relating.

Dioxins and furans, probable human carcinogens, are waste byproducts of the pulping process. In the 1980s the EPA conducted a nationwide study of 104 paper and pulp mills to determine the levels of dioxins and furans such mills generate. The Sitka mill was included in that study.

Since its start-up in 1960, APC had incinerated some of the wastes from its pulping process in power boilers on the mill site, generating both fly ash, which rises in the stacks, and bottom ash, which sinks to the bottom of the boilers. Beginning in 1989, APC installed electrostatic precipitators on its power boilers to collect the escaping fly ash. Mill employees routinely collected this fly ash, combined it with bottom ash, and dumped the dioxin-contaminated substance near the mill, treating it like ordinary solid waste.

On October 31, 1989, the Alaska Department of Environmental Conservation ordered APC to stop disposing of fly ash from its boilers at this site. In response, APC announced plans to truck fly ash to Sitka's lined municipal landfill. But first the DEC wanted the company to test the ash to determine whether it was hazardous. APC employees collected a sample of bottom ash and a sample of fly ash and sent them to a private lab to be tested for the presence of dioxins and furans. Then APC appealed to the city for permission to begin disposing of its ash in the city landfill on an emergency basis while it awaited the test results. The city agreed, and on November 22, mill workers began hauling the combined fly ash and bottom ash to the landfill in open trucks.

On January 7, 1990, the Sitka Right-to-Know Committee, a federally sanctioned citizen advisory body, wrote to the city expressing a concern about this hauling, pointing out that the ash was likely contaminated with dioxin and had not been shown to be non-hazardous as required by the DEC's letter of October 31. On March 7, APC began discharging fly ash through its outfall pipe directly into Silver Bay. Beginning on that day, the mill dumped five to six tons of fly ash daily into the bay.

On March 30, 1990, the lab produced its report. It showed extremely low levels of dioxin in the mill's bottom ash, but levels of 74,600 parts per trillion in the mill's fly ash. The highest dioxin level measured at any of the 104 pulp mills in the EPA study had been 3,000 parts per trillion. After the company received the results of the laboratory analysis, it continued to dump its bottom ash in the landfill and discharge its fly ash into Silver Bay.

When Nancy Hope, chairman of the Right-to-Know Committee, asked Alaska Pulp officials to release the results of the laboratory tests, they stalled for weeks. Finally, they provided the eight-page report, but the page containing the results of the fly ash test was missing. When asked specifically to provide the missing page, they refused. When the city of Sitka asked for the same laboratory test results, company officials again released only the bottom ash test results and withheld the fly ash data.

In May, EPA investigator Irene Alexakos visited the APC mill site and, at the request of the Right-to-Know Committee, asked mill environmental officials Brad Dennison and Edward Oetken to hand over the fly ash test results. They refused; Oetken even questioned her credentials to require their disclosure. Alexakos then telephoned an EPA lawyer, who informed Oetken that disclosure was required. Oetken responded that APC would release the fly ash test results to EPA, but only on condition they be kept confidential and not disclosed to city or state officials. He was informed that there was no legal basis for confidentiality.

On June 12, Danforth Bodien formally notified APC officials that discharging dioxin-contaminated fly ash into the waters of Silver Bay was a violation of the company's permit and the Clean Water Act. He ordered an immediate halt to the discharges. On June 27, APC spokesman Rollo Pool issued a press release putting the company's spin on the incident: APC had begun discharging the ash into Silver Bay after discovering that it was "an economical substitute to neutralize its wastewater before discharging to the ocean." The company had learned only later that the EPA would not allow the practice, Pool said.

In late 1990, the EPA and other agencies conducted a risk screening analysis in and around Sitka to measure levels of dioxins and furans in the soil, water, and water sediments. Inspectors found the cancer-causing chemicals present in soils, marine sediments and sediments in Blue Lake, the source of fresh water for both Sitka and the mill, as well as in the tissues of fish, shellfish, and crabs taken from the mill's receiving waters. Those who ate fish from the affected waters were at highest risk of exposure, the EPA said. For adults consuming one-quarter pound of fish from Silver Bay every other day, the agency placed the cancer risk at two in ten thousand, an astonishing statistic in a community where fresh fish was a food staple. In November of 1991, the EPA issued a proposed water quality regulation for Alaska that prohibited dioxin in marine waters at levels that created a cancer risk higher than one person per million.

The risk screening analysis also found excessive levels of copper, zinc, mercury and lead, all of which pose hazards to marine life. In Sawmill Cove, immediately adjacent to the mill discharge pipes, samplers measured copper levels at sixty-two times the EPA's maximum allowable level. Other studies documented low dissolved oxygen levels, high concentrations of organic compounds, and poor water color and clarity.

BUBBLES AND SLUDGE

In 1990, the Alaska Department of Environmental Conservation conducted its own study of water quality in Silver Bay. The study, DEC said, was prompted by citizen complaints over "a large increase in the amount of floating residue seen in the waters of Silver Bay and washing up on adjoining shorelines; a darkening of Silver Bay's natural color and the possible impacts that the dark color may be having on Silver Bay uses; and a possible connection between deteriorating water quality concerns and a perceived reduction to the fish productivity of Silver Bay."

The DEC reported that a dark reddish-brown plume was visible from the pulp mill discharge point, and that "a large amount of organic residue was observed entrained in the discharge plume," frequently causing it to be 100 percent opaque. State regulations allowed only a five percent degradation of water clarity, yet the DEC found that APC's discharges routinely violated this standard even miles away from the mill. The report noted a dramatic improvement in the color of the water when the mill was not operating. Within a few days of mill shut-down, it was not uncommon to be able to see 60 feet below the surface of the bay.

The DEC report observed that gas bubbles smelling of hydrogen sulfide often broke the surface of Silver Bay, and concluded that "given the history of gas bubbles documented in previous studies, these gas bubbles are a strong indication that an oxygen deficiency may exist on the bottom or in the column of contiguous Sawmill Cove and Silver Bay waters." The Alaska Department of Fish and Game had documented at least two fish kills that occurred after gas bubbles caused part of the waste mat at the bottom of Sawmill Cove to break apart and float to the surface, discharging hydrogen sulfide.

The DEC report also took note of an odorous floating sludge often observed in Sawmill Cove and Silver Bay, which tests had revealed to contain dioxins, furans and hydrocarbons. The U.S. Fish and Wildlife Service had tested samples of the floating residue, including one sample described as "a black fibrous mass" with an extremely strong odor, and had concluded that the stuff would be extremely toxic "to almost any organism encountering it."

NIPPING RESEARCH IN THE BUD

Alaska Pulp Corp. couldn't keep the lid on these major government studies, but it did try to squelch other potentially troublesome research projects. In 1990, the Southeast Alaska Regional Health Corporation (SEARHC) attempted to commission a study of pulp mill air pollution and its possible effects on public health. Alaska Pulp Vice President Frank Roppel intervened with Sen. Frank Murkowski, who put pressure on SEARHC to abandon the study. Lee Schmidt, an early conservationist and an administrator at the hospital operated by SEARHC, made public a letter from Roppel to Murkowski saying the proposed study would "not be in the best interest of Alaska Pulp Corp." Roppel added that the study was "obviously a political ploy carried out in the name of the public good but with conclusions that have already been made." He sent copies of his letter to U.S. Rep. Don Young and Sitka Mayor Dan Keck as well. The health study was abandoned.

Another study, this one involving the effect of air pollution on lichens, also was stillborn after APC officials got wind of it. In 1991 two lichenologists, Linda Geiser and Chiska Derr, visited Sitka while working for the Forest Service on a Tongass-wide baseline study of air quality in pristine airsheds. They decided to include one polluted airshed, Sitka, in their study, and came to Sitka that year for a preliminary survey. Lichens growing on trees are excellent air-pollution indicators, because all of their sustenance comes from the air and precipitation. Analyzing them reveals the presence or absence of sulfur and heavy metals in the atmosphere.

The scientists spent a few days in Sitka, taking photos and tissue samples at one-mile intervals on roads leading from the pulp mill. They found a lichen desert within the first mile of the mill, then faint growth of a single lichen species. As distance from the mill increased, they found more and healthier lichen species. They first observed moss on trees eleven miles from the mill. Not until mile thirteen, beyond the ferry terminal at the end of the road, did they find trees fully covered with diverse lichen communities. The only correlation they could find was the one between the presence of lichens and distance from the mill.

When the lichenologists released their draft study, complete with photos, a hue and cry went up from APC officials, and Gary Morrison, the Forest Service's Chatham area supervisor, announced that he would not allow the researchers to come back to the Chatham area to complete their research. "His only excuse," said Larry Edwards, "was that they had not asked permission to work within his area the previous summer, which was silly, especially considering that their project was Tongass-wide and had been authorized by his agency."

MORE BAD PRESS

In August of 1991 the *Anchorage Times* published the results of its five-month investigation of pollution at the Sitka mill. Reporter Mitch Lipka concluded that the mill had brought not only jobs but serious environmental headaches. Over its life, he wrote, the mill had pumped more than five hundred billion gallons of industrial wastes into Silver Bay, and each day it belched tons of pollutants from its smokestacks into the town's airshed, often covering it in a "smelly haze."

"Mill officials said they have spent nearly $100 million on pollution control since 1968 and $12 million a year to operate it, but the mill has never been in compliance with its pollution permits, always operating under a negotiated agreement or court order to reduce its waste," Lipka wrote. The Japanese-owned mill "has won a reputation among environmental agencies as a combative, recalcitrant street fighter when it comes to regulation," he wrote, and he quoted Danforth Bodien: "They are probably the biggest polluter in the pulp and paper industry. They've used every trick in the books. I guess that's all a part of the game." Bodien later denied that he had called the Sitka mill "the biggest polluter in the pulp and paper industry," however.

Carl Reller, a former Alaska Department of Environmental Conservation official, confirmed to Lipka the magnitude of the problem: "Alaska may be pristine, but where it is polluted it is equal to some of the most polluted areas in the world." APC officials acknowledged that the pulp plant had had an impact on air and water. They said that was the price the community should expect to pay for the jobs the mill had brought. "There's no way to make what we do without polluting," APC spokesman Rollo Pool said.

Seven months later, Larry Edwards filed his class-action suit. Edwards enlisted top-flight lawyers from four firms to represent him. His lead attorney, Terry Reed, had represented APC's union workforce before the National Labor Relations Board. "I feel the case is exceptionally strong, and I feel it's something that should be done," Edwards told the press. "There are a lot of people who have just had it with how the pollution is affecting their lives and the value of their property." However, only 30 percent of eligible waterfront property owners chose to join the class-action suit.

By 1992, others were growing impatient with EPA's failure to enforce the pulp mills' water pollution discharge permits. In July, Eric Jorgensen of the Sierra Club Legal Defense Fund filed notice of intent to sue Ketchikan Pulp Co. and Alaska Pulp Corp. under the Clean Water Act for their failure to meet the limits and conditions set in their permits since 1985. Two months later, the U.S. Department of Justice filed a civil suit against Ketchikan Pulp, alleging hundreds of violations of the Clean Water Act and the Clean Air Act. "We're glad our letter prompted EPA to act," Jorgensen quipped.

THE RAID

Meanwhile, in Ketchikan, the criminal investigation triggered by Kevin James' 1991 whistleblower disclosures was gearing up. On November 16, 1992, thirteen months after James' initial contact with the EPA, the U.S. Department of Justice filed an affidavit for a search warrant to enter the offices and laboratories of Ketchikan Pulp and seize evidence. U.S. Magistrate Harry Branson, who signed the warrant, ordered the affidavit sealed until "such time that the facts contained therein are not considered damaging to further investigation in this case." The next day agents huddled at the Westmark Cape Fox Lodge in Ketchikan to map out their attack plan and draw up a list of the objects they hoped to seize.

At 6:45 a.m. on November 18, when FBI and EPA agents arrived at Ketchikan Pulp's offices to serve the warrant, most KPC administrative and management employees had not yet reported to work. As mill managers arrived, they were presented with the search warrant and a list of property to be seized and advised that employees were free to come and go during the search as long as they didn't interfere or try to remove documents from the premises. KPC officials demanded that their own representatives be allowed to accompany agents throughout the mill and review all documents seized, a request the federal agents denied.

The agents promised managers they would be provided with inventories of the seized documents and allowed to photocopy those they considered essential to day-to-day mill operations. The search lasted two days. In all, agents seized forty-three boxes of documents and shipped them to Seattle by Federal Express. The list of documents ran to nearly 250 items. It included permits, lab reports, consent decrees, computer disks, handwritten memos, environmental compliance documents, maintenance records, reports on plant shutdowns, and files labeled "caustic tank sludge," "toxic chemical releases," "acid spill investigation," "oil spills" and "biological oxygen demand." One file was labeled "environmental control work sheet 'Nasty Day!!!'"

On the second day of the search, KPC sent a letter to all employees advising them that they were not required to talk to investigators unless subpoenaed and offering the services of a company lawyer if they did decide to talk. The letter concluded, "The company does not believe at this time that it or any of its employees have done anything wrong."

On November 20, two days after the raid, Kevin James got a letter from KPC personnel director Michael Baron notifying him that he was being placed on suspension with pay while the company conducted "an internal investigation of pertinent events." On November 21, the Associated Press published a story quoting an unnamed KPC employee who alleged: "Ketchikan Pulp Co. has routinely falsified its records of pollutants discharged into the estuary bordering its pulp mill . . . We can operate clean, but we choose not to. It's a matter of economics. It's the cheapest way."

The unnamed source was Kevin James, who had insisted on anonymity for fear of retribution. James went on to describe precisely how his employer had manipulated records and covered up violations. Ketchikan Pulp was required to keep a record of all pollutants found in the thirty to forty million gallons of wastewater it discharged daily, and to notify the EPA whenever it exceeded limits for pollutants named in its permit. Wastewater was to be monitored for its acidity or alkalinity (pH level), its suspended solids, and its "biological oxygen demand"—its potential to rob receiving waters of oxygen because of high nutrient levels. The pulp mill had been "grossly exceeding" pH levels allowed under the permit, James said. It routinely discharged highly acidic water that posed a severe threat to marine life. But instead of correcting the problems, KPC mill managers simply altered the facts. "We were manipulating our data," James said. "It's routine." Managers knew of the falsifications, he added; one had advised him either to throw away test samples that exceeded EPA levels or to change the numbers.

REPRISAL I

Five months after the raid, on April 19, 1992, KPC's labor relations manager informed James in writing that he was being terminated, ostensibly for filing a false expense report in 1990 after a trip to Utah for surgery to repair a work-related injury. James contacted Sitka attorney James W. McGowan, who promptly filed a complaint with the U.S. Department of Labor asserting that James had been fired for engaging in a "protected activity"—informing a federal regulatory agency of violations of the Clean Water Act. McGowan demanded an investigation. He also demanded that Ketchikan Pulp immediately restore the pay and benefits James had lost since his termination, reimburse him for his legal fees, and continue his pay and fringe benefits for two years from the date of his firing, or until he obtained a comparable job. There was no immediate response.

Daniel J. Roketenetz, a federal administrative law judge, came to Ketchikan in 1994 to hear arguments in the case. The week-long hearing was front-page news in the rabidly pro-pulp industry *Ketchikan Daily News*. The judge was not persuaded by KPC's explanation for the firing. He concluded that James had been terminated "because of his engagement in protected activities, and not because of an insurance claim two and half years earlier." During the hearing, two other former KPC workers, Alfred D. Jackson and Al Roskam, testified that they too had been fired for reporting pollution violations. Roketenetz ordered KPC to pay James' attorney fees but granted him no other compensation.

Meanwhile, the criminal case set in motion by James' disclosures now focused on the actions of six top Ketchikan Pulp Co. officials. Throughout the spring and summer of 1994, KPC and the government skirmished in court over the company's demand for return of the seized documents. In August, all original documents were returned to KPC, but the EPA was allowed to keep copies.

In October, attorneys for KPC and the Department of Justice began meeting to hammer out a settlement in the civil case. One charge alleged that KPC had failed to monitor its discharges for biological oxygen demand on 170 days because of equipment malfunctions. Investigators in the criminal case noted that the dates when monitoring had not occurred corresponded with the dates on which KPC had allegedly tampered with monitoring devices or falsified reports.

The company had strong reason to settle. It was faced with the prospect that file cabinets full of incriminating documents might be made public if the case went to trial. Oral arguments in the case began Jan. 12, 1995, as negotiations continued behind the scenes. On March 6, Ketchikan Pulp Co. agreed to plead guilty to one felony and thirteen misdemeanor violations of the Clean Water Act. In doing so, the company admitted that it had deliberately discharged toxic sludge and wastewater into Ward Cove over five straight days in April of 1990 and had falsified records to cover up the illegal dumping. It also admitted to having discharged highly toxic magnesium oxide directly into Ward Cove several times between 1991 and 1993 while its recovery boilers were off-line for cleaning.

On March 23, the EPA announced that Ketchikan Pulp Co. had agreed to pay $3 million in criminal penalties—the largest successful prosecution of Clean Water Act violations ever in the Northwest. Karen Loeffler, acting U.S. attorney for Alaska, declared, "This case draws the line against environmental crimes. Business as usual is not a license to pollute the environment." In all, the EPA fined Ketchikan Pulp $6 million for civil and criminal violations of federal pollution laws.

But in the end, the company got off with a relative slap on the wrist. In November, at sentencing, the U.S. District Court ordered KPC to pay $1.25 million of its $3 million criminal fine within fifteen days, but allowed it to defer payment of the remaining $1.75 million. As a condition of the settlement, KPC agreed to spend that money on required pollution prevention equipment and upgrades of its wastewater treatment plant.

The original affidavits and other seized and subpoenaed documents remained sealed, precluding disclosure of the names of the Ketchikan Pulp and Louisiana-Pacific officials who had ordered and carried out the environmental crimes, as well as sordid details of mill operations.

To this day, many KPC workers are convinced that if all the information the FBI and EPA obtained when they executed their search warrants had been made public, the Ketchikan mill would have been out of business. "They got a judge to suppress evidence," said longtime KPC employee Gil Smith. "The lawyers sat down with the government and cut a deal. Had the evidence been heard in a court of law, it's very probable that they would have lost their contract."

PAYBACK TIME

Meanwhile, Kevin James had filed a suit for civil damages against KPC's parent company, Louisiana-Pacific Corporation. In his complaint, he alleged that the company had stolen his garbage, tapped his telephone, and sought to dig up dirt on him by contacting his physician and even old friends from high school, all because he had exposed its violations of the Clean Water Act. James McGowan, his attorney, decided to sue in the Alaska state courts but to bring the suit under the federal racketeering law, which provided the opportunity to get access to potentially damning internal documents related to the government's criminal Clean Water Act prosecution of KPC.

L-P's lawyers fought the lawsuit with everything they could muster, eventually bringing in six different law firms and even filing a countersuit against James for alleged violations of his contractual obligations to KPC. They lost at every turn.

Matters came to a head on a week in April of 1996 that played out like a legal thriller. Alaska Superior Court Judge Thomas Jahnke had ordered L-P to turn over a detailed list of environmental records and legal memos that week, and to produce key officials, including the company's in-house legal counsel for environmental affairs, for depositions in Sitka. McGowan didn't know what the documents would show, but he thought they might prove that the decision to attack James had reached the level of L-P's board of directors. Jahnke had also granted McGowan's request to see the potentially incriminating presentencing report prepared by a federal probation officer in the criminal case against KPC. But once in Sitka, L-P's attorneys refused to turn over internal documents, and they filed a motion in federal court to get the entire criminal case record sealed.

On Wednesday of that week Jahnke gave L-P's attorneys until the following Saturday to produce the documents. L-P filed an expedited appeal with the Alaska Supreme Court. On Thursday, two days before the deadline, Supreme Court Justice Dana Fabe upheld Jahnke's ruling. L-P immediately appealed her decision to the full Supreme Court. On Friday the full court concurred. Friday afternoon, L-P's entire legal team caught a plane out of Sitka. At Saturday's deposition they were no-shows. Soon after, settlement negotiations commenced. L-P reached agreement with Kevin James on a settlement in mid-1996. Its terms never were made public, and L-P's internal documents never were released.

A DEAD COVE

By the 1990s, Ward Cove offered mute testimony to KPC's flouting of the nation's environmental laws. Over the years the pulp mill had discharged hundreds of thousands of pounds of solid and liquid waste into the cove. In the four years leading up to the criminal convictions, the cove had received 14.3 million pounds of toxic chemicals directly from the mill, including 6.8 million pounds of methanol, 6.6 million pounds of hydrochloric acid, and heavy metals including arsenic, cadmium and manganese. Over those four years, according to the EPA's Toxics Release Inventory, Ward Cove ranked sixth in the nation for total pounds of toxins discharged directly into a water body, and tenth in the nation for the presence of cancer-causing chemicals. Ward Cove also was on the state of Alaska's list of impaired water bodies for heavy accumulations of sediment, low dissolved oxygen, poor color and elevated levels of toxics.

A mat of contaminated and decomposing wood waste several feet thick lay at the bottom of the cove. Some of the chemicals in the cove were known to bioaccumulate in the tissues and organs of marine animals; others were capable of killing or harming the development of sea urchins, clams, and mussels, and of young salmon, which still passed through Ward Cove to spawn in Ward Creek and still were caught by local fishermen. Crabs in Ward Cove tested for the presence of dioxin were found to contain at least ten times as much of the carcinogen as those at uncontaminated sites. But after 1995 researchers had a hard time finding any crabs to test in Ward Cove.

In a last-ditch attempt to fix the problem, Ketchikan Pulp proposed in 1994 to extend an outfall pipe across Ward Cove to Tongass Narrows, the waterway separating Revillagigedo Island from Gravina Island. The company unveiled a consultant's report showing that such a scheme was feasible. But it withheld the section of the report that predicted the tides would carry the mill effluent into downtown Ketchikan for part of each year. When the information became public, the outfall extension project died a quick death.

16

DEFAULT

The news exploded like a bombshell over Southeast Alaska on June 30, 1993: Alaska Pulp Corporation would close its Sitka pulp mill at the end of September, throwing four hundred people out of work. Although many residents interviewed by a local radio station on the day of the announcement said they were upbeat about Sitka's prospects, news of the impending closure still hit the town hard. Alaska Pulp had an $18 million payroll and accounted for one-sixth of the town's tax base. Local boosters and elected officials forecast an economic meltdown.

Alaska Pulp executives blamed the closure on poor world markets for dissolving pulp. But they said they did not plan to abandon Southeast Alaska. The company would continue logging the Tongass at the maximum rate allowed under its fifty-year contract, feeding the best logs to its sawmill in Wrangell, and using the contract as collateral to get financing for converting the pulp mill to a medium-density fiberboard plant that would employ a hundred workers. In the weeks leading up to the announcement, APC officials had consulted with the Forest Service's Forest Products Research Laboratory in Madison, Wisconsin, to refine their mill conversion plan.

The poor pulp market was indeed a major factor in the decision by Alaska Pulp's primary owner, the Industrial Bank of Japan, to pull the plug on the Sitka mill. As the *Wall Street Journal* noted, the market was suffering from "severe global overcapacity." Alaska Pulp's financial statement revealed that the company had received a low price for dissolving pulp and had run chronic high operating deficits since at least the mid-1980s. Though APC bought its federal timber at a heavily subsidized price, it was still expensive to transport logs from remote areas of the North Tongass to its Sitka mill. Moreover, trees in the north end were generally smaller and less commercially valuable than those in Ketchikan Pulp's South Tongass supply area, a fact that had prompted APC to sue the Forest Service for breach of contract in the mid-1980s over its alleged failure to provide "economic timber."

However, during the Tongass reform campaign, the company had settled the suit and had agreed to pay a substantially higher stumpage rate for Tongass trees in an attempt to win political favor.

Under APC President George Ishiyama, the company had cut management staff and labor costs, eventually breaking the pulp mill's major union. Nonetheless, APC said it had lost $31 million on operation of its pulp mill in the year ending March 31, 1993, and had piled up an accumulated operating deficit of $163 million by the time the closure was announced.

There was more to the story than high operating costs and low prices, however. Forest Service timber appraisers were convinced the corporation's Japanese investors had deliberately drained profits from the pulp mill through complex transactions involving APC's many interlocking corporate partners. Further light was shed on APC's financial affairs in May of 1994, when an Alaska court unsealed records subpoenaed by attorneys for Larry Edwards in his class action suit. The records revealed that while APC's Alaska timber operations were losing money, the corporation had made profitable investments through a subsidiary, AP Financial, under a management services agreement with a separate company owned by George Ishiyama. Annual reports showed that between 1987 and 1990, the value of APC's securities holdings had ballooned from $17 million to $250 million. By 1993, AP Financial's stock holdings were worth $182.4 million and amounted to half of APC's assets.

In January of 1992 APC and Ishiyama had separated their intertwined financial holdings. Then, in early 1993, just a few months before the mill closure announcement, Ishiyama had liquidated AP Financial, transferring it to another company under his control. A liquidation distribution of $20.7 million was made to Ishiyama himself, "as consideration for his personal contributions." APC was left with its rundown Sitka pulp mill, its Wrangell sawmill, and its debts.

A *Sitka Sentinel* report on these financial transactions prompted one reader, Robert Chevalier of Sitka, to write the following letter to the editor: "Mr. Ishiyama has often expressed great concern . . . for the welfare of this community. Why then did he not confide in the hundreds of loggers, tugboatmen, mill workers, etc., when he liquidated and tiptoed away from APC in January 1992, a nice safe 18 months ahead of the announcement of the mill closure? Those who were dependent on APC operations would have been spared a lot of bad luck and trouble had they known they were being sold out."

By 1993, Alaska Pulp's labor practices and its many environmental sins had caught up with it. When the mill closed, Alaska Pulp handed out generous severance checks and pension cash-outs, but only to workers employed on the mill's final day. Many were strike-breakers who had come to work at the mill during the acrimonious 1986 strike. The original workforce had been fired, and the company had not yet paid those workers back pay awarded to them by the National Labor Relations Board, though the board had ordered APC to set aside $10 million to settle the strikers' claims. Cynics said the company was closing its doors to keep from paying this debt.

APC also faced payment of a $5 million fine levied by the U.S. Environmental Protection Agency for longstanding water pollution problems. After the mill closed, the company continued to dump wastes into Silver Bay as it cleaned out its tanks. A year after the closure, the EPA conducted a new investigation and concluded that dioxin-tainted wastes remained both on the mill site and in the bay, largely because of the mill's earlier "deliberate, unpermitted disposal of dioxin-contaminated fly ash."

Also pending was Larry Edwards' class action suit over the pollution of Silver Bay. In October of 1994, a week before trial, APC agreed to settle the lawsuit for $3.3 million. More than a million dollars went to Edwards' legal team. The rest was used to establish a $2 million community trust, half to promote scientific education, primarily through programs at Sitka's high school, and half to support cultural grants. Edwards recalls the debate about naming the trust. Ishiyama and his attorneys insisted on naming it the Sitka, Alaska, Permanent Charitable Trust. Edwards thought that was too wordy. But Ishiyama's strategy became clear when the board of trustees began attracting news coverage. Headlines in the Sitka Sentinel condensed the name of the new charitable institution to the "Sitka APC Trust."

The Alaska Pulp Co. mill near Sitka closed in 1994, a victim of increased competition in the global pulp market. Photo by Kathie Durbin.

APC's woes did not end with the settlement of the class action suit. In July of 1995, the corporation agreed to pay $1.97 million to settle federal pollution charges, including an allegation that the mill had discharged improperly treated wastewater between 1986 and 1990. The EPA documented 250 separate illegal discharges of acidic waste water and water containing solids into Silver Bay.

BREACH OF CONTRACT

Alaska Pulp's decision to close its Sitka mill presented the Clinton administration with a direct challenge. By closing the mill, yet announcing its intention to continue logging, the company was breaking its fifty-year contract with the Forest Service—and daring the government to do anything about it.

U.S. Agriculture Undersecretary Jim Lyons said there was never any doubt in the top echelons of the Forest Service or within the administration that Alaska Pulp had breached its contract. "APC shut their mill down, terminated their employees and gave them severance pay," he said. "It was as clear a closure as could be." As for APC's announced intention to build a medium-density fiberboard plant, "it was a glimmer in their eye," Lyons said. "Our judgment was the company never made a good-faith effort to investigate this option."

In fact, Regional Forester Michael Barton notified APC executive vice president Frank Roppel shortly before the mill closed that the company was likely in violation of its contract, and gave Roppel thirty days to submit a "realistic plan for reopening the existing mill or an alternative facility as soon as possible."

Roppel, however, insisted years later that the Forest Service had given the company no advance warning that its decision to close its pulp mill indefinitely could be construed as a breach of contract. "That question was asked repeatedly by our company of the Forest Service," he said. "We never got a direct answer."

In January of 1994, the Forest Service announced that it had concluded APC was indeed in violation of its contract, and that it was considering canceling it. The announcement triggered frantic efforts by the Alaska congressional delegation to try to salvage the contract, to no avail. In April, Barton advised Alaska Pulp Corporation in writing that he was terminating the contract, and that APC would now have to obtain Tongass timber through the normal competitive bidding process. Soon after, Barton retired.

SHUTTING DOWN WRANGELL

In December of 1994, APC made a clean sweep of its Alaska operations when it closed its sawmill in Wrangell, throwing 230 people out of work in a community of 2,500. Unlike the Sitka mill, the Wrangell sawmill, which trimmed high-grade logs and shipped them to the Far East, had often operated at a profit. But after the Forest Service canceled its fifty-year contract, APC bought no more Tongass timber. It kept the Wrangell mill running only until its supply of logs ran out.

The same month APC closed the Wrangell mill, the company sued the government for more than $1 billion in damages in the U.S. Court of Claims. APC's lawyers argued that although the company's contract required construction of a pulp mill, it did not require the company to operate the mill continuously for fifty years—only to practice "high-level utilization" of timber from the Tongass National Forest and to do primary manufacturing of that timber in Southeast Alaska. The company's lawyers said APC was entitled to compensation for the two billion board feet of timber it was owed under the remaining seventeen years of its contract, as well as for the value of the mill and equipment and foregone profits. In the summer of 1999, that suit was still pending.

The Southeast Alaska Conservation Council speculated in its *Ravencall* newsletter that APC had closed the Wrangell mill to create a jobs crisis, thereby providing political cover for U.S. Senators Ted Stevens and Frank Murkowski to bail the company out with a new mill paid for by taxpayers and a new long-term subsidized timber contract. That didn't happen, but the jobs crisis did. The APC sawmill had generated 20 percent of Wrangell's jobs and 30 percent of its wage earnings. Between 1994 and 1995, annual earnings in Wrangell plummeted. The unemployment rate, always higher in winter because of the seasonal nature of the commercial fishing industry, climbed from 13.4 percent in January of 1993 to 21.6 percent in January of 1994. Worker severance packages ran out within three to six months. Some employees chose to enter retraining programs, but about two hundred families eventually left. However, the town still had a commercial fishing industry, and a few cruise ships stopped off at Wrangell, a rough-edged town in a spectacular setting.

Doug Roberts was elected mayor soon after the mill closed. The immediate challenge, he said, was to replace lost timber jobs. "One of the first things we had to do was hire displaced timber workers and put them on the city payroll to work on various projects. It was a New Deal here for a while." Roberts then set about trying to line up a buyer for the mill and a reliable timber supply that would allow it to reopen, at least on a limited basis. He worked with the Port of Wrangell on a strategy to attract more fishing boats, and with the U.S. Army Corps of Engineers on plans for a new harbor. He organized a group of investors to save the town's fish cannery, which had declared bankruptcy soon after the mill closed. "Wrangell chose to exist as a community," Roberts said.

SITKA REBOUNDS

The situation in Sitka was much rosier. Sitka's unemployment rate shot up temporarily, from 3 percent to nearly 15 percent, but by August of 1994 had dropped to below 7 percent. The town's economy did not collapse. Construction was going full-bore in 1994. Cruise ships and commercial and charter fishing businesses were pumping jobs and money into the town. With two colleges and two hospitals, Sitka was rapidly becoming a regional center for health and education services, sectors that generated new white-collar jobs.

Even pulp mill workers did not feel the impact of the mill closure at once. Most engineers and other professional employees had departed soon after the closure announcement. APC offered free barge service to workers who wanted to leave immediately. Scores of workers took advantage of the chance to ship their possessions back to the Lower 48 free of charge. But most mill employees had children in school. Under a special arrangement with the Alaska Department of Labor, they were able to file backdated unemployment claims even before the mill closed, allowing them to stay in Sitka and collect fifty-two weeks' worth of unemployment checks over the next two years, in addition to their severance pay.

"It was difficult for me to see the trauma because I had seen real trauma," said John Scott of the Alaska Department of Labor, who had worked in Flint, Michigan, a town flattened by the depression in the U.S. auto industry.

It was January of 1995, sixteen months after the mill closure, before most Alaska Pulp workers exhausted their severance pay and unemployment benefits. By then, they were eligible for generous retraining and relocation benefits. Some went to truck-driving school, or got training in operating heavy equipment. Others pursued degrees in teaching or civil engineering or health care. Some bought boats and went into the charter fishing business.

Not all of them found jobs in Sitka, and most who did were forced to make do with a lower standard of living than they had become accustomed to on pulp mill wages. "If you're not in the field of medical care, government, fishing or tourism, you are going to have a difficult time finding a job here," Scott said in August of 1996, nearly three years after the mill's closure. By then, Sitka's unemployment rate hovered at 4.3 percent—two points lower than in Ketchikan, where the pulp mill was still operating.

TOURISM PLAYS ITS CARD

The closure of the Sitka and Wrangell mills threw Tongass National Forest managers a curve. Virtually overnight, the demand for Tongass timber had plummeted. For conservationists, the big question was what would become of timber sales already committed to Alaska Pulp.

When the Forest Service proceeded to transfer many of the APC sales to Ketchikan Pulp, SEACC and the Sitka Conservation Society cried foul. They argued that the closure of the APC mills required the agency to reassess its timber sale program across the Tongass. Legal action would be required. But 1994 was a sensitive time to file a lawsuit over timber. Tony Knowles, a moderate Democrat, was in a tight race for governor of Alaska. SEACC feared a lawsuit to block the transfer of the APC sales would look obstructionist and might backfire, costing Knowles the election.

Fortuitously, a new player had arrived on the scene. In 1992, wilderness outfitters, sea kayak guide services and other small businesses oriented toward wilderness adventure had organized as the Alaska Wilderness Tourism and Recreation Association. The tourism industry had seldom spoken out on resource conservation issues. But that changed in 1993, when AWRTA joined the cruise ship industry in threatening a tourist boycott of Alaska after Governor Wally Hickel announced a plan to shoot wolves from helicopters in order to build up moose and caribou populations in Alaska's Interior. The idea that the state of Alaska would take part in the aerial gunning-down of wolves triggered a nationwide outcry and forced Hickel to drop the plan.

Wilderness outfitters were concerned about the continuing loss of protected, unlogged anchorages in Southeast Alaska, where small boats could put in and kayakers could explore and experience an intact temperate rainforest. People did not spend thousands of dollars flying to Southeast and kayaking into secluded coves to see clearcuts and logging roads. The prospect of getting the APC sales canceled and protecting some of these anchorages was enough to bring AWRTA into the environmental fold.

Even the Forest Service had admitted that its most recent logging plan for the Alaska Pulp supply area would damage tourism and wilderness recreation. But the agency had argued that it could not address that concern, because its first requirement was to meet the terms of the APC long-term contract. That argument no longer held water. "When the mill closed and the contract went away, there was this incongruity," said Steve Behnke, AWRTA's executive director. "The Forest Service still planned to release the sales."

AWRTA agreed to be the lead plaintiff in a lawsuit against the Forest Service, taking some of the heat off SEACC in the months preceding the 1994 election. After the election, at which Knowles was elected governor, SEACC joined the suit, along with the Natural Resources Defense Council, the Wilderness Society and the Organized Community of Kake, a Native village. The roster of plaintiffs was intended to show broad and diverse support for reduced logging on the Tongass.

THE AWRTA SUIT

Tom Waldo of the Sierra Club Legal Defense Fund argued the case. He contended that the Forest Service must withdraw the APC sales and reanalyze them in an environmental impact statement that acknowledged the diminished market for timber in Southeast Alaska. Waldo also argued that the sales violated the Alaska Lands Act by failing to consider the impact of logging on subsistence hunting, fishing, and food-gathering. He lost at district court but prevailed in the 9th U.S. Circuit Court of Appeals.

Waldo believes political developments in Washington, D.C., might have influenced the appeals court ruling. Sen. Ted Stevens had tacked a rider onto a 1995 budget bill that in effect dismissed the AWRTA lawsuit, saying no new Forest Service environmental impact statement was necessary. "I think the court was angered by this rider," Waldo said.

The 9th Circuit ruling sent the case back to an unsympathetic district court judge, James W. Sedwick, for settlement. Waldo and others made the strategic decision that they would be better off negotiating a settlement. "We tried initially to talk to Forest Service folks in Alaska about settling the case, but we could get nowhere," Waldo said. "So some of us went back to D.C. to talk to higher-level people." Lyons and Assistant Attorney General Lois Schiffer became part of the discussion.

At the time, President Clinton was in a showdown with Congress and had vowed to veto a bevy of damaging environmental riders attached to government spending bills. "Some of those riders were Tongass riders," Waldo said. "President Clinton had mentioned the Tongass prominently in explaining why he was vetoing the riders. So the administration paid attention when this case ended up in their laps."

In February of 1996 the negotiators met for three days in Seattle to hammer out a deal. "The administration had goals it wanted to achieve, like meeting its contract obligation to KPC and achieving an independent sales program," Waldo said. The Forest Service wanted to deliver two sales it had auctioned to independent purchasers before the AWRTA case was filed. Canceling those sales would be costly and complicated. And plaintiffs in the case had their own issues. The Native village of Kake wanted to protect subsistence hunting and fishing areas on Kuiu Island. The Boat Company, which offered cruises to pristine anchorages for environmentally minded tourists, wanted protection for Saook Bay on north Baranof Island. Tenakee Springs wanted to keep logging out of Crab Bay on northeast Chichagof Island. "We were trying to get something that was pretty balanced," Waldo said, "so no one was going to take too great a hit. This was a big case. This was every timber sale on the north half of the Tongass, a total of 282 million board feet. These were long, hard negotiations." In the end, the parties agreed that 106 million board feet of timber would be released to the Forest Service for sale.

The settlement was presented to Judge Sedwick as a consent decree enforceable in court. At that point, the timber industry got involved. Jim Clark, attorney for the Alaska Forest Association, requested that the timber industry association be named as an intervenor. Clark raised a series of objections, implying that the Clinton administration was forcing the settlement on local forest managers in Southeast Alaska. Sedwick was sympathetic to the argument, and ordered the environmental groups and administration officials into another round of negotiations, this time with timber at the table.

When those negotiations predictably went nowhere, Sedwick granted the timber industry a two-day hearing, at which industry lawyers argued that the sales released under the proposed settlement were not "economically viable" and could not be profitably logged. In the end, Sedwick ordered a few minor changes in the sales and approved the settlement. It was signed on June 6, 1996.

The settlement was a compromise, but several positive things came out of it, Waldo said. "Because it got so much publicity, and there was such a diverse coalition of plaintiffs, it really helped get across the message that this was not just outside national environmental groups trying to shut down the Tongass. This was lots of local people with concerns of their own, in terms of tourism, cultural concerns in Native villages, and subsistence concerns. It wasn't just jobs versus the environment."

A second plus for environmentalists was the economic analysis the plaintiffs commissioned from an Oregon economist, Ed Whitelaw of Eco Northwest, to help make their case. "In the past, the timber industry had always put forth arguments about how it was the foundation of the economy in Southeast Alaska," Waldo said. "We had never challenged those assertions before. In this case we did. Eco Northwest provided us with an excellent report that showed employment in the timber industry was going down while total employment in the region was going up. Ed Whitelaw predicted that you could reduce logging on the Tongass substantially and the overall economy of the region would continue to grow."

THE RAINFOREST CAMPAIGN

As the AWRTA lawsuit was taking shape, another new player, the Alaska Rainforest Campaign, entered the fray. If SEACC was the quintessential grassroots environmental campaign, fueled by volunteers and run by an underpaid staff, the Alaska Rainforest Campaign was the opposite: a foundation-driven campaign that came into existence because money was available and paid professionals to achieve its goals.

In the early 1990s the Pew Charitable Trusts, based in Philadelphia, had begun funding broad regional conservation campaigns, including the Western Ancient Forest Campaign and Save Our Wild Salmon, both in the Pacific Northwest. Both campaigns depended on the willingness of fiercely independent environmental groups to work together for a common goal. In 1993, the Alaska Conservation Foundation was looking for a reason to ask Pew for a lot of money. John Sisk of SEACC and several other Alaska environmentalists began brainstorming about an Alaska regional forest protection campaign. Its main goals would be to get rid of the pulp mills' long-term contracts and reduce timber sale levels on the Tongass National Forest. Environmentalists also wanted to focus attention on Alaska's other national forest, the Chugach, surrounding Prince William Sound. Millions of dollars had become available through the *Exxon Valdez* Oil Spill settlement for habitat acquisition. There was an opportunity to acquire land owned by two Native corporations in Prince William Sound and to protect those lands from logging.

A meeting was held in Anchorage. Among those in attendance were representatives of SEACC, the Alaska Center for the Environment, the Sierra Club Legal Defense Fund, the Sierra Club, the Wilderness Society and the National Audubon Society. Chuck Clusen, a veteran of the Alaska Lands campaign, facilitated. Jim Stratton of the Alaska Conservation Foundation also attended.

Stratton pointed out that Pew funding came with strings attached. "Pew was only interested in ecosystem-wide campaigns," he said later. "Local groups had to work together, and the nationals also had to be involved. We sat down and talked about, 'Is this something that makes sense? What would its goals be?' We broke for dinner, drank a lot of red wine, worked until the wee hours and had a campaign plan."

Most of the financial and grant-writing responsibility fell to Stratton. "To get the money to fund the next phase we had to create a new widget to sell," he said. "I had a number of discussions with Pew over campaign structure." Tensions with SEACC surfaced immediately. "I warned that if you have a campaign director who can overrule SEACC, SEACC will walk." Pew finally agreed to give SEACC a veto on issues involving the Tongass.

Former SEACC attorney Steve Kallick, who was eager to return to the front lines, agreed to direct the new national campaign. For Kallick, running a well-financed campaign was a new and welcome experience. "Pew insisted we be professional, bring in people with expertise, have real resources. I believed we had to put together a state-of-the-art capacity." The campaign hired scientists, lobbyists and media consultants. At its height, it deployed the equivalent of twenty full-time employees, many of them working within grassroots member groups. Over five years, between 1993 and 1998, Pew and other funders invested $950,000 in the Alaska Rainforest Campaign.

The campaign agenda was a grab-bag. Kallick and his staff took on land acquisitions and buy-backs made possible by the *Exxon Valdez* money, challenged logging on state lands managed in trust for the University of Alaska, and tried to influence development of the Tongass and Chugach national forest management plans. But the campaign soon focused on the most pressing issues at hand: eroding political support for Ketchikan Pulp Co. and pushing for termination of KPC's long-term contract.

17

WHISTLEBLOWERS

I n 1990, when Bill Shoaf applied for a transfer from his high-level
planning position at Forest Service headquarters in Washington, D.C.
to a job on the Tongass National Forest, his colleagues were puzzled.
Why would Shoaf, an intense, ambitious and rigorously professional career
employee, accept what amounted to a demotion to work in Alaska? Shoaf's
reason was simple: he wanted to experience the nation's largest national
forest first-hand. But a few weeks into his first assignment, laying out a
timber sale in the Ketchikan Pulp Co. supply area, he knew that something
was seriously amiss on the Tongass.

Mary Dalton had spent 16 years as a seasonal forestry technician on the
Tongass when, in 1992, she was assigned to document the potential
environmental impacts of an enormous timber sale proposed for Northwest
Baranof Island. She spent four summers in the field, braving rain, rough
terrain and brown bears, to map bear den sites and deer winter range,
discovering previously unknown karst formations in the process. This
hard-won knowledge would prove her undoing.

As Tongass managers prepared huge new timber sales in the 1990s, they
faced increasing dissent from within their ranks. But the timber culture on
the Tongass was too entrenched to tolerate public criticism from its own.
Those who pushed too hard risked retaliation, repudiation, even professional
ruin.

A LEARNING EXPERIENCE

Bill Shoaf's dissent flared into the headlines in 1993, after the Tongass put
up one of the largest timber sales ever offered in the national forest system.
The Central Prince of Wales Project called for logging the heart of the
island to supply Ketchikan Pulp Co. in the second half of the 1990s. Shoaf,

the leader of the Forest Service interdisciplinary team that designed the sale, publicly disagreed with its timber yield estimates and wrote a report that called into question the legality of the entire Tongass timber sale program. His integrity ultimately cost him his career in the Forest Service.

His learning curve began with his first assignment, helping lay out a timber sale on the heavily logged Thorne Bay District. One cutting unit was to be carved out of a 103-acre planning area bordering a salmon stream called Logjam Creek. After extensive field work, in which Shoaf and forest technician Chuck Klee deleted a large area to protect high-value salmon habitat, they laid out a 40-acre unit with 225-foot-wide buffers on both sides of the creek. They made them wide so the trees in the buffers could withstand high winds.

Late that fall, Klee notified Shoaf that a Ketchikan Pulp forester had re-tagged the unit to eliminate their stream buffers. Shoaf reported the incident to Ketchikan Area Supervisor Mike Lunn, and the buffers were restored. But in the end, the KPC forester got his way. The Forest Service engineer and timber sale administrator simply restored ten acres to the unit in the field, including acreage inside the stream buffer, to make up for the "lost" volume Shoaf and Klee had deleted from the unit. After the sale was logged, the narrower buffer blew down in a windstorm.

THE CENTRAL PRINCE OF WALES PROJECT

Shoaf's experience at Logjam Creek would prove instructive in his next assignment. In November of 1990, he was named to head the interdisciplinary team responsible for designing the huge Central Prince of Wales Project, intended to supply KPC's pulp mill and two sawmills for several years. Part of the team's job was to determine how much timber could be cut from the 600,000-acre planning area. Shoaf spent eight months heading the planning effort. He and his team used detailed, site-specific data, combined with topographical maps and old aerial photos, to determine the potential timber yield. They determined that many areas were unsuitable for logging because of potential damage to soils and streams, poor likelihood of tree regeneration, and logistical challenges to logging. Honoring an agreement with the Alaska Department of Fish and Game, Shoaf's team also stayed out of old-growth areas set aside for wildlife and protection of scenic views.

Late in 1991, the Alaska Region office sent Shoaf new aerial photos to replace the 1979 photos his team had been working from—photos the regional office had been reluctant to provide. When Shoaf drew the proposed harvest units onto the new photos, he made a startling discovery: many units had been logged already. Where timber sale records denoted old-growth stands, the photos revealed clearcuts or young regenerating stands. Shoaf's suspicions were aroused further when the Forest Service published a notice in the Federal Register misstating the size of the Central Prince of Wales Project planning area. The map published with the notice accurately depicted a planning area of 600,000 acres, but the text described a planning area of 360,000 acres. When Shoaf pointed out the discrepancy, he was told to proceed with planning on 600,000 acres. No correction to the official record was ever made. Shoaf concluded that his bosses had deliberately understated the size of the project, either to avoid inciting opposition from environmentalists, or to mislead the public into believing that additional timber volume was available on the other 240,000 acres. For Shoaf, the pieces of a disturbing puzzle were starting to fit together.

As Shoaf started analyzing timber yield data and comparing his numbers with volume projections in the Tongass Land Management Plan, he consistently came up short. There was no way, he concluded, that the Central Prince of Wales Project could produce the predicted volume of 290 million board feet. TLMP's timber yield numbers were entirely theoretical—and wildly optimistic. As Shoaf explained in a whistleblower's report: "TLMP had never designed a single unit, looked at a single aerial photograph, or verified any data on the ground, and in fact had no capability of doing so." Instead, the plan assumed that all lands allocated to timber production "were 100 percent harvestable, without any consideration for oversteepened, unstable slopes, high hazard soils, unmapped streamcourses, caves, cultural resources, economic constraints, infeasible logging chances, (or) high elevation areas where it would be difficult if not impossible to regenerate stands."

In fact, Shoaf said, complying with basic environmental protections would require reducing the projected timber volume from the Central Prince of Wales Project by half. He documented similar problems with timber yield projections on two other large projects in the KPC supply area, Control Lake and Lab Bay. Another piece of the puzzle had clicked into place.

The plan Shoaf's team produced was not well-received by the Alaska Region Office. The timber yield data in particular caused Shoaf's bosses heartburn, because they directly contradicted the TLMP projections. In 1993, Shoaf's direct supervisor, David Arrasmith, instructed him to use the theoretical timber yield formulas in TLMP, not the far more accurate and site-specific methodology he had been using, in analyzing timber yields for the Central Price of Wales Project. Shoaf now understood that it was the numbers that mattered, not whether the Forest Service could actually deliver on them. He had promised himself that he would never take part in such a deception. He knew he would eventually have to go public with his findings. But in the meantime, he had been assigned to another project, one that would provide the last missing piece in the puzzle.

REPRISAL II

In June of 1991, Shoaf was asked to analyze the large amount of "falldown," or shortfall, occurring between projected timber volumes and actual timber volumes in the Ketchikan Area. His experience at Logjam Creek had prepared him well for this new task. Shoaf spent a month examining the records. What he found was that the Forest Service consistently overestimated timber yields in the Ketchikan Area, failing to account for the presence of salmon streams, karst formations, goshawk nests, and other features that might be identified in the field. Then, to avoid the inevitable "falldown," timber staff officers routinely borrowed timber from areas scheduled to be logged in the future. They called the practice "unit expansion."

In Shoaf's view, "unit expansion" was a blatant violation of the National Environmental Policy Act. It allowed logging to occur in areas never subjected to an environmental impact statement or to public review. What's more, because these "unit expansions" were not deleted from the timber base, they led to more "unit expansions" on future timber sales, creating a self-perpetuating cycle of overcutting. His investigation found that between 1989 and 1994, Tongass managers had allowed 5,047 acres to be cut outside the boundaries of timber sales, a group of violations he would come to refer to as "the timber sale nobody knew about." Shoaf believed his agency was headed for a showdown by logging unsustainably and failing to admit it. Unit expansion "borrowed timber from the future," he said in an interview. "It masked the falldown. They were cooking the books. Everyone knew it. It wasn't any surprise. No one would say anything. But I wouldn't lie."

Shoaf made sure his work was bulletproof, and in July he submitted his falldown report to David Rittenhouse, the new Ketchikan Area supervisor. In August he provided a copy to Sylvia Geraghty, who had appealed a timber sale on Prince of Wales Island. Shoaf was handling the appeal, and Geraghty had requested the report. She leaked it to the press, and a tempest ensued. In August, two weeks after Shoaf's report made page-one news in Ketchikan, Rittenhouse publicly berated Shoaf at a Forest Service meeting attended by several managers and line employees. Shoaf had been invited to the meeting to present the work of his interdisciplinary team. "Mr. Rittenhouse attacked my competence as a professional in a derisive, hostile tone of voice," Shoaf wrote in his whistleblower's report. "Everyone was shocked, because the onslaught was unexpected and totally out of context with my presentation. This incident was, by far, the most humiliating experience in my entire career with the Forest Service . . . . I was now established as a marked man to be avoided."

Other reprisals followed. In January of 1993, after Shoaf wrote a letter expressing his concern as a private citizen over the draft environmental impact statement for the Central Prince of Wales Project, Arrasmith issued a memo prohibiting Shoaf and other interdisciplinary team leaders from speaking to the media. In his letter, Shoaf had asked the Forest Service to avoid logging one unit near a wolf denning area, establish a five-year moratorium on logging in karst areas so the agency could study the effects of logging and road construction, and eliminate "unit expansion."

Shoaf was steadily pushed aside. In February of 1993, Arrasmith assigned someone else to take over the job of assembling public comments on the Central Prince of Wales Project EIS. The following month, Shoaf and his team were notified that they would not be developing the preferred alternative for the final EIS. In early April Shoaf got his mid-year performance review. For the first time in his Forest Service career, he received unsatisfactory ratings. The categories in which he was judged deficient were team participation and project integration. In May, Shoaf was taken off the team writing the Central Prince of Wales Project record of decision. For Shoaf, the need to get out the truth about dishonesty in the Tongass timber sale program had now become more pressing than the consequences to his own career of doing so.

<u>FIGHTING BACK</u>

In April of 1993, Shoaf co-authored an internal Forest Service report that documented illegally large clearcuts in the Central Prince of Wales Project draft EIS. Federal regulations limited clearcuts on national forests in coastal Alaska to 100 acres, yet Shoaf had determined that individual clearcut units laid out side by side would result in openings far exceeding 100 acres.

That same month, Shoaf and two colleagues published another study that revealed the Forest Service was about to violate the Tongass Timber Reform Act by allowing high-grading of the biggest and best trees in a project on North Prince of Wales Island. They said the Lab Bay sale violated the "proportionality rule" of TTRA, which required that each timber sale include trees of sizes and species that reflected the composition of the standing forest.

And there was more. Shoaf also discovered that in order to make up for the "falldown" in its timber yield projections on the Central Prince of Wales Project, the Ketchikan Area had diverted 110 million board feet of timber originally earmarked for independent purchasers to KPC.

In July of 1993, Shoaf filed a whistleblower disclosure with the Office of Special Counsel under the federal whistleblower protection law. He said he had suffered retaliatory actions after reporting that his supervisors were intentionally overestimating the amount of timber that could be produced in the Ketchikan Area. In September, his position was abolished, and he was assigned to an unfunded, undefined position as "special projects forester."

In a sworn statement prepared for the Government Accountability Project, a whistleblowers' protection group, Shoaf accused Ketchikan Area managers of "gross mismanagement of forest resources." He wrote that he was compelled to speak out, first, because of his love for the Forest Service. "I believe deeply in the agency's mission to provide timber to the nation on a sustained yield basis, while also providing for the sustained multiple use of other forest resources," he wrote. "The current management of the Tongass National Forest is so at odds with the legally mandated mission of the agency that this gross mismanagement must be exposed and corrected for the good of the agency, if not for the good of the nation."

But as much as he loved the agency, Shoaf wrote, he loved the forest more. "The Tongass National Forest is the largest of the remaining temperate rain forest ecosystems. The Tongass Forest is a treasure trove of old-growth timber, fish and wildlife species, paleocultural, geologic, scenic, subsistence, and recreational resources. There are resources on the Tongass, such as the karst ecosystem which contains cave resources of international significance, that scientists are just beginning to discover and understand. This combination of resource values makes the Tongass a forest of national, and indeed global, significance, which must be managed wisely. I believe the current Forest Service management of the Tongass will result in extensive and irreversible damage to the Forest. This must not be allowed to happen."

Shoaf also expressed concern for the communities of Southeast Alaska. "I believe the long-term contracts . . . were established to provide, among other things, community stability in SE Alaska," he wrote. "Since the inception of the long-term contracts, local communities have developed which are heavily timber-dependent. Unfortunately, the level of timber harvest demanded by the long-term contract is not sustainable within the Forest land base. Proposed harvest levels further exacerbate this unsustainable harvest. Inflated projections of future timber supply by local Forest Service managers are deceiving local citizens and businesses into making unwise investments and plans for the future. Local timber dependent communities are bound to suffer greatly in the long term from over-cutting in the near term. Harvest levels on the Tongass National Forest must be reduced immediately, and Forest Service timber supply projections must be corrected, if Southeast Alaska is to avoid the kind of community disruption and human suffering which now plague the Pacific Northwest because of over-cutting there."

In August of 1993, after reviewing Shoaf's twenty-eight-page affidavit and more than a hundred pages of supporting documentation, the U.S. Office of Special Counsel found "a substantial likelihood" that Shoaf's charges were correct, and ordered an investigation.

TRIAGE

Environmentalists appealed the Central Prince of Wales Project, but in November of 1993 Alaska Regional Forester Michael Barton denied their appeal and upheld the decision to go ahead with the project as it had been redesigned by Shoaf's superiors. They appealed again, and the Central Prince of Wales Project landed in the lap of the newly appointed chief of the Forest Service, Jack Ward Thomas. In December of 1993, two days after he arrived in Washington, D.C., Thomas received a letter from U.S. Rep. George Miller, D-California, chairman of the House Natural Resources Committee, asking him to review the Central Prince of Wales Project. The Alaska Rainforest Campaign also called for a delay. Both letters cited Shoaf's whistleblower report. There would be no honeymoon for Jack Ward Thomas.

The new chief ordered a halt to the sale pending a full review of the sale record. That decision drew barbs from Ketchikan Pulp, which accused him of being "a political tool of the environmental special interest groups and Congress." But in February of 1994, Thomas ordered the Alaska Region to proceed with the Central Prince of Wales Project. Though the issues raised by environmentalists on appeal were valid, he said, they did not justify blocking the project. However, he directed the Alaska Region to improve its ability to project timber yields, to base all future timber sales on ground surveys as well as analysis of aerial photos, and to study how the project would affect salmon streams on Prince of Wales Island.

Thomas's boss, U.S. Agriculture Undersecretary Jim Lyons, said that institutional, political and legal issues all played into the decision. The new chief, an intensely loyal career Forest Service employee, was unwilling to second-guess Barton. The prospect that the project might be stalled by environmental appeals "ratcheted up the Alaska delegation's anger over the timber supply issue," Lyons said. Perhaps most important, the Clinton administration was wary of inviting the accusation that it had breached its contract with Ketchikan Pulp by failing to provide the company with enough timber to operate its mills. "If we sent the sale back for revision, there was a serious chance that would shut Ketchikan Pulp down," Lyons said. "Things would begin to grind to a halt in terms of KPC's timber supply. We faced that potential."

However, the decision did mark a turning point for the Forest Service, Lyons said. "We were all concerned about management of the Tongass. We knew we had to reach a resolution. The Central Prince of Wales Project helped bring it to a head. It required us to take a fresh look at how we prepared sales up there."

Back in Ketchikan, Bill Shoaf was frustrated. He believed he had handed Alaska environmentalists a winning case on a silver platter, and he urged them to sue to halt the Central Prince of Wales Project. In June of 1994, after logging in some units had already begun, the Southeast Alaska Conservation Council and other groups did sue. At that point the Forest Service voluntarily halted the logging, pending further study.

But environmentalists in Southeast Alaska didn't relish being involved in another big lawsuit in the summer of 1994. They were already suing the

Forest Service to force cancellation of the Alaska Pulp Corp. timber sales. And the Clinton administration was uncomfortable with the prospect of shutting down logging on the south end of the Tongass. "We were trying to maintain operations for KPC now that the other mill had gone down," Lyons said. "There were some who were arguing, 'You've got them on the ropes. Why not finish them off?' But we were trying to make a sound decision as to what was our obligation under the contracts."

In the end, SEACC and other groups agreed to withdraw from the suit before trial, and the Forest Service agreed to stay out of Honker Divide, the largest pristine watershed remaining on Prince of Wales Island. The deal was spelled out in the final settlement of the suit over the APC sales: if the plaintiffs in that case challenged the Central Prince of Wales Project in court, the Forest Service could withdraw from negotiations over the disposition of the APC sales, leaving the future of those sales in limbo.

It was a straight political tradeoff, and Bill Shoaf never got over it. "If they had litigated Central Prince of Wales there's no way they could have lost," he said years later.

Joe Sebastian, a member of the SEACC board at the time the deal was cut, concedes the point. But he also defends the painful political decision that confronted SEACC: to sacrifice forests on Prince of Wales Island for the chance to save more forests in the North Tongass. "SEACC felt it could not afford to do anything that would threaten the cancellation of those sales," he said. "I tried to explain to Bill Shoaf that APC was bigger than his timber sale. We were talking seventeen years of cutting. Central Prince of Wales was the biggest timber sale in the U.S. It was just a bad deal that those two things came down at the same time."

Shoaf didn't give up. He litigated the case himself, losing in federal district court and appealing his case to the U.S. 9th Circuit, which upheld the lower court ruling.

TIME TO GO

By February of 1995, Shoaf could no longer tolerate his situation as a pariah within the Forest Service. For nearly 18 months he had been given no responsibility. "I came to work and I literally had nothing to do. If they had taken me out to the stocks and put me on display, it would have been better than what they did." He submitted his resignation from the Forest Service, effective March 31, 1995. The following October he filed a formal complaint with the Merit Systems Protection Board, alleging unlawful retaliation, and seeking reinstatement to his former job, payment of back pay and benefits, and reimbursement for attorney fees and other costs.

Out of a job and separated from his girlfriend and business partner, he sold his house in Ketchikan so he could hold onto his fishing boat, the *Blind Faith*, and struggled to make a living as a commercial fisherman.

In a 1997 interview, over a plate of stir-fried vegetables and home-smoked steelhead at his tiny cabin near Ward Cove, he talked of the price he had paid, and of the bitterness he still harbored toward environmentalists for failing to redeem his sacrifice. Because the hard fact was that his truth-telling had failed to halt or significantly alter the largest timber sale in the history of the Forest Service. "I have no love for the greenies," he said. "They cut a deal with the Forest Service."

Shoaf still considered himself a timber beast, and was careful to distinguish his own motives from those of the environmentalists who had let him down. "There's nothing wrong with pushing it to the edge of the envelope," he said. "But not beyond."

THE WOMAN WHO KILLED A BEAR

Mary Dalton came to work on the Tongass in 1979 after four years of forest management studies at Virginia Polytechnical Institute. Her first job was conducting logging road surveys on the Stikine Area, out of Petersburg. In 1981 she was reassigned to the Chatham Area, headquartered in Sitka, where she conducted logging road and forest stand surveys. Except for a brief stint in Hoonah, Sitka is where she stayed, working six months a year as a lowly GS-5 forest technician, and patching together a living from odd jobs the rest of the year.

She built a 10-by-12-foot cedar cabin in the woods near Sitka, where she lived off the grid, without electricity or running water. She threw herself into her job, establishing a reputation as a fearless backwoods forester. During her summers in Alaska, she stayed out in the woods for weeks at a time, conducting surveys, gathering and identifying rare plants, and trying to stay clear of the brown bears of Baranof and Chichagof Islands.

Forest Service employees of both sexes tended to avoid the Chatham Area because of its high concentrations of brown bears. Forest Service parties traveling in brown bear country were required to carry guns. For that reason, Dalton said, many of her supervisors spent little time in the field. "You're carrying a large-caliber elephant gun around with you in the bush. It's murder. And there were horror stories about bear maulings. That bear mentality, that combat mentality, is responsible for the cowboy spirit of the Chatham Area." Because she was in the field so much, Dalton had more than her share of bear encounters. In 1982 she killed a brown bear when it charged her party on a steep mountainside. Another time she was mauled by a brown bear, escaping with minor scratches. In time, she lost her fear of bears.

A round-faced woman with a soft Virginia drawl, Dalton soon gained grudging respect as a tough-minded professional who expected others to meet her own high standards. But her toughness created challenges when she supervised young men in the field. " A lot of people are threatened by competent women," she said. "Young guys especially had an attitude." She dealt with it and didn't complain. "I don't like whiners. Why would you take a job like that, especially if you know you're going to be in charge, if you can't handle the flak from male co-workers?"

Dalton was happiest doing field work. She spent summers in remote camps, far from the prosaic worries of civilization, making trips into town only about once a month. But she didn't let herself get attached to the forest she was surveying. She accepted that its destiny was to be logged.

That began to change in 1989, when after several years as a road surveyor she was assigned to conduct recreational trail surveys in seldom-visited areas. "I got to go into wilderness areas," she said. "They hadn't maintained some of these trails since Civilian Conservation Corps days." She saw places of surpassing beauty, places she felt should not be logged. She fell in love with the Alaska rain forest. The 1989 *Exxon Valdez* disaster also affected her feelings about the uniqueness and fragility of the rain forest, and about the ineffectiveness of government agencies charged with protecting it.

In 1990, the Forest Service was reorganized to comply with a court order requiring ground-based, site-specific surveys, and Dalton was reassigned to the Ground Reconnaissance Inventory Team—GRIT for short. The acronym fit her. Except for a stint conducting biological surveys of state-listed sensitive plants, she stayed with GRIT until 1996. In 1992 she began conducting surveys for the massive Northwest Baranof timber sale project. Timber from Northwest Baranof was destined for the Alaska Pulp Corp. pulp mill in Sitka and its sawmill in Wrangell.

THE NORTHWEST BARANOF PROJECT

For APC, the easy years of high-grading big spruce on gentle terrain were over by the 1990s. Logging had moved into the high country. Timber sales in the Chatham area were more technically difficult than those in the South Tongass, the slopes steeper, the soils more likely to separate from bedrock.

Streams on Northwest Baranof Island had been hammered by logging repeatedly. Dalton talked to old-timers who told her that logging in the 1950s and early 1960s had created so much sediment it had changed the shape of estuaries. In some areas, there was no soil beneath the roots of streamside alders. During the second entry, in the 1960s and 1970s, roads had been built right along streams. The Northwest Baranof Project would be the third entry. Ten miles of new road would be constructed and about sixteen miles rebuilt. "I didn't feel we should be going in and selling more timber until we did some restoration," Dalton said. "I'd never questioned our management before. But now I started to be concerned about our mission."

Dalton threw herself into her work as a forest technician and crew leader. She spent 235 days in the field, and surveyed 475 cutting units over four years. She attended meetings of the interdisciplinary team reviewing the Northwest Baranof Project, even when it meant going into the office on her own time. She took as her model the old-time Forest Service field forester she had read about in forestry school, who stomped through the woods with compass and rifle in the days before computer jockeys used sophisticated software to model timber yield projections. Her own field knowledge made her suspicious of those computer-generated projections.

In fact, Dalton said, computer modeling of the Northwest Baranof Project "did not jibe at all with what we were finding on the ground." One problem in the rugged country she was surveying was landslide potential. Though soil stability is not easily gauged from aerial photos, she learned that planners had field-checked only 10 percent of their soil stability ratings. Dalton's team found that fewer than a quarter of the soil stability ratings they did check were accurate; most understated the risk of landslides.

Dalton had trouble getting accurate information from her own GRIT crew. Some crew members could not locate sites on the ground from aerial photos. People routinely got lost. Some took data from the wrong river drainages. One team member staked out a logging road 25 feet from a sinkhole 75 feet deep and 100 feet wide. Because most of her crew were silviculturists and engineers, not biologists, she was frequently called on to identify winter deer range. "We didn't put people on the ground who knew what they were seeing," she said, "and the real planning team never got on the ground."

Dalton also had trouble getting her supervisors to take her findings seriously. For example, the geology maps she was given showed no karst formations on Baranof Island. But Dalton found the distinctive limestone formations at several sites within a two-square-mile area on Northwest Baranof. When she asked permission to call in James Baichtal, the Forest Service's karst specialist, her boss refused, saying, "It couldn't be karst. It's not on the map." She waited a year for the Chatham Area geologist to come out and see the karst area she had located. When he finally got there, Dalton said, he took a cursory look at one site and dismissed the karst as "insignificant."

When the draft environmental impact statement for the North Baranof Project was issued, Dalton found within it scant evidence that her work had been considered. She turned in more than one hundred pages of notes detailing discrepancies between the EIS and her own observations in the field. She also submitted extensive public comments, and testified at a Sitka hearing attended by Sen. Frank Murkowski. She was slow to realize that her field reports threatened her agency's mission—to meet the timber demands of Alaska Pulp Corp. In 1995, four years after she began working on the Northwest Baranof Project, and two years after APC closed its Sitka mill, Dalton was transferred out of planning and sent to conduct surveys of sensitive plants in logging road rights-of-way. When she questioned her boss, Fred Glenn, about her transfer, he told her, "You have lost your pro-timber views."

When the final EIS for North Baranof was released, she saw with chagrin that her carefully documented findings, especially regarding deer winter range and bear den sites, had once again been disregarded. The wildlife analysis was largely limited to computer model projections and boilerplate text. She was livid. "Why send us out there for four seasons if they're going to base their decisions on computer models?" she said. "I felt we were being used for something that was wrong."

On May 6, 1996, Dalton filed an appeal of the Northwest Baranof Project, asserting that the agency had disregarded most of her research regarding the effect of logging on deer and brown bear habitat. No one, including her immediate supervisor, told her that Forest Service employees were not permitted to appeal agency actions. Nor did anyone tell her it was against Forest Service rules for her to write her appeal on a Forest Service computer and send it on a Forest Service fax machine, even if she did it on her own time. "I honestly thought my appeal would be considered," she said. "It was denied outright."

On May 28 Karen White, the employment officer for the Chatham Area, notified her that she would be suspended for thirty days for "unethical or improper use of official authority," for appealing the project, and for using Forest Service facilities to file her appeal. "Employees have review opportunities at many points in the NEPA process to provide input and express concerns that the public doesn't have," and might also possess sensitive information the public doesn't have, White wrote.

Dalton protested in writing that she had been "blissfully ignorant" of the appeals prohibition and the rule against use of government property, and that a thirty-day suspension was unreasonable and arbitrary. She also defended her right to file an appeal: "(S)omething is obviously very wrong with the planning process on the Chatham Area, as evidenced by the fact that the person who looked at more units in the field than any of the other preparers cannot get their data and concerns into the final document." Her defense was to no avail. In June, Dalton's position was abolished, ostensibly for budgetary reasons, leaving her without a source of income.

"THE FIGHTING FORESTER"

Dalton did not go to the press. But when reporters saw her name on an appeal of the Northwest Baranof Project, the word got out. Gretchen Legler, an Anchorage writer and University of Alaska instructor, hounded her for an interview at a Sitka symposium in June. At first Dalton refused to give her an interview. "I finally agreed, just to get rid of her," she said. Legler interviewed Dalton at her cabin. Dalton showed her some entries in her journal, confided her love of the Alaska wilderness, and read her passages from Walt Whitman. Legler wrote it all down.

Dalton asked Legler to let her see the story before publication, and Legler reluctantly agreed. When Dalton read the finished manuscript, she was flabbergasted. "I said, 'Gretchen, this makes me sound like an idiot. It makes me sound like Ted Kaczinski." But she didn't know where to start in asking for changes, so she finally agreed to allow its publication. "The Fighting Forester: Mary Dalton Jeopardizes Job to Protest Logging," was the cover story in the September 1, 1996, Sunday magazine of the *Anchorage Daily News*. Dalton had become an unwilling martyr. Two weeks later, her thirty-day suspension without pay began.

During her sixteen years on the Tongass, Dalton had received five merit awards, five cash awards, and consistent "above average" to "outstanding" performance reviews. She was widely regarded as one of the agency's most accomplished field foresters. But in October of 1996 Dalton was demoted from a GS-7 to a GS-5 and given the option of transferring to the Coronado National Forest, in the Arizona desert near the Mexican border, or resigning from the Forest Service. With great sadness she packed her books and few possessions and said good-bye to the Tongass, her friends and her cabin in the rain forest.

When Andy Stahl heard about Dalton's case, he contacted her immediately. Stahl, the director of the Eugene, Oregon-based watchdog group Forest Service Employees for Environmental Ethics, offered to take on her cause. In April of 1997, Stahl's organization joined Dalton in filing a lawsuit that challenged the Forest Service prohibition on appeals by agency employees. The following January, the Forest Service backed down and rescinded the rule.

Stahl also agreed to be Dalton's personal representative in hearings before the federal Merit Systems Protection Board. The same month the Forest Service rescinded its prohibition on employee appeals, Alaska Regional Forester Phil Janik paid Dalton a visit in Tucson to meet her and hear her side of the story. Her suspension ultimately was removed from her record. But she didn't get her Alaska job back, nor did she get the Forest Service to reopen the record for the Northwest Baranof Project to incorporate her findings and recommendations.

In October of 1997, a year after her transfer to Arizona, Dalton spoke about her experiences at a conference of environmental journalists in Tucson, Arizona. Her presentation was by turns witty and philosophical, and laced with a surprising dose of humility. "To be very honest, I know if I had offered my criticism in a more tasteful, graceful way, the outcome might have been very different," she said. " I was naive not to realize that my presentation got in the way of the message. I will take a deeper look at the complexity of the situation next time."

She also offered an olive branch to the agency that had vilified her. "I have been witness to some of the finest moments in the Forest Service," she said. "My job has taken me to some remote, beautiful places I would never have seen otherwise. I feel privileged that I can speak out and still have a job." She even expressed gratitude that she was yanked from middle-aged complacency and forced to learn about the unfamiliar plants and ecosystems of the Arizona desert.

However, she confided in an interview that starting over in Arizona had been one of the hardest things she'd ever had to do. In Alaska, she said, "I had grudgingly earned some respect. Down here I don't have that." She was back to taking orders from young men who had been in diapers when she started with the Forest Service.

Dalton was skeptical that her successful challenge of the rule prohibiting employee appeals would make much of a difference. Actions speak louder than words, she said. "When people see what happened to me, it doesn't encourage them to go file appeals even if they do have the right to. But they may start taking people more seriously when they object early in the process. The best outcome may be that planners will be encouraged to present all field data objectively in an environmental impact statement, rather than censoring facts that don't support the proposed action or management strategy."

Dalton understood that she had been caught up in a drama much larger than her own personal struggle. "Forest Service employees have been on the front lines in a protracted ideological battle," she said. "The polarization and controversy around timber sales have created morale problems and an atmosphere of paranoia. There's a climate of retribution and fear. And the Alaska Region is probably the worst case."

18

LAST ASSAULT

Bart Koehler was walking from a Bozeman, Montana, bakery back to his office at the Greater Yellowstone Coalition on the morning of Nov. 5, 1994, when he heard a radio newscaster speak four words that froze his heart: "House Speaker Newt Gingrich." His thoughts raced back to the Tongass. Overnight, with the Republican sweep in the 1994 congressional elections, Alaska's three-man delegation, Sen. Ted Stevens, Sen. Frank Murkowski, and Rep. Don Young, had been handed the keys to the nation's public lands.

Koehler had stayed involved with the Tongass as a member of the SEACC board. Within days, fellow board members were on the phone, pleading with Koehler to come back to Alaska. He took some time to think about it before he said yes. In December he agreed. "I had to weigh everything," Koehler said. "Which place would lose the most the quickest? Could I stay in Montana and watch everything unravel?" The answers, he finally decided, were "Alaska," and "Hell, no."

In January of 1995, by virtue of seniority, Murkowski became the chairman of the Senate Energy and Natural Resources Committee, Stevens became second in command on the Senate Appropriations Committee, and Young seized the reins of the House Natural Resources Committee, which in an act of naked symbolism he promptly renamed the House Resources Committee. "The most difficult thing I've ever had to do," Koehler said later, "was to go back into this issue and go head-to-head with these guys who suddenly had so much power."

The views of the Alaska delegation on environmental and public land issues placed them beyond the pale of the American mainstream. In 1994 rankings of their voting records, the League of Conservation Voters had given Stevens a 7, Murkowski a 3 and Young a 2 on a scale of 1 to 100. But the Republican Party's right wing was in control now. And for the Alaska delegation, it was payback time. This was their opportunity to roll back environmental protection for Alaska lands. And the 1990 Tongass Timber Reform Act would be their first target.

"LANDLESS NATIVES"

Murkowski didn't wait for January to flex his new political muscle. In November of 1994, in the final weeks of the 103rd Congress, he introduced the Alaska Landless Natives Act, a bill ostensibly intended to resolve lingering Native land claims. Murkowski's bill proposed to create five new village corporations representing Alaska Natives, in Haines, Tenakee, Wrangell, Petersburg and Ketchikan. Some Native residents of these towns claimed they had been left "landless" because their communities had failed to qualify as Native villages under the 1971 Alaska Native Claims Settlement Act. In fact, they were not landless; they were shareholders in Sealaska, the regional Native corporation, which held title to 267,250 acres in Southeast Alaska.

Even a cursory reading revealed that the real intent of Murkowski's bill was to reopen areas of the Tongass that had been placed off-limits to logging by the Tongass Timber Reform Act. The bill was a transparent attempt by Alaska timber interests and their newly powerful friends in Congress to get their hands on more Tongass timber. Under Murkowski's bill, 645,000 acres of the Tongass set aside in 1990 for recreation, subsistence hunting and fishing and food-gathering would become available for selection by the new Native corporations.

Several Southeast Alaska communities were quick to denounce Murkowski's ploy. "The Senator's motives are thinly veiled attempts to placate an aggressive timber industry lobby, which apparently had more to do with the drafting of this legislation than the Natives themselves," wrote David Beebe, the mayor of Kupreanof, in a January 1995 letter to Alaska Governor Tony Knowles. "The ramifications of this bill, if enacted, would raise a host of divisive issues, threatening the communities of Southeast Alaska. The impacts span the spectrum of life in our region, from commercial fishing to subsistence, and from fragile cultural relations to sustainable economic policy of Southeast." Other small tourism-dependent communities warned that increased clearcutting would discourage visitors who came to Southeast Alaska seeking a pristine wilderness experience.

Commercial fishermen were adamantly opposed to reopening large areas of the Tongass to logging. The Ketchikan Trollers Committee adopted a resolution declaring: "It is absolutely clear that opening another 600,000 acres in Southeast Alaska for large scale logging operations could be devastating to many, many salmon runs, especially the coho stocks that have become the backbone of the troll industry." SEACC and the Alaska Rainforest Campaign launched their own offensive, calling the bill a raid on the public lands that would further fragment the rain forest ecosystem and close public access to large sections of the Tongass. Most significantly, traditional Alaska Native groups, including the Alaska Native Brotherhood, the Alaska Native Sisterhood, the Haida Tribe and the Hoonah Indian Association, protested that "Landless Natives" would spell the end of their subsistence economy.

There was ample evidence that Murkowski was using Alaska Natives as pawns in an attempt to benefit his timber industry friends. In January, Joseph Henri, an Anchorage investor, wrote to all three members of the delegation telling them he wanted to buy and reopen the Wrangell mill, but only with a guaranteed timber supply. "If that sawtimber is to come out of the Tongass Forest," he wrote, "the Forest Service must be given a direct congressional command to make 130 million board feet available to the Wrangell Mill each year until the Landless Native timber becomes available in at least the same volume."

And Robert Willard, the chairman of an association representing the "landless" Natives, acknowledged in a 1994 letter to a member that the timber industry's hunger for Tongass trees was driving the Landless Natives bill in the same way the petroleum industry's lust for Arctic oil had driven the 1971 Alaska Native Claims Settlement Act. "Without the press for timber, the prospects for a bill at all are likely very dim," Willard wrote, as the bill was being hammered out behind closed doors.

Willard had his own motives for supporting a bill of some kind. He wanted the new corporations to be required to mill their timber in Southeast Alaska, creating jobs for Natives, even if they could make a bigger profit by exporting their logs. "The greatest dividend is not the dividend check," he said in an interview. "It's the economic development and opportunity for our children." ANCSA had failed to emphasize job creation, he said. Only one small mill had been built to process timber from Native corporation lands.

Stung by criticism from within the Native community, Willard eventually backed away from the Murkowski bill and promised to consult with environmentalists, the Forest Service and other Native groups before supporting a revised draft.

SEACC saw "Landless Natives" as a portent of things to come. "It was clear to me from the get-go that we would have to fight this thing," Bart Koehler said. In June of 1995, when Murkowski held a field hearing on his bill in Wrangell, SEACC was ready. Koehler had organized a panel of eleven speakers who opposed the bill. He had jousted with Mark Rey, a former timber lobbyist tapped by Murkowski to administer the Senate Energy and Natural Resources Committee, over how much time the SEACC panel would be allotted to speak. Wrangell was still reeling from the closure of its sawmill, and Murkowski played to the fear and uncertainty in the community, all but promising that his bill would lead to the reopening of the mill. He also declared: "Alaskans have an accountability to the rest of the world to produce timber. We can't protect our favorite areas as long as we have this responsibility."

But for Murkowski, the Wrangell hearing turned into a rout. And he faced organized opposition at hearings in Ketchikan and Sitka as well. In Washington, he faced opposition from fellow senators, including Bennett Johnston, who thought he had decided the future of the Tongass in 1990. "Johnston told Murkowski he would fall on his sword over this," said Steve Kallick, director of the Alaska Rainforest Campaign. "Johnston told him, 'Don't undo TTRA. That's my legacy. Don't touch it.'" Faced with a storm of opposition, Murkowski quietly withdrew his bill. But the "Landless Natives" debacle was just the beginning.

FENDING OFF ATTACKS

The next two years unfolded like a rolling nightmare for Tongass defenders. The delegation introduced seventeen bills and held fifteen hearings in an effort to turn back the clock on Tongass reform, delay the release of a new Tongass Land Management Plan, and extend the life of Ketchikan Pulp's fifty-year contract. For Alaska Regional Forester Phil Janik and his Tongass planning team, the effort to produce a defensible new forest plan while fending off political attacks from the delegation and court rulings demanding more protection for wildlife became an intricate political ballet.

In February of 1995, the Alaska regional office of the U.S. Fish and Wildlife Service overruled its Juneau field office and declined to list the Alexander Archipelago wolf as a threatened species. Regional Fish and Wildlife Service Director David Allen said there was insufficient scientific information to support a listing, and that anyway the Forest Service had promised to take another look at the wolf in its new Tongass plan. But Allen added, "It is clear by our analysis that without significant changes to the existing TLMP, the long-term viability of the Alexander Archipelago wolf is seriously imperiled."

In May, the agency released a nearly identical decision on the Queen Charlotte goshawk, noting the Forest Service's intention to increase protection for goshawk habitat. Again, the agency added a warning: without significant changes to the existing Tongass plan, "the long-term viability of the Queen Charlotte goshawk may be seriously imperiled." Janik had already ordered temporary measures to protect goshawk nest sites and habitat reserves across the Tongass. But the announcement by the Fish and Wildlife Service seemed to embolden the delegation.

In July, Congress passed and President Clinton signed the 1995 Budget Rescission Act, cutting money already appropriated for fiscal 1995. Stevens attached several provisions designed to undermine the evolving Tongass plan, about which he appeared to have inside knowledge. One eliminated all funding for the development of habitat conservation areas on the Tongass. Another limited the size of buffer zones around goshawk nests to a maximum of three hundred acres, though some leading biologists had recommended buffers at least a hundred times as large.

Allen of the Fish and Wildlife Service noted that it was the Forest Service's proposed habitat conservation areas and goshawk nest buffers that had persuaded him not to list the goshawk. "If the HCAs were taken out, then we would have to take another look at the situation," he warned.

Stevens' bill, which expired two months later, was mainly symbolic. But it got Phil Janik's attention.

INTO THE COURTS

In September, the Southwest Biodiversity Project sued the Fish and Wildlife Service over its decision not to list the goshawk as an endangered species. Two months later, the Biodiversity Legal Foundation filed a nearly identical lawsuit challenging the agency's decision not to list the Alexander Archipelago wolf. Both lawsuits made the same argument: The Endangered Species Act requires agencies to make listing decisions based on the best available scientific knowledge about the status of the species at the time, not on an agency's promise to manage its habitat differently in the future.

In December, shortly after the second lawsuit was filed, SEACC attorney Buck Lindekugel wrote a letter to newspapers in Southeast Alaska, disavowing the lawsuits and disassociating SEACC from them. "While we care about the future of goshawks and wolves, we don't feel the management of the Tongass should be focused on a single critter," he wrote. "We are extremely concerned about the bigger picture: the current rate of logging will have serious negative impacts forest-wide on deer, bear, salmon, and other wildlife we all depend on in our home region."

Kieran Suckling of the Southwest Biodiversity Project was astonished that SEACC would publicly criticize his suit. He had filed at least three dozen endangered species petitions, he said. "They're all controversial. There are often environmental groups that would prefer it not happen. But this was the first time one actually came out against us." SEACC and the Alaska Rainforest Campaign saw things differently. They were acutely aware of the open warfare that had broken out in the Pacific Northwest following the listing of the northern spotted owl. Alaska's environment was under attack in the 104th Congress. They feared a backlash from Stevens might undo all they had accomplished. "I didn't believe we could sustain a defensive campaign," Steve Kallick said. "We thought the petitions would provoke a rider from Stevens that we couldn't stop."

SEACC's public denunciation of the listing lawsuits opened a schism in the ranks of Southeast Alaska's close-knit environmental movement. While SEACC was intent on holding together its blue-collar, grassroots coalition, and fending off attacks in Congress, dissident activists, led by Don Muller and Larry Edwards of the Sitka Conservation Society, believed it was time to adopt a more adversarial approach to protecting the Alaska rain forest.

A FRONTAL ASSAULT

In Washington, the siege of the 104th Congress continued. Stevens introduced a bill requiring the Forest Service to sell 418 million board feet of timber annually over the next two years—the target set in the preferred "Alternative P" of the now discredited 1991 Tongass plan. Regional Forester Phil Janik disavowed Alternative P, calling it legally and scientifically indefensible. Alaska Governor Tony Knowles also opposed it, and announced that he favored establishing large habitat conservation areas across the Tongass to head off endangered species listings.

Murkowski introduced a self-standing bill requiring the Tongass to sell even more timber—enough to support 2,400 direct timber jobs, or about 500 million board feet annually. Rep. Don Young introduced a bill proposing to turn over the entire Tongass National Forest to the state of Alaska. Neither bill made it to a floor vote. Murkowski also introduced a bill to extend Ketchikan Pulp Co.'s fifty-year contract by fifteen years. The contract still had ten years to run, but Louisiana-Pacific officials said that without a guarantee of adequate timber for another fifteen years beyond that, L-P would be unable to borrow the money to invest in pollution control equipment and necessary mill maintenance, and would be forced to close the Ketchikan pulp mill for good. It was a familiar refrain.

Things got nasty at the first Forest Service oversight hearing, on May 18. Stevens called Koehler a liar and accused SEACC of being responsible for ten thousand lost jobs in Southeast Alaska, then stormed out of the hearing room. Alaska's senior senator had been angered by SEACC's testimony, which included a letter from Koehler reminding Stevens of his hope back in 1990 that the Forest Service would find "workable solutions" to the remaining problems on the Tongass. Koehler wrote that SEACC still harbored that hope, but that Alaska's senators had refused to give Forest Service managers a fair chance to implement reform. "Let's not kid ourselves, we know what this hearing is really all about," he added in his formal testimony. "Alaska's senators are here to bash the Forest Service and start an attack to roll back the Tongass reform law. They want to put areas that they had once voted to protect back on the chopping block."

COUNTER-OFFENSIVE

The Alaska Rainforest Campaign went all out to counter the delegation's frontal assault, mobilizing public opinion against the delegation's pro-logging initiatives, working to erode support for Ketchikan Pulp Co. by planting damaging stories with the news media, and pushing for termination, not extension, of KPC's long-term contract. The campaign hired a media consultant, Michael Finkelstein, to meet with editorial boards around the country. Over nine months, the campaign got 130 editorials opposing the contract extension and the Tongass riders.

In August of 1995, Murkowski angered constituents when at the last minute he downgraded a formal committee hearing in Washington, D.C., to an off-the-record work session after he learned that several witnesses from Southeast Alaska communities and a spokesman for the governor's office planned to testify against his timber jobs bill. By the time he announced the change, most of the witnesses were in jets on their way to Washington, D.C.

Murkowski's own ethical standards were called into question the following month, when he announced that he had sold his shares in Chevron Oil, Louisiana-Pacific and other publicly traded natural resource companies— four days before he introduced his timber jobs bill.

Murkowski got still more bad press in August, when the U.S. Environmental Protection Agency began the process of adding Alaska Pulp Corp.'s closed Sitka mill site to its Superfund National Priorities List. To head off the listing, Murkowski came up with the idea of attaching a rider to another bill prohibiting the EPA from adding any new sites to the list for one year without the express request of the governor of the affected state. But the ploy backfired when a member of Murkowski's staff left a threatening message on the voice-mail system at the EPA's regional office in Seattle, saying the senator hoped the matter would not have to be handled through a rider. The EPA leaked the message to the *New York Times*, which called the incident an "unabashed level of interference with the executive branch." EPA Superfund manager John R. Meyer told the *Times*: "What you have here is one of the most blatant and obvious examples of discharge of a hazardous substance into a bay that is a commercial fishery. There's people who eat that stuff, and we can't tell them whether there's a problem or not."

DETOURS AND DELAYS

In August, Forest Service Chief Jack Ward Thomas made a week-long trip through Southeast Alaska to assure people that the Tongass was large enough to accommodate logging, fishing and tourism. He asked business leaders to be patient as the Forest Service wrapped up years of work on a new plan, and predicted it would be done in one more year.

Phil Janik was feeling pressure to speed up the pace of the TLMP planning process, and asked the planning team to give him a framework for developing forest plan alternatives based on the information the research scientists had in hand. On a Friday in August of 1995, three or four scientists met in Juneau to brainstorm. Using scratch boards, flow charts and the map prepared by the VPOP team, they came up with several options for addressing concerns about protection of fish, wildlife, and karstlands across the Tongass. The approaches included various combinations of light-touch logging across the forest, small clearcuts that mimicked natural windthrow, extended logging rotations of 200 to 300 years, and large reserves.

That meeting was a catalyst. In the first two weeks of September the process became unstuck. The team produced ten preliminary alternatives, complete with assessments of the level of protection each would provide. "It was a quantum leap forward," said Pamela Finney, the team's spokeswoman.

It was at about that time that Steve Brink was removed from the TLMP team and made deputy director of timber management. Brink was widely believed to be the source of leaks from inside the TLMP team to Alaska congressional delegation staffers on Capitol Hill, and his ouster prompted a protest from the delegation, which demanded that Agriculture Secretary Dan Glickman investigate "apparent irregularities in personnel procedures."

On November 6 and 7, 1995, the research scientists convened the first of ten panels of experts to review their findings. Then the government shut down. The shutdown, and the resulting furlough of 800,000 federal employees, were triggered in part by an impasse between President Clinton and congressional Republicans over anti-environmental riders attached to spending bills. And the Tongass played a key role in the donnybrook.

Stevens had attached his "Alternative P" rider to the 1996 Senate Interior appropriations bill funding the Forest Service. Clinton announced that he would veto the appropriations bill, and let the entire Interior Department shut down, unless the Tongass language and other objectionable riders were removed. And he did. On November 15, after a week-long government shutdown, the House blinked. By a vote of 230 to 199, with 48 Republicans on the winning side, the House stripped away all of Stevens' riders, including the Tongass timber quota. Stevens, showing a streak of pragmatism, got Leon Panetta, Clinton's chief of staff, to agree to a $110 million appropriation for the communities of Southeast Alaska, which they could spend in any way they chose.In the end, not one of the Tongass bills introduced in 1995 became law.

"It's absolutely amazing to me that we're still in the old congressional ballgame," Koehler wrote in SEACC's *Ravencall* that winter. "As we dive back into the fray, remember that we have risen to the challenges, we have flatly refused to give up the ship, and amazingly, Tongass defenders are still standing our ground and holding our own."

The government shutdown threw the scientists' assessment panel process into chaos. TLMP team co-leader Doug Swanston was declared a critical employee so the work could continue, but the furlough forced the rescheduling of several key panels dealing with wildlife issues. Somehow, between November 1995 and February 1996, all ten panels did manage to convene. The scientists scrambled to write their reports. Simultaneously, the team of forest managers writing the TLMP environmental impact statement was at work on a draft environmental impact statement. By February the team had a completed draft and was preparing to fly to Washington, D.C., to brief top Forest Service and administration officials. But on February 12, Murkowski, who had been given a leaked copy of the document, fired off a missive to Agriculture Secretary Dan Glickman asserting that the alternatives the Forest Service was considering would kill the timber industry in Southeast Alaska. At the last minute, the trip to Washington, D.C. was abruptly scrubbed and the team went back to the drawing board.

At this point the three Tongass area supervisors, who answered only to Janik, were brought into the process. They decided not to select any of the ten alternatives the assessment panels had so meticulously analyzed. Instead, they took bits and pieces from various alternatives and cobbled them together into a preferred alternative that research scientists had no opportunity to review before its release.

Janik outfoxed Murkowski in the end. His office was on the verge of releasing this new draft EIS when Murkowski scheduled an April 18 hearing in Washington, D.C. to grill the TLMP team about the basic science underlying the plan. Murkowski had asked Glickman not to distribute the draft EIS until he held his hearing. Janik decided to release the report on the day of the hearing. At 5:30 a.m. Juneau time, while Murkowski's inquisition of the TLMP team was going on four time zones away, Forest Service employees in Juneau were faxing a press release that described the preferred alternative in detail.

"At the hearing we revealed the substance of our draft, every decision," Janik said. "All three area supervisors were there. They presented in great detail each recommendation the public would be commenting on." Murkowski got his inquisition, but it was too late. The draft plan was on the street.

It was not the good news conservationists had hoped for. Its preferred alternative failed to include large habitat reserves for wildlife or adequate buffers around goshawk nests. It was weak on protection of subsistence hunting, fishing, and food-gathering areas. And it called for an annual timber sale level of 357 million board feet—far more than the Tongass was likely ever to sell again, now that only one pulp mill was operating in Southeast Alaska..

At public hearings throughout Southeast Alaska, citizens voiced strong reactions to the plan. On the north end of the Tongass, where timber had never been a dominant part of the economy, many speakers called for greater protection of fish and wildlife habitat. In Ketchikan and Wrangell, the plan got a hostile reception. Overall, two-thirds of Southeast Alaskans who testified asked for more and better land protection. And reaction was not limited to Southeast Alaska; the Forest Service received 22,000 comments from across the nation. Most demanded strong protections for the nation's largest national forest.

Enter the ESA

Between draft and final, the world changed dramatically, and so did TLMP. In September of 1996 U.S. District Judge Stanley Sporkin of the District Court for Washington, D.C., ruling in a lawsuit brought by the petitioners, said the U.S. Fish and Wildlife Service had erred in deciding not to list the Queen Charlotte goshawk. The following month he made an identical ruling regarding the agency's dismissal of the Alexander Archipelago wolf petition.

Sporkin agreed with the plaintiffs that the Endangered Species Act required the agency to base its decisions not on promises made in an unadopted plan but on the current status of the species. He noted that biologists had found strong evidence of threats to the survival of both species, and noted in his wolf decision that the U.S. Interior Secretary, the official ultimately responsible for enforcing the act, "cannot use promises of proposed future actions as an excuse for not making a determination based on the existing record." In a footnote, he added: "Clearly, in passing the ESA, Congress did not intend the Secretary to wait until the particular species is on the verge of extinction before taking action. If, with the continuation of current circumstances, the wolf will be 'endangered' in the future, it is clearly 'threatened' today." In Alaska, Judge Sporkin's rulings instantly put the goshawk and the wolf in the driver's seat as the Forest Service set about writing a final Tongass plan.

Through the fall of 1996 Janik's staff and Allen's staff huddled to make the final Tongass plan listing-proof. Five-hundred-foot beach fringes became one thousand-foot beach fringes to accommodate the goshawk, which forages along beaches. Large habitat reserves were set aside, including a 200,000-acre reserve on Prince of Wales Island, to protect habitat and a prey base for wolves. Those wolf reserves became de facto deer reserves as well.

THE POLITICAL MOOD SHIFTS

The barrage of pro-logging bills from the Alaska delegation did not let up. In 1996 Murkowski introduced a bill to expand University of Alaska Trust lands by allowing the state to select land from the Tongass National Forest. Murkowski also introduced legislation to block designation of wild and scenic rivers and habitat reserves on the Tongass through an amendment to the 1980 Alaska Lands Act. Young revived the effort to establish new Native corporations and let them select prime timberland on the Tongass. He also pushed for a bill that would transfer the entire Tongass to the state of Alaska. Stevens, seeking to delay release of the new Tongass Land Management Plan, asked for a General Accounting Office investigation of the Tongass planning process.

"We were being hit by so many bills," Bart Koehler said. "It was fill-in-the-blanks legislation. Give the Tongass to the university, to the landless Natives, to the state. We had to keep swatting these bills down. We had to take them seriously. With a Republican-controlled Congress, you never knew what might happen."

But by the end of the 104th Congress, the nation's mood was changing. Even by the free-wheeling standards of the Gingrich revolution, it was clear that the Alaska delegation had overreached. As the respected *National Journal* commented, "Stevens and Young alienated Republican moderates by trying to ram their proposals through." Their attacks on popular environmental laws, the *Journal* said, "made the Republicans vulnerable to charges that Congress was pursuing an extremist environmental agenda."

19

ENDGAME

In April of 1996, Chuck Cushman, a white-bearded circuit rider for the pro-development wise use movement, set up shop in Ketchikan. Cushman had earned the nickname "Rent-a-Riot" for his adeptness at riling up fearful working-class communities by blaming environmentalists and federal agencies for their economic woes. Local supporters of Ketchikan Pulp Co. soon announced the formation of a new pro-timber group, Concerned Alaskans for Resources and Environment, or CARE. Businesses and individuals in Ketchikan quickly raised more than $200,000 for the CARE campaign.

CARE's goal was to pressure Congress and the Clinton administration to grant Ketchikan Pulp a fifteen-year extension of its contract, which was to expire in 2004. In fact, Louisiana-Pacific had been looking for a way out since at least 1994, when L-P President Harry Merlo announced that the company might sell a majority share of the Ketchikan mill, noting that its pulp operations were "no longer part of what we would consider our core business focus."

Louisiana-Pacific was awash in legal problems. The $6 million in criminal and civil fines it owed the EPA in connection with violations of the Clean Water Act at its Ketchikan mill were only a small piece of the mess the company had created for itself during Harry Merlo's eighteen-year reign. In 1993, the EPA had fined L-P $11 million, the largest pollution penalty ever levied by the agency under the Clean Air Act, for violating its air pollution permit at fifteen mills in eleven states, and for giving misleading information to federal investigators. Then, in 1995, L-P suffered a huge financial and public relations disaster when it was revealed that the company had taken shortcuts in manufacturing an exterior siding called Inner Seal, which Merlo had promoted, and which had become one of the company's top-selling products. Distraught homeowners reported that the siding, manufactured from a plywood alternative known as oriented strandboard, sprouted mushrooms in wet weather. Thousands joined a class-action suit to recover damages. In addition, the company faced a federal grand jury indictment for alleged fraud and Clean Air Act violations in connection with operations at its Montrose, Colorado, waferboard plant.

In April of 1995, five members of L-P's board of directors asked for an internal investigation of Merlo's management record, and in July the board voted unanimously to oust Merlo and two other senior executives. Merlo resigned on July 28, ending one of the most ruthless, flamboyant and controversial reigns in the annals of the timber industry.

The following January the board hired Mark Suwyn, a low-key executive with extensive experience in the timber and chemical industries, to restore the company's credibility and bolster its bottom line. At the company's annual meeting, in May, Suwyn predicted that L-P would grow dramatically through acquisitions and introduction of new products by the end of the decade. When it came to L-P's Alaska operations, however, Suwyn sang a familiar tune. Faced with escalating environmental liabilities and the collapse of the world pulp market, he warned that without a contract extension and other favors from the Clinton administration, L-P would be unable to attract financing to install $200 million in required pollution control equipment at the Ketchikan pulp mill and would have to shut it down.

Tensions escalated in Ketchikan as the delegation and timber industry supporters pulled out all the stops to win the contract extension. CARE organized demonstrations of support for Ketchikan Pulp and placed a half-page ad in the *Anchorage Daily News* warning: "If this disaster occurs, it's going to hit families in Southeast Alaska as hard as flood, fire or quakes." CARE boosters also pressured Alaska Governor Tony Knowles to use his influence with the Clinton administration to win the contract extension. Knowles refused.

By the summer of 1996, the precariousness of the timber industry's future in Southeast Alaska was evident even in remote logging camps. Silver Bay Logging Co., the dominant logging contractor in Southeast, was cutting logs it couldn't sell. In Appleton Cove, logging supervisor Dave Bannister had two barges loaded with a half-million board feet of pulp logs he could not get rid of because Ketchikan Pulp was not buying. "In the twenty years I've been here it's never been this bad," he said.

A LINE IN THE FOREST

Bart Koehler headed back to Washington in September armed with a modest proposal: a plan that would allow Ketchikan Pulp to keep buying timber and operating its pulp mill for three more years while the town adjusted to the reality of a post-pulp economy. This "transition alternative" had cost SEACC support from some of its members. Koehler defended SEACC's political pragmatism with his trademark rejoinder: "It's the real world, muchacho, and you're in it." When he got to D.C., however, things started moving fast—in a direction he had not expected. On September 12, Mark Suwyn announced that he would shut down Ketchikan Pulp Co. operations within weeks unless Congress and the Clinton administration agreed to modify and extend KPC's long-term contract.

It was two months until election day. President Clinton had damaged his credibility with western environmentalists by signing a bill that temporarily suspended environmental laws across the nation in an effort to jump-start the salvage of damaged timber. The "timber salvage rider" had reopened the slowly healing wounds left by the Northwest old-growth wars. Mainstream activists, even gray-haired grandmothers, were blocking logging roads and getting arrested. The president needed something to refurbish his environmental record.

Six years after passage of the Tongass Timber Reform Act, the fate of the Alaska rain forest remained a national issue. Clinton knew his Republican opponent, Bob Dole, would carry Alaska. The political risks of defying the Alaska delegation were negligible, the potential gains high. Clinton drew a line in the forest. There would be no emergency extension of Ketchikan Pulp's contract—at least not until the new Tongass forest plan was done.

Agriculture Undersecretary Jim Lyons, Clinton's top forest policy advisor, said later it was clear that acquiescing to an extension would simply prolong a failed policy, while allowing the contract to expire would allow the Forest Service to move forward with a new vision for the Tongass. "This was the only remaining long-term sale contract of its kind in existence in the national forest system," Lyons said. "Essentially what they were looking for was favored treatment unlike that any other timber purchaser was getting. The obligation to meet the contract was driving the entire program on the Tongass. It was inappropriate to extend the pain any longer."

The administration was obligated to fulfill its fifty-year contract with KPC, Lyons said. "But we knew the obligation to provide a certain amount of timber would supersede any attempt to come up with a comprehensive ecosystem management plan on the forest. It meant we had to produce more timber than was ecologically sustainable." Louisiana-Pacific's reaction to the administration's hard line was predictable, he said. "There was a period of time in which they vilified us, then Mr. Suwyn called and said, 'Let's talk.'"

On September 19, a week after he delivered his ultimatum, Suwyn made a formal written proffer to Agriculture Secretary Glickman, Lyons' boss. He was silent on the contract extension demand. Instead, Suwyn offered to negotiate a settlement of KPC's breach-of-contract suit against the government in exchange for an agreement that would allow KPC to close its Ketchikan pulp mill but keep its two Alaska sawmills running on Tongass timber, at least for a while. "This proposal is offered in good faith as a route to maintain a portion of the economy of southeast Alaska despite the shutdown of the pulp mill which is the centerpiece around which the economy has been built over the past forty-two years," Suwyn wrote.

Bart Koehler had met Suwyn only once, in July, when the new CEO agreed to sit down with Alaska Rainforest Campaign lobbyists in Washington, D.C. "He declared that closing the pulp mill was not a threat, it was a fact of life," Koehler recalled. "We asked him if he had an exit strategy for his workers in Ketchikan. He told us, 'No, we have no strategy. We have a month, then we're going to shut it down.' They hadn't talked about severance or retraining. It was clear to us that we cared more about those workers than he did. Suwyn was looking for a way to close the mill and blame everyone else but himself. He clearly wanted to get the best deal possible and get the hell out of Dodge."

KPC CUTS ITS LOSSES

When Sen. Frank Murkowski saw that a self-standing contract extension bill would not pass the Senate, he attached his measure to a popular Omnibus Parks Bill that provided financing for the federal purchase of a number of land parcels, including the Presidio in San Francisco, a tallgrass prairie preserve in Kansas, an old-growth forest in Oregon, and the 20,000-acre Sterling Forest on the New York–New Jersey border. The White House threatened to veto the parks bill unless the contract extension provision was deleted. The move held up adjournment of Congress for several days. On Ocober 3, Murkowski finally pulled it, under pressure from Senate Majority Leader Trent Lott.

In exchange, he got a letter from Leon Panetta, President Clinton's chief of staff, stating the administration's willingness to begin negotiations on mutual cancellation of Ketchikan Pulp Company's contract. Under this non-binding side agreement, if the negotiations produced a settlement, KPC would be allowed to log nearly 300 million board feet of timber already under contract to supply its two sawmills.

On October 7, Suwyn announced at a Portland press conference that Louisiana-Pacific would close its Ketchikan pulp mill the following March, throwing five hundred people out of work. He informed shareholders that L-P would spend $188 million of its third-quarter earnings on closure and cleanup costs.

In Ketchikan, the news was greeted with anxiety, restrained joy and a sense of inevitability. The mill's closure would mean the loss of five hundred family-wage pulp mill jobs in a town of fourteen thousand, with ripple effects on school enrollment, real estate values and the town's tax base. But it was clear that Ketchikan Pulp had played out its string.

"The mill's demise shows Alaskans that there's a limit to what even powerful congressional advocates can accomplish," the *Anchorage Daily News* editorialized on October 20. "Our congressional delegation can take credit for waging a vigorous campaign against long odds to save jobs in Ketchikan . . . For all the economic benefits it delivered, though, the pulp mill also teaches Alaskans a sad lesson about caring for the environment. The mill's legacy to Alaska includes a toxic mess in the waters of Ward Cove and land sites contaminated by toxic dredging materials."

Though Koehler had been closely involved in the negotiations that produced the Panetta side agreement, he still found it hard to believe that the end game finally had arrived. "This was an opportunity to close a chapter on the pulp mills that would be fair to the pulp mills," he said. "One billion board feet of timber would be spared that would have been cut if the contract had continued for the full fifty years."

HIGH-STAKES POKER

In the fall of 1996, the real deal-making began. During closed-door negotiations in Portland, Suwyn, Lyons, Lois Schiffer of the Department of Justice and Greg Frazier of Agriculture Secretary Glickman's staff began hammering out an agreement that would cancel KPC's long-term contract, provide a short-term guarantee of timber for KPC's two Alaska sawmills, assure a full environmental cleanup at Ward Cove, and resolve the company's longstanding $400 million breach-of-contract suit against the government, which stemmed from passage of the 1990 Tongass Timber Reform Act. L-P's lawyers argued that the Forest Service, in implementing the law, had unilaterally changed the terms of KPC's long-term contract, creating timber shortages that contributed to a decline in timber jobs. The Clinton administration, already the defendant in a $1 billion suit for civil damages over its cancellation of the Alaska Pulp Corp. long-term contract, had much to gain by settling. The Justice Department feared the government might be held legally liable if the L-P case went to trial.

But Louisiana-Pacific had far more at stake than the government in this poker game. Suwyn was eager to cut L-P's losses in Southeast Alaska. The outlook for dissolving pulp on the highly competitive and rapidly evolving world market was dismal. Production of pulpwood was moving to the boreal forests of the northern interior, and to fast-growing hardwoods like cottonwood, which could be grown like crops and harvested in a few years. The obsolete Ketchikan mill could not compete with new dissolving pulp mills in Brazil, Austria and Indonesia. And a major expansion of the giant Sappi Saiccor Ltd. mill in South Africa had increased the world capacity for dissolving pulp dramatically.

L-P had lost $40 million on operation of its antiquated pulp mill in the first nine months of 1996. The company faced a $200 million investment in environmental upgrades and other deferred maintenance costs. Appeals and lawsuits over future timber sales on the Tongass seemed likely. And during the mill's last year of operation, its already tarnished image had been further blackened by disclosures over its poor record on environmental compliance, worker safety and public health. Despite continuing worker complaints, KPC mill managers had failed to address the problem of sulfur dioxide leaks at the mill—until January of 1997, when sixty feet of titanium pipe blew up. The company hired a consultant from Anchorage, who told astonished mill managers that hydrogen explosions were occurring inside the fourteen-year-old pipes. At first, they refused to believe it. The federal Occupational Safety and Health Administration finally ordered KPC to replace the titanium pipes.

The work began shortly before the mill closed for good. At closure the company had invested $150,000 to $180,000 in labor and $100,000 in stainless steel pipes. "They decided to go ahead even after the closure decision in case they blew a pipe during the closure process," said Mike Speelman, the manager hired to convert the doomed mill from titanium pipes to stainless steel.

The Alaska Rainforest Campaign mounted a campaign to publicize the company's continuing violations of the Clean Water Act and Clean Air Act, paying staff members in other organizations to work exclusively on KPC's pollution record. One of those was former EPA official Irene Alexakos, who had written most of the notices of KPC's Clean Water Act violations, and who was now working for the Alaska Clean Water Alliance. The pulp mill was in violation of its federal water pollution discharge permit and was operating under a consent decree that required it to undertake a cleanup of Ward Cove. In January of 1996 the Rainforest Campaign and other groups filed a lawsuit against EPA challenging Ketchikan Pulp's permit and asking the government to require the company to spend as much as $180 million on pollution control equipment.

The Rainforest Campaign also hit Louisiana-Pacific where it lived, feeding information about air pollution problems near the Ketchikan pulp mill to a reporter in Portland, L-P's corporate home. "We went after Mark Suwyn on his home turf," Steve Kallick said. "We bombarded Suwyn in Portland all the time. We wanted to embarrass him and make him hate that mill." In Ketchikan, grassroots activists Eric Hummel and Marg Clabby had been poring through state and federal environmental documents on their own time, trying to draw attention to serious air and water pollution caused by pulp mill operations—but with little success. They found themselves lumped together with forest activists and accused of working to close the mill. In 1996 they got a small grant and formed the Citizens Health Action Network to inform people about the extent of pulp mill pollution and to get the state to enforce environmental laws.

In August of 1996, over protests from local environmentalists, the Alaska Department of Environmental Conservation issued KPC a new air pollution discharge permit. However, the state also announced that it had reached a settlement with KPC in a civil suit that would require the company to reduce emissions of hazardous air pollutants, control releases of sulfur dioxide to the atmosphere, and meet standards limiting visible emissions from its boilers. Within two weeks after the settlement was announced, a sulfur dioxide leak at the mill sent nearby residents to the hospital, bringing to twelve the number of workers and neighbors who had recently been sickened by gas leaks.

Neighbors of the pulp mill also turned up the heat. Carol Murray and Leslee Engler had bought a house near Ward Cove in May of 1995. Within days of moving in, they were gassed with sulfur dioxide. They set about documenting the emissions, which smelled variously of acetone, vinegar and rotten egg, and began videotaping the black stuff coming out of the pulp mill stacks. They organized their neighbors to complain to KPC about the black soot that was falling into the open barrels they used to collect rainwater for drinking. In response, KPC managers offered to deliver bottled water to houses downwind of the mill.

THE SETTLEMENT

The pulp mill was history, but there were still profits to be made at KPC's Alaska sawmills—if the company could be sure of a log supply. Suwyn hoped to be able to operate its sawmills at Ward Cove and nearby Annette Island with timber the company had already purchased, keeping 400 sawmill workers employed and providing a soft landing for Ketchikan's economy. If negotiations failed, the company would forfeit that timber and be forced to compete for Tongass logs on an equal footing with other bidders.

The hard decision to close the pulp mill had been made. Negotiations moved ahead in a businesslike way. "What we did, in a stepwise fashion, was to figure out the timber volume, what was available, what guarantees we wanted from KPC regarding maintaining a level of employment," Agriculture Undersecretary Lyons recalled. "There were a host of environmental issues. Then we got down to what was the money value of the damages."

The deal was sealed in early February of 1997 and formally announced by the parties on February 21. Louisiana-Pacific got $140 million in settlement of its breach-of-contract lawsuit and the right to log 300 million board feet of timber it had previously contracted for—enough to keep its sawmills running for three more years. After that, if L-P wanted to stay in Alaska, it would have to bid for timber at auction like any other federal purchaser. The settlement also affirmed the company's responsibility to clean up the heavily polluted pulp mill site. Louisiana-Pacific would face no sanctions for breach of contract. In turn, L-P would drop its lawsuit against the government. The settlement, said Mark Suwyn, "avoids a lengthy, contentious and distracting claims process with an uncertain outcome."

A BITTERSWEET OCCASION

On March 2, 1997, a Sunday, one hundred local, state and federal officials, among them Murkowski, Lyons, Schiffer, and Governor Knowles, held a ceremonial signing at Ketchikan's Ted Ferry Civic Center to seal the settlement. The mood of the event was sad and celebratory at once, offering a poignant closure to the era inaugurated on that day in 1954 when the pulp mill had been dedicated with such festivity, such high hopes. KPC President Ralph Lewis served as master of ceremonies. "We all feel the sorrow for the mill going down," he said. "At the same time, we've got to turn the page, we have to move forward, we have to make things happen." Murkowski described the occasion as "bittersweet." He promised to work with the Forest Service to help develop an industrial use for the low-grade fiber once fed to the pulp mill. Suwyn proclaimed his satisfaction with the pact, vowing that Louisiana-Pacific would not abandon Ketchikan, but would help to "build an ongoing economic miracle in this community."

"Quite honestly, if I hadn't been sitting there in the back of the room, I wouldn't have believed it," Bart Koehler said. "Ketchikan had turned out to celebrate the closure of the pulp mill. They were happy they had timber for three years, for the sawmills." In keeping with the spirit of the occasion, Koehler went up to Murkowski and shook his hand.

Some environmentalists and even some KPC workers criticized the settlement, calling it yet another huge taxpayer subsidy for Ketchikan Pulp. But Rep. George Miller, the California Democrat who had done as much as anyone to bring reform to the Tongass, called it a bargain for taxpayers. "If you look at how much it cost to maintain the long-term contract," he said, "the settlement pays off in very short order." Alaska environmentalists said it was a small price to pay. Koehler declared: "The true transition from the pulp mill era to a community-based future for Southeast Alaska begins today."

Lyons, who had been dealing with the Tongass since his days staffing the House Agriculture Committee in the 1980s, said later that the settlement was one of the most satisfying moments of his career. "When I was on Capitol Hill there were two long-term timber sale contracts and the Tongass was a subject of perennial debate on the floor of the House," he said. "Within five years both contacts were eliminated, and we got a new Tongass plan that is not constrained by the need to meet a long-term contract. I look at this as a part of the legacy I'm proudest of. I'm proud of the administration's role here."

THE LAST ROLL OF PULP

Despite the appearance of good will, nerves were raw in Ketchikan in the days leading up to the actual mill closure. In March, days before the pulp mill ceased operating, the hostility that had divided Ketchikan for the last year boiled over. In that final week, someone circulated a flyer announcing that there would be a "victory party" on the day the mill shut down. The event was to be held at a local hall, the flyer said, with proceeds going to defray legal costs incurred by Forest Service whistleblower Bill Shoaf. At the mill, twenty or thirty grim workers vowed to crash the party. The town's embattled environment activists hunkered down. But the flyer was a hoax. As the *Ketchikan Daily News* reported, the hall in question had been closed for months. Local conservationists disavowed the rumored event. So did Shoaf. The community took a collective deep breath. It seemed possible that in this polarized town of millworkers and fishermen, the season of blame finally had passed.

Early on the morning of March 25, as the last roll of pulp came off the production line, a cold Southeast Alaska monsoon swept people indoors. The atmosphere in Ketchikan was subdued. If some people celebrated, they did it discreetly. Most workers had a clear-eyed view of the reasons for the closure. In the mill cafeteria, and later at a bowling alley in a Ketchikan shopping mall, a few of them saluted the mill's final day of operation and shared their views. Their consensus: years of short-sighted management by Louisiana-Pacific was most to blame for the closure.

"Personally, I don't believe government or environmentalists have as much to do with this plant closing as management itself, or mismanagement," said Russell Mock, a millwright and machinist at the mill for eleven years. "It didn't take a high IQ to see this was the way it would turn out. They did no more than they were forced to do. In times of economic boom they should have been striving to get into environmental compliance, but they waited until charges were filed against them. There was a lot of money dumped into the plant at the last, but I believe they should have headed this off from the beginning. If they'd done a better job of maintaining the plant, I think they would have had a better leg to stand on with environmentalists."

"When Harry Merlo was getting $1,500 a ton for pulp he wasn't investing in the mill," agreed longtime employee Gil Smith. "The profits were being drained out of the mill."

Ironically, even as the mill's impending closure was announced, KPC was completing work on a spill containment wall around the perimeter of the mill site. The wall had been constructed to comply with the consent decree resulting from KPC's criminal conviction for violations of the Clean Water Act. It was designed to allow testing of all liquid waste, even rainwater runoff, before it was piped to the mill's water treatment plant. The company also was in the process of converting to an elementally chlorine-free mill. The $6 million conversion, scheduled to come on line the following month, would have reduced the mill's use of chlorine by 80 percent.

HARD FEELINGS

The attitude of KPC managers toward their workers inspired little loyalty at the end. Mike Speelman, hired in 1994 as the mill's central maintenance supervisor, had previously worked as a master mechanic and foreman supervisor at Portland General Electric, an Oregon utility. Speelman was accustomed, he said, to working in a place where "you treated your people like human beings, treated them like you would like to be treated." He was appalled at the attitude he encountered among top managers at Ketchikan Pulp. "I could not believe how they treated their people," he said. "They

Gil Smith (left) and John Wolon, longtime Ketchikan Pulp workers, on the eve of the mill's closing in March 1997. Photo by Kathie Durbin.

treated them as thieves, as crooks, as liars. It came from mid-level supervisors all the way up to (KPC President) Ralph Lewis." Speelman was shocked as well by the waste of material and equipment. "I walked into the mill and I said, 'How in the hell is it running?' Pumps were just sitting out in the weather, rusting. Then I saw the real waste, the waste of personnel."

KPC had been uncooperative with efforts by the Association of Western Pulp and Paper Workers to apply for federal job retraining and relocation benefits under the Trade Adjustment Act. Because the act's benefits were available to workers whose jobs were eliminated due to foreign competition, KPC's workers clearly were eligible. But initially KPC wouldn't even provide the U.S. Department of Labor with a list of the company's customers, said union representative Paul Lamm; he got the list through the back door, from a company computer base. "The application was filed by AWPPW," Lamm said. "The carpenter's union lobbied for the benefit. So did Gov. Tony Knowles and the entire Alaska delegation. But the company didn't cooperate."

Workers covered by the Trade Adjustment Act were entitled to receive paid relocation costs if they found jobs anywhere in the United States. But Lamm said most Ketchikan Pulp workers didn't want to move. A survey of three hundred hourly and salaried KPC employees revealed that 77 percent preferred to stay in Ketchikan. "The sad reality is that if they want to maintain a wage, they're not going to find it in Ketchikan," Lamm said. "Realistically, it's going to be tough for some of the unemployed once the benefits run out. The average wage at the pulp mill is $15 an hour. There's nothing to take the place of those high-wage jobs."

Still, many workers saw the mill's closure as an opportunity to start over. John Wolon, an employee of KPC since 1976, was apprenticing as a news photographer at the *Ketchikan Daily News*. He hoped the job transition benefit the union had secured would allow him to study photography at the prestigious Brooks Institute in California. In the meantime, Wolon, who had only a high school diploma, was taking college English courses at the local campus of the University of Alaska. "We all feel bad about the mill closing," he said. "A lot of families will be put out by this. But if the education benefit does come through, and doesn't all go to bureaucracy, there could be opportunities for a lot of people. We're only going to get one chance at retraining."

Rick Benner, the mill's operations manager, led a tour of the mill three days before it closed. The phase-down had begun; already the mill was being operated by a skeleton crew. He was business-like, even cheerfully resigned to the impending closure. Morale was "not too bad," he said. About half his workers had made plans for education or training or intended to return to the Lower 48. He would be around for a while, overseeing the shutdown. Thirty Boy Scouts had come through the mill the previous week, taking the tour so they could get their pulp and paper merit badges. That's when the reality of the closure had hit him, he said. "They asked me, 'What are you going to do for a job?' I got a little emotional then."

Guarded optimism

Leslee Engler noticed the difference in the air immediately after the pulp mill shut down. Her chronic headache had vanished. "It's just unbelievable," she said a few days later. "There's no nasty vinegar smell, no rotten egg smell. I'm feeling so much better. I didn't realize how oppressive it was to walk outside and be hit with air I couldn't breathe."

For conservationists, in Alaska and across the nation, there was relief and guarded optimism: relief that the era of pulp was over, and optimism that the Forest Service might now begin managing the Tongass for fish and wildlife, recreation and tourism, subsistence and a scaled-down timber industry focused on production of value-added wood products. "The Forest Service is no longer saddled with this albatross, and can manage this tremendous forest for all the people who use it," SEACC attorney Buck Lindekugel said.

Ketchikan's fourteen thousand residents knew they had just witnessed history in the making. But the shape of things to come was less clear. The talk in shops and restaurants was of severance checks and job retraining, plummeting property values and new economic development prospects. For city officials, there was the challenge of charting a new course for a town dominated for forty-three years by a single industry. Already, in Ketchikan, change was in the wind.

In October of 1996, Jack Shay, a moderate, had defeated J.C. Conely, a Ketchikan Borough assemblyman and the chief drumbeater for CARE. Shay immediately established a committee to recommend priorities and programs for Ketchikan's future. "I came here on a platform of, 'We're not going to die,'" the quixotic new mayor said. "My agenda is, 'Try to get on with life without making pulp.'"

20

HOONAH

F loyd Peterson steered his skiff out of Hoonah Harbor and pointed it west across Port Frederick. It was a mid-September day in 1997, the last sunny day before the onset of fall rains. Coho salmon jumped and kittiwakes scattered before the boat.

On the far side, Peterson turned south and followed the shoreline below a dirt-brown hillside. Only the thinnest crown of trees at the ridgetop and a skinny beach strip remained of the rain forest that had blanketed this slope not long ago The clearcut stretched south for ten miles, to the national forest boundary at Neka Bay. Peterson pointed out the fringe of trees along the water with scorn: "They leave a sixty-foot buffer along the beach. Deer die by the hundreds within these buffers." In another area, he nodded toward a greening patch facing saltwater that had been beach-logged in the 1940s and had grown back to tall young spruce. Reforestation is a slow process in this land of short growing seasons. Trees in one fourteen-year-old clearcut were only five feet high.

Peterson and his neighbors in the Tlingit village of Hoonah used to call West Port Frederick "the meat locker" for its abundant Sitka black-tailed deer. This was their traditional hunting ground, just across the water. But the meat locker was erased in two seasons of logging by the regional Native corporation Sealaska and its contractor, Whitestone Logging Company. Hoonah's residents had a ringside seat as it happened. From their front doors they could watch the progress of the bulldozers and hear the chainsaw's whine.

By the summer of 1997 the logging had reached Hoonah's back yard as well. Whitestone Logging was clearcutting the Spasski Creek watershed behind the village on the north end of Chichagof Island. Spasski Creek is a salmon spawning stream, and its watershed had always been an incubator for deer and brown bear, which foraged in the fresh clearcuts. But once the second-growth thickets close over, they would find little cover and less food.

Peterson's leg was amputated above the knee and he walked stiffly, pulling his wooden leg around in front with his hands when he sat. But neither his handicap nor the clearcutting had kept him from hunting. He had outfitted an aluminum skiff as a landing craft so he could take his all-terrain vehicle ashore to track deer. Following a route unknown to the hunters who arrived on the ferry from Juneau to drive the backroads around Hoonah, he pointed out the place at the head of Port Frederick where he hunts now, a place accessible only by boat. Peterson also knew the locations of the best fishing holes—away from the clearcuts, back in the heads of inlets along Chichagof Island's serrated north coast.

Early in the evening, after the log trucks had headed back to camp, Peterson drove his pickup into the scalped hills behind Hoonah. On the way the pickup passed muskeg bogs where stunted bull pines, arranged as if by a Japanese landscape artist, stood in stark relief. Because the pines have no commercial value, they had been left behind, along with some scraggly hemlocks along the larger streams. Not many deer remained in these hills, Peterson said: "The road hunters got them all." Atop a slash-piled landing high on a ridge, the 360-degree view encompassed clearcuts and logging roads, the blue waters of Port Frederick and the sea-and-landscape beyond. The logging scars went on and on into the back country, leading from one denuded drainage to the next, deep into the heart of Chichagof Island.

For Hoonah's thousand residents, nearly two decades of industrial logging, first by the Forest Service, which presided over the removal of hundreds of millions of board feet of the best timber on the Hoonah Ranger District, then by Sealaska and the village's own Native corporation, Huna Totem, had taken their toll. And even Peterson, Hoonah's most outspoken logging critic, felt powerless to stop the destruction.

PETERSON'S FATHER, A SWEDE, came to Hoonah in the 1930s on a purse seiner and ran a crab cannery for twenty-five years. His mother was half Tlingit, half Norwegian. Floyd lived easily in both worlds. He went to high school in Juneau, and to boat-building school in Tacoma. He returned to Hoonah, became a successful commercial fisherman, and married Marge, an Alaska Native from Bethel. For thirty years they lived in a big double-wide manufactured home overlooking West Port Frederick. They moved into their new house next door, a big modern house with a deck and view windows, just as logging commenced across the water. They had the best view in town of the logging, and watched the destruction of Hoonah's primary hunting ground with growing anger.

In the spare room of his house Peterson stored what he called his "political work": correspondence, government reports, news clippings about his battle against the logging, stories from national magazines about the campaign to save the Tongass. There was nothing subtle about his brand of activism. "I went to the *Juneau Empire* and said, 'We're getting national coverage but you guys are ignoring this. What's wrong with you?' At first they wouldn't print my letters to the editor." It's no coincidence, he contended, that Sealaska was a major newspaper advertiser.

Peterson is proudest of "Hoonah's Legacy," the video he helped to create. Filmed by Homer, Alaska, videographer Daniel Zatz, with a camera strapped to an airplane wing, it is a damning and irrefutable indictment of logging by Native corporations surrounding Hoonah. Peterson took Zatz to see the logging on the ground and helped edit the images. The video has no spoken words, only mournful music and the corporate slogans of Sealaska and Huna Totem, juxtaposed against scenes of the naked landscape.

ANCSA's LEGACY

Hoonah's Natives are descended from people who lived for millennia along the northeast coast of Chichagof Island and across Icy Strait at Glacier Bay. They fished for salmon in the strait, hunted seals in the bay, and took their deer from the forests that blanketed the low hills. The 1980 Alaska Lands Act guaranteed the people of Hoonah and all other rural Alaska residents the right to a subsistence harvest of fish, game and wild plants on their traditional lands. Under the law, when deer or salmon are scarce, the subsistence harvest takes precedence over hunting or fishing for sport.

Yet the Forest Service and the Native corporations have seldom restrained their logging to protect subsistence hunting and food gathering. Though the Forest Service acknowledged in its 1997 Tongass Land Management Plan that its planned timber harvest on the Hoonah Ranger District would further damage subsistence areas used by Hoonah residents, the agency planned further incursions into what was left of the village's customary hunting grounds. Sealaska expected to log extensively in the Spasski Creek and Gartina Creek watersheds and on West Port Frederick. By 1997, Sealaska had already cut its way across the northern end of Chichagof Island almost all the way to Lisianski Inlet. "If that is gone, we don't know where we'll go," said Frank Wright Jr. president of the Hoonah Tlingit and Haida Community Council. "We're literally surrounded by logging. The effects are right before our eyes."

The tragedy facing Hoonah and other Alaska Native villages began with passage of the Alaska Native Claims Settlement Act. The 1971 law brought economic development to some Native communities in Southeast. But it also created a system of disenfranchisement. "Tribal governments are not recognized in Alaska, and Native corporations are not responsive," said Wanda Culp, a Tlingit from Juneau who owns a cabin across Icy Strait from Hoonah. "We have to do petitions and letter drives to influence the corporations. They aren't under tribal jurisdiction; they're under state jurisdiction."

"Hoonah is the largest Tlingit community in Southeast Alaska," Floyd Peterson agreed. "But we don't have any input, any recourse. It's almost like we're under a dictatorship."

Part of the problem is absentee management. Only a small number of Sealaska's 16,000 shareholders, and only 350 of Huna Totem's original 867 shareholders, still lived in Hoonah by 1997. No member of the Sealaska board of directors lived there. Huna Totem built its new corporate office in Juneau. It is a typical situation throughout Alaska. By the 1990s, only about one-third of village corporation shareholders actually lived in Native villages; the rest lived elsewhere, even outside Alaska, and had no direct stake in the environmental impacts of resource extraction.

HISTORY OF A DISASTER

The disaster at Hoonah began to unfold in the 1960s, even before the passage of ANCSA, with the opening of Northeast Chichagof Island to road-building and industrial logging under the Alaska Pulp Corp. long-term contract. In the early 1970s, after Congress passed ANCSA, Hoonah's leaders established Huna Totem, a village corporation of 920 shareholders, which selected 23,000 acres from the Tongass National Forest adjacent to the village. Like many Alaska Natives, Peterson didn't pay much attention to the land selection process. "Ninety percent of the community was fishing," he said. "We all thought the land was being put in the hands of the corporations to manage it wisely for us. Why not select land around your village?"

At first, the corporation's prospects looked bright. But Huna Totem's first timber harvest, a joint venture with Sealaska, was a fiasco. As cutting was about to begin, the market for softwood timber plummeted and Sealaska backed out, leaving Huna Totem with a $1.5 million debt for roads and start-up costs for a harvest that didn't happen.

To recoup its losses, Huna Totem formed a new joint venture, Huna Pacific, with Jim Clevenger, a logging contractor from the Pacific Northwest. The venture was financed by a $5.2 million loan from the Federal Land Bank of Spokane, which also invested in four other Native corporations in Southeast Alaska, committing a total of $25 million to the startup of logging on Native corporation lands. Huna Totem board members thought the standing timber would be their collateral, but the bank wanted the land itself put up as security for the loan. Village leaders opposed using Native land as collateral, but they had few options.

In the spring of 1982 Huna Totem's joint venture began its first timber harvest with a crew recruited largely from the fishermen of Hoonah. But eighteen months later, after more than a thousand acres around the village had been logged, the venture was abandoned. Instead of turning a profit, Huna Totem had plunged deeper into debt. Moreover, the logging angered many village shareholders. "It basically goes against the nature of our people to cut the trees," Huna Totem Chairman Frank O. Williams told the *Anchorage Daily News*. "There were protests not to cut a single tree. But the protests didn't stop the logging."

One day soon after logging began, Wanda Culp drove with her children to a food-gathering area on Hoonah Mountain and discovered that the forests were gone. She recalls seeing an elderly woman standing in the road looking shell-shocked. "She just had her hand over her heart."

After the joint venture with the Washington firm collapsed, Whitestone Logging was hired to finish the job. The Huna Totem board held a retreat to figure out what had gone wrong. It concluded that inexperienced Native logging crews, problems with the logging contractor and a continuing fall in lumber prices were all to blame. "We tried to accomplish too many things too soon," Williams conceded. "We tried to make loggers out of fishermen without giving them any training. We just put them out in the woods."

In March of 1985, a month before logging was to begin on another 600-acre unit near Hoonah, the Huna Totem directors decided to cut overhead, sell off subsidiaries and double the pace of logging to pay off a bank loan that threatened to linger on long after the last of the marketable timber was gone from Huna Totem lands. The corporation wanted to get out of debt and head off any effort to foreclose on the 1,900 acres it had put up as collateral on its loan. "We made a decision that the corporation would survive," Williams said. Huna Totem was not unique; by the mid-1980s, at least six Southeast Native corporations faced a combined debt of more than $30 million collateralized by at least 60,000 acres of their timberlands.

The pace of logging did increase, and Huna Totem's debt did dwindle—temporarily. The corporation hoped to be profitable by the end of 1986, and to stop clearcutting at that point. More than three hundred loggers and truck drivers were put to work felling the forests behind the village and hauling logs to the harbor, where the logs were loaded onto Filipino freighters and shipped off to Japanese mills. Tom Mills, a Hoonah Tlingit supervising the stevedore loading crew, was asked his view of the logging by Hal Bernton of the *Anchorage Daily News*. Mills shook his head in embarrassment. "I've hunted and fished here all my life," he said. "I don't want to see the land cut. All the eagles are out on the breakwater because there are so few trees left on the hill."

Then, in 1986, Congress passed the Tax Reform Act, with its provision allowing Alaska Native corporations to sell their net operating losses to profitable companies. Huna Totem, like most other Native corporations in Southeast, logged heavily in the late 1980s to take advantage of the tax loophole. But after Congress plugged it four years later, the corporation could not make a profit on its logging operations. In 1994, facing bankruptcy, Huna Totem sold its stumpage on West Port Frederick to Sealaska, and the meat locker's fate was sealed.

In January of 1995, the city of Hoonah and the Hoonah Indian Association passed resolutions opposing "any and all logging in and around the entire Port Frederick drainage area" because of its importance to wildlife and its significance as a cultural and historic site. Nonetheless, logging began the following year.

Rick Harris, Sealaska's senior president for resources, conceded the concern by Sealaska shareholders over "the intensity of harvest and its effect on wildlife," especially near Hoonah. He defended Sealaska's forest practices on its own land. As a matter of corporate policy, he said, Sealaska retains beach buffers and migration corridors for wildlife and leaves eight-acre buffers around eagle nests. But there were special circumstances at West Port Frederick, he said, because Huna Totem sold its stumpage and retained the land. "They basically sold everything. We had to buy everything." To recoup its costs, he said, Sealaska had to liquidate the timber.

Harris was not blind to the anger Sealaska's handiwork had provoked. "I've had to battle with myself over the visual appearance," he admitted. But he added that stream buffers seemed to be protecting salmon, and loggers routinely reported large numbers of brown bear and Sitka black-tailed deer in the clearcuts. Wildlife still used this land, Harris said. The question he could not answer was: for how long?

'A CRIME AGAINST OUR CULTURE"

Frank Wright Jr. wants to know the answer to that question. Wright lives with his wife and children in a small house on Hoonah's main street. His living room, like Floyd Peterson's, looks out on the West Port Frederick clearcut. To him, the view represents a promise broken.

Wright' grew up in this house in a family of fourteen. His father pumped gas for an oil company, but his real job was obtaining food for his family. "He fished in summer and hunted in winter," Wright said. "He fed us on fish and deer meat and seal. Now I wonder where people will go to get their game."

Wright has carried on his father's tradition, gathering food not only for his family but for the people of his village. Each fall he takes his purse seiner out to Excursion Inlet and does a "net set" for the community. In September of 1997 he caught a thousand dog salmon in one day and donated them to Hoonah's residents. Winter unemployment in the village reaches 70 percent. Some of the fish would be eaten by families without salmon of their own. Some would be smoked and set out at traditional festivals.

When Huna Totem was getting started, Wright took a job as the corporation's personnel manager. He proposed that Huna Totem buy the local cold storage locker, which served the village's thriving commercial fishing industry. "The board of directors rejected it, wouldn't even consider it," Wright recalled. "They said fishing is going down anyway." The storage locker, now owned by Icicle Seafoods of Petersburg, survived and flourished. But Huna Totem decided to put all its eggs into the timber basket. When Wright learned that Huna Pacific, the new joint venture, planned to liquidate all the timber on Huna Totem lands within twenty-five years, he quit his job.

In 1986 Wright got himself elected to the board of the Hoonah Indian Association, the village's tribal government. The association, federally recognized since 1939, was struggling to survive on a budget of $36,000.

At the time, Sealaska and Huna Totem had just begun building logging roads. Neither corporation bothered to notify the village or the tribal government of its logging plans. The association found out about them from the loggers themselves. In response, its board petitioned Huna Totem to save the ten-mile stretch of forest extending from Neka Point to Chris Point—the meat locker—to protect Hoonah's view and critical deer habitat. The village corporation promised never to log it.

By 1988 the tribal government had barely enough money to keep the lights on in the ramshackle cultural center that served as its headquarters. It became inactive, and the one voice in Hoonah willing to speak out against the activities of the Native corporations was silenced.

Wright recognized that reconstituting tribal government was essential if Hoonah was to have a voice independent of the corporations. "I knew a government-to-government relationship with the U.S. government was necessary if we were going to be able to work together," Wright said. "With it, we have authority. Without it, no one would talk to us." In 1992 he invested $400 of his own money to rent a polling place and pay for election materials so the association could elect a new tribal council. Ten tribal members ran for the seven council seats. With federal assistance, the reconstituted tribal government hired an executive director and fixed up the cultural center, and the Hoonah Indian Association became a vocal adversary of Native corporation logging.

Its first challenge was to distinguish itself from Huna Totem in the minds of government agencies, the press and the public. "A lot of people had the misconception that the Native corporations are the voice of the tribal governments," Wright said. "We needed to educate people that the corporations do not speak for the tribes." The recent clearcutting was so visible from the ferry, and from Hoonah's main street, that Wright had been asked by one visitor, "Why are you Natives doing this to your land?" He had tried, he said, to explain: "Some of us are fighting this. We aren't responsible."

In taking a strong stand against further destruction of fish and game habitat around the village, the Hoonah Indian Association was not alone. The Alaska Native Brotherhood and the Tlingit and Haida Association petitioned for sharp reductions in logging. Hoonah adopted a coastal management plan recommending that no more than 30 million board feet of timber be logged annually from all ownerships in the Hoonah area. All these petitions were ignored. In 1996, Native corporations cut 130 million

A ship takes on logs for export at West Port Frederick, near Hoonah. Photo by James R. Mackovjak.

board feet of timber around Hoonah. In 1997, Sealaska planned to log 67 million board feet, most of it in the Spasski Creek watershed, where logging already had eliminated forests that provided critical winter cover for deer.

But for Wright, the clearcut across West Port Frederick was the biggest betrayal. Snow piled up in the clearcuts now, he said. Soon the deer would have no winter cover. He never went into that country anymore. "Huna Totem told us they would never log it," he said. "It turns my gut every time I look at it."

The scarcity of nearby deer increased the risk for Hoonah hunters, Wright said, forcing them out into the treacherous waters of Icy Strait. "You have to go from here to Point Adolphus to hunt now. Point Adolphus is twenty miles over open water with heavy tides. It's not safe to go out to Icy Strait in winter."

Wright described his feelings on seeing a bear caught between a logging tower on West Port Frederick and a boat full of people, including a Juneau radio reporter. Trapped, the bear had no place to go, he said, and finally lay down in the forest.

It was too soon to know how the logging would affect Hoonah's fisheries, but Wright worried about that too. "You can see through the buffer strips. There are little streams that are totally wiped out."

Wright had confronted other Sealaska shareholders, trying to raise the level of awareness about the impact of logging. "I asked, 'Do you have any idea what effect this will have on Hoonah?' The simplest answer they had was, "We are a profit-making organization. It doesn't matter.'"

The economic benefits Hoonah residents have realized from the destruction of their traditional lands are slight, however. The Whitestone Logging camp is five miles from town, and loggers and their families rarely come into Hoonah. Few loggers or truck drivers are local hires. There is no large sawmill in town, only a small mill that cuts rough green lumber. Hoonah shareholders receive a few hundred dollars from Huna Totem and about $1,000 from Sealaska annually. Wright scoffs at the notion that these dividend checks should silence opposition. "You can't equate our dividend checks with the loss of habitat for game. It doesn't make up for the loss of the continued existence of a tribe. People don't like it when I call it an act of genocide. They don't realize that when they take the land we used for centuries, it's a crime against our culture."

FROM THE WINDOWS OF FLOYD AND MARGE Peterson's house the clearcuts across West Port Frederick stand out vividly in the morning sun. It is hard not to despair. But this is Southeast Alaska. The land is resilient. Afternoon shadows swallow the scars, and by dusk the hills are dark shapes across the water. When the fog rolls in, it obscures even the large log ship anchored in the harbor, and the wild beauty of this land reasserts itself. In the forest, the boughs of the spruces and hemlocks drip with condensed fog. Coho salmon still spawn in Spasski Creek. The air is alive with the smell of the sea. Even in Hoonah, hope survives.

A NEW ERA

As the shore road curving south out of Sitka rounds a bend, the partially dismantled pulp mill looms into view on the shore of Silver Bay. It is a reminder now of an era many Sitkans would like to forget. The end of pulp mill operations had a dramatic effect on the bay. "The water is unbelievably crystal clear now," bookstore owner Don Muller said three years after the mill's closure. "We didn't know what clear was before the mill closed. Populations of mussels near the pulp mill had been essentially wiped out. Now they're coming back."

At Ward Cove north of Ketchikan, hundreds of people gathered on April 1, 1999, to watch the pulp mill's bleach plant collapse in a cloud of dust and smoke. Like the mill's dedication, its demise was a public event. A raffle was held to decide who would set off the charges. A former pulp mill worker, Dan Eichner, was the lucky winner. A month later, Louisiana-Pacific Corporation announced that it was selling its two sawmills as well and leaving Alaska once and for all.

IN SOUTHEAST ALASKA, THE FUTURE began to come clear only after the water and the air came clear. The future would be built not upon one large industry, but upon many smaller enterprises. Community leaders in Sitka and Ketchikan had predicted economic disaster when the mills closed. What occurred was worker dislocation, more painful for some than for others, followed by a surprising economic rebound.

Three years after the Alaska Pulp Corporation mill closed, not even Sitka's most ardent boosters suggested it should ever reopen. "There is a consensus that we need a much smaller timber industry," Mayor Pete Hallgren said in 1996. "Something the size of the pulp mill would be very destructive to the community now."

With the departure of the pulp industry, Sitka became distinctly more white-collar. Between 1993 and 1996 the number of manufacturing jobs dropped by more than half, and though unemployment levels returned to pre-pulp mill closure levels by 1995, the average monthly wage fell slightly between 1993 and 1996, reflecting the loss of the high-paying pulp mill jobs. The city of 8,800 began looking for ways to attract small wood products manufacturers to round out its economy, which was humming along on commercial and sport fishing, tourism, and jobs in government and health services. By 1997, Sitka's growing health care sector employed 675 people and contributed an annual payroll of $21 million to the town's economy.

In the summer of 1996 throngs of summer tourists filled Sitka's downtown, construction was booming and the real estate market was hot. Along the road to the ferry landing north of town, gleaming new houses looked out over Sitka Sound. A new marina had a seven-year waiting list for moorages.

Commercial tourism was booming; in fact, it threatened to overwhelm the town. More than two hundred cruise ships spilled tourists onto its narrow streets. Locals avoided the downtown area as thousands of tourists disembarked to flood gift shops and crowd into Russian Orthodox St. Michael's Cathedral with its onion-shaped dome. Mayor Hallgren admitted that Sitka had reached its tourism carrying capacity. "Cruise line spending got us through the mill shutdown," he said, "but whenever you have increased economic activity, you have an impact on quality of life." Yet tourism is a fickle suitor. In 1997 Holland America Lines bypassed Sitka on several cruise ship itineraries. Sitka experienced a 30 percent drop in visitors and a $3.5 million reduction in tourism-related business.

After the pulp mill closed, Sitka saw a surge of citizen activism and growing opposition to the return of big timber. In November of 1995 Sitkans came within four votes of passing a measure to prohibit clearcutting in areas where Sitka residents engaged in subsistence hunting, fishing and food-gathering.

IN KETCHIKAN, ONE YEAR AFTER the pulp mill closed, the town's population and school enrollment had dropped slightly, and the unemployment rate had edged up from 8.7 percent to 9.1 percent. But gross business sales had actually jumped by 3.7 percent, to $452 million. Construction, tourism and shipyard operations had enjoyed a strong year. Tourism in particular was exploding; in 1997, 480,000 cruise ship passengers streamed into Ketchikan to get a look at the town's weathered ambiance. And automobile sales unaccountably leaped by 37 percent in the year following the mill's closure.

UNLIKE SITKA, KETCHIKAN still had a timber industry. Louisiana-Pacific Corporation's two sawmills, at Ward Cove and nearby Metlakatla, continued to cut timber from the Tongass National Forest. Meanwhile, community leaders debated how to spend their $25 million share of the $110 million economic development fund U.S. Sen. Ted Stevens had secured for Southeast Alaska. There were proposals for new salmon canneries, a large vessel moorage, an aquarium, and a dry kiln for the manufacture of veneer and plywood.

In 1998, the Ketchikan- Gateway Borough voted to give Louisiana-Pacific Corp. $7 million to study construction of a veneer mill on the pulp mill site at Ward Cove. The Southeast Alaska Conservation Council opposed the project, observing that it would consume large quantities of wood fiber but create few jobs. Throughout 1998 and early 1999 L-P officials and the Alaska congressional delegation tried to win another contract extension that would allow KPC additional time to log the timber it had been guaranteed under its settlement with the federal government. They also tried to get a guarantee of federal timber to supply the proposed veneer mill. But the Clinton administration refused to reopen negotiations.

IN WRANGELL, CITY OFFICIALS and business leaders launched a marketing campaign to attract new employers. A promotional packet featuring stunning photos of the town's scenic backdrop and a breaching humpback whale promoted the town's deep water port, its strategic location, its available job force, its mineral potential, its abundant hydroelectric power. The town's leaders chose not to focus on tourism, despite Wrangell's spectacular scenery. They concentrated on keeping the salmon cannery open, building a new boat harbor, and maintaining a timber industry of some kind. In 1997, Silver Bay Logging Co. bought the Wrangell mill from Alaska Pulp Corporation and started operating it on a limited basis, with a workforce of fifty.

Yet despite heroic efforts by community leaders, and a substantial infusion of state and federal economic assistance, Wrangell was slow to rebound after its old-growth sawmill closed in 1994. Over the next three years the number of people employed dropped from 12,672 to 10,079, and the annual payroll plummeted from $31.2 million to $23.7 million. "Wrangell has had a tough, tough situation," former mayor Doug Roberts said at the end of 1998. "We still have a lot of work to do."

The wave of the future in Southeast Alaska's timber industry appeared to be smaller-scale mills. In 1997 Steve Seley, a long-time Ketchikan logging contractor, broke ground for a new cedar mill near the Ketchikan airport.

He hoped to buy half the 14 million board feet of timber his mill would require yearly from state lands, and to employ sixty workers when it was running at full capacity. He planned to install a dry kiln and planer and produce finished lumber for sale in Alaska and elsewhere. He wanted to experiment with selection cutting and helicopter logging to reduce the impact on the land.

Seley's project attracted strong support from local and state officials, Alaska's congressional delegation, and the Southeast Alaska Conservation Council, which urged the U.S. Army Corps of Engineers to grant the required permits. "The concepts that serve as the foundation for this proposal are sound ones, and represent ideas that we believe the new timber industry for Southeast Alaska should follow in the future," SEACC Executive Director Bart Koehler wrote.

Pete Smith belonged to an even smaller-scale class of timber entrepreneurs. In 1990, Smith and his wife Valery White moved to Whale Pass on the northeast coast of Prince of Wales Island, cleared a plot of land, and built a large house of cedar and fir. Smith set about making a living by milling fine yellow cedar salvaged from beaches or bought from other small purchasers. Using a portable sawmill, he cut the cedar into custom-milled planks, which he sold to boat-builders all over the country through an ad in *Wooden Boat* magazine. Even the smallest Forest Service timber sales, averaging 150,000 board feet, were too big for him. "We don't go through a lot of volume here," Smith said. "If we have 40,000 board feet of timber, that's easily enough to keep us happy for a year. And we make a very good living."

IN BOTH SITKA AND KETCHIKAN, there were unresolved issues regarding the cleanup of the polluted mill sites and what should be done with the land. Alaska Pulp Corporation had escaped a federal Superfund designation for its Sitka mill only through the direct intervention of the Alaska delegation. Instead, the Alaska Department of Environmental Conservation supervised the monitoring of water and soil pollution and the development of a cleanup plan. APC initially committed just $6 million to the cleanup, however—a pittance to restore one of the nation's most polluted sites. In 1998, Alaska Pulp offered to give the mill site to the city and borough of Sitka, thereby escaping legal liability for future cleanup costs. Then, in early 1999, a private party came forward and offered to lease the land for a water bottling plant, tapping the pulp mill's upstream fresh water supply at Blue Lake. By mid-1999 community leaders were still mulling what to do with the site on Silver Bay.

Ketchikan Pulp Co. had less flexibility in the cleanup of its pulp mill site at Ward Cove. Standards for the cleanup had been specified in the 1997 settlement between the government and Louisiana-Pacific. The cost was expected to approach $200 million. Yet the future of the Ward Cove property too was still up in the air by mid-1999.

FOR FORTY-THREE YEARS, THE TONGASS National Forest was an instrument of the pulp industry. The closure of the last pulp mill in Southeast Alaska left the Forest Service at first unable to adapt to changing times.

In May of 1997, Alaska Regional Forester Phil Janik signed the long-awaited, much-delayed Tongass Land Management Plan. In many respects, the plan signaled a remarkable departure from the old way of doing business on the Tongass. It designated an additional 1.1 million acres of mapped reserves across the forest to protect wildlife habitat, subsistence use and recreation. It established thousand-foot-wide buffers bordering beaches and river mouths to preserve wildlife travel corridors. It recommended protection for more than five hundred river miles on thirty-two proposed wild and scenic rivers. It added buffer zones around the most sensitive cave and karst formations.

Yet the Forest Service adopted these reforms only when it could no longer ignore scientific research on the longterm threats logging posed to wildlife, and only when it realized that without reform, it might face even more severe logging restrictions under the Endangered Species Act. And though the plan represented a leap, it was hardly the perfect blueprint to lead the Tongass Forest Service into the new millennium.

For one thing, the 1997 plan's maximum timber sale level of 267 million board feet was no longer supported by market demand. With both pulp mills closed, the demand for Tongass timber collapsed. Forest Service research economists Richard Haynes and David Brooks predicted in a 1997 study that even under the most optimistic scenario, demand in the post-pulp era would not exceed 171 million board feet until after the year 2007. "(I)t is our judgment that the derived demand for National Forest timber will be substantially lower than previously projected, and is likely to increase only slightly over the next two decades," they concluded.

Neither was the 1997 plan embraced by scientists. Its habitat conservation areas were smaller and further apart than many conservation biologists had recommended. Leading wildlife biologists said the reserves were especially deficient as sanctuaries for the Queen Charlotte goshawk. Others said the

100-year cutting cycles called for in the plan were inadequate to assure adequate habitat for Sitka black-tailed deer.

Yet despite these scientific misgivings, in September of 1997 the U.S. Fish and Wildlife Service reaffirmed that the listing of the Queen Charlotte goshawk was "not warranted" based on the habitat protection measures in the new Tongass plan. Protesters from Alaska and Arizona occupied the agency's regional office in Anchorage to protest the decision, and soon after, the Southwest Biodiversity Project and SEACC filed a new lawsuit challenging the agency's failure to list the goshawk.

For SEACC and other environmental groups, the biggest disappointment was that Janik's plan called for logging to commence in some of the last large unprotected roadless areas in Southeast Alaska, including the Cleveland Peninsula, East Kuiu Island, and Port Houghton. Environmentalists appealed the plan to Forest Service Chief Mike Dombeck. The 1997 plan also drew appeals from timber industry groups, Alaska Natives and others— thirty-three appeals in all.

Janik soon moved on to a position in Washington, D.C. , and his deputy, Jim Caplan, was appointed acting regional forester. To help resolve ongoing conflicts, Caplan adopted a policy of "collaborative stewardship," which he defined as "community-based decision making." Caplan encouraged forest managers to reach out to concerned citizens in Southeast Alaska. "There will always be people opposed to some aspects of timber management, and we will still put up timber sales," he said. "But there's a willingness by the Forest Service to be a partner, not a leader."

But the 1997 Tongass Land Management Plan was not to be the last word. On November 14, 1998, Agriculture Secretary Dan Glickman received an extraordinary letter signed by ninety-three members of Congress urging him to improve the 1997 plan. The Tongass, they wrote, "is a splendid, untamed expanse of forest like nothing else remaining in our country, and a central part of our national heritage." It was time, they said, to recognize its ecological value—and to acknowledge the new economic reality in Southeast Alaska. "The pulp mills are closed, timber demand at current levels meets the need for sustainable market utilization, the regional economy is increasingly diversified, and despite logging's inroads, the Tongass remains— unlike many National Forests—largely intact and ecologically healthy."

The lawmakers acknowledged that the 1997 plan was an improvement over past plans. But they questioned the wisdom as well as the economics of continued road construction and clearcutting in pristine watersheds. They also reminded Glickman that, in 1989, as a member of the U.S. House of Representatives, he himself had voted for a Tongass reform bill that proposed to protect more than 1.8 million roadless acres. "The current Tongass plan fails to protect many of the important areas identified in that bill," they wrote. They urged Glickman to use his review authority under the federal appeals process to produce a plan worthy of the Tongass.

Five months later, on April 14, 1999, Agriculture Undersecretary Jim Lyons, Glickman's deputy, announced that he had resolved the many appeals of the 1997 Tongass plan by revising it to protect an additional 500,000 roadless acres from logging during the ten-year life of the plan. The eighteen areas Lyons placed under the ten-year logging moratorium included most of the areas conservationists had fought to save since the Tongass timber reform campaign of the late 1980s. And there was more. Lyons announced that he had doubled the logging rotation in critical wildlife areas from 100 to 200 years to increase winter cover for deer and other species. And he said that he had ordered a reduction in road densities to protect wolves, brown bears, and other species vulnerable to poaching and overhunting. It was a bold and surprising move.

"This is not a step I take lightly," Lyons wrote in the record of decision. "It is my belief that the continuing controversy and exceptional circumstances surrounding the Tongass Land and Resource Management Plan warrant my direct and immediate participation in order to bring this controversy to closure as quickly as possible so that the Forest Service can move forward . . . " The new plan, Lyons said, would provide greater balance among uses of the Tongass, including the needs of subsistence hunters and fishermen, while still providing an adequate timber supply to meet demand in the foreseeable future. Under Lyons' plan, the acreage available for logging would decline by 15 percent, and the maximum annual timber harvest would drop from 267 million board feet to 187 million board feet—still an adequate level to meet projected demand for a decade.

Reaction from the timber industry and the Alaska delegation was predictably irate. Sen. Frank Murkowski called Lyons' plan "a scientific insult, a legal affront and an economic crime." Others on Capitol Hill raised the possibility of a lawsuit or a congressional override of the plan.

In late April, on the heels of Lyons' announcement, Louisiana-Pacific Chief Executive Officer Mark Suwyn announced that L-P was giving up on its plan to build a veneer mill in Ketchikan. Instead the company would proceed with plans to build four new mills in northeastern British Columbia to manufacture veneer and engineered wood products. Then, on May 6, Suwyn announced that L-P was negotiating to sell its sawmills and what remained of its pulp mill to a consortium of Alaska timber executives under the name Gateway Forest Products. The company had concluded that it could not buy enough Tongass timber to keep operating the mills, Suwyn said. "While the region has a plentiful supply of renewable resources and an excellent workforce, we were not able to justify a continued presence given recently reduced levels of timber available from the U.S. Forest Service."

TIMES OF ECONOMIC TRANSITION are difficult for communities. Yet the path to a sustainable economy for Southeast Alaska is no mystery. The region remains richly endowed. Its fish and wildlife are abundant. Its scenery and its opportunities for wilderness adventure are matchless. It still has its rainforest, tattered in many places, yet capable of supporting those uses and a timber industry of appropriate scale as well.

With so much land, so many resources and so few people, Southeast has an opportunity to build a sustainable economy that could become a model for other sparsely populated, resource-rich regions. Its first task will be to decide how much taking the land can support. How much timber, how many salmon and deer and brown bears, how many cruise ships disgorging passengers, how many kayakers paddling into quiet coves? Answering those questions will require a shared sense of identity, a shared sense of destiny.

Bart Koehler believes if it can happen anywhere, it can happen in Southeast Alaska. "What our board has always held dear is the tremendous sense of place, of caring, here, and also the sense of a broader community, because there aren't many of us here," he says. "People need to recognize each other's basic human dignity. Loggers have their own history, traditions and culture. So do commercial fishermen, and so do conservation groups. And almost everywhere you look, there's the Tongass. We're all here together out on the edge of the earth."

LATE AUGUST IS SPAWNING SEASON for pink and chum salmon in Southeast Alaska. In years of strong runs, rotting fish carcasses and dessicated skeletons litter the beaches and grassy meadows of inlets like Saook Bay, a small indentation on the north coast of Baranof Island.

In the summer of 1996 I visited Saook Bay. I walked over grasses flattened by bears, entered the rain forest, and emerged in a meadow of nagoonberry, fiddlehead fern and wild celery, all edible plants still used by Alaska Natives and other subsistence food-gatherers. I skirted a pond, observed the mark

*Quiet estuary in El
Capitan Passage, off the
west coast of Prince of
Wales Island. Photo by
Trygve Steen.*

of beaver on downed trees, and pushed through high grass to a stand of huge spruce inhabited by hungry mosquitoes. The light was soft through lifting clouds. Everything sang its song: maggots crawling over salmon carcasses; exhausted fish, swimming lethargically just below the surface of the clear stream, no longer bright but dull with approaching death; the bald eagle that soared from a high spruce at our approach; the stream itself, busily decomposing the bodies it had nurtured as smolts; the mountain that loomed behind clouds; alders displaying the claw marks of grizzlies eight feet up their trunks; spikes of Devil's club, fresh bear scat beneath our rubber boots, fish heads bright with blood, the toed roots of spruces clutching forest duff.

The forest seemed so engaged in its cycles of life and death that I might have entered a land never set food on by humans. Yet this inlet was well known to the Tlingit and other subsistence food-gatherers, and a slope thick with alder marked the place where loggers had entered years ago. In 1996, Saook Bay was scheduled for another entry, more road-building, new clearcuts. It was hard to imagine the roar of bulldozers, the whine of chainsaws, the thunder of toppled trees echoing across calm water.

In April of 1999, when the revised Tongass Land Management Plan was released, East Saook Bay and seventeen other places, all unique and irreplaceable, won a ten-year stay of execution. Saook Bay was granted its reprieve because of its importance to subsistence users and to wolf, deer, marten and goshawk. For me, Saook Bay will always be as it was on that late summer afternoon in 1996: fragrant with rotting salmon, bathed in a muted sunshine that filtered through fog and lit the kelp-strewn beach.

FIVE YEARS AFTER: AN UPDATE

On a morning in late September of 2004, as thick clouds begin to break up over Tongass Narrows, a DeHavilland Beaver floatplane takes off from a downtown Ketchikan dock. It crosses a saltwater channel, flies over muskeg bogs and the shallow waters of Bostwick Inlet, then turns north up a river valley into the untouched heart of Gravina Island, a sweep of green that extends from ridge to ridge. Sunlight and shadows play over the slopes of this unprotected wilderness where deer and wolves roam just a ten-minute flight from Ketchikan.

The pristine beauty of the landscape reminds me that I have been away from Southeast Alaska for too long. Forest Service District Ranger Jerry Ingersoll describes his agency's plan to carve 60,000-acre Gravina Island with 21 miles of roads and 58 clearcuts, but I am distracted by the shifting mosaic of light and cloud, forest and water. At the head of the valley the pilot banks and turns the plane back toward the inlet. We set down on the water and climb out onto the pontoons. The plane rocks gently; the only sound is the muted shriek of gulls.

I ask, "Do you feel any ambivalence about what you are about to do to this gorgeous island?" Ingersoll, who is departing for a desk job in Wash-

Bostwick Inlet, Gravina Island. Photo by Kathie Durbin.

ington, D.C., in four days, answers as I expected: Yes, the island is gorgeous, but many places in the Tongass National Forest are gorgeous, and we can't save them all. The 1997 management plan designates this land for logging. And the 1990 Tongass Timber Reform Act requires the Forest Service to "seek to meet market demand."

In fall of 2004, the market for Tongass timber is depressed. Only three large sawmills still operate in Southeast Alaska. It will cost federal taxpayers $5.5 million to sell the 38 million board feet of hemlock, spruce, and cedar in the Gravina Island sale, an expenditure that won't be recouped by timber revenue. But Ingersoll says generating revenue isn't the point. The sale will employ 240 workers and keep a local timber industry alive.

Offering this timber will encourage investment in new mills and mill equipment, breathing new life into a moribund industry, predicts Ingersoll's boss, Tongass Supervisor Forrest Cole. Though the closure of two Southeast Alaska pulp mills in the 1990s eliminated the most important market for Tongass timber, Cole also blames a decade and a half of litigation by environmentalists for deterring new investment. "Since 1990, the land base has been in a constant state of flux," he says. "You can't expect investments to be made in existing mills when no stability exists."

It's a chicken-and-egg argument: Why punch roads into pristine Alaska wilderness when there is so little market for the wood? How can a market be developed when potential investors have no guaranteed timber supply?

In fall of 2004, that debate was playing out in the courts. In September, a federal judge upheld the 1997 Tongass plan, rejecting a broad legal challenge brought by environmental groups. But the Southeast Alaska Conservation Council appealed to the 9th U.S. Circuit Court of Appeals and won a new injunction. A three-judge panel said SEACC was "likely to prevail" at trial. Fifty timber sales in roadless areas were once again on hold, some much larger than the Gravina Island project.

On November 2, President George W. Bush won reelection, guaranteeing four more years of pro-logging federal forest policy. But in Southeast Alaska, conservationists already had experienced a swift political reversal of the victories they had won during President Bill Clinton's two terms in office.

Two weeks before leaving office in January 2001, Clinton had signed the Roadless Area Conservation Rule, placing 58.5 million acres of roadless national forest land, including 9.6 million acres of the 17-million-acre Tongass, off-limits to commercial logging for at least a decade.

But on January 20, 2001, his first day in office, President Bush issued a directive postponing the effective date of the roadless rule. Soon after, the timber industry and the state of Idaho sued to prevent the rule's implementation and won an injunction in a federal district court in Idaho. U.S. Attorney General John Ashcroft declined to defend the roadless rule in court, breaking a promise he had made during his Senate confirmation hearings to let the rule become law.

The environmental law firm Earthjustice stepped into the breach, appealing the Idaho court ruling and winning a reversal in the 9th Circuit. But in 2003, another federal judge, this time in Wyoming, overturned the roadless rule and tried to block its implementation nationwide. The rule was in legal limbo.

Then, on Christmas Eve 2003, U.S. Agriculture Undersecretary Mark Rey, the former timber industry lobbyist who now oversaw the Forest Service, announced that he was temporarily exempting the Tongass from the roadless rule. That allowed the agency to move forward with planning new sales. In July 2004, the administration proposed repeal of the roadless rule nationwide.

Meanwhile, legal challenges of the 1997 Tongass plan and the 1999 revised plan were working their way through the courts. In 2001, the U.S. District Court for Alaska overturned the 1999 Tongass plan with its broad wildlife protections, saying the Clinton administration had failed to seek public comment on the revision. Earthjustice appealed. The same court ruled that the Forest Service had erred in adopting the 1997 plan by failing to review more than one hundred roadless areas on the Tongass to determine whether they warranted permanent wilderness protection by Congress.

In response, Tongass officials drew up several alternatives for designating new wilderness. Hearings were held in twenty Southeast Alaska communities and Anchorage. Environmentalists mobilized their supporters. Testimony, even in the timber towns of Ketchikan and Wrangell, overwhelmingly favored more wilderness protection. Yet at the end of the process, the Forest Service recommended not a single acre of new wilderness.

"We know there was a concerted effort to organize testimony," explained Larry Lunde, the Tongass official who oversaw the process. "Some people were not informed."

*

At the state level, the election of U.S. Sen. Frank Murkowski as governor in 2002 portended big changes for communities in Southeast Alaska. The following year Murkowski proposed major changes to the Southeast Alaska Transportation Plan. The four-year-old plan, developed with involvement by community leaders, promised more frequent and convenient ferry service and improvements to local airports. Murkowski wanted to add several expensive and controversial road-construction projects, including a highway up the east side of Lynn Canal that would connect Juneau with the historic gold-mining town of Skagway. Environmentalists had long fought the road, which would open pristine Berner's Bay, north of Juneau, to development. The governor also proposed a road connection from Wrangell to the British Columbia highway system, opposed by the Canadian province because it would take business away from the B.C. port of Prince Rupert; a road across rugged Baranof Island to shorten the ferry connection to Sitka on the island's west coast; and completion of a road link between Hoonah and Tenakee Springs on Chichagof Island, which would end Tenakee's hard-fought isolation once and for all.

The price tag for these roads, which would penetrate some of the most rugged and least-populated lands in North America, was conservatively estimated at $1.8 billion. But with Sen. Ted Stevens of Alaska chairing the Senate Appropriations Committee and Rep. Don Young heading the House Transportation Committee, the Alaska delegation was poised to deliver federal appropriations to begin planning these mega-projects.

Young, Alaska's only congressman, was pushing another expensive transportation project: a two-bridge, $230-million land link between Ketchikan and its airport on Gravina Island, ostensibly to replace a seven-minute ferry shuttle. One span would rise 250 feet, rivaling the height of the Golden Gate Bridge. In fact, the bridges were part of a larger plan by the governor and the Alaska delegation to open Gravina Island to vehicles and development. The roads built to provide access to Tongass timber would also reach timber on adjacent state trust land.

Floatplane pilots, cruise ship operators, and the U.S. Coast Guard opposed the bridges as navigation hazards. Subsistence hunters warned that the bridge link would open the island's herds of Sitka black-tailed deer to poachers. The national organization Taxpayers for Common Sense gave the project its 2003 Golden Fleece Award. A New York *Times* editorial scorned it as a "bridge to nowhere." Nonetheless, in September 2004, the Federal Highway Administration signed off on the project.

*

With the Bush administration and Alaska elected officials united on an agenda of resource extraction, forest activists appeared to be losing ground. But economic forces were pushing Southeast Alaska toward a different future.

By 2003, timber jobs accounted for less than 1 percent of the region's employment. Tourism, including an explosion of cruise ship visits, now was driving the region's economy.

More than eight hundred thousand cruise ship passengers came ashore in Ketchikan during the 2004 season, double the number a decade earlier. When the ships were in port, five thousand tourists spilled out onto Ketchikan's streets to buy smoked salmon and expensive jewelry, walk the historic streets surrounding the wharf, visit totem pole parks, and fly over nearby wilderness areas.

Between 1993 and 2003, revenue from tourism in Ketchikan nearly tripled, to $117 million, due mainly to retail sales, which quadrupled from $22 million to $87 million over the decade. Revenue from sales taxes paid by visitors jumped from $198,000 to more than $6 million.

Sitka and Juneau reaped the benefits of the tourist boom too. But the remote Alaska Native community of Hoonah, in the north end of the

Cruise ship passengers come ashore in Ketchikan. Photo by Kathie Durbin.

Tongass, was the newest and most improbable cruise ship destination. In 2004, the gritty town of 860, surrounded by national forest and Native corporation clearcuts, was reborn as an authentic outpost on the Alaska frontier. A refurbished old cannery opened as a cultural museum and craft bazaar. The summer unemployment rate dropped from 60 percent to zero overnight as residents sold handmade sealskin moccasins to tourists and entrepreneurs offered bear tours and charter fishing excursions.

*

At the end of September 2004, as the five-month tourist season comes to a close, four huge cruise ships are docked at Ketchikan. No one knows how long the cruise ship boom will last. Tongass Supervisor Cole says the seasonal jobs it has generated are no substitute for year-round jobs. "You can't support a family selling trinkets," he says.

Patti Mackey, executive director of the Alaska Visitors Bureau, is grateful for the flood of visitors. "Too much of anything can be annoying," she says. "It's not a perfect industry. But the taxes that have been generated from retail sales have helped make up for the family-wage jobs that were lost."

Wayne Weihing, a former Ketchikan Pulp Co. worker and one of the town's most vocal environmentalists, is convinced that the cruise ship trade is creating ripples in the local economy. "Somehow people have money for remodeling, money for late-model SUVs," he says. "When that last ship leaves, those tourism-related businesses plan for external and internal remodeling work. That's driving freight shipments and providing winter jobs for carpenters."

While the boom lasts, Cape Fox Corporation is cashing in. The Alaska Native corporation, based in the village of Saxman, near Ketchikan, cut all its timber in thirty years. The steep hillsides surrounding Ketchikan bear the scars of its logging. In 2004 its board hired business developer Bruce Borup to lead the transition from logging to tourism and government services. A new upscale gift shop near the Ketchikan docks is the corporation's latest investment.

Cape Fox Corporation owns the Cape Fox Hotel, Ketchikan's premier accommodation. Its portfolio now also includes Cape Fox Tours, five retail stores, a title company, and construction companies in Fairbanks and Los Angeles that compete for federal contract as minority-owned businesses. Borup borrowed from the corporation's permanent fund to establish the new ventures. The fund pays each of the corporation's 287 shareholders an annual dividend. In 2004, the dividend was $2,240, income desperately needed in Saxman, where the unemployment rate topped 25 percent.

"Let's cut to the chase; Ketchikan would be dead without tourism," Borup says. "There is nothing else. But tourism is fickle. If we don't do something about our docks, the cruise ships will move to Prince Rupert." Because the town's docks can accommodate only three cruise ships at a time, other ships must anchor offshore and ferry their passengers ashore, making the town less desirable in the view of the cruise ship industry.

Cape Fox is not giving up on timber, Borup says, but its second-growth cedars will have no commercial value for eighty years, when they begin producing the chemicals that give cedar its natural preservative. Borup is trying to negotiate land exchanges with the Forest Service that would give Cape Fox a new source of timber until its own stands mature. But the conservationists at SEACC vow to fight any deal that trades cutover corporate land for unlogged national forests.

Some Cape Fox directors now regret that Cape Fox did not log its lands sustainably, Borup says. "Their use for subsistence has been greatly reduced. The logging hasn't advanced other goals, such as subsistence fishing and hunting and berry gathering. The whole premise should have been to maximize revenue over the long term."

*

By 2004, logging is increasingly at odds with tourism. Cruise ship passengers drawn to Southeast Alaska by the promise of pristine wilderness and visitors who pay thousands of dollars to stay at remote fishing lodges don't expect to witness industrial logging.

In late September of 2004, his busy charter fishing season at an end, Larry McQuarrie makes a run into McKenzie Inlet near the resort to check his shrimp pots, carrying chunks of frozen bait fish in his skiff.

In 1989, McQuarrie opened Sportsman's Cove Lodge, a rustic fishing lodge in remote Saltery Cove, on eastern Prince of Wales Island. For seven years, he has been at war with the Forest Service over its Cholmondeley Timber Sale, which proposes to log on a peninsula bordering his resort. Steering his skiff up the inlet, he points out where the log-transfer facility will go and the route a logging road will take up a hillside through a notch leading to the back of his property.

Larry McQuarrie. Photo by Mike Greene.

McKenzie Inlet is not untouched by logging. But to visitors from the Lower 48, it's pristine enough. The lodge's location is a drawing card, McQuarrie said. Clearcuts will hurt his business.

"When we take them out on the McKenzie Inlet cruise, our customers thank us," he says. "We do a whole natural history cruise, pointing out bears, eagles, landslides, describing how the forest regenerates and explaining the geology, how the landforms were carved by glaciers. If we brought folks in here with an expectation of a pristine Alaska and there were log trucks running by and the water was muddy and you couldn't go hike up to that beautiful lake up there, that would impact us."

Yet scenery is not McQuarrie's biggest concern. His water supply is. His Class B water system, drawn from two small creeks that flow down slopes above his property, provides all the lodge's water needs—for cooking, drinking, doing laundry, and cleaning the salmon and halibut his guests catch each day. At Saltery Cove, which gets 165 inches of rainfall annually, water bubbles from springs and cracks in the ground. He fears that logging and road building in these wet drainages will destroy his source of pure water, and thus his lodge, which depends on return customers for 80 percent of its business. Not only is that unfair, he says, but it makes no sense economically.

McQuarrie estimates that his business returns $1 million annually to the local economy. "We buy fuel, we buy services, we have a maintenance base in Ketchikan. Ninety-seven percent of our guests spend their last night in Ketchikan. Everything we buy in Ketchikan we pay taxes on. We also pay a business income tax to the state."

Operating a lodge off the grid means being self-sufficient and therefore vulnerable, McQuarrie says. If something goes wrong with the water supply, there is no backup. For example, if construction of a logging road resulted in an oil spill during his charter fishing season, "it could shut us down." He also worries about soil erosion on steep slopes. The buffers the Forest Service proposes to leave along the streams "are meaningless," he says. "Mass wasting will occur."

Tongass Supervisor Forrest Cole says state and Forest Service hydrologists have concluded that a logging road could be built across the streams without affecting water quality. But McQuarrie says the Forest Service deliberately suppressed reports that concluded logging in the watershed would irreparably harm the fragile water system. In expectation of a lawsuit, he is paying $5,000 for baseline water-quality studies to document any future deterioration of the streams that supply his lodge and the home of his neighbors, Ron and Joan Leighton.

Ron Leighton, a Tsimshian Indian chief who retired to Saltery Cove after a career as a Ketchikan police officer, leads a hike up a steep, wet slope to show the source of the water—hundreds of tiny springs that trickle into the small creek. The creek not only provides the Leightons with water, it also powers a Pelton wheel that generates most of the electricity they need.

The pipes have been there, serving first a salmon saltery and then a salmon cannery, since 1901, Leighton says. In researching water rights at Saltery Cove, he discovered a 1902 water rights declaration that preceded by five years President Theodore Roosevelt's establishment of the Tongass National Forest. "Roosevelt granted the cannery the right to reservoirs up on the hill," he says. "There is a presidential citation that says this water right is for perpetuity."

Cole intends to proceed with the sale. He says that McQuarrie should have done more research before buying the property. "We've got folks who have made large investments in a piece of real estate and expect the surrounding land to stay the same. He chose to put his resort next to a timber harvest."

"In the Forest Service's view, the forest has no value other than the timber," McQuarrie counters. "The forest has intrinsic value in just being a forest. In some cases, it is not in the best interest of the forest to log."

*

The Tongass timber sale program has always been heavily subsidized by American taxpayers. By one estimate, the program lost $750 million between 1982 and 2002. Those subsidies continued after the pulp mills closed in the 1990s, as Ketchikan tried to lure new investors with offers of Tongass timber. Between 1999 and 2003, Sen. Ted Stevens added $36 million to the Forest Service's budget to prop up the program.

In 2003, SEACC released a report documenting that the subsidies were accelerating. The report calculated that the Forest Service had spent more than $36 million preparing timber sales and building logging roads on the Tongass in 2002. In return, it had received $1.2 million from private purchasers for a thousand acres of old-growth timber. In effect, taxpayers had paid $178,000 for each timber job generated by the logging.

According to the report, more than half the sales offered between 1998 and 2002 attracted only a single bidder, and the market was so depressed during the period that the Forest Service gave timber purchasers three-year extensions on their contracts, allowing them to hold onto their timber rather than cut it at a loss.

The numbers startled even Republicans in Congress and prompted indignant newspaper editorials. In June 2004, the House passed a resolution forbidding the Forest Service to spend any money building new logging roads on the Tongass in 2005. Environmentalists claimed a major victory. In late November, Stevens used his clout as Appropriations Committee chairman to strip the language from a huge federal spending bill. Still, it was clear that the taxpayer subsidy issue remained politically potent.

The demise of the two pulp mills that consumed billions of board feet of Tongass timber over more than four decades has changed the political cli-

Many buildings at the former Ketchikan Pulp Co. mill have been torn down. The Ketchikan-Gateway Borough bought the Ward Cove property and is trying to find a buyer for the site. Photo by Kathie Durbin.

mate in Southeast Alaska, says Tim Bristol, executive director of the Alaska Coalition and a former SEACC grass-roots organizer. "Outside of Wrangell and Ketchikan, and to some extent Prince of Wales Island, most people don't think about logging anymore," he says.

In Ketchikan, however, a phantom timber industry survives. After Louisiana-Pacific left in the late 1990s, former pulp mill executives founded Gateway Forest Products. With a $7 million loan from the Ketchikan Gateway Borough Assembly, the company bought 150 acres at Ward Cove, the site of the old pulp mill, and built a veneer mill. But the mill lost money from the start, and in 2001 the company filed for liquidation under federal bankruptcy laws. The borough bought the land and the veneer mill for $2.2 million and has been trying to attract a buyer ever since.

When borough officials began courting an Oregon company as a potential purchaser, however, conservationists began calling the company's owners with the message, "We don't want you to come up here and cut Tongass timber." Soon after, the company ended discussions with the borough, triggering bitter resentment by Ketchikan officials.

In fall of 2004, the Pacific Log and Lumber sawmill, which opened in the late 1990s, is still in business. At its mill near the Ketchikan airport on Gravina Island, it produces ship masts and rough-sawn logs that are barged south to the Pacific Northwest for drying and finishing. Viking Lumber, on Prince of Wales Island, sells green lumber to a door and window manufacturer in the Lower 48. But in 2004, residents of Southeast Alaska still cannot buy finished lumber for home remodeling projects from local mills.

*

A vision of a different kind of timber industry is rising from the rubble of the Ward Cove pulp mill complex. In the cavernous building that housed the mill's pipe-welding shop, now the Ketchikan Wood Technology Center, researchers are discovering the remarkable strength of Alaska wood.

Engineers demonstrate by placing a 16-foot-long, two-by-six Sitka spruce board into a long box called a tension proof tester. Grips hold the board at each end as motorized heads pull it in opposite directions. As the pressure increases, the board stretches two and a half inches, finally cracking at 51,000 pounds per square inch. The stress record is held by a board that withstood pressure of 90,000 pounds per square inch, the weight of a loaded rail car.

Researchers, supported by grants from the Forest Service and the University of Alaska, plan to test 4,500 spruce boards cut from trees all over

Alaska. Old-growth Alaska hemlock and Alaska yellow cedar have been put through the same rigorous test. The results prove that lumber from these slow-growing Alaska species possesses strength unmatched by conifers grown on industrial tree farms in the Lower 48. Alaska yellow cedars average forty growth rings per inch; hemlocks average twenty-six. In contrast, plantation-grown trees in the Pacific Northwest typically average three growth rings per inch.

Based on their superior strength and stiffness, the American Lumber Standard Committee has recently designated Alaska yellow cedar and Alaska hemlock as unique products with their own grades. A specific grade for Alaska Sitka spruce is expected next.

Kevin Curtis, the technology center's director, says the strength of Alaska lumber makes it an excellent choice for decking, siding, and glued laminated beams. He is convinced that the future of the timber industry in Southeast Alaska lies in marketing the unique properties of Alaska wood worldwide, not in competing with the lower 48 to produce two-by-fours.

"What we have is a small amount of high-grade material that is wasted in the commodity market," he says. "Let's take this tree and harvest the largest recoverable amount of wood we can get. Let's put the pieces to-

Stress tests done at the Ketchikan Wood Technology Center reveal the amazing strength of lumber from Alaska old-growth spruce, cedar, and hemlock. Photo by Kathie Durbin.

gether not as nature makes a wood product but as intelligent engineering makes a wood product."

In a sense, Alaska never had a true timber industry, Curtis says. For nearly a half-century, the vast majority of Alaska timber was chipped for pulp or exported in the round. "We had a third-world colonial resource-extraction industry. The world changed and our large sawmills were no longer economically viable."

Because Alaska yellow cedar was thought to have no commercial value, the Forest Service was allowed to export yellow cedar logs unprocessed. Now the value of that species has been documented, Curtis says. "Yellow cedar doesn't decay. The Forest Service cut a yellow cedar that had been standing dead for eighty years and a green tree. They had exactly the same strength." It's that kind of research-based knowledge, he says, that will make it possible to market Alaska wood for its highest purpose. "If I can show them this piece of wood is four times as valuable, I can make it worth four times as much. But if we don't know what our resource is worth, when someone comes up here with a suitcase full of money, we'll take it."

Across a potholed parking lot from the technology center, in a corner of the old pulp warehouse, Larry Jackson is putting these concepts into practice with a pile of logs scrounged from old mill yards and a makeshift kiln dryer that can dry western red cedar to a moisture content of 10 percent in three days. In 2004, Jackson bought a portable mill called a wood miser, which cuts logs into boards with minimal waste, and invested $80,000 in a fancy molder-planer that makes trim, moldings, and flooring.

Four months after he started, he is already recouping his investment. Over the summer of 2004, he sold thirty cases of cedar planks for grilling salmon. He has sold some "music wood," Sitka spruce billets prized for making musical instruments. With his new planer, he is turning out tongue-and-groove siding and hemlock flooring—products not often available in Ketchikan. "My whole concept here is low volume, high margin," Jackson said. "Hopefully, when you mill a log, you get money from every part of the tree."

*

Change is occurring within the Forest Service itself. Downsized dramatically after the closure of the pulp mills, the staff of the Tongass now spends some of its time planning and carrying out projects to restore streams ravaged by logging, repair poorly built logging roads, and thin second-growth stands. Responding to lobbying by SEACC and requests from small operators, the agency has begun offering small-volume "micro-sales" in areas like Thorne Bay on Prince of Wales Island, though critics say the program still takes a back seat to planning large sales in roadless areas.

"Because it's been forced to, the Forest Service has become a good manager in Southeast Alaska," Curtis says. "They learned from the egregious practices of the past."

Tim Bristol believes the pace of change has been too slow. "The Forest Service has become the problem. They aid and abet the subsidies." Nor is he convinced that the agency is committed to a smaller, more strategic timber sale program. "On the one hand, they are trying to bring innovation to the wood products industry. On the other hand they are saying, 'We need a bigger chunk of the forest if we are ever to get to where we want to be.' I think those are competing visions."

Russell Heath, SEACC's executive director, also faults Cole for outdated thinking on what a twenty-first-century timber program on the Tongass should look like. "For him, 'value added' is a high-volume mill that makes two-by-fours, and the only way to get the timber is by going into roadless areas," he says. In contrast, SEACC supports a program that takes timber only from the existing 5,000 miles of logging roads, exports no raw logs, supports value-added manufacturing, and focuses on meeting local market demand.

Cole says his goal for the Tongass always has been to provide year-round jobs and community stability. "You're not going to see a semiconductor industry start up in Thorne Bay. The timber industry is ten months of employment. The cruise ships end today."

But he insists that pressure to get out the cut no longer drives management of the Tongass. "The timber industry in Southeast is a very small part of what we do. We have a huge fishery, a huge wilderness program. The vastness of the wilderness is why the cruise ships come here."

What seems clear in the fall of 2004 is that tourist-dependent businesses, conservationists, and, increasingly, the native Tlingit, Haida, and Tsimshian people of Southeast Alaska will be monitoring the agency's plans for the Tongass more closely than ever before.

In October of 2004, Alaska Native leaders in Saxman and the Metlakatla Indian Community of Annette Island filed an appeal of the Gravina Island sale, saying the Forest Service failed to properly consult with them about the impact of the sale on deer, salmon, and shellfish-gathering areas. Nora

DeWitt of Saxman called the project "a direct attack and desecration of our traditional areas."

Tongass officials countered that they had addressed Alaska Natives' concerns by abandoning plans for a log-transfer facility in Bostwick Inlet and by agreeing to close logging roads during deer-hunting season. Soon after, however, Cole withdrew the Gravina Island sale temporarily to reanalyze its impacts on wildlife.

As for conservationists, their immediate challenge is to develop a strategy for defending their gains and limiting their losses in the face of a rightward shift in the electorate. "I'm trying to reposition SEACC so it's not as beholden to the Democrats," Heath says. "We don't know how long our legal tools will work for us. What is working for now is that there is no market for this timber."

In the long run, Heath says, he trusts the entrepreneurial genius of Americans to determine Southeast Alaska's economic future. In the meantime, the one thing the nation is not growing more of is forest wilderness. "We need to educate people about the nature of their economy," he says. "The greatest treasure we have is a standing, healthy Tongass National Forest."

ACKNOWLEDGMENTS

THE GENESIS of this book was a trip by floatplane, cruise boat and ferry through the north end of Southeast Alaska in August of 1996, as the fate of Southeast Alaska's last pulp mill hung in the balance.

I had visited the Tongass National Forest before: on a week-long reporting trip for *The Oregonian*, in 1989, during the height of the debate over reform of the Tongass timber program, and in the early 1990s, when I traveled from Juneau to Haines aboard *Crusader*, a schooner operated as a floating seminar by the Seattle-based Resources Institute.

On my first trip, immersed in getting "the story," I toured the pulp mills, interviewed loggers, millworkers and community leaders, got a first-hand look at logging on Chichagof Island, and visited the world's largest log-sorting yard at Thorne Bay. Forest Service officials were my guides, though I also found time to interview pulp mill workers, environmentalists, community leaders, wildlife biologists and mill managers. From that trip, I remember the smell of freshly sawn cedar in an open-air mill on Prince of Wales Island, the allure of a path through lush old-growth forest I wasn't allowed to take (too many bears, too little time), and the sight of mountain goats on rocky outcrops in the South Baranof Wilderness as I flew in a pulp company helicopter to a remote logging camp.

On *Crusader*, traveling up Lynn Canal from Juneau to Haines, and listening to Nora Marks Dauenhauer tell traditional stories from Glacier Bay in the original Tlingit, I began to understand the long history of human settlement in the Alexander Archipelago.

The 1996 media tour, organized and funded by Conservation International, began to fill many gaps in my understanding of the history and culture of Southeast Alaska. Our boat, the *Observer*, anchored in protected coves—Saook Bay, Trap Bay, Poison Cove, Hoonah Sound— where we could go ashore and explore forest, river and saltwater marsh. In Angoon, Tlingit leaders described their fight to keep logging off Admiralty Island. At Tenakee Springs, residents told of their campaign to stop a Forest Service road. At Appleton Cove, I visited a floating logging camp to talk to loggers and timber managers. In Sitka, I spent four days interviewing everyone I could find about how the town was faring nearly three years after the closure of the pulp mill there.

The following March I returned to Southeast Alaska the week the Ketchikan Pulp Co. pulp mill closed for good. I talked to workers, mill managers, city officials and environmentalists. On that trip I also toured Prince of Wales Island, and took a ferry to Petersburg to meet with Glenn and Martha Reid.

In September of 1997 I spent two weeks in Juneau, interviewing Forest Service officials and longtime forest activists, with side trips to Angoon and Hoonah, Native villages that have followed different paths since passage of the Alaska Native Claims Settlement Act. As an unexpected bonus, I explored Juneau's wonderful trail system, accompanied by an eager German shepherd named Mayday, in glorious weather.

In August of 1998, I attended a conference on Alaska environmental history at the University of Alaska-Anchorage. The conference, organized by UAA historian Steve Haycox, helped me understand how the story of the Tongass National Forest fits within the still-unfolding history of Alaska.

Each trip has added layers of understanding and appreciation for this place called Southeast Alaska and its temperate rain forest. Yet I am acutely aware that to Alaskans I remain an Outsider, an interloper from the Lower 48. For helping me to overcome this obstacle by supporting the time I needed to travel, read and understand, I am indebted to the following people and institutions: Ted Smith, president of the Henry P. Kendall Foundation, for offering encouragement, advice and the seed money that made this book more than an unrealized dream; Conservation International, for inviting me along on the 1996 *Observer* tour; and Jim Compton of the Compton Foundation, Donald Ross of the Rockefeller Family Fund, and Bill Lazar of the Lazar Foundation, who provided the means for me to complete the book. These funders attached no strings to their support, but wanted only to see a full and complete story told.

A number of sources provided not only their personal stories but essential perspective: Bern Johnson, Jim Stratton, John Sisk, Steve Kallick, Matthew Kirchhoff, Joe Sebastian, Alan Stein, Jack Gustafson, Larry Edwards and Don Muller. Bart Koehler spent long hours helping me to reconstruct the six-year congressional Tongass timber reform campaign. Larry Edwards lent me his entire Sitka file. Mary Anne Stewart put me in touch with Ed and Peggy Wayburn, who graciously gave me a four-hour interview in their San Francisco home. Mary Anne also suggested that I might find useful information in the Sierra Club Collection at the University of California's Bancroft Library, as indeed I did. Tavia Hollenkamp and Pamela Finney of the Forest Service organized two days of marathon interviews with Forest Service employees in Juneau, which contributed essential historical and scientific perspective to this story. The *Anchorage Daily News* library provided stories from its archives. Steve Haycox offered perspectives on Alaska history, constructive criticism of an early partial manuscript, and a scrupulous academic critique of the full text.

Several Ketchikan Pulp Co. workers, including Charlie Stout, Gil Smith, Paul Lamm, Bruce Romine, and Mike Speelman, shared stories and pizza with me on the evening the pulp mill closed. Glenn and Martha Reid spent an entire day with me at their home in Petersburg, reliving their experiences as independent loggers and making copies of documents I needed on their fax machine. Chuck Clusen sent me a copy of "The Fight for Wild Alaska," by the late Robert Cahn, an out-of-print history of the Alaska lands campaign. Terry Shaw provided me with photocopies of key scientific documents on a quick turnaround. Bill Shoaf and Mary Dalton took the time to tell me their painful stories.

Excerpts from the work of Richard Nelson and Robert B. Weeden are used with the kind permission of the authors. Trygve Steen, Jack Gustafson, James Mackovjak, John Schoen, David Person, and Craig Flatten generously donated photographs. For an understanding of Alaska Native corporations and pulp mill pollution, I depended on the excellent work of newspaper reporters Hal Bernton and Mitch Lipka, respectively.

Travel in the Southeast Alaska backcountry depends on the hospitality of strangers. For a fascinating tour of North Prince of Wales Island I am indebted to Tim Bristol, who provided transportation, and to Joe Sebastian, Joan Kautzer, Pete Smith and Valerie White, who offered food, lodging and a glimpse of the good life. K.J. and Peggy Metcalf put me up in Angoon and showed me a small part of Admiralty Island by boat. Claire Johnson helped me find the people I needed to talk to in Sitka and provided a home-cooked meal of black cod. I am grateful as well for the hospitality of Floyd and Marge Peterson in Hoonah, Al and Signe Wilson in Sitka, and my hosts at the New York Hotel in Ketchikan and the Cozy Lodge Bed and Breakfast in Juneau.

Finally, I wish to thank the editors at Oregon State University Press for seeing the value in telling this story, and for their enthusiasm as we worked to bring this book to fruition, and for their decision to keep *Tongass* in print by publishing this second edition with its five-year update.

Sources and Bibliography

Sources

PROLOGUE: PRINCE OF WALES ISLAND

The description of Prince of Wales Island is from a tour by the author in March 1997. Background on the ecology and extent of the Alaska rainforest comes from USDA Forest Service technical reports; *Tongass: Alaska's Vanishing Rainforest,* by Robert Glenn Ketchum and Carey D. Ketchum; "The Rain Forests of Home: An Atlas of People and Place," published by Ecotrust, Conservation International and Pacific GIS; and Richard Carstensen's essay in *The Enduring Forests,* among other sources. Lawrence Rakestraw's "A History of the United States Forest Service in Alaska" informed the discussion of early logging. *The Social Economy of the Tlingit Indians,* by Kalervo Obert, provided background on the indigenous people of Southeast Alaska. Richard Carstensen described the search for the giant trees of Southeast Alaska during a September 1997 talk in Juneau. John Muir's description of Southeast Alaska is excerpted from "The Alexander Archipelago," in *Travels in Alaska,* a 1988 collection of Muir's essays published by Sierra Club Books.

PART I

1 THE CONTRACTS

The description of the opening of the Ketchikan pulp mill is drawn from accounts in the *Ketchikan Daily News, Time* magazine and the October 1954 issue of *Pulp and Paper* magazine. Descriptions of early efforts by the Forest Service to attract a pulp industry to Southeast Alaska are from numerous historical accounts, including Rakestraw's history; articles by B. Frank Heintzleman, including "The Forests of Alaska as a Basis for Permanent Development," in the April 1927 issue of *Alaska* magazine; and newspapers, including 1902 issues of the *Alaska Record Miner* and 1923 issues of the *Alaska Daily Empire.* Other sources include Clause-M. Naske's *An Interpretive History of Alaskan Statehood;* Stephen W. Haycox's "Economic Development and Indian Land Rights in Modern Alaska: The 1947 Tongass Timber Act; *Spirit! Historic Ketchikan, Alaska,* compiled by June Allen, edited by Patricia Charles; "History of Alaska Lumber and Pulp Co. Inc.," by Alaska Lumber and Pulp Co; and an interview with Roland Stanton. Excerpted material on Admiralty Island is from *The Wild Grizzlies of Alaska,* by John Holzworth, and "Lost Paradise," by Corey Frank and Frank DuFresne, in *Field and Stream, 1956.*

2 THE CONSERVATIONISTS

This history of the early conservation movement in Southeast Alaska was reconstructed from news stories, especially in the *Juneau Empire* and the *Ketchikan Daily News;* correspondence among early organizers of the Tongass Conservation Society, the Sitka Conservation Society and the Southeast Alaska Conservation Council; interviews with Larry Edwards, Don Muller, Richard Gordon, Joe Sebastian, Alan Stein, Charles Zieske, Kay Greenough, and Edgar and Peggy Wayburn; and reports and correspondence in the Sierra Club Collection at the Bancroft Library, University of California at Berkeley.

3 ANGOON

For background on the Tlingit people of Angoon, the author relied primarily on interviews with Matthew Fred, Gilbert Fred, Edward Gambel Sr., Pauline Jim and K.J. Metcalf, and on "Admiralty Island: Fortress of the Bears," in *Alaska Geographic, 1991.* John Strohmeyer's *Extreme Conditions: Big Oil and the Transformation of Alaska* provided background on the campaign to settle Alaska Native land claims. Gunnar Knapp's "Native Timber Harvests in Southeast Alaska," published by the Forest Service, provided a useful description of Native land selections.

4 THE BIG SQUEEZE

This chapter is based on extensive interviews with Glenn and Martha Reid and Joe Pentilla at the Reid home in Petersburg, Alaska; interviews with two of their attorneys, William Dwyer and Peter Vial, and court documents in *Reid Brothers Logging Company v. Ketchikan Pulp Company and Alaska Lumber and Pulp Company*, including, but not limited to, internal company memos, correspondence, briefs, findings of fact, appeals and federal court rulings. The account of the fire that nearly destroyed documents critical to the Reid Brothers case is from Glenn and Martha Reid, and from accounts in February 1976 editions of the *Ketchikan Daily News.*

5 OPENING UP THE COUNTRY

Current and retired Forest Service employees, including Ron Skillings, Joe Kennedy, Ron Dippold, Rai Behnert, and K.J. Metcalf, described Forest Service management practices and perspectives on the Tongass National Forest in the 1960s and 1970s. Metcalf provided internal correspondence on the agency's road-building plan. The history of Tenakee Springs is from a chapter by Vicki Wisenbaugh in "Tenakee Times: An Informational Booklet on Tenakee Springs, Alaska." The discussion of the Wallmo-Schoen study is from an interview with co-author John Schoen, and from the study, "Response of Deer to Secondary Forest Succession in Southeast Alaska," *Forest Science,* 1980. Matthew Kirchhoff of the Alaska Department of Fish and Game provided valuable background on early biological research studies in Southeast Alaska.

6 THE BACKROOM DEAL

For specific details of the Alaska Lands campaign, the author relied on copies of correspondence among environmental groups; accounts in *Ravencall,* the newspaper of the Southeast Alaska Conservation Council; Robert Cahn's "The Fight to Save Wild Alaska," published by the National Audubon Society; and *Alaska Geographic's* "Alaska National Interest Lands." The account of efforts by conservationists to get Tongass wilderness included in the 1980 law is based on interviews with Ted Whitesell, Richard Gordon, Ed Wayburn, Kay Greenough, Paul Peyton and Leonard Steinberg .

PART II

7 PICKING UP THE PIECES

This chapter is based on extensive interviews with Jim Stratton, Steve Kallick and John Sisk of the Southeast Alaska Conservation Council, and on SEACC reports, correspondence and other documents provided by Jim Stratton.

8 COVERUP

This account of the Reid Brothers ruling and its aftermath is based on an extensive interview with retired Forest Service employee Ron Galdabini; correspondence, internal company memos and other documents entered into evidence in *Reid Brothers Logging v. Ketchikan Pulp Co. and Alaska Lumber and Pulp;* rulings by U.S. District Judge Barbara Rothstein and the 9th U.S. Circuit Court of Appeals in the *Reid Brothers* case; reports of Forest Service investigations into pulp mill activities following the Rothstein ruling, including the report of the Reid Brothers Anti-Trust Case Review Team; and correspondence between the Office of General Counsel and the U.S. Department of Justice. The account of U.S. Rep. Jim Weaver's effort to expose pulp mill violations is from an interview with Bern Johnson; stories in the *New York Times* and *The Washington Post;* a December 1982 column by syndicated columnist Jack Anderson; and a transcript of the June 29, 1983 hearing of the House Interior Subcommittee on Mining, Forest Management, and Bonneville Power Administration.

9 TIMBER MINING

The account of the early years of logging by Native corporations in Southeast Alaska is drawn from Gunnar Knapp's Forest Service history of Native corporation logging; interviews with Alaska state habitat biologists Don Cornelius and Jack Gustafson; and a series of stories on Native corporation logging by Hal Bernton of the *Anchorage Daily News.* Background on litigation over the Shee-Atika Corporation land claims on Admiralty Island is from the Sierra Club Collection at the UC-Berkeley Bancroft Library. Quoted testimony from Alaska Natives is excerpted from Thomas R. Berger's *A Village Journey: The Report of the Alaska Native Review Commission.* The discussion of net operating losses is from the Knapp history and stories by Hal Bernton in the *Anchorage Daily News.*

10 UNION BUSTING

The perspective of millworkers and loggers employed in Southeast Alaska is based largely on interviews with Ketchikan Pulp Co. workers, including Gil Smith, Charlie Stout, John Wolon, Paul Lamm, Bruce Romine and Mike Speelman. The account of management changes at Alaska Pulp Co. is from the *Los Angeles Times.* The account of the failed worker buyout and mill closure in Ketchikan is from an interview with Paul Lamm, stories in the *Ketchikan Daily News,* and a transcript of testimony by KPC worker Wayne Weihing before the House Committee on Resources and the House Committee on Agriculture on July 11, 1996. Harry Merlo's perspective on controlling labor costs is from a June 1984 story in the *Seattle Post-Intelligencer.* The strike against the Alaska Pulp Co. mill in Sitka and Florian Sever's testimony before Congress were widely reported. Sever described his subsequent dealings with APC in an interview and provided National Labor Relations Board documents. Background on the world pulp market is from *Pulp & Paper 1999 North American Factbook.* The account of asbestos exposure violations by Ketchikan Pulp is from an interview with Bruce Romine and a report of the Alaska Occupational Safety and Health Review Board based on an Alaska Department of Labor investigation of an asbestos exposure incident at the KPC mill in September of 1993. Accounts of life in the logging camps are from visits by the author to Rowan Bay in 1989, and to Appleton Cove in 1996.

11 CONFRONTING THE BEAST

The account of efforts by the Southeast Alaska Conservation Council to document overcutting of the Tongass after 1980 is from interviews with Jim Stratton, Steve Kallick and John Sisk, and from SEACC reports, including "The Tongass Accountability Report," by Joseph Cone, and "Last Stand for the Tongass," by Kallick and Bart Koehler. Timber sale figures are from the U.S. Forest Service Alaska Region and news accounts. Background on Bart Koehler is from interviews and from Susan Zakin's *Coyotes and Town Dogs: Earth First! and the Environmental Movement.* The account of early efforts to build support for reform in Congress is based on interviews with Sisk, Kallick, Koehler, Joe Sebastian and Scott Highleyman. Testimony at the oversight hearing on the Tongass before the House Interior Subcommittee on Public Lands, on May 8 and 9, 1986, is excerpted from the hearing transcript. The account of the entry of national conservation foundations into the Tongass campaign is based on interviews with Stratton, Koehler and Donald Ross.

12 SMOKED SALMON AND ALASKAN BEER

This reconstruction of the first three years of the Tongass timber reform campaign is based on interviews with Scott Highleyman, Bart Koehler, Steve Kallick, and Jeff Petrich; transcripts of congressional hearings in 1987, 1988 and 1989; news accounts, and correspondence. Descriptions of Forest Service expenditures after establishment of the Tongass Timber Supply Fund were detailed in the 1988 U.S. General Accounting Office study, "Tongass National Forest: Timber Provision of the Alaska Lands Act Needs Clarification." The description of Florian Sever's battle to get his job back is from news accounts and a column by syndicated columnist Jack Anderson. The discussion of *People of the Tongass: Alaska Forestry Under Attack,* is based on a 1989 interview with Ron Arnold.

13 FIRST VICTORY

The description of the North Prince of Wales Island tour is from an interview with Jack Gustafson; reports and correspondence by Gustafson and Don Cornelius submitted to Forest Service and the Alaska Department of Fish and Game officials; and news accounts. The story of the Salmon Bay Lake lawsuit comes from interviews with Alan Stein and Robert "Buck" Lindekugel. The account of the final push for passage of the Tongass Timber Reform Act is from Bart Koehler, Scott Highleyman and Steve Kallick. Excerpted comments from members of Congress upon passage of the Tongass Timber Reform Act are from transcripts of House and Senate floor sessions.

PART III

14 SCIENCE UNMUZZLED

Tongass National Forest timber sale statistics were obtained from the Forest Service, Alaska Region. Background on establishment of the Viable Populations Committee is from interviews with Matthew Kirchhoff and Chris Iverson; "Tongass in Transition: Blueprint for a Sustainable Future," by the Association of Forest Service Employees for Environmental Ethics; news accounts, especially Bridget Schulte's December 27, 1992, story for States News Service; and the committee's 1993 draft report, "A Strategy for Maintaining Well-Distributed, Viable Populations of Wildlife Associated with

Old-Growth Forests in Southeast Alaska," together with surveys of the status of individual species, especially Kirchhoff's report on the Alexander Archipelago wolf, D. Cole Crocker-Bedford's report on the Queen Charlotte goshawk, and the John Schoen-Kimberly Titus report on the brown bear. Additional background is from Forest Service technical reports published in 1996 by the Pacific Northwest Research Station, including "The Alexander Archipelago Wolf: A Conservation Assessment," and "Conservation Assessment for the Northern Goshawk in Southeast Alaska." Jasper Carlton, Eric Holle and Kieran Suckling provided background on petitions to list the wolf and goshawk under the Endangered Species Act. Background on Tongass cave and karst resources is from the Forest Service technical report "Karst Landscapes and Associated Resources: A Resource Assessment," by James F. Baichtal and Douglas N. Swanston. Perspectives on Forest Service management of karst and caves are from interviews with Kevin Allred and Pete Smith, and from an article by Allred, Smith, Kris Esterson and Steve Lewis for the National Speleological Society. Alaska Regional Forester Phil Janik and Forest Service research biologist Fred Everest described efforts to bring greater scientific credibility to the Tongass Land Management Plan.

15 TOXIC BEHAVIOR

Kevin James' whistleblower disclosures of criminal violations of the Clean Water Act by Ketchikan Pulp Co. are contained in a U.S. Environmental Protection Agency criminal file obtained by the author through the federal Freedom of Information Act, with key names redacted. KPC's lengthy record of civil violations of the Clean Water Act and Clean Air Act is well-documented in news accounts; in complaints, consent decrees, biological studies, correspondence and press releases from the EPA and the Alaska Department of Environmental Conservation; in a summary of a 1991 EPA Superfund Program preliminary assessment of the Ketchikan Pulp Co. mill site; and in the EPA's Toxics Release Inventory. Additional information was provided by Ketchikan residents, including Eric Hummel and Marg Clabby, and by Danforth Bodien of the EPA. The account of efforts by the pulp mills to win waivers from provisions of the Clean Water Act is from an interview with Bodien, and accounts in the *Ketchikan Daily News.* The account of Alaska Pulp Corporation's record of violations of the Clean Water Act and Clean Air Act was compiled from similar state and federal agency documents; from news accounts, including a series by Mitch Lipka, "A Mill Town Torn: Pulp, Poison and Paychecks," in the *Anchorage Times,* August 1991; and from the Complaint and Requests for Admission, *Larry Edwards v. Alaska Pulp Corporation,* a class action suit filed Feb. 28, 1992, in Superior Court for the State of Alaska, which also documents efforts by Alaska Pulp Corporation officials to cut off funding for research on the environmental and human health effects of air pollution in Sitka. The account of Kevin James' lawsuit alleging wrongful termination from KPC is from James' September 7, 1993 complaint, filed with the U.S. Department of Labor; correspondence between James' attorney, James McGowan, and lawyers for Louisiana Pacific Corporation; and accounts in the *Ketchikan Daily News.* The account of events leading up to L-P's settlement with James in his civil damages suit is from an extensive interview with McGowan.

16 DEFAULT

The account of the closure of the Alaska Pulp Corporation mill in Sitka and of financial and other decisions by APC executives preceding the closure was compiled from news stories, including accounts in the *Wall Street Journal,* the *Los Angeles Times,* the *Sitka Sentinel* and *Ravencall.* Assistant U.S. Agriculture Secretary Jim Lyons and APC executive vice president Frank Roppel discussed aspects of pending litigation concerning the Clinton administration's finding that APC defaulted on its contract by closing the Sitka mill. Tom Waldo of the Earthjustice Legal Defense Fund recounted the lengthy negotiations between environmentalists, timber industry representatives and the Clinton administration over what would happen to timber sales purchased by APC. John Scott of the Alaska Department of Labor described the effect of the mill closure on workers. Former Wrangell Mayor Doug Roberts detailed efforts to keep Wrangell's economy alive after APC closed its Wrangell sawmill. Steve Kallick and Jim Stratton provided background on the creation of the Alaska Rainforest Campaign.

17 WHISTLEBLOWERS

Bill Shoaf's story is based on a lengthy interview with Shoaf at his home in March of 1997, and on *William R. Shoaf v. United States Department of Agriculture Forest Service*, Before the Merit Systems Protections Board, Complaint and Exhibits, October 31, 1996. Mary Dalton's story is based on Dalton's presentation before the Society of Environmental Journalists in Tucson, Arizona, in October 1997, and follow-up interviews; news stories, correspondence between Dalton and her supervisors in the Chatham Area of the Tongass National Forest, and Dalton's appeal of the Northwest Baranof Project; and "The Fighting Forester: Mary Dalton Jeopardizes Job to Protest Logging," by Gretchen Legler, in *We Alaskans*, the Sunday magazine of the *Anchorage Daily News*, September 1, 1996.

18 LAST ASSAULT

The account of the Landless Natives bill is drawn from news stories, correspondence and resolutions provided by the Alaska Rainforest Campaign, and from interviews with Buck Lindekugel, Robert Willard and Frank Wright Jr. Descriptions of the power of the Alaska delegation in the 104th Congress and its efforts to legislate more logging on the Tongass National Forest were widely reported by the national and Alaska media. Bart Koehler and Steve Kallick provided background on efforts by environmental activists to block these efforts in Congress. Behind-the-scenes accounts of efforts to complete a Tongass Land Management Plan (TLMP) in 1995 and 1996 are based on interviews with several members of the TLMP team, including Terry Shaw, Doug Swanston, Pamela Finney, Chris Iverson, Fred Everest and Steve Kessler, and with Alaska Regional Forester Phil Janik.

19 ENDGAME

Descriptions of the campaign to win an extension of the Ketchikan Pulp Co. contract are drawn from the *Ketchikan Daily News* and other newspapers, and from interviews with Ketchikan Mayor Jack Shay and other Ketchikan residents. The account of negotiations between Louisiana-Pacific Co. and the Clinton administration is based on correspondence between L-P President Mark Suwyn and U.S. Secretary of Agriculture Dan Glickman, interviews with Bart Koehler and Jim Lyons, and news accounts. Steve Kallick provided background on the role of the Alaska Rainforest Campaign in weakening support for KPC. Eric Hummel, Marg Clabby, Leslee Engler and Carol Murray described the impact of pulp mill pollution in Ketchikan. The account of the ceremony marking the negotiated settlement between Louisiana- Pacific and the Clinton administration appeared in the March 3, 1997 issue of the *Ketchikan Daily News*. Several KPC workers, including Russell Mock, Paul Lamm, Gil Smith, Charlie Stout, Mike Speelman and John Wolon, shared their views of the pulp mill closure. Rick Benner of KPC led a private tour of the pulp mill three days before it produced its last roll of pulp.

20 HOONAH

This chapter is based on interviews with Floyd Peterson, Frank Wright Jr., Johanna Dybdahl, and Wanda Culp during a visit to Hoonah in September of 1997. The *Juneau Empire* and a 1985 series by Hal Bernton of the *Anchorage Daily News* provided background on the history of Native corporation logging in the Hoonah area. The perspective of Sealaska Corporation was provided by Rick Harris, the corporation's senior vice president for resources.

EPILOGUE: A NEW ERA

The account of Sitka's adjustment to the closure of its pulp mill is based on interviews with numerous Sitka community leaders during an August 1996 visit, including Mayor Pete Hallgren, Chamber of Commerce President Dan Keck, City Assembly members Ann Morrison and Kathy Wasserman, John Scott of the Alaska Department of Labor, and environmental activist and bookstore owner Don Muller. The January 1998 edition of *Alaska Economic Trends*, published by the Alaska Department of Labor, provided an updated assessment, especially "Sitka: Coping With Structural Change," by John Boucher, and "Case Study of a Layoff: Work Life After Sitka's Pulp Mill Closure," by Kristen Tromble. For an assessment of Ketchikan's adjustment to the closure of its pulp mill, I relied on news accounts, including "A Year Later: Ketchikan Weathers Mill Closure," by the Associated Press, March 12, 1998, and "Life After Logging," by Jeanine Pohl Smith, in the *Juneau Empire*, Aug. 10, 1997. Mike McNulty described Steve Seley's secondary wood manufacturing project in the August 21, 1997, *Ketchikan Daily News*. The description of Wrangell's effort to keep its economy alive is baed on an interview with Doug Roberts and on state and local economic reports. The account of the Clinton administration's April 1999 revision of the 1997 Tongass Land Management Plan is from news accounts and press releases from the U.S. Department of Agriculture and SEACC.

BIBLIOGRAPHY

"Admiralty Island, Fortress of the Bears," *Alaska Geographic*, Vol. 18, No. 3, 1991.

Alaska Conservation Review: Special Tongass Issue, Alaska Conservation Society, Winter 1975.

"Alaska National Interest Lands," *Alaska Geographic*, Vol. 8, No. 4, 1981.

"America's Vanishing Rain Forest: A Report on Federal Timber Management in Southeast Alaska," The Wilderness Society, Washington, DC, April 1986.

AFSEEE (Association of Forest Service Employees for Environmental Ethics), "The Tongass National Forest: Under Siege," *Inner Voice*, Eugene, OR, Vol. 2, No. 1, Winter 1990.

AFSEEE, "Tongass in Transition: Blueprint for a Sustainable Future," Eugene, OR, 1996.

Baichtal, James F., and Douglas N. Swanston, "Karst Landscapes and Associated Resources: A Resource Assessment," USDA Forest Service Pacific Northwest Research Station, Portlan,d OR, 1996.

Berger, Thomas R., *A Village Journey: The Report of the Alaska Native Review Commission*, Hill and Wang, New York, 1985.

Bernton, Hal, "Native Logging: Windfall or Downfall?" *Anchorage Daily News*, August 1985.

"Between Worlds: How the Alaska Native Claims Settlement Act reshaped the destinies of Alaska's Native people," *Juneau Empire* Special Report, January 31, 1999.

Cahn, Robert, "The Fight to Save Wild Alaska," National Audubon Society, New York, 1982.

"Can We Save the Tongass?" *Defenders* Special Issue, Vol. 69, No. 2, Spring 1994.

Carstensen, Richard, "Southeast Alaska," in *The Enduring Forests*, The Mountaineers, Seattle, WA, 1996.

Cornelius, Don, "Alaska's Tongass National Forest: A View from the Top," *Inner Voice*,, Vol. 8, No. 5, September/October 1996.

Cornelius, Don, "Conflict in Alaska's Rainforest," *Defenders,* Spring 1996.

Dauenhauer, Nora Marks, and Richard Dauenhauer, *Haa Shuka', Our Ancestors: Tlingit Oral Narratives,* University of Washington Press, Seattle, WA, and Sealaska Heritage Foundation, Juneau, AK, 1987.

Durbin, Kathie, "End of an Era: Southeast Alaska Braces for Life After the Pulp Mills," Cascadia Times, Vol. 2, No. 7, December 1996.

Durbin, Kathie, "Sawdust Memories," *Amicus Journal,* Vol. 19, No. 3, Fall 1997.

Durbin, Kathie, "Tongass forest focus of dispute," *The Oregonian,* October 29-30, 1989.

Durbin, Kathie, "A Tongass Tale," *Inner Voice,*, Vol. 10, No. 2, March/April1998.

Durbin, Kathie, "Too Close to Home: Logging Threatens Native Way of Life in the Alaska Rainforest," *Cascadia Times,* Vol. 1, No. 2, May 1995.

Dwyer, William L, Richard C. Yarmuth and Peter M. Vial, *Reid Brothers Logging Company v. Ketchikan Pulp Company and Alaska Lumber and Pulp Co.,* Brief of Appellee, May 7, 1982.

Frank, Corey, and Frank DuFresne, "Lost Paradise," *Field and Stream*, September 1956.

Haycox, Stephen W. "Economic Development and Indian Land Rights in Modern Alaska: The 1947 Tongass Timber Act," *Western Historical Quarterly,* 1990, reprinted in *An Alaska Anthology: Interpreting the Past,* University of Washington Press, Seattle, WA, 1996.

Heintzleman, B. Frank, "The Forests of Alaska as a Basis for Permanent Development," *Alaska* magazine, April 1927.

Holzworth, John M., *The Wild Grizzlies of Alaska,* G. P. Putnam's Sons, New York, 1930.

Iverson, George C., Gregory D. Hayward, Kimberly Titus, Eugene DeGayner, Richard E. Lowell, D. Coleman Crocker-Bedford, Philip F. Schempf, and John Lindell, "Conservation Assessment for the Northern Goshawk in Southeast Alaska," USDA Forest Service Pacific Northwest Research Station, Portland, OR, 1996.

Kallick, Steve, and Bart Koehler, "Last Stand for the Tongass," Southeast Alaska Conservation Council, Juneau, AK, 1986.

Ketchum, Robert Glenn, and Carey D. Ketchum, *The Tongass: Alaska's Vanishing Rain Forest,* Aperture Foundation, Inc., New York, 1987.

Knapp, Gunnar, "Native Timber Harvests in Southeast Alaska," USDA Forest Service Pacific Northwest Research Station, Portland, OR, 1992.

Larry Edwards v. Alaska Pulp Corporation, Complaint and Exhibit list, filed Feb. 28, 1992, in Superior Court for State of Alaska.

Larsen, Jonathan Z., "Going, going . . . America's majestic rain forest, at two bucks a tree," *Conde' Nast's Traveler,* Vol. 22, No. 11, November 1987.

Legler, Gretchen, "The Fighting Forester: Mary Dalton Jeopardizes Job to Protest Logging," *We Alaskans* magazine, *Anchorage Daily News,* September 1, 1996.

Lipka, Mitch, "A Mill Town Torn: Pulp, Poison and Paychecks," *Anchorage Times,* August 1991.

Mitchell, Donald Craig, *Sold America: The Story of Alaska Natives and Their Land,* 1867-1959, Hanover Press of New England, Hanover, NH, 1997.

Muir, John, "The Alexander Archipelago," in *Travels in Alaska,* Sierra Club Books, San Francisco, CA, 1988.

Naske, Clause-M., *An Interpretive History of Alaskan Statehood,* Alaska Northwest Publishing Co., Anchorage, AK, 1973.

Nelson, Richard, *The Island Within,* North Point Press, San Francisco, CA, 1989.

Obert, Kalervo, *The Social Economy of the Tlingit Indians,* University of Washington Press, Seattle, WA, 1973.

Person, David K., Matthew Kirchhoff, Victor Van Ballenberghe, George C. Iverson, and Edward Grossman, "The Alexander Archipelago Wolf: A Conservation Assessment," USDA Forest Service Pacific Northwest Research Station, Portland, OR, 1996.

Pulp and Paper, "The Ketchikan Story," October 1954.

"The Rain Forests of Home: An Atlas of People and Place," Ecotrust, Pacific GIS, and Conservation International, Portland, OR, 1995.

Rakestraw, Lawrence, "A History of the United States Forest Service in Alaska," U.S. Department of Agriculture, 1981. Reprinted by USDA Forest Service, Alaska Region, Anchorage, AK, 1994.

Ravencall, Southeast Alaska Conservation Council, Juneau, AK, 1977-1999

Rothstein, Barbara J, U.S. District Judge, *Reid Brothers Logging Company v. Ketchikan Pulp Company and Alaska Lumber and Pulp Company,* Findings of Fact and Conclusions of Law, June 5, 1981.

Shoaf, William R., *William R. Shoaf v. United States Department of Agriculture Forest Service,* Before the Merit Systems Protection Board, Complaint and Exhibits, October 31, 1996.

Sierra Club Collection, Bancroft Library, University of California at Berkeley.

Skow, John, "Forest Service Follies," *Sports Illustrated,* Vol. 68, No. 11, March 14, 1988.

Soderberg, K.A., and Jackie DuRette, *People of the Tongass: Alaska Forestry Under Attack,* Free Enterprise Press, Bellevue, WA, 1988.

Southeast Alaska Conservation Council, "The Tongass Timber Problem: The Full Report of the Tongass Accountability Project," Juneau, AK, 1985.

Spirit! Historic Ketchikan, Alaska, compiled by June Allen, edited by Patricia Charles, Lind Printing, Ketchikan, AK, 1992.

Strohmeyer, John, *Extreme Conditions: Big Oil and the Transformation of Alaska,* Simon and Schuster, New York, 1993.

Suring, Lowell H., D. Coleman Crocker-Bedford, Rodney W. Flynn, Carol S. Hale, G. Chris Iverson, Matthew D. Kirchoff, Theron E. Schenck II, Lana C. Shea, and Kimberly Titus, "A Proposed Strategy for Maintaining Well-Distributed, Viable Populations of Wildlife Associated With Old-Growth Forests in Southeast Alaska, USDA Forest Service, Portland, OR, May 1993.

USDA Forest Service, Alaska Region, "Multiple Use Management Guide for the Alaska Region," Juneau, AK, 1964.

USDA Forest Service, Alaska Region, "Tongass National Forest Land and Resource Management Plan," Juneau, AK, 1997.

U.S. General Accounting Office, "Tongass National Forest: Timber Provision of the Alaska Lands Act Needs Clarification," April 1988.

Wallmo, Olof C., and John W. Schoen, "Response of Deer to Secondary Forest Succession in Southeast Alaska," in *Forest Science,* Vol. 26, No. 3, 1980.

Weeden, Robert B., *Messages from Earth: Nature and the Human Prospect in Alaska,* University of Alaska Press, Fairbanks, AK, 1992.

Zakin, Susan, *Coyotes and Town Dogs: Earth First! and the Environmental Movement,* Viking, New York, 1993.